Negotiation and Dispute Resolution

First Edition

Beverly J. DeMarr, Ph.D.
Ferris State University

Suzanne C. de Janasz, Ph.D.
IMD—Institute for Management Development

D1319233

PEARSON

Boston   Columbus   Indianapolis   New York   San Francisco   Upper Saddle River
Amsterdam   Cape Town   Dubai   London   Madrid   Milan   Munich   Paris   Montreal   Toronto
Delhi   Mexico City   Sao Paulo   Sydney   Hong Kong   Seoul   Singapore   Taipei   Tokyo

Editorial Director: Vernon Anthony
Executive Editor: Gary Bauer
Editorial Project Manager: Linda Cupp
Editorial Assistant: Tanika Henderson
Director of Marketing: David Gesell
Marketing Manager: Stacy Martinez
Senior Marketing Coordinator: Alicia Wozniak
Senior Marketing Assistant: Les Roberts
Senior Managing Editor: JoEllen Gohr
Production Project Manager: Debbie Ryan
Art Director: Jayne Conte
Cover Designer: Bruce Kenselaar
Permission Research: Jodi Rhinehart-Doty
Cover Art: Shutterstock
Media Project Manager: Karen Bretz
Full-Service Project Management: Revathi Viswanathan
Composition: PreMediaGlobal
Printer/Binder: Edwards Brothers
Cover Printer: Lehigh-Phoenix Color/Hagerstown
Text Font: 10/12 Palatino

Credits and acknowledgments borrowed from other sources and reproduced, with permission, in this textbook appear on appropriate page within text (or on page xvii).

Library of Congress Cataloging-in-Publication Data

DeMarr, Beverly J.
  Negotiation and dispute resolution / Beverly J. DeMarr, Suzanne C. de Janasz. — 1st ed.
    p. cm.
  Includes index.
  ISBN-13: 978-0-13-157753-4
  ISBN-10: 0-13-157753-0
 1. Negotiation.   2. Conflict management.   3. Mediation.   I. De Janasz, Suzanne C. II. Title.
  BF637.N4D46 2012
  302.3—dc23

                                                          2011038766

10 9 8 7 6 5 4 3 2 1

ISBN 10:   0-13-157753-0
ISBN 13: 978-0-13-157753-4

Dedication

*To my parents, Arthur and Hazel DeMarr, who raised me to believe
I could do anything in life and to my children, Melita and Eric Cioe,
who give me the reason for doing it. ~Bev*

*To my father, Stan Cooper, who was a model of strength, courage,
and perseverance; you are forever in my heart. To my children, Gabby and Alex,
who continue to make me proud in so many ways. To my mother, my friends,
and my colleagues, who have been a source of inspiration,
renewal, and support. ~Suzanne*

BRIEF CONTENTS

CONTENTS

PREFACE

WHY THIS BOOK?

This book represents a culmination of the authors' teaching and professional experiences. We first decided to write this text some years ago when we realized that the texts on negotiation currently available didn't quite suit our needs. We were looking for a book that did a good job of covering basic concepts and also presented the broad range of topics students need in order to be successful in a complex, global, and increasingly competitive environment. We also wanted a full complement of experiential exercises and assessments without requiring an additional purchase of either individual exercises or a second book. This book was written to fit these requirements.

Contemporary organizations look different than those of a few decades ago. Structures are flatter and require more team-based work and a greater need for influence without authority—increasing the interaction between co-workers and the need for persuasion, negotiation, and conflict resolution within organizations. Competitive forces have increased the need for higher order negotiation skills within and between organizations. Organizations are engaging in outsourcing and sending work offshore—which necessitates negotiation and conflict resolution with a wide variety of domestic and global subcontractors, and formal and informal partnerships, such as those in the defense industry between Northrop Grumman and Boeing and Lockheed and General Dynamics. Doing business this way means more negotiations ... and potentially more conflict between customers, vendors, and business partners. Furthermore, with the sharpened focus on unethical behavior and the fact that business practices and expectations for ethical behavior vary across cultures and continents, employees need to understand the role of ethics and develop principle-centered negotiation skills now more than ever.

To address these needs, we have created a resource that contains sufficient depth and breadth of coverage of critical topics and skills in negotiation and dispute resolution. And, because conceptual knowledge is a necessary but not sufficient ingredient for becoming a masterful negotiator, we have augmented the concepts with numerous experiential exercises, activities, and self-assessments that provide students with the opportunity to apply the material in meaningful ways to hone their negotiation and conflict resolution skills.

DESIGN OF THE BOOK

To develop a skill requires a solid foundation. The first two chapters (Part I) do just that, provide a solid foundation which covers the concepts and terminology used in negotiation. We cover the overall process of negotiation, from preparation through bargaining and agreement. The next three chapters (Part II) take a closer look at the actual processes involved in negotiation and dispute resolution. Chapter 3 examines distributive negotiation—where negotiators view the outcome as fixed and attempt to gain as much from the "pie" as possible. Chapter 4 examines integrative negotiation, where the focus is on creating value and building long-term relationships among negotiators and the organizations they represent. Because negotiations are not always amicable or fruitful, in Chapter 5, we address conflict and dispute resolution techniques and tools, both informal and formal.

The processes of negotiation and conflict/dispute resolution are affected by the individuals involved, the relationship between those individuals (interpersonal processes), and the context in which the processes exist. The six chapters of Part III examine these characteristics, beginning with individual effects (understanding yourself), interpersonal processes (communication, persuasion, and the nature of relationships in negotiation), and the context (team/multiparty negotiations, global negotiations).

Finally, we take a broad view of applications of these concepts and processes as they relate to one's professional and personal affairs. The four chapters of Part IV focus on applying negotiation skills as an employee (e.g., negotiating the terms and conditions of your job and negotiating on behalf of your employer) and to situations you are likely to encounter as a small business owner or in your personal life (e.g., negotiations involving automobiles and real estate), as well as when negotiating your future.

Model of the Book

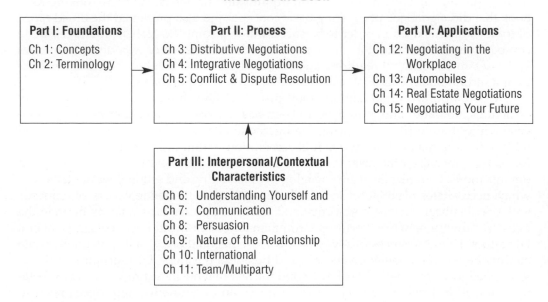

Part I: Foundations
Ch 1: Concepts
Ch 2: Terminology

Part II: Process
Ch 3: Distributive Negotiations
Ch 4: Integrative Negotiations
Ch 5: Conflict & Dispute Resolution

Part IV: Applications
Ch 12: Negotiating in the Workplace
Ch 13: Automobiles
Ch 14: Real Estate Negotiations
Ch 15: Negotiating Your Future

Part III: Interpersonal/Contextual Characteristics
Ch 6: Understanding Yourself and
Ch 7: Communication
Ch 8: Persuasion
Ch 9: Nature of the Relationship
Ch 10: International
Ch 11: Team/Multiparty

Each chapter:

- begins with a scenario to motivate and integrate the material for that chapter;
- contains appropriate and relevant theoretical information;
- contains assessments and experiential exercises so you can immediately apply and practice skills and techniques in a wide variety of negotiation and conflict resolution situations with different types of people, goals, and challenges;
- asks you to reflect on what you have learned and how you will use the information, and identify opportunities for future development;
- identifies resources available to research in preparation for a negotiation;
- includes an "ethical dilemma" that encourages you to think about ethical issues that may arise in negotiation.

We hope you find this book a valuable means for developing your ability to competently and confidently negotiate and resolve professional and personal conflicts—skills more critical than ever in the current environment.

RESOURCES FOR STUDENTS

Companion Website

The Companion Website contains copies of worksheets for all exercises and assessments in the text so students can download and print the worksheets for inclusion in a portfolio.

The Golden Personality Type Profiler

This popular personality assessment, similar to the full Myers-Briggs assessment program, but oriented toward workplace behavioral assessment, provides students with information about fundamental personality dimensions. It takes about 15–20 minutes to complete and students receive an easy-to-use and practical feedback report based on their results. This tool helps students improve their self-knowledge and ability to work effectively with others by providing students with feedback on their leadership and organizational strengths, communication and teamwork preferences, motivation and learning style, and opportunities for personal growth. An access code for the Golden Personality Type Profiler can be value packaged with the textbook at low cost or purchased online at www.pearsonhighered.com.

RESOURCES FOR INSTRUCTORS

To access supplementary materials online, instructors need to request an instructor access code. Go to **www.pearsonhighered.com/irc**, where you can register for an instructor access code. Within 48 hours of registering you will receive a confirmation email including an instructor access code. Once you have received your code, locate your text in the online catalog, and click on the Instructor Resources button on the left side of the catalog product page. Select a supplement and a log-in page will appear. Once you have logged in, you can access instructor material for all Prentice Hall textbooks.

Instructor's Manual

The Instructor's Manual contains teaching notes for all experiential exercises, confidential role information for all role plays, chapter outlines, sample syllabi for a variety of delivery formats, and sample test questions.

Pearson MyTest Electronic Testing Program

Pearson MyTest is an assessment generation program that helps instructors easily create and print quizzes and exams. Questions and tests can be authored online, allowing instructors ultimate flexibility and the ability to efficiently manage assessments anytime, anywhere.

PowerPoint Lecture Presentation Package

The package contains lecture presentation screens for each chapter.

ABOUT THE AUTHORS

Beverly J. DeMarr, Ph.D., is a Professor of Management at Ferris State University. She received her Doctorate in Organizational Behavior and Human Resource Management from Michigan State University. She currently teaches courses in Negotiation, Human Resource Management, and Compensation, and has been recognized for excellence in online teaching. She has published in Personnel Psychology, Journal of Business Ethics, Human Relations, Public Personnel Management, and International Journal of Conflict Management. She is a member of the Organizational Behavior Teaching Society and the Academy of Management where she serves as an invited member of the Teaching Theme Committee.

Beverly has been actively involved in mediation since 2004. She has mediated numerous general civil, employment, civil rights, domestic relations (divorce, parenting time), and restorative justice (victim-offender) cases and conducted a variety of training sessions for mediators. She is a volunteer mediator for the Dispute Resolution Center of West Michigan and was a member of the Board of Directors of the Westshore Dispute Resolution Center from 2007 until 2011. She was also an elected union representative for eight years, negotiating labor contracts and representing constituents in a wide variety of disputes.

In addition to her Ph.D., Beverly earned a Master of Labor and Industrial Relations from Michigan State University, a Master of Business Administration from Grand Valley State University, and a Bachelor of Science in Business Administration from Aquinas College. She is an Ambassador of the Community Foundation for Muskegon County and a member of the Women's Division Chamber of Commerce.

Suzanne C. de Janasz, Ph.D., is Professor of Leadership and Organization Development at IMD—Institute for Management Development—in Lausanne, Switzerland. As a Fulbright Fellow, she taught at Warsaw University in Warsaw, Poland, and has had visiting stints there and at ALBA Graduate Business School in Vouliagmeni, Greece. An award-winning instructor, Suzanne specializes in the areas of leadership, negotiations, organizational behavior, creativity/innovation, entrepreneurship, and interpersonal/managerial skills.

Suzanne's research on mentoring, careers, authenticity, work–family conflict, and leadership appears in such journals as *Academy of Management Executive, Journal of Organizational Behavior, Journal of Vocational Behavior, Career Development International and Journal of Management Education* and has been featured in domestic and international newspapers and radio programs. Her text, *Interpersonal Skills in Organizations (now in its fourth edition),* is used throughout the world. In addition to her Fulbright Fellowship, Suzanne received the New Educator Award from the Organizational Behavior Teaching Society (OBTS) and the Jepson fellowship from her previous university. Suzanne is currently serving as the Past Chair for the Careers Division in the Academy of Management and has held leadership roles in the Southern Management Association and the OBTS. She also serves on the boards of several nonprofit organizations.

After earning an undergraduate music degree from the University of Miami, Suzanne earned her MBA and Ph.D. degrees from the Marshall School of Business at the University of Southern California (USC). Between the two degrees, she worked for five years as an organizational consultant in the aerospace industry. Prior to joining the faculty of IMD, Suzanne taught at James Madison University and the University of Mary Washington's College of Graduate and Professional Studies, both in Virginia.

ACKNOWLEDGMENTS

Taking an idea for a book through the writing, revision, and production processes requires the efforts of many people without whom this book would not have been possible. We would like to thank the following reviewers for their thoughtful comments and suggestions:

Mark Alexander, Indiana Wesleyan University
Roger N. Blakeney, University of Houston
Joanne S. Bochis, Montclair State University
Eugene P. Buccini, Western Connecticut State University
Joseph F. Byrnes, Bentley University
Maxine Christenson, Aims Community College
Mark Davis, Harding University
Laura Dendinger, Wayne State College
Kerry Fina, Doane College
Andrew Herdman, East Carolina University
Amy Kenworthy, Bond University, Australia
Chalmer E. Labig, Jr., Oklahoma State University
Roger C. Mayer, University of Akron
William F. Morrison, San Jose State University
Martin Otto, Dakota County Technical College
Abe Qastin, Lakeland College
Malika Richards, Pennsylvania State University
Joyce A. Russell, University of Maryland
Nan Stager, Indiana University, Bloomington
Alexander D. Stein, Temple University
Lorenn Walker, University of Hawaii
Jason Kanov, Western Washington University
Jennifer K. Wood, Penn State, New Kensington

We thank our colleagues Sharon Bell, Maury Peiperl, and Ed Wertheim for their contributions to the book, as well as our friends at OBTC for their feedback and support in the early stages of this project.

We appreciate everyone we have worked with at Pearson Prentice-Hall from development through the production of the text and supplements. In particular, we thank Shelia Deininger for taking the initiative to connect us with an editor based on a chance five-minute phone conversation and to that editor, Gary Bauer, for his superhuman response to the proposal. That we had signed contracts within two weeks from our first contact with him was truly miraculous. Throughout the project he has remained responsive and dedicated to getting this book into production. A special thanks to Linda Cupp, whose help in navigating the review and production process was invaluable. We were fortunate to have her join our team.

We would also like to thank our permissions researcher Jodi Rhinehart-Doty for tracking down and obtaining all needed permissions, and Sharon Jones at JetBlue Airlines for her assistance in obtaining their permission.

Finally, we thank the students who initially suggested writing the book and the students and participants in the United States and abroad whose valuable feedback on the text, exercises, and assignments helped shape the final product.

Beverly J. DeMarr
Ferris State University

Suzanne C. de Janasz
IMD—Institute for Management Development

PART I

Foundations of Negotiation and Dispute Resolution

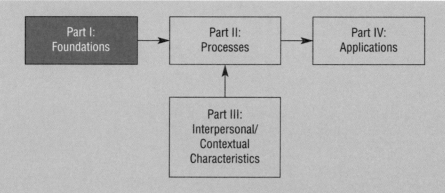

Chapter 1 Introduction

Chapter 2 The Language of Negotiation

Introduction

Chapter Objectives

After studying this chapter and completing the exercises you should be able to:

- Identify a variety of situations where negotiation takes place.
- Describe the characteristics of negotiation.
- Distinguish between interests and issues.
- Evaluate the role of incentives in negotiation.
- Understand the importance of being prepared.
- Identify various types of conflict.

What do you think of when you think of negotiation? Do you think of Donald Trump negotiating multi-million dollar business deals or the legendary Kofi A. Annan negotiating international peace agreements? Do you think of police negotiating with a suicidal person to get him off a bridge or government agents negotiating the release of hostages? Do you think of Kyle MacDonald and the red paperclip? Kyle who? What red paperclip?

Chapter Scenario

You may have seen the story on TV or the Internet. You may have even visited the website. Kyle MacDonald, a 26-year-old Canadian, negotiated his way from owning a single red paperclip to owning a house. It took almost a year, but what started as a hobby turned into something much bigger that brought him a house and a great deal of media attention. It began with the paperclip and a website. The first trade was the paperclip for a pen that looked like a fish, which he traded for a doorknob that he traded for a camping stove that he traded for a generator that he traded for an "instant party." The party was traded for a snowmobile, which he traded for a trip to Yahk, British Columbia, that he traded for a truck. He traded the truck for a recording contract that he traded for a year's rent in Phoenix that he traded for an afternoon with Alice Cooper. He traded the afternoon with the rock star for a snow globe that he traded for a role in a movie that he traded with the town of Kipling, Saskatchewan for—a house.[1]

While the story of Kyle and the red paperclip is amazing, negotiations occur more frequently than the high-profile examples reported in the media. Where there is negotiation there is also the possibility of conflict because the parties involved may have different wants and needs. Similarly, conflicts can be effectively resolved through negotiation. Thus, the two topics are inextricably intertwined. Without a doubt negotiation skills are a core competency needed by everyone to be successful. In the workplace, whether you are an employee, manager, executive, or business owner, you will negotiate and resolve disputes virtually every day and in a variety of contexts. Not only do you negotiate in your professional life, but in your personal life as well.

The good news is that negotiation is a learnable, transferable skill—regardless of what you are negotiating or with whom you are negotiating, the process is the same. Even if you've never been particularly proficient or comfortable negotiating, you can learn. As you practice your negotiating skills you will become more comfortable with the process. What initially may feel stilted becomes more fluid and natural with practice. Once you learn the process, you can apply it to most any situation, professional or personal. That is the goal of this book—to increase your comfort with and mastery of the negotiation process by providing the necessary conceptual material and giving you numerous opportunities to apply your knowledge and skill in a variety of situations. We will encourage you to view negotiations from the other party's perspective to gain a better understanding of her actual needs. Helping the other party to meet his needs typically helps you to get your needs met and improves the relationship in both professional and personal contexts.

With that we would like to officially welcome you to *Negotiation and Dispute Resolution*. We know that you are likely to put more time and effort into courses you believe are relevant and useful in your life. Thus, throughout the book we use examples and exercises dealing with a wide variety of topics and situations that you are likely to encounter in both the workplace and your personal life. We also hope to make learning about negotiation and conflict resolution enjoyable, even fun. Experienced negotiators and mediators generally enjoy the process. Kyle MacDonald said that he had fun while negotiating his way from a paperclip to a house.[2] In addition to providing the necessary material to inform the what, how, and why of negotiation and conflict resolution, we provide a wide variety of opportunities to practice applying the concepts. You may never negotiate your way from a red paperclip to a house, but you will improve your negotiation and conflict resolution skills for use in all areas of your life—and hopefully have a little fun in the process.

WHY STUDY NEGOTIATION?

In their bestselling book, *Freakonomics*,[3] Steven Levitt and Stephen Dubner show that incentives are what drive people to do just about everything in life. Remember what we said about students putting more effort into classes they see as relevant and providing useful skills? This is because the students see those classes as providing value to them in the future. It explains why accounting majors typically put more effort into an accounting class than marketing majors, and marketing majors put more effort into a marketing class than accounting majors. A purely economic point of view says that we don't do anything unless there is an incentive.[4] In other words, we do things because we receive something in return. We go to college because it positions us to get a better job than we could get with a high school diploma. Even when we love our jobs, ultimately we go to work every day because we get paid. On the job we work hard and put forth extra effort to get promoted or recognized. Throughout our career we engage in continuing education—or at least we should—to keep ourselves marketable. We volunteer because it will look good on our resume or because it helps us feel good about ourselves. So what will you gain by putting time and effort into improving your negotiation and conflict resolution skills? There are a number of things.

Negotiation can be profitable.[5] Good negotiation skills lead to better deals in everything from your salary[6] and benefits to anything you purchase or sell. Over your lifetime, the dollar value of financial gains resulting from successful negotiation can be tremendous.

Negotiation can result in a wide variety of positive and negative emotions.[7] Negotiation can be liberating. Has anyone ever talked you into doing something that you really didn't want to do? Have you ever bought something only to realize later that it really wasn't what you wanted? Better negotiation skills will make it less likely that you will feel like someone took advantage of you. It can be comforting when you use your negotiation skills to resolve a conflict with someone close to you and salvage the relationship. Negotiation can also be frustrating if the other party isn't cooperative or completely above board; however, being able to recognize and successfully deal with such people can reduce the time and resources you expend. Negotiation can be good for your ego. When you negotiate well you feel a sense of accomplishment, especially if you are a bit competitive. Participating in negotiation role plays can even help develop your critical thinking skills,[8] which transfer to a variety of other situations in life. If none of this has you hooked yet, consider this—you really don't have a choice. Like it or not you negotiate virtually every day in practically every aspect of your life, even if you don't think of it as such.

NEGOTIATION: IT'S EVERYWHERE

In organizations, managers negotiate when hiring employees and continue to negotiate with them throughout their employment over subjects that run the gamut from work assignments to time-off to resolving conflicts between coworkers. They negotiate budget allocations with senior management and labor contracts and grievances with unions. Non-management employees negotiate and resolve conflicts with customers, suppliers, coworkers, or even other departments within the organization. Today, as more organizations are moving toward team-based work environments, there is increased interaction between coworkers. As the interaction with others increases, particularly in the absence of positional authority, so does the need for negotiation and conflict resolution skills.

Beyond the negotiations that every employee encounters on a regular basis, an increasing number of employees negotiate as a formal part of their jobs. In addition to the usual jobs in sales and purchasing, employees in operations, program management, engineering, finance, human resources, and other functional areas find themselves negotiating more frequently. One reason for this change is the increase in outsourcing and offshoring, which requires negotiation and subsequently conflict resolution with a wide variety of subcontractors, both domestic and international. There is also an increase in companies, even those that have historically been competitors, engaging in joint efforts to produce products. This is especially true in the defense industry, where partnerships such as those between General Dynamics and United Defense, and Lockheed and General Dynamics are becoming more the norm than the exception due to continued and drastic cuts in government-approved budgets. All of these negotiations may result in conflict with customers, vendors, and business partners. In some cases, U.S. companies are even partnering with foreign companies (e.g., Chrysler and Fiat; General Dynamics and MTU, a German company), further complicating matters with issues ranging from linguistic and cultural differences to logistical challenges. Moreover, with the increased focus on exposing and punishing unethical behavior in organizations, the need to understand the role of ethics—and develop principle-centered skills[9]—is essential in negotiation.

If you are a small business owner, you may negotiate with representatives of your local government for licenses, zoning variances, or a host of other issues. You will likely negotiate the lease or purchase of real estate to house your business, company vehicles to transport products, and a variety of office equipment. You may negotiate with other businesses for materials and supplies, landscape and parking lot maintenance, as well as cleaning, refuse, and recycling services. Any of these transactions could result in a dispute over merchandise or services. You might even find yourself in the midst of a dispute with a neighboring business over the use of an adjoining parking lot or a landlord who is not living up to the terms of your lease or even a customer who is not paying his bill. Historically, if the disputed amount was under a certain dollar value (e.g., $2,000), the dispute would be resolved in small claims court. If the disputed amount was above the minimum for small claims, there would be a lawsuit. Today, however, there is a trend toward replacing the more formal and expensive avenue of legal action with methods that fall under the generic label of Alternative Dispute Resolution (ADR), the most common of which are mediation and arbitration. Of course, ideally you wouldn't need a third party because you would be able to negotiate directly with the other party to resolve the dispute, which would be the least formal and costly alternative.

Even if you aren't a business owner, you are likely to buy automobiles, real estate, and a variety of other big ticket items in your personal life. Good negotiation skills can make the difference between getting a good deal and paying far too much. Over the course of your lifetime, this can easily amount to tens of thousands of dollars. Outside of work you will negotiate and resolve conflicts with business associates, family members, friends, neighbors, and even total strangers. Here your negotiation and conflict resolution skills can be the difference between preserving—or even improving—a relationship and ending it.

Clearly, negotiation and conflict resolution are a part of daily life. In the workplace, good negotiation skills can result in better terms and conditions of employment and greater success when representing your employer. Similarly, the ability to resolve conflicts with or between others leads to a more harmonious work environment. Outside of work, these skills are equally beneficial. For example, we have seen that most consumers look at contracts as done deals. You either sign the contract or walk away from the deal. This is simply not true. In many transactions, terms can and should be negotiated, such as the price of a service, what's included in your new car purchase, even a contract with a book publisher! Similarly, when people have a conflict with someone, they may simply end the relationship, even when the relationship would be mutually beneficial. Thus, improving your negotiation and conflict resolution skills will lead to increased success in both your work and personal lives. But what if you aren't comfortable negotiating or think that you aren't very good at it? Can everyone become a better negotiator?

Points to Ponder

1. What type of things have you negotiated?
2. Was it easy for you?
3. Do you enjoy negotiating with others?
4. What would you like to learn about negotiating?

NEGOTIATION: IT'S FOR EVERYONE

We all know some people who always seem to get good deals when they negotiate. Whoever the other party may be and whatever the subject is, they get what they want, when they want it, and they get it on their terms. Some people are able to do this while maintaining or even improving their relationship with the other party. They are respected and well liked, and people want to associate with them in and out of the workplace. There are other people, however, who may get their way but damage the relationship in the process. These people are often labeled bullies or tyrants. They are the boss that no one wants to work for, the coworker that no one wants to work with, and the customer no one wants to serve. We look at their families and feel sorry for them.

We also all know people who never seem to get what they want. They are the workers who get stuck with menial tasks no one else wants to do and work longer and harder than their coworkers, yet never get any recognition for their hard work and dedication. They are the people who are repeatedly passed over for promotion. Sometimes we feel sorry for these people and want to help them and other times we wonder why they won't stand up for themselves. We may even begin to think they enjoy being a victim. Yet the answers are often more complex. Perhaps they haven't really thought about what they really want or if it is even realistic. Maybe they are too timid or don't know how to ask for what they want. They may not have reflected on why they should get what they want or developed convincing arguments. It's likely that such people don't understand the process or value of negotiating.

But it is not simply that a person is always a good negotiator or always a poor negotiator. Often people do well in certain contexts but not others. Some people drive a hard bargain in the workplace but acquiesce to anything when it comes to family. Others might always get their way with family—albeit sometimes by whining—but be reluctant to ask for what they want at work. Sometimes people do well with certain types of negotiations but not others. For example, an individual might negotiate great deals with suppliers but be hesitant to ask for a raise he clearly deserves. People may be more assertive negotiators when they are acting on behalf of another person than when they are representing themselves.

What is the difference between those who negotiate well and those who don't? In being effective in some situations but not others? With some people but not others? Can everyone learn to become a better negotiator in all situations with all people? Yes! If you are someone who is very uncomfortable with the idea of negotiating, with practice, you can increase your comfort level. If you are someone who is already comfortable with negotiation, you can improve and refine your skills. If you do well in some situations but not others, you can learn to apply the process in a variety of situations and transfer your skills from the workplace to the marketplace to the home front. You can even learn to deal more effectively with those with whom you are not comfortable negotiating.

CHARACTERISTICS OF NEGOTIATION

Experts have identified six characteristics of negotiation.[10] First, you must have two or more parties. While people sometimes strike deals with themselves (e.g., if I lose ten pounds, I will buy myself a new outfit; when I finish writing this chapter, I will take a day off), this is not considered a true negotiation. Second, there must be a conflict of interest. Obviously if everyone was already in agreement there would be nothing to negotiate. The conflict can range from something relatively minor without much at stake to something that can impact the lives of millions of people. Minor conflicts can arise between friends, such as where to go for lunch or what movie to see. In all likelihood if one party doesn't get what he wants, it will not have a major impact on his life. At the other end of the continuum, major conflicts can have a life-changing impact, such as the conflict between the United States and Saddam Hussein, which led to a war where thousands of people died and the lives of millions more were affected.

The third characteristic is that you should expect a better outcome as a result of the negotiation. If you can't get a better deal by negotiating, why put any effort into the process? There are a number of reasons why people don't negotiate.[11] Some may assume they can't do any better than the stated offer so they don't try to negotiate. Some people are embarrassed to ask for a better price on something. They think the seller or others will think they are poor or cheap if they ask. Some may be willing to attempt negotiation in one context but not another.[12] The reality is that you will never get a better outcome unless you ask. That doesn't mean that you have to be rude or antagonistic about it. Indeed a politely asked "Is that the best you can do?" will often be greeted with a better offer. You just have to get in the habit of asking.

Asking can be especially hard for job applicants when an employer offers them a job. Often they are afraid the employer will get mad and rescind the offer; however, it is highly unlikely that an employer would respond in such a harsh manner to a politely asked "Is that the best you can do?" Research suggests that an employer will come back with a higher offer,[13] even an offer of several thousand dollars more, which can amount to a substantial difference over time. Let's take the example of Jill, who posed that simple question to her last employer when she was offered a job. The employer immediately increased the base salary offered by $3000. On the surface it appears that Jill gained $3000, which for most people isn't a trivial amount. But if you look deeper, Jill gained substantially more than that. Over time it could amount to tens of thousands of dollars. If Jill stays with the employer for ten years the difference is $30,000. If she stays 20 years it is $60,000. If she ends up spending her entire career (from college graduation at age 22 to retirement at age 67) with this employer it is $135,000, an amazing amount for asking the simple question "Is that the best you can do?" If she changes employers a few times and gets more than initially offered each time, the numbers can go even higher. And this is when you keep the calculation to simple math.

If you wanted greater accuracy you would factor in the increased amount that would accumulate with raises. In essence, this is the same principle as compound interest. If you get raises that are a percentage of your base salary and your base salary is higher, your raise will be higher. In Jill's case, assuming she gets an annual raise of 3%, the raise on the additional $3000 would amount to a raise that was $90 more in the first year. While this might not seem like much initially, it adds up by compounding over time. Add to that the increased amount attributed to all forms of compensation and benefits that may be calculated as a percentage of base pay (overtime pay, employer contributions to your retirement plan, life or disability insurance, social security, etc.) and you see the impact of negotiation.

The fourth characteristic is that the parties prefer mutual agreement as opposed to giving in, fighting, walking away from the relationship, or appealing to a higher authority. Imagine you live next door to someone who goes to bed early and likes to get up with the sun to take care of outdoor chores with big noisy power tools. You on the other hand work nights, like to have friends over after work to listen to music, and sleep later in the morning. These differences have left you and your neighbor on less than friendly terms. Your options are to stop entertaining after work, declare all out war with your neighbor, move to a rural area where you are a half mile from your closest neighbor, call the police when your neighbor starts the lawnmower at 7:00 in the morning, or negotiate a mutually agreeable solution with your neighbor. While there is no guarantee that you will be able to work things out, you will never know unless you try.

The fifth characteristic of negotiation is that there is an implied quid pro quo. In other words, both parties need to be willing to give something to get something. You can't realistically expect your up-with-the-sun neighbor to give up his power tools and start partying with you at four in the morning to the latest Top 40 music. What is more realistic is that you agree to hold down the noise late at night in return for your neighbor showing you the same courtesy early in the morning. You may not become friends, but you might be able to find a way to peacefully co-exist.

The last characteristic of negotiation is that it will involve both tangible and intangible components. Staying with the example of the neighbor, he might agree to keep his power tools in the garage until 9:00 if you agree to keep the volume of your music down and limit the number of people you entertain. Alternatively you might both agree to limit the activities the other finds offensive to certain days of the week. Either way you both get tangible results as well as the intangible reduction in stress caused by the conflict.

THE NATURE OF NEGOTIATION

The basic characteristics of negotiation help identify situations where negotiating may prove fruitful, but they are only the beginning. There are other fundamental concepts that must be understood if one is to become a successful negotiator.

Interdependence

Implicit in all negotiations is that the parties have some level of **interdependence** (i.e., they are neither completely dependent nor completely independent), and that by working together, all will benefit. While there are many examples of interdependence, Sly and the Family Stone give a good musical example in their rock and roll classic *"Dance to the Music"*: "All we need is a drummer for people who only need a beat. I'm gonna add a little guitar and make it easy to move your feet. I'm gonna add some bottom, so that the dancers just won't hide. You might like to hear my organ playing 'Ride Sally Ride.' You might like to hear the horns blowin'. . ." and the song continues with the contribution of the various musicians in the group. Without offending the drummers out there who live for their drum solos, most people wouldn't attend a concert or buy a CD that contained only drum solos. That is because the music is better, as judged by concert attendance and CD sales, when all members of the band play together.

Such is the nature of interdependence; we have both something to contribute and something to attain. It is rare indeed that we are either completely dependent or independent. This is true in the workplace where we depend on others within and outside the organization. We depend on virtually everyone in our own organization to help us accomplish our work. If we work in manufacturing, we depend on people in sales and marketing to obtain orders for our products, engineers to determine how to build the products, buyers to obtain the raw materials to make the products, and people in accounting to collect the payments for the products and track the company's financials, just to name a few. Outside of the organization, we depend on suppliers to provide the goods and services we need and customers to purchase our goods and services. Even those who are self-employed depend on a variety of suppliers and customers to provide materials and services. Similarly, in our communities we depend on each other to make a variety of contributions, ranging from volunteer work to the simple acts of voting and paying our taxes. In both our work and personal lives, we depend on friends and family members to help us out in times of difficulty and share our happiness during good times. These interdependencies both influence the balance of power in negotiations and are often more effectively managed by negotiating. We explore this in detail in Chapter 3.

Issues vs. Interests

When negotiating, it is important to distinguish between issues and interests. **Issues** are the specific items or terms you actually negotiate and are generally the first thing that we think of when we anticipate negotiating. This includes what is or is not going to happen, who will be responsible, when it will or will not happen, how it will be done, and what happens if one of the parties doesn't live up to the agreement. In the example of the neighbors, the issues might include the time at which your neighbor starts using his power tools, the days or the frequency when the tools would be used, a curfew on your parties, and/or a limit on the frequency or days when you can have them. There are a multitude of issues that are negotiated depending on the situation; however, in all cases the issues we negotiate need to satisfy our interests.

Interests are what you hope to accomplish to address your underlying concerns, needs, desires, or fears. Interests may include substantive issues, procedures used, maintaining the relationship, and matters of principle.[14] Fisher and colleagues[15] maintain that the most powerful human interests are basic human needs that include security; economic well-being; and a sense of belonging, recognition, and control over one's life. These interests permeate one's entire life and transcend the boundaries between our work and personal lives. For example, having job security and adequate compensation provides a sense of economic well-being that influences our standard of living and how we spend our time outside of work (e.g., exercising, playing sports). At the same time what we do outside of work (i.e., living a healthy lifestyle) can influence work-related factors (e.g., absenteeism).

In the example of the neighbors, the interests may include each party's need to get adequate sleep (control over one's life), especially on days they have to work (economic well-being). Your neighbor may also have a strong desire to have a well-maintained home and yard (to maintain or increase the value of the home and recognition from others), and to get the work done early to avoid the mid-day heat (to minimize health risks) or to allow time for other activities in the afternoon (control over one's life). You may have a need to unwind after work or to maintain social contact with your friends (a sense of belonging), which may be difficult because of your work schedule. You may both have a desire to resolve this in a fair manner that respects the rights of all parties to keep this conflict from escalating (security). You may also both wish to get along with the other since you are neighbors (a sense of belonging).

The Role of Incentives

The best possible outcomes in negotiations are usually realized when all parties' interests are satisfied to some extent. Thus, negotiation is not just about pounding your fists on the table and getting everything you want while the other party limps away empty-handed licking his wounds. This may be the makings for a classic Hollywood drama, but in real life it typically doesn't work, especially when you need to deal with the other party again in the future. But if it isn't about pounding your fists to frighten your opponent into submission, what is it? According to the dictionary, to **negotiate** is "to arrange for or bring about by discussion and settlement of terms."[16] But negotiation isn't just about being a smooth talker either. Beyond having good communication skills, truly successful negotiators understand the process of negotiation, particularly the role of incentives and persuasion tactics, the parties involved, the subject of the negotiation, and the specific situation.

Successful negotiators know that people respond to incentives and that you can often get more for yourself by understanding and offering the other party what she wants. We see this in practice every day in a variety of situations. One example is new car sales. When the economy is bad, people don't spend as much money. To encourage people to buy new cars the automakers offer no-interest or low-interest financing or rebates, and sometimes even both. The automakers understand that even when the economy is bad, there are people who would like a new car and that offering a great deal may provide the incentive people need to spend money when they otherwise wouldn't. On a smaller scale, retailers advertise "buy one get one free" or "buy one get half off" offers on everything from groceries to apparel to recliners. When consumers think they are getting a deal they often buy more, sometimes whether they actually need the product or not.

When there is tough competition in a labor market, employers use incentives to attract employees. With the ongoing shortage of nurses and other health care professionals, hospitals sometimes encourage prospective employees to work for them with signing bonuses. Some offer to pay off student loan debt as an incentive to get people to move to less desirable geographic areas to alleviate a shortage. This is especially true with physicians, who often graduate with large amounts of debt, making such an incentive even more appealing. In some cases employers offer incentives, typically in the form of a raise, to retain employees who have let the employer know that they are seeking other employment. This, however, does not mean that if you threaten to quit, your employer will automatically offer you more money to stay. Indeed most of us know someone who has threatened to quit in an attempt to pressure an employer for a pay increase, only to have the employer wish her well in her new endeavors.

Similarly, offering incentives does not guarantee that everyone will jump at the offer. A particular incentive may work for one person but not another. When automakers offer incentives, some people buy cars while others do not. When a remote town in the middle of nowhere offers to pay off a physician's student loans, not all newly minted MDs eagerly apply. So how do you know if an incentive is going to be effective? You typically don't know for sure, but you can make fairly accurate predictions if you understand the other party and what she wants or needs. To do this you must accept that we are all different and value different things. It is human nature to assume that others have the same values and priorities in life that you have, but this is not accurate. Psychologists even have a name for this: fundamental attribution error. While you may place a high value on driving a new car or living in the city of your choice, others may place a higher value on having money in the bank for a rainy day or having their student loans paid. To understand the other party's needs, you need to get to know him and his history, and be able to view the situation from his perspective. And yes, this all takes time and effort.

Negotiators also need to understand the subject of the negotiation. If you are negotiating to purchase steel for use in the manufacture of your company's products, you need to be well versed in the technical specifications of steel, as well as the requirements for your particular application. If you are negotiating a job offer you need to understand the demand for your knowledge, skills, and abilities in the relevant labor market and the various aspects of compensation and benefits. If the negotiation involves buying a vehicle, you need to understand the makes, models, and options available. Whatever the subject of the negotiation, you need to be able to identify and understand a wide range of alternatives because research and preparation is vital to success in negotiation. As with understanding the other party, understanding the subject of the negotiation and researching alternatives takes time and effort.

Finally, successful negotiators understand the specific situation. What works with a particular person in one situation may not work in another. For example, a person who would normally be inclined to take advantage of great financing and instant rebates on a new car may not be if she is concerned about being laid off from her job. Indeed economists track a variety of statistics on peoples' behavior from consumer spending to new construction of residential housing to use when making predictions about the economy. In a similar vein, someone who may be tempted to move away to a remote location if he was single may not be willing to do so if he has small children or ailing parents. Successful negotiators make an effort to understand the situation from the perspective of the other party, and offer solutions and options that would be perceived as valuable or desirable. This is not always as easy as you might think.

A further complication is that situations change, sometimes dramatically and rapidly. Take the case of Elizabeth Vargas and Bob Woodruff, who in 2006 accepted positions as coanchors of the ABC nightly news in the United States. Shortly after accepting these highly coveted positions, the situation changed dramatically for both coanchors, albeit for very different reasons. Elizabeth was surprised to discover that she was expecting a child. About the same time Bob was critically injured while covering the war in Iraq. Due to unforeseen circumstances, Bob was left fighting for his life and Elizabeth in effect became the sole anchor. As a result of the unplanned pregnancy and the added job responsibility, Elizabeth made the difficult decision to step down from what had been a fabulous career opportunity.

While situations may change unexpectedly, successful negotiators understand this and work with it. They may even be able to influence the situation to make it more favorable. Despite resigning her position as coanchor, Elizabeth Vargas stayed with ABC, returning to a position with the news program 20/20. In the end she had a position that provided a better fit with her personal life given the altered situation and ABC kept an employee they clearly saw as valuable. Similarly Bob Woodruff fought his way back from his injuries and was able to return to work in early 2007. Many of his reports now deal with situations faced by returning veterans and he is making a difference in many of their lives through his reporting. The evening news is now anchored by Diane Sawyer, but both Elizabeth and Bob adapted and made the best of their respective situations. This is what successful negotiators do; they adapt to changing circumstances and find alternatives that meet their needs. But even successful negotiators sometimes encounter difficult situations or people and have to deal with conflict

Conflict

Conflict can be defined as a fight, battle, or struggle; a controversy or quarrel; discord of action, feeling, or effect; or incompatibility or interference.[17] It can be intra- or interpersonal or group. Intrapersonal conflict is the conflict a person feels within himself or herself. A common example is work–family conflict where a person is trying to fulfill the roles of employee and parent simultaneously and feels torn between the two roles. While this is a serious issue, it does not fit our requirement that there be two or more individuals for negotiation to occur. Interpersonal conflict is conflict between two people and includes conflict between coworkers, business acquaintances, neighbors, or friends. Intragroup conflict occurs when there is conflict between people within a group. This could be a within a work team, family unit, or social group. Intergroup conflict is conflict between groups and can include conflicts between departments, teams, or even countries.

In general conflict can be functional or dysfunctional and you need an appropriate amount; too much or too little is not good. If the conflict is managed well, it facilitates innovation and change, and results in better-quality decisions. It can also bring previously ignored problems into the open so they can be addressed while clarifying individuals' expectations and enhancing organizational commitment. It also tends to pique employee interest and increase understanding of why things are the way they are. If the conflict is not well managed and gets out of control, the result is a high level of personal stress, anxiety, and burnout. At an organizational level, it usually creates a climate of mistrust where individuals engage in defensive risk-avoiding behaviors, and there is reduced cooperation and sharing of resources. In negotiations, poorly managed conflict often leads to a breakdown in the negotiation process and may result in the parties not reaching an agreement. We address the issue of conflict and approaches to resolving it in detail in Chapter 5.

Whether you are a novice or an experienced negotiator you can always improve your negotiation and conflict resolution skills. Our goal is to help you do that by helping you to understand the processes involved and become proficient in gathering, assembling, and using relevant information so you are well prepared and equipped for success in negotiating and resolving conflicts in a wide variety of settings.

Points to Ponder

1. Have you or someone you have known ended a relationship where there was conflict that might have been repaired?
2. What kinds of things have you done to repair a broken relationship?
3. What would you like to learn about resolving conflict?

PREPARATION: CLARIFYING GOALS AND INTERESTS

In most cases, successful negotiators, regardless of their experience level, spend more time preparing for a negotiation than they actually do negotiating. They are also more likely to approach it from a problem-solving perspective instead of as a competitive game. The first step is to identify the potential interests and issues involved, tangible and intangible. Understanding your needs leads to higher aspirations,[18] which leads to more favorable outcomes.[19] When you are identifying issues it is important to think beyond what is important to you and consider issues that may be important to the other party.

Let's say you are planning a vacation to Hawaii with a friend. The obvious tangible issues that are likely to come to mind first are when you will go, where you will stay, and how much it will cost. You have to come up with a time for the trip that takes both your school schedule and your friend's work schedule into consideration. You will also have to decide where to stay: will it be a five star resort on the beach or an economy motel a few blocks away? This is likely to be influenced by your respective finances. If your working friend has cash in the bank and you are struggling to pay your tuition, the answer is unlikely to be easy.

But you need to go beyond obvious issues and address the interests of everyone involved. You may be looking at it as an opportunity to see the sights and participate in all the activities, while your friend may want to spend serious time on the beach. On the surface this could play out as a difference in what each party likes to do—sightseeing versus tanning—but the underlying interests may be quite different. You may want to tour Pearl Harbor because you plan to take a class on the history of World War II and want to use this as an opportunity to tour one of the most significant sites involved. Your friend may be looking at the vacation as an opportunity to recover from a very busy work schedule. Thus, a less obvious concern that you should address is why you want to go and what you want to accomplish while you are there. By doing so you will have an increased likelihood of coming up with a plan that meets both of your needs.

Once the interests and issues are identified you need to prioritize them. One way to think about it is what you must have, what you would like to have, and things you could care less about. Staying with the example of your Hawaiian vacation, you might list all the activities and attractions that you and your friend might possibly do and then classify the issues as high, medium, or low priority from your perspective. From there you can estimate the priority your friend places on each of the activities. In doing this you need to keep in mind your friend's and your underlying interests, that is, taking in the relaxing and, sights respectively. Of course at this point you are only estimating your friend's priorities, but this estimation can give you a sense of where there might be common ground when the actual negotiation begins. While you might think this is excessively detailed, it really helps to put your list in writing so you and your friend can visually identify the alternatives and your priorities. Table 1.1 is an example of how this might look.

Laying out the alternatives in this way makes it easy to see the possibilities. It doesn't provide one solution, indeed there are several very plausible solutions. You might decide to do the helicopter tour of the island because you both really want to do

TABLE 1.1 Prioritizing Issues for Your Hawaiian Vacation

Activity	Your priority	Friend's priority
Beach time	Low	High
Pearl Harbor	High	Low
Atlantis submarine	Low	Low
Hawaiian luau	Medium	Medium
Pineapple plantation tour	Medium	Low
Catamaran dinner cruise	Medium	Medium
Shopping	Low	Medium
Zoo/aquarium	Low	Low
Helicopter tour of island	High	High
Hiking Diamond Head	Medium	Low

it (and because it is very cool). You might also decide to spend time on the beach and tour Pearl Harbor together because each is a high priority to one of you. Conversely, you could agree to tour Pearl Harbor while your friend spends time at the beach, and then do the Hawaiian luau or the Catamaran dinner cruise together because it is something in which you are both moderately interested. And these are just a few possibilities. While this example is very simplistic, you could easily add other factors to consider. If cost were an issue you could include a column for the estimated cost of each activity so you could estimate budget requirements.

Once you have identified and prioritized the relevant issues and interests, you need to consider your alternatives. If you don't come to a negotiated agreement with your friend, what are your options? One alternative would be to go alone. This would likely increase your cost because you wouldn't be sharing a room. Besides, most people find it more fun to travel with someone. You might also find someone else to go. Here you need to consider people who might be interested, have the time and financial resources available, and who might be more like-minded in terms of what activities they would enjoy. You might even find a group tour that you could join. Of course another alternative is that you simply don't go.

Your approach to the negotiation is going to depend on how much you want to go and how attractive your alternatives are. If the idea came up one night after a few cocktails and you aren't 100% committed to going, you might decide it's not worth a lot of effort. On the other hand, if you really want to go and don't have anyone else with whom to travel, you would probably be willing to put more effort into reaching an agreement. Of course you also have to think about these things from your friend's perspective. How much does she want to go? What are her alternatives? Often it helps to put yourself in your friend's shoes to try to understand her perspective.

Once you have identified your friend's and your alternatives, you need to think about what you want to say and how you will say it. You may even practice this with another person to get feedback. If you think this is overkill, think about your worst classroom presentation. We have all had them. You go in very confident in your ability to "wing it" only to find yourself in the middle of your speech stumbling and wishing it were over. While you probably won't have an audience when you are negotiating, you do want to get your point across effectively.

Your preparation should also include anticipating what the other party might say and how she might react. You don't want to inadvertently say or do something that is going to anger the other party, especially if you care about maintaining the relationship after the negotiation. Even if you don't care about the relationship, making the other party angry is going to diminish the chance of negotiating an agreement. Anticipating the other party's reaction is often easier when you are rehearsing with another person because you can get his opinion on your approach and assumptions. Of course another person's opinion isn't a substitute for good research.

PREPARATION: THE IMPORTANCE OF RESEARCH

Whether you are planning a vacation or preparing for some other negotiation, a big part of the preparation process is research to help you understand what your alternatives are and to help predict what to expect from the other party. Fortunately, today the Internet makes many resources available for gathering information. Before the Internet you had to physically go to a bank or credit union to look up the "book value" of used cars in Kelly's "blue book." Today you can access this information online at Kelly's Blue Book website (www.kbb.com) or one of several other such sites (Chapter 13 provides detailed information on negotiations involving automobiles). But the information available today isn't just limited to automobiles. There is a wealth of information available to help you prepare for a variety of negotiations.

If you were planning to buy a house ten years ago, you had to rely on a real estate agent to give you access to their multiple listing book; a three-ring notebook containing a page of information on each home for sale in a particular area. If you were planning to sell your house, you had to rely on the same real estate agent to give you information on the sale price of other comparable homes in the area that had recently been sold. Today most realtors' websites are linked to the multiple listing database of all properties for sale in an area (see Chapter 14 for more on real estate negotiations). The information available goes beyond autos and houses.

When your parents were looking for their first job, they likely scoured the "help wanted" section of the Sunday newspapers. If they were wondering about average salaries and benefit packages in their field, they would either rely on word of mouth or get information from a headhunter (i.e., professional recruiter). Today you can simply go online and access one of the websites containing salary survey information such as www.salary.com or www.monster.com (see Chapter 12 for more on workplace negotiations). If you are thinking about relocating, there are also sites available that show you the difference in cost of living from one geographic area to another, which can make a big difference in whether relocation is a smart move from a financial standpoint.

Research takes negotiation from "I want a raise because I want/need more money" to "I deserve a raise because the going market rate in our area for people with my credentials and experience is 15% higher than what I am currently making." Having appropriate documentation helps focus the negotiation on facts and logical conclusions instead of emotions. In doing so you increase the likelihood of arriving at an agreement that meets the needs of all parties and avoiding conflict.

ETHICS IN NEGOTIATION

Negotiation is a form of social exchange, which means there is a possibility that one party will exploit, or attempt to exploit, the other.[20] Thus, an issue that may arise in negotiation is whether or not a person is behaving ethically or using negotiation tactics that are ethically questionable. One's ethics are personal and based on one's value system. A tactic one person views as ethically appropriate may not be viewed that way by others. Even if you always behave in a highly ethical manner, others with whom you negotiate or have conflicts may not. Thus, it is important to assess not only your behavior in a particular situation, but how others might act as well. To facilitate this we include one or more ethical dilemmas at the end of every chapter to provide you an opportunity to assess numerous behaviors in a wide variety of settings.

There are a number of approaches that may be used when assessing whether a person is behaving ethically or if a particular negotiation tactic is considered ethical, and not all produce the same results. We consider the three most commonly used approaches in the business ethics literature—utilitarian, rights, and justice.[21] The **utilitarian**[22] approach maintains that the best alternative is the one that provides the greatest good and least harm for the greatest number, although individuals may suffer as a result. An example of this would be when a local government forces a landowner to sell her property to make way for an airport expansion or new highway. In these situations, the individual homeowner's interests are deemed less important than the interests of the general public. When evaluating a situation using the utilitarian approach the questions to ask are: who is being helped by the action, and, who is being harmed? If there are more people being helped than harmed, the utilitarian perspective would hold that the action is justified.

The **rights** approach to ethics holds that ethical decisions are ones that protect the rights of individuals (e.g., privacy, free speech), although it might not result in the greatest efficiency or total value.[23] The issues to address are: what rights are being exercised, by whom, and whether there are any rights being denied; if yes, then which ones and whose? Consider the example of the two neighbors discussed earlier. Does one neighbor's right to peace and quiet outweigh the other's right to do as he pleases on his own property? As you might guess, this example could be argued either way depending on whose rights you are most concerned with, and perhaps, even if you are a morning or a night person.

The **justice** perspective focuses on the fair and impartial creation and application of rules.[24] An example would be an employer who refuses to make any exceptions to a policy regardless of the situation. If you are an employee in such an organization it will likely be much more challenging to negotiate creative working arrangements than it would be otherwise. Relevant issues to address when evaluating situations with this approach are: Are any laws, policies, or rules being violated? Which ones? By whom? In the example of the neighbors, the outcome would be influenced by any local noise ordinances.

OVERVIEW OF THE BOOK

As shown in Figure 1.1, we have divided this book into four sections that provide an appropriate theoretical background in negotiation and conflict resolution, and numerous opportunities to practice and develop your negotiation and conflict resolution skills for use in a wide variety of business and personal situations. Part I is the foundation. It provides an overview of negotiations in general, and defines the language used in negotiation and conflict resolution. Part II covers the processes involved in distributive and integrative negotiation and conflict resolution. Part III considers the interpersonal and contextual characteristics of negotiation, ranging from the impact of personalities, communication, and relationships to the impact of culture and involvement of additional parties in a negotiation.

After introducing the basic premises of negotiation and conflict resolution, in Part IV we shift our focus to the application of what you have learned. Here we delve more deeply into the specifics of negotiations that you are likely to encounter in the workplace, as well as negotiations involving automobiles and real estate that may occur in both your personal and professional lives. This "deep dive" into the research, planning, and execution of these common negotiations provides a greater depth of experience with the negotiation process that you will be able to transfer to other settings.

FIGURE 1.1 Organization of the Book

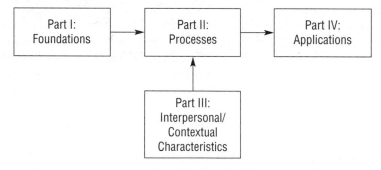

Summary

Whether we realize it or not, we negotiate something almost every day of our lives. We negotiate and attempt to resolve conflict at work and in our personal lives. Some of us are highly skilled negotiators who enjoy the process, and others are not. Some of us are good in certain situations or with certain subjects but not others. However, regardless of our skill or comfort level, we can all improve. To be more successful we need to understand the role of incentives, the interest of the parties involved, the issues involved in the negotiation, and the importance of preparation prior to a negotiation. If we become skilled in the process, we will achieve better substantive outcomes and enjoy better relationships with others.

Summary: The Big Picture

Negotiation and dispute resolution	Negotiation and conflict resolution are learnable, transferable skills.
	The processes can be used in a multitude of work-related and non-work-related situations to obtain better outcomes and improve relationships.
	One's comfort level with negotiation and dispute resolution can be context dependent.
Negotiation characteristics	Two or more parties.
	Conflict of interest.
	Expectation of a better outcome.
	Prefer mutual agreement.
	Implied quid pro quo.
	Tangible and intangible components.
Interdependence	We need others and others need us.
Interests and issues	Interests are basic needs.
	Issues are what we negotiate to meet our needs.
Incentives	Incentives motivate human behavior.
	Offering incentives that meet the other party's needs increases the likelihood of the other party agreeing to your proposals.
	Need to understand the other party's wants and needs, the subject of the negotiation, and the specific situation.
Conflict	Can be inter- or intrapersonal, or group; functional or dysfunctional.
Preparing to negotiate	Clarify goals and interests, and prioritize.
	Identify issues and prioritize.
	Explore alternatives.
	Plan what you will say.
	Anticipate what the other party will say and how she will react to your proposal(s).
Research	Research all alternatives.
Ethics in negotiation	Utilitarian approach seeks the greatest good for the greatest number.
	Rights approach focuses on protecting individual's rights.
	Justice approach applies fair and impartial rules for decision making

Key Terms and Concepts

Conflict   A discord of action, feeling, or effect; or incompatibility or interference.

Interdependence   A state of mutual dependence, neither completely dependent nor completely independent.

Interests   What you hope to accomplish to address your underlying concerns, needs, desires, or fears.

Issues   The specific items or terms you negotiate.

Justice   An approach to ethics that focuses on the fair and impartial creation and application of rules.

Negotiate   To arrange for or bring about by discussion and settlement of terms.

Rights   An approach to ethics that holds that ethical decisions are ones that protect the rights of individuals (e.g., privacy and free speech), although this approach might not result in the greatest efficiency or total value.

Utilitarian   An approach to ethics where the best alternative is the one that provides the greatest good and the least harm for the greatest number, although individuals may suffer as a result.

Discussion Questions

1. Identify situations where negotiation is likely in the workplace and in your personal life.
2. Using a negotiation with which you are familiar, describe the characteristics of negotiation.
3. Using a negotiation with which you are familiar, discuss how the issues that were negotiated related to the parties' interests.
4. Describe how incentives influence your behavior at school or work and in your personal life.
5. Using a negotiation with which you are familiar, identify the preparation involved and the extent to which it was successful. What else might have been done?
6. Identify possible conflicts that you may experience in the workplace and in your personal life.
7. Discuss your level of comfort in negotiating with others at school, work, and home.

Ethical Dilemma: The Research Project

Bill and Rachael are both analysts in the market research department at ABC Company. Bill is generally viewed as a top performer. Objectively his work is good, but he really excels at self-promotion. When dealing with others he is a tough negotiator, confident to the point of being cocky. He likes to win and win big. He is unafraid of stepping on anyone's toes and lives by the motto that it is easier to beg forgiveness than to ask permission.

Rachael is bright and hard-working; however, she is modest and relies on others to notice the good work she does. She believes it's more important to spend her time working than promoting herself and publicizing her accomplishments. She views conflict as a complete waste of time and has a difficult time standing up for herself. This often results in others taking advantage of her.

Bill and Rachael have recently been assigned to work together on what has the potential to be a highly visible project. The project involves a lot of research, writing a report, and presenting the findings to the senior executives. They just finished meeting to lay out the tasks involved and establish a plan for the project. In their meeting Bill told Rachael that she can do the research and draft the report, and he will make the presentation. When Rachael suggested they work together on the research and jointly make the presentation, Bill told her that she needs to do the research and draft the report because she is better at "that sort of thing," while he needs to make the presentation because of his superior presentation skills.

Bill left the meeting satisfied that he had won yet again and believing that since he will be making the presentation he will get the majority of the credit for the project. This is important to him because he has heard there will be an opening in the near future for a senior analyst. He wants the promotion and thinks the visibility of this project will make him a shoo-in for the job.

Rachael left their meeting feeling resentful and put upon but not knowing what to do about it. While this sort of thing has happened to her in the past she was especially upset this time because she has heard there will soon be an opening for a senior analyst and she is very interested in the position.

Questions

1. Is Bill behaving ethically?
2. What do you think he should do in this situation?
3. How might Rachael negotiate an outcome that better meets her needs?

Endnotes

1. www.oneredpaperclip.com (accessed August 4, 2010).
2. *Ibid.*
3. Levitt, Steven D., and Stephen J. Dubner. *Freakonomics.* New York: William Morrow (Harper Collins), 2005.
4. Wheelan, Charles. *Naked Economics: Undressing the Dismal Science.* New York: W. W. Norton & Company, 2002.
5. Zetik, D. C., and A. F. Stuhlmacher. "Goal Setting and Negotiation Performance: A Meta-Analysis." *Group Processes & Intergroup Relations* 5(1) (2002): 35–52.
6. Barron, A. Lisa. "Ask and You Shall Receive? Gender Differences in Negotiators' Beliefs about Requests for a Higher Salary." *Human Relations* 56 (6) (2003): 635–662.
7. Kumar, Rajesh. "The Role of Affect in Negotiations: An Integrative Overview." *The Journal of Applied Behavioral Science* 33 (1) (1997): 84–100.
8. Page, D., and A. Mukherjee. "Promoting Critical-Thinking Skills by Using Negotiation Exercises." *Journal of Education for Business* 82 (5) (2007): 251–257.
9. Fisher, Roger, William Ury, and Bruce Patton. *Getting to Yes* (2nd ed.). Boston: Houghton-Mifflin, 1991.
10. Lewicki, Roy J., Bruce Barry, and David M. Saunders. *Negotiation* (6th ed.). Boston: McGraw-Hill Irwin, 2010.
11. Terri Kurtzberg, and Victoria Husted Medvec. "Can We Negotiate and Still Be Friends?" *Negotiation Journal* 15 (4) (1999): 355–61.
12. Sillence, John A A. "Organizational Context and the Discursive Construction of Organizing." *Management Communication Quarterly* 20 (4) (2007): 363–394.
13. Barron, Lisa A. "Ask and you shall receive? Gender differences in negotiators' beliefs about requests for a higher salary." *Human Relations* 56 (6) (2003): 635–662.
14. Lax, D., and J. Sebenius. *The Manager as Negotiator: Bargaining for Cooperation and Competitive Gain.* New York: Free Press, 1986.
15. Fisher, Roger, William Ury, and Bruce Patton. *Getting to Yes* (2nd ed.). Boston: Houghton-Mifflin, 1991, p. 48.

16. *The American Heritage® Dictionary of the English Language, Fourth Edition.* Retrieved June 8, 2009, from Dictionary.com website: http://dictionary.reference.com/browse/negotiate

17. *The American Heritage® Dictionary of the English Language, Fourth Edition.* Retrieved June 8, 2009, from Dictionary.com website: http://dictionary.reference.com/browse/conflict

18. Stuhlmacher, Alice F., and Matthew V. Champagne. "The Impact of Time Pressure and Information on Negotiation Process and Decisions." *Group Decision and Negotiation* 9 (6) (2000): 471–491.

19. Zetik, D. C., and A. F. Stuhlmacher. "Goal Setting and Negotiation Performance: A Meta-Analysis." *Group Processes & Intergroup Relations* 5 (1) (2002): 35–52.

20. Olekalns, Mara, and Philip L. Smith. "Mutually Dependent: Power, Trust, Affect and the Use of Deception in Negotiation." *Journal of Business Ethics* 85 (3) (2009): 347–365.

21. Whittier, Nathan C., Scott Williams, and Todd C. Dewett. "Evaluating Ethical Decision-Making Models: A Review and Application." *Society and Business Review* 1 (3) (2006): 235–247.

22. Mill, John Stuart. *Utilitarianism, On Liberty, Essay on Bentham.* New York: New American Library, 1962.

23. Kant, Immanuel. *Lectures on Ethics.* New York: Harper & Row, 1963.

24. Rawls, John. *A Theory of Justice.* Boston: Harvard University Press, 1971.

Exercise 1.1   A Trip Down Memory Lane

For this exercise, you need to think of times in your life when you have negotiated or attempted to resolve a conflict, and were successful or unsuccessful. The negotiations could be when you have purchased or sold something, where you have attempted to get something you want, or when you tried to get someone to do what you wanted. The conflict resolution examples could be when you tried to resolve a conflict you had with another person or when you attempted to resolve a conflict between other people. Your examples can be from work, school, or your personal life.

For each example try to remember as much detail as possible—the who, what, where, and when of the situation. What, if anything, had you done to prepare or get yourself psyched up? What was the substantive outcome? What was the effect on your relationship with the other party? To organize the examples for further analysis, complete the worksheet on the following pages. For each of the categories, record the details of at least one example where you were successful and one where you were not.

After you have recorded the details of each example, identify commonalities in the situations where you were successful and the situations where you were unsuccessful. For example, are you generally more or less successful when dealing with family members or strangers? Are you more or less successful with particular topics (e.g., buying/selling vs. interpersonal conflicts)? Is there anything you do to prepare that seems to help?

Worksheet: Exercise 1.1 A Trip Down Memory Lane

1. Examples of when you purchased or attempted to purchase something and wanted to get a good deal on it.

Successful	Unsuccessful
Who: _____	Who: _____
What: _____	What: _____
Where: _____	Where: _____
When: _____	When: _____
Preparation: _____	Preparation: _____
Outcome: _____	Outcome: _____
Comments: _____	Comments: _____

2. Examples of when you sold or tried to sell something and wanted to maximize your outcome.

Successful	**Unsuccessful**
Who: _____	Who: _____
What: _____	What: _____
Where: _____	Where: _____
When: _____	When: _____
Preparation: _____	Preparation: _____
_____	_____
_____	_____
Outcome: _____	Outcome: _____
_____	_____
_____	_____
Comments: _____	Comments: _____
_____	_____

3. Examples of when you attempted to persuade others (relatives, friends, coworkers, or strangers) to do what you want.

Successful	**Unsuccessful**
Who: _____	Who: _____
What: _____	What: _____
Where: _____	Where: _____
When: _____	When: _____
Preparation: _____	Preparation: _____
_____	_____
_____	_____
Outcome: _____	Outcome: _____
_____	_____
_____	_____
Comments: _____	Comments: _____
_____	_____

4. Examples of when you attempted to resolve a conflict with another person (relative, friend, coworker, or stranger).

Successful	Unsuccessful
Who: _____	Who: _____
What: _____	What: _____
Where: _____	Where: _____
When: _____	When: _____
Preparation: _____	Preparation: _____
_____	_____
_____	_____
Outcome: _____	Outcome: _____
_____	_____
_____	_____
Comments: _____	Comments: _____
_____	_____

Considering the examples you have identified, complete the following paragraphs.

In general I am more successful negotiating when: _____

_____

_____

_____

In general I am less successful negotiating when: _____

_____

_____

_____

In general I am more successful resolving conflict when: _____

_____

_____

_____

In general I am less successful resolving conflict when: _____

_____

_____

_____

_____

Exercise 1.2   Mirror, Mirror on the Wall/Initial Self Evaluation

In this exercise, you will be assessing your negotiation and conflict resolution skills. To help you start thinking about this in more detail, complete the questionnaire on the following page and draft a paragraph that describes how you see yourself as a negotiator.

In class you will form small groups and share your Individual Bargaining Statements. Group members will provide feedback that you may use to revise your Individual Bargaining Statement.

Next, you will write an Initial Self Evaluation paper that addresses the following:

1. Individual Bargaining Statement/paragraph describing yourself as a negotiator.
2. How comfortable are you negotiating? How easy do you find it to ask for what you want?
3. How comfortable are you in situations of moderate conflict? How do you typically react to conflict?
4. How effective are you in persuading others? If you are going to try to persuade someone, how do you typically prepare?
5. What do you hope to learn in this class?

Worksheet: Exercise 1.2 Mirror, Mirror on the Wall/Initial Self Evaluation

Self-Assessment Questionnaire

Rate each of the following on a scale of 1–5 where 1 = strongly disagree and 5 = strongly agree.

Rating

_____	1. I usually enjoy trying to get a good deal when I buy or sell something.
_____	2. I am generally comfortable asking for a better price on something I want to buy.
_____	3. I am typically comfortable talking to people I don't know well.
_____	4. I frequently use humor to make my point.
_____	5. I am generally comfortable in new environments.
_____	6. I can typically maintain a poker face when I need to.
_____	7. I can usually understand another person's point of view.
_____	8. For the most part I enjoy persuading others.
_____	9. I am usually comfortable in situations where there is mild to moderate conflict.
_____	10. In most situations I am generally competitive.
_____	11. I can be very persistent when it comes to getting what I want.
_____	12. I have negotiated a number of times in my life.
_____	13. I am frequently successful in making things happen and getting what I want.
_____	14. I typically aim high when setting goals.
_____ Total points	

Based on your responses, draft a paragraph that describes how you see yourself as a negotiator.

_____

_____

_____

_____

_____

_____

_____

_____

_____

_____

_____

Exercise 1.3   How Do Others See You as a Negotiator?

For this exercise, you will be interviewing others who know you in various capacities (relatives, friends, coworkers, roommates, etc.) to develop a profile of how others see you as a negotiator.

Talk to at least three people who know you in different capacities. Explain to them that you are taking a class in negotiations and you would like to ask them some questions to help you better understand your negotiation and conflict resolution skills. Ask them to be very candid in their responses so you will know what you need to work on in the class.

Interview Questions

1. How persistent am I when I want something?
2. How easily do I give up?
3. How competitive am I?
4. How likely am I to use:
   a. Guilt or emotional appeal ("Please!")
   b. Logical explanation ("You should do this because ....")
   c. Exchange ("I'll do _____ for you if you do _____ for me.")
5. What do you think would make me a better negotiator?

Summary of Results

1. How did others describe you? _____

_____

_____

_____

_____

2. Were the descriptions what you expected? _____

_____

_____

_____

_____

3. What, if anything, did they say that surprised you? _____

_____

_____

_____

_____

Exercise 1.4   Freeze Frame/The Poker Face

Freeze! Don't move! Seriously, keep breathing but don't move any body parts. Take an inventory of your body. Are your muscles tense? Are your hands clenched? What is your posture like? What is your facial expression? What are your hands doing? Keep breathing and be aware of your body. Are you relaxed? If not, consciously let the muscles relax. Let a small smile come to your face. Become aware of others around you. Do they seem relaxed? Are their hands clenched? Do their faces look tense? What is their posture like?

This is an exercise that you will practice many times throughout this course as a way to become more aware of, and over time learn to control, the messages you are sending to others via your body language. It is most helpful to practice this in tense situations as that is when our nonverbal messages are most likely to be different than our verbal messages.

Your instructor may assign this as an out-of-class activity and have you record your observations for later discussion in class and/or periodically stop the class and have everyone quickly assess their body language.

CHAPTER 2

The Language of Negotiation

Chapter Objectives

After studying this chapter and completing the exercises you should be able to:

- Identify the issues that would constitute the bargaining mix in a variety of negotiations.

- Apply proper terminology when preparing for and executing a negotiation.

- Identify opening offers, and target and resistance points.

- Understand the role of a negotiator's Best Alternative to a Negotiated Agreement (BATNA) and its impact on negotiation.

- Assess the impact of framing in negotiating and resolving conflict.

- Understand the role of reciprocity in negotiations.

egotiations occur in a wide variety of situations. Often when people think of negotiating, they think about buying or selling material items such as cars, electronics, or appliances; however, as we know from the field of labor economics, the notion of buying and selling also applies in an employment setting, where the employee is selling his labor (i.e., knowledge, skills, and abilities) and the employer is purchasing it. Even in our personal relationships, we want what another has to offer, whether that is their help, friendship, love, respect, and/or approval. In return, the other person wants what we have to offer. Whether or not we label these exchanges as negotiations, for all practical purposes, that is what they are. If we are to be successful, we need to understand the process and all that is involved.

Chapter Scenario, Part I

Katherine, a recent college graduate, has just been offered a job at a medium-sized company in her hometown. She has no idea if the offer is a good one or not. She doesn't want to settle for less than she's worth, but she is also a bit worried that she won't get a better offer and certainly doesn't want to anger the prospective employer. Katherine's uncle Art, who has negotiated labor contracts for many years, told her that she should negotiate the job offer with the prospective employer. He said she should start with an aggressive opening demand and be sure not to set her resistance point too low. Katherine, who has always been a little intimidated by Uncle Art, smiled and nodded in agreement, but really had no idea what he was talking about.

Clearly Katherine has much to learn if she is going to try to negotiate a better offer. Being well prepared will increase the probability that she will negotiate an outcome that better meets her needs.[1,2] In the process she may even impress her new employer with her level of preparation and professionalism. But first she will need to assess her priorities and alternatives, and investigate the level of salary and types of benefits local employers are paying recent college grads in her field. She will have to understand what types of things might be negotiable and develop opening offers and target and resistance points for each issue in the bargaining mix. But before all this, she will need to understand what all those things mean!

BARGAINING MIX

All of the issues involved in a negotiation are collectively referred to as the **bargaining mix**. The type and scope of the issues can vary dramatically depending on the type of negotiation. In a negotiation involving the purchase of raw materials to be used in the manufacture of a company's products, the issues will likely include product specifications, price, various discounts, and how and when the products will be shipped. If you are buying a building to house your small business, the issues will probably include closing costs, allowances, repairs, and the date the buyer takes possession, in addition to purchase price. When you are negotiating vacation plans with a friend or family member, you are apt to address where to go, how long to stay, where to stay, what to do/see, how to get there, and how much to spend, among other things. In all negotiations the importance each party places on each of the issues can be quite different as well. Knowing and communicating these priorities can lead to more satisfying outcomes for all involved.

In general, the more issues there are the better the chance the parties will walk away happy. As you will learn in Chapter 4, a key principle of integrative negotiation is "expanding the pie," in other words, creating more value so there is more for everyone involved. This often means increasing the number of issues in the bargaining mix. If there is only one issue involved, the negotiation is viewed as an all-or-nothing interaction. If the other party gets what he wants, you don't, and vice versa. On the other hand, if there are two issues, you could each get something. If of the two issues only one is very important to you and the other issue is of primary importance to the other party, both parties have the capacity to achieve their desired outcome. Taking it a step further, if there are ten issues, each party can obtain multiple desired goals. Of course there comes a point where there are so many issues that the negotiation becomes unwieldy, but within reason, more issues mean that the parties have a greater probability of satisfying their interests. The likelihood of doing so increases when parties preparing for negotiation establish an initial offer, target, and resistance point for each issue that is likely to be in the bargaining mix.

INITIAL OFFERS

An **initial offer**, sometimes referred to as an **opening offer**, is the first offer made by a party in any negotiation and serves as an anchor in that it sets a boundary on the negotiation. From the seller's standpoint this is the asking price. From the buyer's standpoint this is the first offer made. Sometimes the asking price is referred to as the list price or Manufacturer's Suggested Retail Price (MSRP). This is commonly cited in retail on everything from cars to cosmetics. With many products it is highly unusual for someone to pay list price as many stores use sales to lure customers to buy their products. The more cynical among us might even argue that the list price is a fictitious number posted only to make customers think they are getting a great deal. Think about your local appliance and clothing stores that seem to have a sale advertising "the lowest prices of the season" every week. How could they be offering the lowest prices of the season this week when they just offered them last week?

This also happens outside of retail sales. If you have ever sold a car or house, you probably set the price higher than what you realistically expected to get to create room to negotiate. In some cases you might even get lucky and have someone offer to pay your asking price, but this is rare. Most buyers know that sellers will likely take less than the asking price and, playing their part in the negotiation process, they make an opening offer that is lower than they are actually willing to pay. Buyers—like sellers— want to leave themselves room to negotiate, but hope to get lucky and have the seller accept their initial offer.

Who makes the first offer often depends on the type of negotiation. In most sales transactions the seller effectively makes the initial offer when he names a price. The exception to this is in an auction where the buyers place bids that start low and increase until no one is willing to go any higher. In employment negotiations, employers extend an offer to an applicant; however, when union contracts are negotiated, the union usually makes the first offer, sometimes referred to as an opening demand. While some people are reluctant to make the first offer in a negotiation, research suggests that because making the first offer anchors the negotiation, it can give the party making the offer an advantage.[3]

The question then becomes how do you choose your opening demand? Research shows that knowledge of the other party's best alternative is the strongest determinant of one's initial offer.[4] Initial offers should be chosen carefully as they provide signals to the other party. If you are a seller and you set your asking price too high, prospective buyers may decide that your price is unreasonable and simply walk away. If you are a job applicant and you ask for an extremely high salary, the employer may conclude that you either aren't interested in working there, have an unjustifiably inflated view of yourself, or that you would be difficult to work with in the future. Conversely, if your initial offer is too low, you may needlessly forego the additional compensation you could have easily, and perhaps rightfully, received. Thus, it is imperative that you do your research up front and find out what is reasonable given the current situation. Are the products/services that you are offering in high demand? What is the typical price being paid in the market today? Just because something was worth a certain amount in the past does not mean it is worth as much or even more today. Many people were confronted with this harsh reality during the collapse of the housing market in 2008 when they learned they owed more for their houses than they were currently worth due to declining home values. While that was a dismal situation for the homeowners, it was good news for home buyers who understood that banks that owned foreclosed houses were very anxious to sell them. Thus, people who wanted to buy a house would often make a very low initial offer and end up purchasing the house at a deep discount.

TARGET POINT

The **target point**, sometimes referred to as an **aspiration**, is the best outcome each party can reasonably and realistically expect to obtain as a result of the negotiation[5] and can be an important anchor for negotiators.[6] Research shows that negotiators who set challenging goals consistently achieve better outcomes than those who don't.[7] As with initial offers, a target point for each issue should be established before commencing negotiations as it provides focus for the negotiator.[8] Target points are generally not shared with the other party, at least not initially. As a negotiation progresses the parties sometimes make statements like "I was really hoping to get . . ." or "I was hoping not to spend more than . . ." as a way of signaling the other party; however, they are very unlikely to say "My target point is . . ." at the beginning of a negotiation.

In the case of monetary issues, target points should be quantified and based on factual information identified through research. For example, if you are negotiating a labor contract for a group of unionized workers you need to be realistic in your expectations. While most people believe they are over-worked and underpaid, and would love to see a 10% pay increase, that may or may not be realistic given the economy and the financial health of the organization. You might be surprised to learn that 10% pay increases were actually quite common in the early 1980s when there was double-digit inflation and many companies were doing well financially. However, if inflation is around 3% and budgets are very tight, a union's expectation of a 10% across-the-board pay increase would leave most employers stunned. In this example a more realistic target would be in the 2–4% range, depending on the specific circumstances of the employer, industry, and local economy.

In the case of non-monetary issues, target points should be based on as much factual information as possible. Let's say you are on a business trip with a colleague and are trying to decide where to go for dinner. You might consider whether your colleague has any food allergies or dietary restrictions. If your colleague is a vegetarian, the local steakhouse is probably not as good a target as if he follows a low-carb diet. Similarly, if your colleague has a limited travel budget, a gourmet five-star restaurant is likely out of the question—unless of course you are willing to pay the bill.

RESISTANCE POINT

The **resistance point**, sometimes referred to as a **reservation price**, is a negotiator's bottom line or the point beyond which she will not go. Walton and McKersie refer to resistance points as the "most pessimistic assumptions about what is possible."[9] From the seller's standpoint, it is the least he will accept before walking away from the negotiation. From the buyer's standpoint it is the most she will pay for whatever is being negotiated. During a negotiation, the resistance point is the reference point for rejecting or considering the other party's offer.[10] Like the target point, the resistance point is typically not revealed to the other party, especially during the early stages of negotiation. Occasionally one party may state "I will not take less than __" or "__ is my final offer," but such a statement would come as the negotiation nears an end and might even help to achieve settlement when the parties are close. However, be aware that not all buyers or sellers will have the same resistance point because one's resistance point is often influenced by many factors.

Consider the following example. Let's say I have a very large dog (who uses the fenced-in yard when nature calls) and live where much snow falls during the winter months. Come springtime, the yard is filled with unwanted deposits. You live nearby and I offer to pay you $5 per hour to clean up my yard. Most people would turn this down; however, if you were really strapped for cash and had a strong stomach you just might do it. What if I offered to pay $15 per hour? What about $50 per hour? Depending on your financial condition, you may or may not be interested at any price. What if the payment were a guaranteed "A" in this class? What if in return for the spring cleaning you were able to get an inside track on your dream job? While these are purely hypothetical examples, the point is that we all have different resistance points depending on our circumstances. With few exceptions—things we find morally reprehensible—everyone has his price. This is evidenced by some reality TV shows (e.g., *Fear Factor, Survivor*) where contestants do things most of us wouldn't, like eat worms and other slimy creatures, for the chance to win a very large sum of money.

BEST ALTERNATIVE TO A NEGOTIATED AGREEMENT (BATNA)

A person's resistance point is usually directly related to her **Best Alternative to a Negotiated Agreement** or **BATNA**.[11] It is quite literally the most ideal alternative outcome one party to a negotiation could get without negotiating with the other party. In general the better the alternatives, the stronger the negotiator's bargaining position and the more likely she is to make the first offer.[12] Fisher and colleagues maintain it is the

FIGURE 2.1 WATNA: The Flip Side of BATNA

While BATNA is more commonly discussed in negotiations, it is also useful to consider your **Worst Alternative to a Negotiated Agreement (WATNA)**. Essentially, it is the worst outcome you might face if you do not come to a negotiated agreement. It is used most often in conflict resolution and can be particularly useful when emotions are running high. For example, if you are involved in a divorce and you are unable to come to an agreement over the division of property, you would consider the costs involved, both monetary and emotional, of having to go through a trial in court. If the dispute is over who gets the television and who gets the sofa, objectively it would not be worth the cost of having the items appraised and hiring an attorney to represent you in court where the likelihood of "winning" your case is uncertain. Even if the judge decides in your favor, you may end up incurring more in appraisal and legal fees than the item is actually worth. Add to that the emotional costs of extending an already difficult situation and people typically become much less attached to the items in question.

true measure by which you should judge any proposed agreement.[13] A common problem is that negotiators don't identify and consider enough alternatives. As a result, they have less leverage when they negotiate—if they negotiate at all. The consequences of this weakness can have a major impact over the course of one's life. Some people stay in jobs where they are not happy because they believe they don't have other alternatives. Instead of looking for other possibilities (e.g., returning to school to acquire additional skills or relocating for a new career opportunity) they stay where they are, resolved that this is their lot in life. Sadly, many of these people experience regret later in life. One reason for the success of early retirement/buyout programs, offered by employers to entice long-term employees to leave the organization, is that employees see them as an opportunity to do something different with their lives. The offer provides the extra incentive that gets employees to consider other alternatives that might better satisfy their interests.

The concept isn't limited to jobs though, it also applies to relationships. There are people who stay in unsatisfying, bad, or even dangerous relationships because they think they have no alternative. This sometimes happens in abusive relationships where the abused person stays because she thinks she can't afford to leave. Instead of looking for ways to increase her income such as pursuing additional education or training, she resigns herself to the current situation. Another example is the person who stays in a less than fulfilling relationship because he thinks he won't find anyone else. No matter what your situation, you will always be in a better position to satisfy your interests in both your work and non-work lives, if you thoroughly investigate all possible alternatives, bearing in mind that not beginning or completing the negotiation may be an alternative as well. For example, let's say you are interested in purchasing a new car. You find one that you like and you make an offer. You negotiate with the seller, but he is not willing to come down enough in price to meet your resistance point. If the car you currently own runs well and meets your needs, keeping it a while longer may be the best alternative. It may also be helpful if you consider the worst case scenario as suggested in Figure 2.1.

Chapter Scenario, Part II

After much thought about what she really needed from a job and considerable research on what employers were typically offering to recent college graduates in her field, Katherine felt more confident about negotiating with her prospective employer. She realized that while a starting salary that would allow her to meet her living expenses was necessary, the opportunity to gain experience and progress in her career were most important for her in the long term. She evaluated her alternatives to accepting this offer. Her research into typical starting salaries for those in her field showed that the offer the employer had made was a little low. She planned to use that information to negotiate a higher starting salary. She decided to ask if the employer would provide tuition reimbursement so she could pursue an MBA to increase her value to the employer—and help her progress in her career. She also planned to discuss the types of assignments that she would be given so she could gain experience. It was time for her to negotiate the job offer—and she was now ready!

BARGAINING RANGE/SETTLEMENT ZONE

The area between parties' resistance points is referred to as the **bargaining range** or **settlement zone**. If there is overlap between the two resistance points, the settlement zone is positive and settlement can occur, provided the parties exchange enough information to signal the other party that settlement is possible. Consider the example shown in Figure 2.2. Julie has a car that she wants to sell. She has advertised the car for $8,000 and thinks she can get at least $7,500. She has decided that she will not take less than $7,000 for it. John is considering buying Julie's car. He has offered Julie $6,800 hoping that she would accept his low offer. Realistically, he expects to get the car for $7,300 but would go as high as $7,600. In this example, the bargaining range is the area between $7,000 and $7,600, or $600. There is a good chance of reaching agreement if during the course of the negotiation, Julie lets John know that she will take less than $8,000, which is more than his resistance point, and John lets Julie know that he is willing to pay more than $6800, which is less than her resistance point.

FIGURE 2.2   Positive Bargaining Range

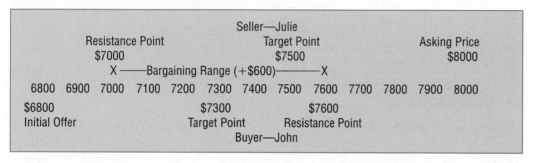

If the resistance points of the parties are identical, the bargaining range is zero and settlement can only occur at that point, as shown in Figure 2.3. Since there is only one possible settlement point, the likelihood of settlement decreases. For settlement to occur, the parties have to be willing to exchange enough information to let each other know how low (or high) they will go. Without this, settlement will not occur. Staying with the car example, let's say Julie is still asking $8,000 for her car, but this time she thinks she can get $7,800 and will not accept less than $7,600. John still offers $6,800, hopes to get it for $7,300, and won't pay more than $7,600. The bargaining range is zero. Settlement can only happen at $7,600, but for that to occur Julie and John need to let each other know that they are willing to settle at that amount.

FIGURE 2.3   Non-Overlapping Bargaining Range

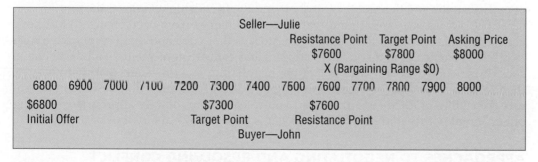

If there is no overlap of the resistance points, the settlement range is negative and there will be no settlement unless one (or both) of the parties adjusts his or her resistance point. To continue with the same car example in Figure 2.4: this time Julie is still asking $8,000, hoping to get $7,800, and won't take less than $7,600. John offers $6,800, hopes to get it for $7,000 and won't pay more than $7,200. In this example there is a negative settlement range of $400 between the two resistance points and settlement will not occur.

FIGURE 2.4   **Negative Bargaining Range**

	Seller—Julie		
	Resistance Point	Target Point	Asking Price
	$7600	$7800	$8000

(Bargaining Range –$400)

| 6800 | 6900 | 7000 | 7100 | 7200 | 7300 | 7400 | 7500 | 7600 | 7700 | 7800 | 7900 | 8000 |

| $6800 | | $7000 | | $7200 | | | | | | | | |
| Initial Offer | | Target Point | | Resistance Point | | | | | | | | |

Buyer—John

We must acknowledge that resistance points occasionally may change due to changing circumstances. In the various car scenarios, Julie established her resistance point and we assumed that it was firm. Let's say, however, that a great deal of time passed and Julie had numerous calls, but no offers, on her car. She may have grown tired of dealing with people calling or something may have come up that required some quick cash. In either case, she may decide to reevaluate her position on the price of the car. Similarly, John may not be having any luck finding a car he wants within his price range or perhaps his current vehicle has broken down. Thus, he may also reevaluate how much he is willing and/or able to spend.

SETTLEMENT POINT

The **settlement point** is what the parties actually agree upon. In a multi-issue negotiation there is a settlement point for each issue. Sometimes there are issues that should be included, but are overlooked. On a whim, Melissa and Carrie, two friends from college, decided to take a trip to southern Florida. Before going they agreed that they would split the cost of transportation, lodging, and food, and keep it within a certain dollar amount; not become separated; and not party so much that they wouldn't be able to go out the next day. Both lived up to the agreement and were still good friends when they came back. Unfortunately this isn't always the case.

Brian and Sam decided to take a summer road trip and spend a month driving cross country. While they had planned their route and agreed that each would pay his own way, they failed to discuss their respective expectations about the kinds of places where they would eat and how much would be spent on entertainment along the way. Brian spent his money quickly, splurging on food and double mocha lattes, while Sam opted for the daily specials and drank regular coffee. When Brian ran out of money before the end of the trip, he wanted to go early. Sam still had money and wanted to continue the trip as planned; however, he couldn't take Brian's constant complaining about being out of money. In the end they cut the trip short and the friendship was never the same.

The stories are similar (and real except the names have been changed) but have very different outcomes. The moral of the story is that you should not be in such a rush to reach a conclusion that you fail to address and come to agreement on all pertinent issues. It is better to spend additional time negotiating an agreement that will hold up, than to rush to conclusion on something that could prove quite troublesome in the future. Once the issues are identified and you research and identify appropriate opening offers, target points, and resistance points, it is time to think about your basic approach.

APPROACHES TO NEGOTIATING AND RESOLVING CONFLICT

Researchers have developed models that identify several general approaches to a negotiation or conflict situation. Although the terminology is different, the concepts are the same: a two-dimensional model with four or five general areas representing the various approaches. In the Thomas-Kilmann conflict style model,[14] the dimensions are assertiveness/concern for one's own outcomes and cooperativeness/concern for other's outcomes, and the approaches to handling conflict are referred to as avoiding, accommodating, competing, collaborating, and compromising. We will explore this model in greater detail in Chapter 6, but at this juncture, we simply highlight the similarities of this model with the Dual Concerns Model.[15,16] The Dual Concerns Model identifies the dimensions as concern for one's own outcomes and concern for the other party's outcomes; the possible approaches are called inaction, yielding, contending, and problem solving. The Rubin et al.[17] "concern for your own outcomes" dimension can be thought of in terms of the Thomas-Kilmann "assertiveness" dimension, while the "concern for the other's outcomes" can be thought of in terms of the cooperativeness dimension. A comparison of the models is shown in Figure 2.5.

FIGURE 2.5   Comparison of Models

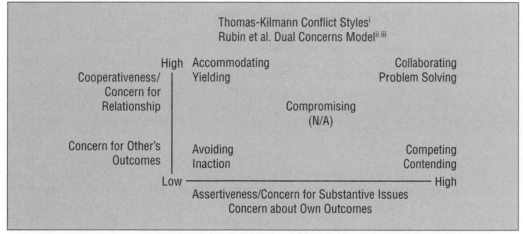

[i] Thomas, K. W., and R. H. Kilmann. *Thomas-Kilmann Conflict Mode Survey.* Tuxedo, NY: Xicom, 1974.
[ii] Pruitt, D. G., and J. Z. Rubin. *Social Conflict: Escalation, Stalemate and Settlement.* New York: Random House, 1986.
[iii] Rubin, J. Z., D. G. Pruitt, and S. H. Kim. *Social Conflict: Escalation, Stalemate and Settlement* (2nd ed.). New York: McGraw-Hill, 1994.

Regardless of which terminology you use, the basic concepts are the same. If you really don't care about the issue and your relationship with the other party, there is no reason to negotiate or try to resolve the conflict—it would only be a waste of your time and energy. If the issue is really important and the relationship isn't, you will approach the negotiation more competitively. An example is making a major purchase from a salesperson you really don't know or care about. Most people in this situation just want to get the best price on what they are purchasing and care little about how much profit the store makes or the size of the salesperson's commission check. If you are very concerned about the other party and her happiness (e.g., with very close friends or family members), you will approach the situation much more cooperatively, and will likely adopt a yielding/accommodating strategy. This is also likely when the issue isn't important or the time pressures are high.[18]

On the other hand, if you are concerned about both maintaining the relationship and the substantive outcome, your approach will likely be one of collaboration where you try to arrive at a solution that makes everyone happy. This typically takes more time and effort, but the end result is well worth it. Let's say you are planning a wedding and your parents and your future in-laws have very different ideas about everything from how many people to invite to whether there should be a sit-down dinner or a buffet to whether or not alcoholic beverages should be served at the reception. The tension has been building ever since you announced the engagement. This is "your day" and you want it to be perfect, but you also know that you are going to have to live with your parents and in-laws. While you might be tempted to elope to the Caribbean, taking a collaborative approach to negotiating the details of the ceremony and reception will likely bode better for the long term, considering what is at stake.

While there is general agreement that collaboration/problem solving is the best approach when trying to satisfy your own needs while maintaining the relationship, there is some disagreement on the validity of compromising where the parties both get and give up some of what they want. The Thomas-Kilmann Conflict model includes compromise; the Dual Concerns Model does not. Instead, the Dual Concerns Model views compromising as either joint yielding or a failure in problem solving.[19] It has even been referred to as "lazy problem-solving involving a half-hearted attempt to satisfy both parties' interests."[20] Whether you view it as a valid approach or a lack of forethought, the reality is that people regularly compromise to resolve a wide variety of conflicts. It may be an efficient, though not entirely effective approach. Thus, we treat it as valid. People plan to give something in order to get something. Indeed this is a fairly common approach in traditional negotiations between employers and labor unions where both parties may bring issues to the table that they either don't care much about, or know they will never get, so they have something to trade for what they really want.

Points to Ponder

1. Where do you see yourself in terms of the Thomas-Killmann and Dual Concerns models? To what extent is your answer influenced by the situation?
2. How comfortable are you in moving outside your usual position?

We do not all approach negotiation in the same way, nor do any of us approach all negotiation situations in the same way. While one may persist with a basic approach for a period of time, it may change, sometimes rapidly.[21] Generally speaking, negotiations are either distributive or integrative in nature. Distributive negotiations generally involve more competitive behavior, where there is a winner and a loser, and little concern for the relationship. Integrative negotiations are characterized by more cooperation, meeting the needs of both parties, and more concern for maintaining the relationship after the negotiation concludes. We will examine these two approaches and their differences in greater detail in Chapters 3 and 4, respectively.

One's approach to negotiation is also influenced to some extent by one's personality,[22] which we cover in detail in Chapter 6. For now, think about how different people you know typically approach conflict. You likely can think of some people who are very competitive in everything they do. Similarly, you probably know some people who do everything in their power to avoid conflict and others who are quick to give in. Hopefully, you also know some people who try to find solutions that satisfy everyone involved. But personality alone doesn't predict exactly how a person will behave in a negotiation. The strategy a person employs in a negotiation also depends on how he frames the situation.

FRAMING

A **frame** is the lens through which you view a negotiation, which also influences your behavior in a negotiation.[23] Think about framing in a negotiation the same way you would if you were taking a photo. You can use a wide angle lens to get the big picture or a telephoto lens to focus in more specifically on some aspect of the subject. Let's say the subject of the photo is a house that is in very good condition, except for one broken shutter. If you view the whole house, it looks pretty good; however, if you zoom in on the broken shutter, it doesn't. Similarly, you can position the subject against a variety of backgrounds, each of which affects how the subject appears to the viewers. Imagine you are taking a photo of a friend. If the photo is taken with your friend sitting on a horse he would appear to be more of an outdoors type than if he were sitting in a sporty car. Framing is the basic premise behind dressing for success when interviewing for a job or making an important presentation to your superiors. In the same manner you can frame the subject of a negotiation to make it appear different than it really is.

Research shows that how a negotiation is framed is related to the final outcome.[24,25] In general, positive frames lead to more successful outcomes than negative frames.[26] If one party is convinced he is getting a good deal, he is more likely to accept the offer presented. On the other hand, if he thinks he is being taken advantage of, he is much less likely to accept the offer, even if it means he ends up worse off. Indeed, the more negatively you frame a situation the more risk you are likely to accept because you believe you have less to lose. Imagine you are working for an organization that is offering a buyout. Essentially they are offering to pay you to leave your job. If you are an employee who hates your job or believes that you will be laid off permanently, you are more likely to accept the buyout, even if you don't have another job lined up. In this example, you are risking a job that leaves much to be desired that you may lose anyway. On the other hand, if you like your job and don't believe that you personally will be laid off, you probably won't accept the buyout offer because there would be more to lose.

Consider the case of the union negotiating a new faculty contract at a regional state university where there had been animosity between the union and the administration in the past. The union sent regular newsletters to the faculty to update them on progress at the bargaining table, most of which painted the administration in very negative terms. In one of the updates, the union lamented that the administration was not serious about coming to agreement because they had offered only a 2% increase in base pay and offered no increase in the retirement contribution. While you can debate whether a 2% increase is a serious offer, in this example the retirement contribution was already calculated as a percentage of base pay. Thus, if base pay increases, the retirement contribution automatically increases by the same percentage. Presumably the union understood the math involved and was just framing the report in a negative way to garner support from the faculty for a potential strike. The more negatively something is framed, the more likely there is to be conflict that can quickly escalate.[27]

But what if something is framed in such a way that it is not to your advantage? The answer is simply to reframe it. Assume you are negotiating to buy the house with the broken shutter and the seller is using a wide angle lens to present the house as being in very good condition and negotiate a higher selling price. Instead of jumping into negotiating the price, you should first point out the need for repairs—the shutter and other items needing attention. This approach can reframe the negotiation from one over a house in very good condition that should command a premium price to a negotiation over a house that needs potentially costly repairs that suggests a discounted price.

RECIPROCITY

Reciprocity—the notion that if someone does something for you, you owe them—is one of the most powerful principles there is in negotiation according to social psychologist and internationally respected expert on negotiation, Robert Cialdini.[28] If someone buys you lunch, the next time it is your turn to pick up the tab. If someone gives you a birthday gift, you feel an obligation to give them one on their birthday. Indeed most of us know someone who has wanted to stop buying gifts for someone, but struggled with actually doing it. People may say they are going to stop, but when they receive a gift, they may begin to feel guilty. Some people are able to hang tough, while others back down and begrudgingly continue.

Often one of the biggest chores for graduates and newlyweds is sending thank you notes. When someone gives you a gift to commemorate your special day, it creates an obligation for you to thank them for it. This is such a cultural tradition that there are even rules as to how it should be done. The thank you notes must be hand-written, personal, and timely, according to etiquette expert, Letitia Baldrige.[29] While it's likely that people who receive thank you notes throw them away after reading them, the point is that the gift giver is likely to remember who has—and hasn't—sent a thank you note.

Similarly, grocery stores use reciprocity to increase sales. Think of the times you have been shopping only to be offered a taste of something you don't normally buy. If you try the sample, you feel more obligated to purchase the product than if you hadn't tried it. Stores know this and use it to their advantage, especially at times when there is a high level of traffic in the store (e.g., weekends) and customers are more likely to be a bit hungry (e.g., lunchtime and mid-afternoon). Reciprocity isn't limited to your personal life; you see it in the workplace as well.

If a coworker helps you when you are buried in work, you are most likely to reciprocate when your coworker needs help. If there isn't an immediate opportunity to reciprocate, there is usually an implied IOU. Sometimes the party receiving the help will even say something like, "I really owe you one," but even if words aren't exchanged, there is usually an unspoken understanding that she will reciprocate. Think about this the next time someone needs your help. Even if you are busy, helping others can pay dividends in the long run if you have the reputation of always going the extra mile for your coworkers.

In a negotiation, reciprocity may be either helpful or harmful depending on the behavior that is reciprocated.[30] If one party agrees to something the other party wants, the other party is likely to reciprocate. It may even start a chain reaction of sorts—often referred to as the snowball effect—where the parties start agreeing on relatively small issues and work their way up to the bigger issues until they have a full agreement. Conversely, if one party takes a hard-line approach or behaves badly in a negotiation, the other party likely will mirror that behavior and the result can be a complete breakdown in the negotiation. Strategies and tactics for resolving conflict in negotiation are addressed in detail in Chapter 5.

Points to Ponder

1. Think of something you do out of a sense of obligation that you would prefer not to do.
2. How difficult would it be for you to stop?

Summary

In this chapter we have introduced you to the basic language of negotiation beginning with definitions of bargaining mix, opening offers, and target and resistance points. Next we explored the concept of BATNA and its role in negotiations. From there, we turned to the concept of the settlement or bargaining zone and its impact on the potential for reaching an agreement.

We defined settlement point and explored the Thomas-Kilmann Conflict Styles and the Dual Concerns Model for approaching conflict and negotiation. Finally, we introduced you to the impact of framing and reciprocity in negotiation.

Summary: The Big Picture

Bargaining mix	All of the issues in a negotiation.
Initial offers, and target and resistance points	Need to define them for each issue when preparing to negotiate.
BATNA	The better your BATNA the stronger your position in a negotiation.
Settlement zone/bargaining range	The area between the parties' resistance points where settlement may occur.
Settlement point	The point of final agreement on each issue in a negotiation.
Approaches to negotiating and resolving conflict	Your approach will depend on your level of assertiveness and concern for substantive issues and the relationship with the other party and concern for her outcomes.
Framing	How an issue is framed influences your behavior in a negotiation.
Reciprocity	Negotiators often reciprocate the other party's behaviors, both positive and negative.

Key Terms and Concepts

Bargaining mix   All of the issues involved in a negotiation.

Bargaining range/settlement zone   The area between parties' resistance points.

Best Alternative to a Negotiated Agreement (BATNA)   The most ideal alternative outcome one party to a negotiation could get without negotiating with the other party.

Frame   The lens through which you view a negotiation.

Initial/opening offer   The first offer made by a party in a negotiation.

Reciprocity   The notion that if someone does something for you, you owe them.

Resistance point/reservation price   A negotiator's bottom line; the point beyond which she will not go.

Settlement point   What the parties actually agree upon.

Target point/aspiration   The best outcome each party can reasonably and realistically expect to obtain as a result of the negotiation.

Worst Alternative to a Negotiated Agreement (WATNA)   The worst outcome you might face if you do not come to a negotiated agreement.

Discussion Questions

1. Identify the issues that might constitute the bargaining mix in an initial employment negotiation such as Katherine's in the chapter scenario.
2. Explain the differences between opening offers, target and resistance points, and their role in negotiation.
3. Discuss the role of a negotiator's alternatives in a negotiation.
4. Describe the impact of how an issue is framed on the final outcome in a negotiation.
5. Citing examples from your school, work, and personal lives, discuss the role of reciprocity in your daily relationships.

Ethical Dilemma: To Reciprocate or Not to Reciprocate?

You are negotiating to buy a house. So far the sellers have been very cooperative in working out the terms of the sale and engaged in an integrative style of negotiation. Now however there is a problem. There is a wrought iron horse mounted on the exterior of the house on the chimney. The seller did not specifically exclude this on the sale agreement but now wants to keep it, saying it was a birthday gift from a family member. You like the horse and would like to have it remain with the house, but because the seller has been so cooperative on everything else, you aren't sure whether to pursue this.

Questions

1. Do you have any obligation, moral or otherwise, to cooperate with the sellers since they have been cooperative with you?
2. If the sellers had engaged in distributive bargaining tactics and were generally uncooperative would your answer to question 1 be different? How?
3. To what extent, if any, should you reciprocate the other party's behavior when negotiating?

Ethical Dilemma: You Heard It through the Grapevine

You are in the market for a new-to-you car. There is one in particular that you are interested in that is for sale by a friend of a friend. You have driven it and had it checked out by a friend of the family who is a mechanic. Based on your research you have determined the car is worth $8,000 and you are prepared to pay that much to get the car. The day before you planned to close the deal you heard through the grapevine that the seller has some unexpected legal problems that could land him in jail if he doesn't come up with $6,000 to pay the fines very soon. This news has you wondering if you could get the car for even less than you were willing to pay.

Questions

1. How might you use the information about the seller's legal problems?
2. What could you gain by using the information?
3. What could you lose by using the information?
4. Is it ethical to use the information about the seller's legal problems to get the car for less than you determined to be a fair market price?

Endnotes

1. Zetik, D. C., and A. F. Stuhlmacher. "Goal Setting and Negotiation Performance: A Meta-Analysis." *Group Processes & Intergroup Relations* 5(1) (2002): 35–52.
2. Ertel, D. "Turning Negotiation into a Corporate Capability." *Harvard Business Review* May 1999, p. 55.
3. Galinsky, A. D., and T. Mussweiler. "First Offers as Anchors: The Role of Perspective-Taking and Negotiator Focus." *Journal of Personality and Social Psychology* 81(4) (2001): 657–669.
4. Buelens, M., and D. Van Poucke. "Determinants of a Negotiator's Initial Opening Offer." *Journal of Business and Psychology* 19(1) (2004): 23–35.
5. Blount, S., M. C. Thomas-Hunt, and M. A. Neale. "The Price Is Right—Or Is It? A Reference Point Model of Two-Party Price Negotiations." *Organizational Behavior and Human Decision Processes* 68(1) (1996): 1–12.
6. White, S. B., and M. A. Neale. "Reservation Prices, Resistance Points and BATNAs: Determining the Parameters of Acceptable Negotiated Outcomes." *Negotiation Journal* 7(4) (1991): 379–388.
7. Zetik, D. C., and A. F. Stuhlmacher. "Goal Setting and Negotiation Performance: A Meta-Analysis." *Group Processes & Intergroup Relations* 5(1) (2002): 35–52.
8. Fells, R. "Preparation for Negotiation Issue and Process." *Personnel Review* 25(2) (1996): 50–60.
9. Walton, R. E., and McKersie, R. B. *A Behavioral Theory of Labor Negotiations: An Analysis of a Social Interaction System.* New York: McGraw-Hill, 1965, p. 42.
10. Fells, R. "Preparation for Negotiation Issue and Process." *Personnel Review* 25(2) (1996): 50–60.
11. Fisher, R., W. Ury, and B. Patton. *Getting to Yes* (2nd ed.). Boston: Houghton-Mifflin, 1991, p. 97.
12. Magee, J. C., A. D. Galinsky, and D. Gruenfeld. "Power, Propensity to Negotiate, and Moving First in Competitive Actions." *Personality and Social Psychology Bulletin* 33(2) (2007): 200–212.
13. Fisher, R., W. Ury, and B. Patton. *Getting to Yes* (2nd ed.). Boston: Houghton-Mifflin, 1991, p. 101.
14. Thomas, K. W., and R. H. Kilmann. *Thomas-Kilmann Conflict Mode Survey.* Tuxedo, NY: Xicom, 1974.
15. Pruitt, D. G., and J. Z. Rubin, J. Z. *Social Conflict: Escalation, Stalemate and Settlement.* New York: Random House, 1986.
16. Rubin, J. Z., D. Pruitt, and S. H. Kim. *Social Conflict: Escalation, Stalemate and Settlement* (2nd ed.). New York: McGraw-Hill, 1994.
17. *Ibid.*
18. Pruitt, D. G. "Strategic Choice in Negotiation." *The American Behavioral Scientist* 27(2) (1983): 167.
19. Pruitt, D. G., and J. Z. Rubin. *Social Conflict: Escalation, Stalemate and Settlement.* New York: Random House, 1986.
20. Pruitt, D. G. "Strategic Choice in Negotiation." *The American Behavioral Scientist* 27(2) (1983): 167.
21. *Ibid.*
22. Olekalns, M., and P. L. Smith. "Loose with the Truth: Predicting Deception in Negotiation." *Journal of Business Ethics* 76(2) (2007): 225–238.
23. Neale, M. A., and M. H. Bazerman. "The Effects of Framing and Negotiator Overconfidence on Bargaining Behaviors and Outcomes." *Academy of Management Journal* 28(1) (1985): 34.
24. Ghosh, D., and M. N. Boldt. "The Effect of Framing and Compensation Structure on Seller's Negotiated Transfer Price." *Journal of Managerial Issues* 18(4) (2006): 453–467, 429–430.
25. Carnevale, P. J. "Positive Affect and Decision Frame in Negotiation." *Group Decision and Negotiation* 17(1) (2008): 51–63.
26. Neale, M. A., and M. H. Bazerman. "The Effects of Framing and Negotiator Overconfidence on Bargaining Behaviors and Outcomes." *Academy of Management Journal* 28(1) (1985): 34–49.
27. Bazerman, M. H., and M. A. Neale. *Negotiating Rationally.* New York: The Free Press, 1992.
28. Cialdini, R. B. *Influence: Science and Practice* (4th ed.). Boston: Allyn & Bacon, 2001.
29. Baldrige, L. *New Complete Guide to Executive Manners.* New York: Simon & Schuster, 1993.
30. Brett, J. M., D. L. Shapiro, and A. L. Lytle. "Breaking the Bonds of Reciprocity in Negotiations." *Academy of Management Journal* 41 (1998): 410–424.

Exercise 2.1   An Amp on the Internet

Rick is an 18 year old who is getting ready to go away to college where he will be living in a dorm. He has played bass guitar for six years and wants to be able to continue that while he is away at school. The problem is that the amplifiers that he has are all too large for a small dorm room and transporting conveniently. He wants to buy a small amp, but as a college student, his funds are very limited. He searched the Internet for amps for sale and found one that is just what he wants that is for sale by Alan.

Alan, a drummer, was in a band that recently split up in a very unpleasant way. To protect his credit rating, Alan paid the debts the band had accumulated and ended up with a variety of miscellaneous musical equipment which he has put up for sale on the Internet. At this point he is very frustrated and wants to be done with the whole ordeal, but needs to recover some of his money by selling the equipment. He has just been contacted by Rick who is interested in one of his amps.

Instructions:

1. Identify the involved parties, their potential interests, and possible alternatives to a negotiated agreement.
2. Identify the issues that would likely be part of the negotiation.
3. For each issue, establish a plausible initial offer, target, and resistance point.
4. Describe one way the situation could be framed.
5. Describe how your response to the previous question could be reframed.

Party: _____

Interests: _____

_____

Alternatives to a negotiated agreement: _____

_____

Party: _____

Interests: _____

_____

Alternatives to a negotiated agreement: _____

_____

Party: _____

Interests: _____

_____

Alternatives to a negotiated agreement: _____

_____

Party: _____

Interests: _____

_____

Alternatives to a negotiated agreement: _____

_____

Issue: _____

Initial offer: _____ Target: _____ Resistance point: _____

Issue: _____

Initial offer: _____ Target: _____ Resistance point: _____

Issue: _____

Initial offer: _____ Target: _____ Resistance point: _____

Issue: _____

Initial offer: _____ Target: _____ Resistance point: _____

Issue: _____

Initial offer: _____ Target: _____ Resistance point: _____

Issue: _____

Initial offer: _____ Target: _____ Resistance point: _____

Issue: _____

Initial offer: _____ Target: _____ Resistance point: _____

Issue: _____

Initial offer: _____ Target: _____ Resistance point: _____

Issue: _____

Initial offer: _____ Target: _____ Resistance point: _____

Issue: _____

Initial offer: _____ Target: _____ Resistance point: _____

How could the situation be framed? _____

_____

_____

_____

_____

How could the situation be reframed? _____

_____

_____

_____

_____

Exercise 2.2   Four Is a Crowd?

Lisa lives in a five-bedroom rental house with two other college students, Max and Donnie. Lisa's good friend Rita lived in the house for the past two years, but moved out when her lease was up last spring because she was finished with school, except for her student teaching. At the time Rita was hoping to be able to do her student teaching in her home town so she could stay with her parents. Unfortunately, that didn't work out and she had to return to the college town for three months to complete her student teaching. She knew there was room available in the house with Lisa and was willing to pay her share of rent and expenses. She discussed it with Lisa, who thought it was a great idea since they had the room, and the money Rita would pay would help reduce costs for everyone currently in the house.

Lisa was very excited about having her good friend around again and thought Max and Donnie would be happy to reduce their expenses, but when she discussed it with them, they were less than enthusiastic. Donnie in particular, who had just moved into the house, was very much against it saying only that he "didn't care for" Rita. Lisa was very surprised at Donnie's reaction because Donnie had quite a bit of credit card debt and she had thought that he would appreciate the reduced living expenses.

Instructions:

1. Identify the involved parties, their potential interests, and possible alternatives to a negotiated agreement.
2. Identify the issues that would likely be part of the negotiation.
3. For each issue establish a plausible initial offer, target, and resistance point.
4. Describe one way the situation could be framed.
5. Describe how your response to the previous question could be reframed.

Party: _____

Interests: _____

_____

Alternatives to a negotiated agreement: _____

_____

Party: _____

Interests: _____

_____

Alternatives to a negotiated agreement: _____

_____

Party: _____

Interests: _____

_____

Alternatives to a negotiated agreement: _____

_____

Party: _____

Interests: _____

_____

Alternatives to a negotiated agreement: _____

_____

Issue: _____

Initial offer: _____ Target: _____ Resistance point: _____

Issue: _____

Initial offer: _____ Target: _____ Resistance point: _____

Issue: _____

Initial offer: _____ Target: _____ Resistance point: _____

Issue: _____

Initial offer: _____ Target: _____ Resistance point: _____

Issue: _____

Initial offer: _____ Target: _____ Resistance point: _____

Issue: _____

Initial offer: _____ Target: _____ Resistance point: _____

Issue: _____

Initial offer: _____ Target: _____ Resistance point: _____

Issue: _____

Initial offer: _____ Target: _____ Resistance point: _____

Issue: _____

Initial offer: _____ Target: _____ Resistance point: _____

Issue: _____

Initial offer: _____ Target: _____ Resistance point: _____

How could the situation be framed? _____

_____

_____

_____

_____

How could the situation be reframed? _____

_____

_____

_____

_____

Exercise 2.3   Hot Fun in the Summertime

Scott, a college freshman who wants to become a lawyer, is getting ready to return home for the summer. His mother has made it clear that he needs to do something productive with his time and that he has to earn enough to cover his summer spending. Ideally, Scott would find a paid internship in his field. He talked to a local judge to see if there were any internships available. While the judge would like to have Scott work for the summer, he made it clear that he has no money to pay for an internship. Since a paid internship with the judge didn't work out, Scott is leaning toward Plan B, working for a friend of the family. It would put money in his pocket, but no relevant experience on his resume.

Instructions:

1. Identify the involved parties, their potential interests, and possible alternatives to a negotiated agreement.
2. Identify the issues that would likely be part of the negotiation.
3. For each issue establish a plausible initial offer, target, and resistance point.
4. Describe one way the situation could be framed.
5. Describe how your response to the previous question could be reframed.

Party: _____

Interests: _____

_____

Alternatives to a negotiated agreement: _____

_____

Party: _____

Interests: _____

_____

Alternatives to a negotiated agreement: _____

_____

Party: _____

Interests: _____

_____

Alternatives to a negotiated agreement: _____

_____

Party: _____

Interests: _____

_____

Alternatives to a negotiated agreement: _____

_____

Issue: _____

Initial offer: _____ Target: _____ Resistance point: _____

Issue: _____

Initial offer: _____ Target: _____ Resistance point: _____

Issue: _____

Initial offer: _____ Target: _____ Resistance point: _____

Issue: _____

Initial offer: _____ Target: _____ Resistance point: _____

Issue: _____

Initial offer: _____ Target: _____ Resistance point: _____

Issue: _____

Initial offer: _____ Target: _____ Resistance point: _____

Issue: _____

Initial offer: _____ Target: _____ Resistance point: _____

Issue: _____

Initial offer: _____ Target: _____ Resistance point: _____

Issue: _____

Initial offer: _____ Target: _____ Resistance point: _____

Issue: _____

Initial offer: _____ Target: _____ Resistance point: _____

How could the situation be framed? _____

_____

_____

_____

_____

How could the situation be reframed? _____

_____

_____

_____

_____

Exercise 2.4   Neither a Borrower nor a Lender Be

Bill borrowed $4,000 from Barbara to pay for some repair work on his car and to pay off some high-interest credit-card debt. He said he would pay her back at the rate of $300 per month. He just lost his job and is concerned that he won't have enough money coming in to live comfortably and still pay her back. Bill would like to drastically reduce the amount he is paying to Barbara each month so he has a cushion in case he has unexpected expenses.

Barbara is planning to purchase her first house. She wants to minimize her mortgage and needs the money Bill owes her to put toward her down payment. She has known Bill for quite a while and has come to believe that Bill cares only about himself.

Instructions:

1. Identify the involved parties, their potential interests, and possible alternatives to a negotiated agreement.
2. Identify the issues that would likely be part of the negotiation.
3. For each issue establish a plausible initial offer, target, and resistance point.
4. Describe one way the situation could be framed.
5. Describe how your response to the previous question could be reframed.

Party: _____

Interests: _____

_____

Alternatives to a negotiated agreement: _____

_____

Party: _____

Interests: _____

_____

Alternatives to a negotiated agreement: _____

_____

Party: _____

Interests: _____

_____

Alternatives to a negotiated agreement: _____

_____

Party: _____

Interests: _____

_____

Alternatives to a negotiated agreement: _____

_____

Issue: _____

Initial offer: _____ Target: _____ Resistance point: _____

Issue: _____

Initial offer: _____ Target: _____ Resistance point: _____

Issue: _____

Initial offer: _____ Target: _____ Resistance point: _____

Issue: _____

Initial offer: _____ Target: _____ Resistance point: _____

Issue: _____

Initial offer: _____ Target: _____ Resistance point: _____

Issue: _____

Initial offer: _____ Target: _____ Resistance point: _____

Issue: _____

Initial offer: _____ Target: _____ Resistance point: _____

Issue: _____

Initial offer: _____ Target: _____ Resistance point: _____

Issue: _____

Initial offer: _____ Target: _____ Resistance point: _____

Issue: _____

Initial offer: _____ Target: _____ Resistance point: _____

How could the situation be framed? _____

_____

_____

_____

_____

How could the situation be reframed? _____

_____

_____

_____

_____

Exercise 2.5   Stretched Too Thin

Stephanie works in a hospital that is currently short-staffed. Because of this she is often asked to work double shifts and come in on her days off. She usually agrees because she is a dedicated employee and the extra money comes in handy since she just bought a new house. Lately, she has been working so many hours that she is getting burned out. She needs to get away from the hospital and spend some time with her family, but her boss keeps calling her and asking her to come in.

Dale is Stephanie's supervisor at the hospital. He relies on her a lot when he needs someone to cover a shift for someone who is unable to work his regular shift. Lately this seems to be happening more often. He knows that Stephanie is stretched very thin, but he has to have coverage for the patients and other employees are not as willing as Stephanie is to work extra shifts.

Instructions:

1. Identify the involved parties, their potential interests, and possible alternatives to a negotiated agreement.
2. Identify the issues that would likely be part of the negotiation.
3. For each issue establish a plausible initial offer, target, and resistance point.
4. Describe one way the situation could be framed.
5. Describe how your response to the previous question could be reframed.

Party: _____

Interests: _____

_____

Alternatives to a negotiated agreement: _____

_____

Party: _____

Interests: _____

_____

Alternatives to a negotiated agreement: _____

_____

Party: _____

Interests: _____

_____

Alternatives to a negotiated agreement: _____

_____

Party: _____

Interests: _____

_____

Alternatives to a negotiated agreement: _____

_____

Issue: _____

Initial offer: _____   Target: _____   Resistance point: _____

Issue: _____

Initial offer: _____ Target: _____ Resistance point: _____

Issue: _____

Initial offer: _____ Target: _____ Resistance point: _____

Issue: _____

Initial offer: _____ Target: _____ Resistance point: _____

Issue: _____

Initial offer: _____ Target: _____ Resistance point: _____

Issue: _____

Initial offer: _____ Target: _____ Resistance point: _____

Issue: _____

Initial offer: _____ Target: _____ Resistance point: _____

Issue: _____

Initial offer: _____ Target: _____ Resistance point: _____

Issue: _____

Initial offer: _____ Target: _____ Resistance point: _____

How could the situation be framed? _____

_____

_____

_____

_____

How could the situation be reframed? _____

_____

_____

_____

_____

PART II

Negotiation Processes

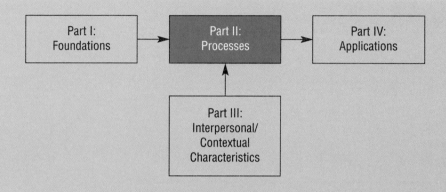

Chapter 3 Distributive Negotiations

Chapter 4 Integrative Negotiations

Chapter 5 Conflict and Dispute Resolution

Distributive Negotiations

Chapter Objectives

After studying this chapter and completing the exercises you should be able to:

- Develop strategies for distributive negotiations.
- Evaluate the use of power tactics in negotiation.
- Identify the use of hardball tactics in negotiation and develop effective responses to counter their use by others.
- Apply the concept of claiming value in negotiations.
- Assess the role of concessions in negotiations.
- Evaluate the effectiveness of various tactics for obtaining commitment in a negotiation.

I f you were asked to identify a famous negotiator who would it be? If you are a history buff you might think of Nobel Peace Prize winner Henry Kissinger discussed in Figure 3.1. If you are a movie fan you might think of the character played by Bruce Willis in the cult classic movie *The Fifth Element* who is sent in to negotiate the release of a hostage, but instead walks in, shoots, and kills the other party. Obviously, this is a very extreme example. That said, you are likely at some point to find yourself negotiating with people who are far more competitive than cooperative. Indeed negotiation has been described as "a mixture of information exchange, discovering interests, reshaping alternatives, applying pressure, finding new solutions, and making compromises."[1] But what constitutes pressure and how much is appropriate?

FIGURE 3.1 Famous Negotiator Henry Kissinger

Henry Kissinger (1923–) is arguably the most famous international negotiator of all time. He was born to a family of German Jews who fled to the United States in 1938 to avoid Nazi persecution. In World War II he was assigned to work in military intelligence where his knowledge of German society and command of the German language helped him work successfully with the Germans to restore peace and order in war torn areas. After the war he completed a Ph.D. at Harvard where he studied political science, specifically peace processes, which led to his work on U.S. foreign policy. Kissinger played a critical role in U.S. foreign policy during the Nixon and Ford presidencies negotiating a myriad of situations, including the end of the Vietnam War, the softening of the U.S. relationship with the Soviet Union, a reopening of relations with the Peoples Republic of China, and the end to the 1973 war between Egypt and Israel.

Chapter Scenario, Part I

Sally has been having problems with her car for some time. She has paid for a number of repairs but it just seems to be one thing after another. She finally decided that it is time to get a different car, even though she doesn't have a lot of money and doesn't want to take on a lot of debt. She has been looking at cars but hasn't found anything. She really wants to just get another car and be done with the hassle. She stops at yet another car lot today and sees a car that she thinks might be the one for her. The salesman comes out to talk to her. She explains that she wants to buy the car, but is on a tight budget and wants to keep her payments as low as possible. He won't lower the price of the car and insists that she can qualify for a larger loan. He is unrelenting. She thinks he is trying to take advantage of her (after all, she has heard that women tend to pay more for cars than men), but doesn't know how to get him to stop badgering her for the sale.

Even though Sally would like to negotiate with the salesman to buy the car at a good price, he is not making it easy. Ideally for Sally, the salesperson would explore various alternatives that would allow Sally to meet her need to keep her payments low. Instead, the salesman is using high-pressure tactics to get Sally to buy the car at the highest possible price, thus insuring the largest possible profit for the dealership and the highest commission for him. He is using tactics common in distributive bargaining.

DISTRIBUTIVE NEGOTIATION

The objective of **distributive negotiation** is to achieve an efficient compromise[2] by focusing on the distribution of outcomes as opposed to meeting the needs of the parties involved. If you picture the issues or value at stake in a negotiation as a pie, distributive negotiation is essentially a contest to see who gets the biggest share. It assumes that there are finite resources available (i.e., a "fixed pie") and that what one party gains comes at the expense of the other party. The relationship between the parties is generally an adversarial one where one party wins and the other loses. This is sometimes referred to as a zero-sum game. It most often happens in situations where you want the best outcome possible for yourself and don't care about the relationship with the other party. In negotiation, strategies are middle range goals that organize a negotiator's approach.[3] The strategies employed in distributive negotiations are typically very competitive, where one party pushes to get as much of the settlement range as possible with little or no regard for what the other party gets.

In the chapter scenario, the car salesman was using a distributive strategy to obtain as much profit as possible by any means necessary, without concern for Sally's need to keep her payments low or the potential benefit from building a relationship for the future. While this approach is not hard to find, over time there has been a gradual shift toward more integrative approaches. People generally want to be—and be thought of as—nice. As a result, more attention has been devoted to developing cooperative, integrative approaches to negotiating.[4] There are many advantages to an integrative approach to negotiations and we will cover the topic in detail in Chapter 4. However, negotiators need to become more strategic in the selection and implementation of approaches to negotiation, rather than merely sticking to one familiar approach or being reactive to the provocation of the other party.[5] Indeed distributive and integrative approaches are each appropriate in certain circumstances.[6]

Negotiations can be distributive as a result of the people or the situation involved. The social motives of the parties in a negotiation influence their choice of strategy such that cooperatively motivated people (i.e., those who are concerned about others' outcomes) are more likely to adopt integrative strategies, while individualistic people (i.e., those who are more concerned with their own outcomes) tend to use more distributive strategies.[7] In the chapter scenario, the car salesman was likely more individualistic, while Sally's nature was more cooperative. Even if you want to be cooperative, you can't control how others behave, so you need to be able to recognize and respond effectively in situations where the other party is engaging in distributive behaviors. Being able to use different approaches strategically, particularly confronting rights and power strategies when they are used against you, is an important negotiation skill.[8]

A negotiator's perception of the situation also leads him or her to focus on either distributive or integrative tactics.[9] Purchasing a car or major appliance are typical examples of situations that often result in distributive bargaining. In most cases, you do not know the salesperson and probably aren't interested in becoming friends. On the other hand, assuming you have limited financial resources, you probably are concerned about getting the best price possible. These types of situations are inherently distributive.

If in the chapter scenario it was the last day of the month and the salesman needed to sell the car at a certain price to meet his sales quota for the month, he would have more incentive to use distributive tactics than if he had already achieved his sales quota. At the same time, Sally may have had visions of establishing a good relationship with a salesperson that she could use in the future. Of course one's perceptions may not be accurate. Research has shown that we may perceive integrative potential when it does not exist,[10] which seems to be true for Sally. Similarly, even when the parties enter negotiations with the view that it is a fundamentally distributive situation, in the end they often believe their own negotiated agreements yield roughly equal payoffs to both negotiators, whether or not that is actually the case.[11] Thus, if Sally purchased the car at a high price, the salesman would likely believe that the car provided her with as much value as the higher price provided the dealership and the salesman.

In purely distributive negotiations, technology in the form of Negotiation Software Agents (NSAs) or multi-attribute auctions* may be used to assist in the negotiation process.[12] Consider the case of eBay, shown in Figure 3.2, the world's largest marketplace with 88 million active users.[13]

FIGURE 3.2 eBay: Automating Distributive Bargaining

You are almost certainly familiar with eBay and likely have used it to buy or sell something, but you may not have thought about it in the context of distributive negotiations. However, as a multi-attribute auction, that is essentially what eBay is.[14] Sellers seek to sell their wares to the highest bidder, while buyers are attempting to get what they want at the lowest possible price. The eBay website even makes numerous references to "winning" and uses the phrase "in it to win it."

When sellers specify a minimum bid they are stating their resistance point. When they offer an item that can be purchased immediately for a specified price, they essentially state their target point. Buyers can place each bid themselves or allow the system to automatically generate bids up to a specified amount, which is essentially their resistance point. While buyers are able to rate the sellers—fundamentally a relationship issue—the primary focus is clearly on the substantive outcome (i.e., price).

---
*In procurement negotiations, a protocol that takes crucial non-price attributes into account.

MIXED-MOTIVE BARGAINING

Even in situations that aren't completely distributive, there are distributive components in most negotiations. Walton and McKersie used the term **mixed-motive bargaining** to describe a situation when the negotiating agenda has "significant elements of conflict and considerable potential for integration."[15] Typically, negotiations that involve money tend to be distributive unless the parties can find a way to generate more value or identify non-financial interests. The classic example of mixed-motive bargaining is found in industrial relations.[16] When negotiating with a union, the employer wants to keep labor costs as low as possible so as to maximize profits. At the same time, the union wants to negotiate the highest wages and best benefits possible for its members. They are interdependent because both parties need each other to survive; without employees the employer cannot remain in business and without the employer the employees won't have jobs. Thus, it is in their mutual best interests to work together. If they can do that and come up with ways to increase efficiency, the employer can reap higher profits and afford to pay the employees more. In the end both will be better off.

A mixed strategy of integrative bargaining to establish the maximum total sum, followed by relatively hard distributive bargaining to claim the largest share may be the most attractive strategy, but the most difficult strategy to implement.[17] Basically, the parties would work cooperatively to generate alternatives and explore possible solutions for resolving the situation, which would result in more possibilities from which to choose and more value to claim. For a mixed strategy to be effective there needs to be an ongoing relationship between the parties and multiple issues on the table.[18] The ongoing relationship provides an incentive to work together, while multiple issues increase the likelihood that each party will meet at least some of his needs. Remember: the more issues there are in a negotiation, the greater the probability of getting more of what you want.

As noted earlier, social motives influence negotiators' actions and reactions. In mixed-motive situations, negotiators do better when their strategies are consistent with their social motives.[19] Thus, while mixed-motive situations require the use of both distributive and integrative strategies, cooperative negotiators will likely be more effective, and comfortable, in generating options, while individualistic negotiators will have an edge in claiming value. One way to capitalize on this when there are multiple negotiators on each side is to have a cooperative negotiator take the lead during the value creation stage and an individualistic negotiator take over during the value claiming stage. This is important because engaging in a completely cooperative approach to negotiation leaves one vulnerable to last-minute power plays by the other party.[20]

LEVERAGE/POWER

At the most basic level there are two components of **leverage** or power in a negotiation: the benefits the negotiator brings to the table and the counterpart's BATNA (Best Alternative to a Negotiated Agreement).[21] The more a negotiator's offer is valued by the other party, the more power the negotiator will have. Similarly, the better a negotiator's BATNA, the more power she will have. Essentially it comes down to the economic principle of supply and demand. The higher the demand and lower the supply for an item, the better the BATNA (because there will be other customers) and the stronger the seller's position in a negotiation. Conversely, the buyer will have a better BATNA and be in a stronger position to negotiate when the demand is low and the supply is large. Take the case of the H-1 Hummer that had a list price of over $140,000. When they were first introduced in 1992 the supply was relatively low, and because it was a new and unique vehicle, the demand was fairly high. There weren't many, if any, comparable alternatives for the buyers and if someone really wanted one of the vehicles, his resistance point would typically be higher. At the same time, there were other buyers who wanted the product. Thus, the dealers had good alternatives so their resistance points were higher. Because of the disparity in BATNAs, people were initially paying close to list price for Hummers. Over time, however, the situation changed. Following the invasion of Iraq, gas prices increased dramatically and demand dropped off for the behemoths that averaged around 11 miles per gallon. Car dealers found themselves trying to sell a product that people no longer desired. Sales dropped off so much that in June 2006, General Motors ceased production of the largest of the Hummers.

This sales example applies to employment situations as well. When the demand for employees with a particular skill exceeds the supply, an individual's BATNA is better and his bargaining power increases. Applicants who possess knowledge, skills, and abilities that are in high demand are in a much stronger position to find employment and negotiate better salaries and benefits than those with skills that are in lower demand. For example, for a number of years there has been a shortage of nurses in most parts of the United States. As a result, wages and benefits have increased for nurses at a faster rate than for many other occupations. Conversely, when a factory closes, leaving many unskilled or semi-skilled workers looking for work, these workers often remain unemployed for long periods of time. When they do find work, it often provides lower wages and fewer benefits than their former jobs. Because these workers have fewer employment alternatives, they have little power to negotiate job offers and may take any job they are offered just to have an income.

POWER TACTICS IN NEGOTIATION

In addition to the power that a negotiator has related to the situation and her BATNA, there are a variety of power tactics that can be used to gain an advantage. Tactics are the specific behaviors used by a party in a negotiation.[22] Which tactics are used will likely depend on whether the situation is viewed as distributive or integrative, the parties and personalities involved, and the unique characteristics of the situation. The tactics in distributive negotiations tend to be more direct and assertive because there is little emphasis on the relationship between the parties. Similarly, there are often natural differences in the basic personalities of negotiators. Some people are naturally more concerned about their relationships with others,[23] making them less likely to engage in particularly direct and assertive tactics that might offend the other party.

While your preferred tactics are related to your personality and value system, we commonly use different tactics when dealing with different people, organizations, and cultures. The tactics you use when negotiating with your boss are unlikely the same that you use with your coworkers. Similarly, you probably wouldn't use the same tactics when resolving a conflict with your friends as those you would use with your spouse. Different situations also call for different tactics. You are likely to use different tactics with a police officer who has come to investigate the theft of your property than one who has just pulled you over for speeding. Research has also found that women typically use less competitive tactics than men, unless they are negotiating on behalf of someone else, in which case their styles are the same as men's.[24] Generally recognized power tactics include rationality, ingratiation, coalition building, exchange, assertiveness, upward appeal, and imposing sanctions.

Rationality is a generic tactic used across various contexts[25] that involves the use of reason and logical presentation of facts or data. In short, you appeal to the other party's sense of logic and reason. If they don't agree with you, they seem illogical and unreasonable. Let's say that it is Saturday and Brenda wants to spend the day working in the garden while Eddie mows the lawn. Eddie isn't particularly anxious to mow the lawn and instead wants to go to the boat show at the local arena. Brenda points out to Eddie that the weather forecast is calling for a 90% chance of rain on Sunday so they should do their outdoor chores today and go to the boat show tomorrow. Unless Eddie literally doesn't know enough to come in out of the rain, it would be illogical for him not to agree with Brenda.

Ingratiation is another generic tactic used in a variety of settings[26] that involves being friendly to the other party to get him to like you. When you like someone, you are more likely to be cooperative and agreeable. When someone is being friendly she is generally humble and may flatter the other person with compliments. She may also do favors for the other person to win him over. This often results in the other person reciprocating the friendly and helpful behaviors, making ingratiation an effective tactic when negotiating.

It is important to note, though, that there is a fine line between friendliness and what most people consider sucking up. While most people appreciate others who are friendly to them, they are also generally annoyed by those who they perceive to be disingenuous or even trying to manipulate them. Most professors can recall students who at the end of the semester tell them how much they have learned and enjoyed the class and that the professor is the best they have encountered in their entire college career. While this is sometimes sincere, when it comes from a student who rarely attended class and did very poorly on assignments and exams, it is more likely viewed as a transparent attempt to influence the final grade. Needless to say, in this situation the friendliness is unlikely to be effective.

Coalition building involves obtaining the support of and forming an alliance with others. It's based on the notion that there is strength in numbers and is most often used when you don't think you have enough influence to get what you want on your own. The alliance may be with people who are directly involved in the situation or with those who are more removed. For example, let's say your office is on a traditional 8 a.m. to 5 p.m. Monday through Friday work schedule. You would like to have some flexibility in your schedule, but aren't sure that your boss will be receptive to your idea. Before going to your boss, you talk with your coworkers to see if they would like flexibility in their work hours, so when you approach your boss you can say that a number of employees want to be able to vary their work schedule. Another example is when a teachers' union or a school district is involved in labor contract negotiations and seeks the support of parent groups and taxpayers in the community to bolster their position at the bargaining table.

Exchange is **quid pro quo bargaining**—you scratch my back and I'll scratch yours—and is the basis for barter systems. Success with this tactic depends on each party having something to offer that the other party wants. If you have nothing the other party desires, she has no incentive to give you what you want. Conversely, if you have something the other person values, your power is increased and there is a greater probability of getting what you want from her. Imagine you have a roommate who is very good at calculus, but doesn't have much of a social life. On the other hand, you have a very full social calendar, but are struggling in your required calculus class and fear that if you don't do well on the final, you may fail the class. You need help with calculus and your roommate needs a social life. You tell your roommate that if she helps you with your studies, you will take her to the local pub with you on Thursday night when many college students gather to toast their professors.

Assertiveness involves using a direct and forceful approach to push your own agenda and/or attack the other party's position. In organizations, assertiveness is more often used by persons who are higher in the organizational hierarchy.[27] As with friendliness, people use this tactic to different degrees with different results. At a minimum, taking a firm stand will prevent others from seeing you as a pushover and taking advantage of you. At the other end of the continuum, others may view you as a bully. Success in using this tactic depends on knowing where to draw the line between being assertive and overly aggressive. Let's say you are on vacation in another country and are approached by locals trying to sell you trinkets. You really don't want their wares and want to be left alone. A firmly spoken "No" will often achieve the desired results without having to pull out your trusty pepper spray. At the other extreme, it can include disruptive action such as shouting or storming out of a negotiation.

Upward appeal involves obtaining support for your position from people in higher positions of authority. For a child it is often "I'm going to tell my Mom." For a neighbor having a loud party at 3 a.m. it could be calling the police. For a company you hired to work on your house it might be filing a complaint with the Better Business Bureau or taking the contractor to court. In the workplace it might involve going to your boss for support in a dispute with a coworker. In general, your relationship with the other party will be better in the long run if you can resolve the situation without involving a higher authority.

Imposing sanctions involves the use of coercive power to achieve the desired results. If you think about it, this is actually a fairly common practice in business. Think of all those bills you get—utilities, taxes, credit cards—most stipulate that if they are not paid by the due date listed you will be assessed a late fee. The farther behind you get in your payments, the more severe the penalty becomes. Utilities might be shut off, credit cards can be cancelled, cars repossessed, and homes foreclosed. You comply with the other party to avoid the penalties. In some cases, the penalty is framed as an incentive, as with the once-standard industry terms "2/10 net 30," where the full amount was due in 30 days, but if you paid within 10 days you received a 2% discount.

In some cases, one of the parties manipulates the timing of the negotiations so that a type of sanction on the other party occurs naturally if the parties fail to reach an agreement. An example of this is when an employer is successful in having a labor contract expire just before Christmas. If the union fails to reach an agreement the workers are faced with going on strike, thereby losing their income at a time when most people are spending more money than they normally would because of the holidays. Similarly, teacher unions, whose contracts typically expire at the end of the school year, may take their time negotiating until it gets close to the time for school to start in order to garner the support of parents who are anxious for their children to return to school.

Points to Ponder

1. Which power tactics do you use most often?
2. What factors influence your choice of power tactics?
3. Which power tactics are you least comfortable with? Why?

TACTICS TO CHANGE POWER

Table 3.1 identifies the four basic tactics for changing the balance of power in a negotiation: improve the quality of your own BATNA, decrease the quality of the other party's BATNA, decrease your value of the other party's contribution, and increase the value of your contribution.[28] Two of the tactics deal with the parties' BATNAs and two deal with their contributions. Improving the quality of your BATNA involves increasing the attractiveness of your best alternative or finding another more attractive alternative, thereby decreasing the other party's power by making you less dependent on what he has to offer. For example, if you are buying a vehicle, you would search out other vehicles that provide similar value at a lower cost.

The second tactic also deals with BATNA but has to do with the other party's best alternative. You increase your power by decreasing the value of the other party's best alternative, making him more dependent on what you have to offer. A common example is found in labor-management negotiations. If the parties come to impasse, the union typically pickets the employer to bring attention to their plight and to discourage replacement workers from crossing the picket line. To the extent the union is successful, the employer's alternative of continuing production through the use of replacement workers is diminished, which increases the union's power.

Similarly, you can alter the balance of power by changing the value of the other party's or your contributions. Decreasing the value you place on the other party's

---

TABLE 3.1	Tactics to Increase Your Power in a Negotiation	
	BATNA	**Contributions**
Your	Increase the quality of your BATNA.	Increase the value of your contributions.
Other party	Decrease the quality of the other party's BATNA.	Decrease the value of the other party's contributions.

contribution decreases her power. A common method of doing this is to find flaws in what the other party has to offer. For example, if you are buying a house you may find and draw attention to repairs that need to be done. Generally, the seller will reduce the price by some amount to avoid having to make the repairs himself. This tactic is also common in a wide variety of retail settings where you find "scratch and dent" sales on appliances, discounted prices on "floor models," and reduced prices on clothing that may be soiled or missing a button.

The final tactic to increase your power in a negotiation is to increase the value of your contribution. Another example from retail is offering to pay with cash instead of a credit card. This is especially effective if you are purchasing a big-ticket item. As a buyer this doesn't cost you any additional money, but from the seller's standpoint it eliminates the fee charged by the credit card company, usually 3% to 5%, for processing the transaction. Another example is if you have a house and are going to rent a room to someone who is moving to the area beginning the first of the month. You might offer to let your new tenant move some things in early to reduce the amount of things he has to move all at once. Since the tenant will not actually be staying there, your expenses won't increase but you are providing additional value to him by making his move more convenient.

In addition to the four basic tactics for changing the balance of power in a negotiation there are others that may be used, either by you or against you. Most are considered hardball tactics and are used in distributive situations to show the other party that you are a tough negotiator. The goal of all of these tactics is to get the other party to make concessions.

HARDBALL TACTICS

The first hardball tactic is **highball/lowball** where one party makes an extreme opening offer in an attempt to throw the other party off balance and get him to believe that he is not being realistic with his opening offer. If it is successful the other party alters his position, sometimes dramatically. The risk is that the other party will assume that there is no point in negotiating since you are so far apart. With the collapse of the housing market in 2008, there were far fewer buyers, which strengthened their bargaining position. At the same time there were many more homes for sale as a result of the many foreclosures, which put the sellers in a weaker bargaining position. As a result, many buyers would make very low offers in hopes that the seller would accept it just to be free of the house. In many cases this tactic was effective, and buyers were able to acquire a home at a much reduced price. Even when the initial low offer was not immediately accepted, it often served to anchor the price in the negotiation at a much lower amount than the initial asking price. Of course this tactic has very little chance of success during good economic times.

Another common hardball tactic is **bluffing**, sometimes referred to as playing "**chicken**." Basically it involves going head to head with the other party to see who will back down first. It may involve exaggerating your position or even making false threats to convince the other party that you have the upper hand. This is a common tactic when playing poker and some people are very good at it. These people are often referred to as having a poker face and are able to withhold any display of emotion so the other party is unable to determine if they are bluffing or not. Of course there are risks involved. The first is that the other party won't back down and the negotiation becomes deadlocked, resulting in a failed negotiation. Another risk that can have longer-term consequences for your reputation is when you bluff but don't follow through with your threat when the other party doesn't acquiesce. In a personal context, an example is the parent who threatens punishment if his teenager doesn't improve her grades but then doesn't follow through when there is no improvement. Similarly, in the workplace an example is the employee who tells his boss that if he doesn't get a substantial raise he is going to quit, but fails to follow through. In both cases the person who bluffs and subsequently backs down loses credibility with the other party.

Intimidation, or engaging in aggressive behavior, is another fairly common hardball tactic. It may involve name-dropping to imply a closer relationship with those in power or statements like "this is the right thing to do" or "policy requires that . . ." to make a negotiator's position seem more legitimate. In some cases one party may try to get the other to feel guilty for something she has or hasn't done. Statements like "You did. . . ." or "You were supposed to. . . ." are generally intended to put the other party on the defensive so the negotiator can gain an advantage. It may also include behaviors ranging from raising one's voice or pounding one's fist on the table to making threats toward the other party.

Some hardball tactics are not as obviously aggressive as others. The **bogey** involves including issues in your opening offer that are really not important to you, but give you something to trade later. This has often been used in labor negotiations where there are typically many issues involved. In one case, the unionized faculty at a private college always included as one of the issues in their opening demand that a union representative be given a seat on the college's board of trustees. The faculty knew that this was something the administration would never agree to but they still brought it up in every contract negotiation, in part to have something to trade and in part to rattle the cage of the administration. While this may have initially passed as a legitimate request worthy of a concession, over time it became more of an irritation that could potentially harm the relationship between the parties. Obviously the union did not use this tactic judiciously.

The **"nibble"** involves asking for additional small things after negotiation has begun or even reached tentative agreement on the main issues. One example is asking for free delivery on furniture that you already negotiated to purchase at a very good price. Another is asking for free accessories such as free gloves when buying a coat or free earrings when buying a necklace. Different people view this in different ways. Some see this as being a smart negotiator who keeps trying to get more. Others see this as annoying behavior or perhaps even being a bit disingenuous. How the party on the receiving end of the nibble reacts often depends on how persistent the person doing the nibbling is. If she takes no for an answer and gracefully lets it drop, the other party is unlikely to take issue with it. On the other hand, if she threatens to renege on the deal demanding to get her own way, the other party might just end the negotiation.

Overwhelming the other party with information, sometimes referred to as a **"snow job"** or creating a **"blizzard**," can also be used as a hardball tactic. It involves providing the other party with so much information that he is left feeling distracted and overwhelmed so he will agree to what you want just to avoid wading through all the information. Essentially, he agrees just so he doesn't have to deal with it—or you—any more. While this may be effective in some cases, in others it simply serves to make the other party dig in his heels and come back with even more information supporting his position, all of which leads to protracted negotiations.

The final hardball tactic is commonly referred to as **good cop/bad cop** and requires two negotiators. It is rooted in the scenario of two police officers trying to convince a suspect to confess. It begins with one officer taking the role of the hardnosed, "bad cop" who is very tough on the suspect, demanding answers and threatening the suspect with possible punishments. The other officer follows in the role of the "good cop" who in contrast appears reasonable so that the suspect wants to cooperate with him. But this tactic isn't limited to gangsters and high-drama television. A much less dramatic albeit common example is the couple who is shopping. The wife, taking the role of the good cop, finds something she wants to purchase but says she has to get her husband's approval. The husband, taking the role of the bad cop, cites all the reasons that they shouldn't make the purchase. Perhaps the item is too expensive or that he just doesn't find the product appealing. If it is successful, the seller lowers the price in an attempt to appease the husband to gain his approval on the sale.

Points to Ponder

1. Which hardball tactics might you use?
2. Are there any hardball tactics that you would never use? Why?
3. What types of situations might make you more inclined to use hardball tactics?

We would be remiss if we didn't offer a word of caution about the use of hardball tactics in negotiation. While the judicious use of these tactics in certain situations can prove effective in the short term, negotiators take the risk that the other party may respond with an equally or even more aggressive tactic of her own. Even when the parties are aware of the costs and consequences of such behavior, they may not be able to avoid getting drawn into a downward spiral and respond without a great deal of forethought about the implications for how the ensuing negotiation is likely to evolve.[29]

That said, many of these tactics may be effectively used in small doses. It comes down to a matter of degree and with whom you are dealing. For example, providing the other party with information is generally viewed positively, but at some point it becomes a hardball tactic. What may be the norm in one culture may be unacceptable in another. Even within a particular culture, what one person with whom you negotiate finds acceptable, another may not. Some people are simply more easily offended than others. While one person may have no problem with mildly aggressive behavior, another may view it as completely inappropriate. Generally speaking, men can get away with behaving more aggressively than women.[30] In the end you have to understand the party with whom you are dealing and choose your tactics accordingly. But what if the other party is using hardball tactics against you?

HARDBALL TACTICS: RESPONSES

While we choose our own behaviors when negotiating, we can't control what behaviors the other party employs. To be effective we need to be prepared for dealing with all types of bargaining behaviors including hardball tactics. There are four basic tactics for responding to hardball tactics: preventing it, ignoring it, discussing it, and responding with hardball tactics of your own. Many times the use of hardball tactics can be prevented altogether by befriending the other party early in the negotiation. People are generally less likely to use hardball tactics on someone they like or whom they consider a friend or ally. It is also helpful to shift the focus from the differences between you and the other party to a common threat. You and the other party become a team working together to overcome the threat, as opposed to opponents trying to best each other.

In some cases ignoring a hardball tactic can neutralize its effect. You might deflect the tactic by pretending you didn't hear or understand it, or by treating it as a joke that couldn't possibly be serious. You might also change the subject or take a break in an attempt to get the other party to drop it. If the other party sees that his attempts at intimidating or provoking you are not working, he may abandon the tactic. While ignoring one hardball tactic may not stop the other party from trying another, ignoring several can send a clear message that you won't be taken in by them.

If the other party persists in the use of hardball tactics, it may be necessary to discuss the behavior and establish ground rules for behavior during the negotiation. While you might be a bit uncomfortable confronting the other party about his behavior, experts herald this as an effective approach.[31] For example, if the other party is shouting, you might say "I can see this is a very important issue to you, but let's see if we can resolve this without raising our voices." Similarly, proposing that you work together to resolve the dispute makes it difficult for the other party to continue using the hardball tactic without appearing unreasonable.

The final option is to respond with a hardball tactic of your own. If you do this, it is imperative that you understand what you are doing and why. While there may be a real temptation to get even with the other party, you run the risk of making the situation even worse by getting drawn in to a downward spiral of increasingly negative behaviors.[32] Thus, you must be very cautious in using hardball tactics. That said, in some cases responding to a hardball tactic with a hardball tactic sends the message that you will not be intimidated and is enough to stop the use of such tactics, especially if the other party was using the tactic to test your resolve.

Chapter Scenario, Part II

Finally, Sally had enough of the salesman's high-pressure sales tactics. As he was going on and on about how much she could afford, she interrupted him with: "Excuse me, this is my money and I will be the one to decide how much I wish to spend on a car and your high-pressure sales tactics are not going to change that. If you are unwilling or unable to show me cars that are within the parameters that I have set, then I will have no choice but to take my business elsewhere." The salesman was taken aback that Sally had called out his behavior. Not wanting to lose a possible sale, he backtracked saying: "I'm sorry; of course it is your decision. I would really like to help you find the car that is right for you. Let's take a look at some of the cars over here."

INFORMATION SHARING IN A DISTRIBUTIVE NEGOTIATION

The sharing of information in distributive negotiations is quite different than in integrative negotiations. In integrative negotiations, information sharing is a crucial component in the creating value stage where it is necessary to identify alternatives for meeting the needs of both parties. Since distributive negotiations are competitive in nature, the sharing of information is more guarded so as to protect one's position. In addressing the issues, a distributive negotiator focuses on facts, asks miscellaneous task-related questions, and suggests the discussion of individual issues.[33] A distributive negotiator would not ask questions about the other party's needs or put effort into building a relationship. Similarly she wouldn't try to combine various issues in an attempt to meet the needs of the other party. When responding to proposals from the other party, she will generally engage in negative behaviors such as displaying negative reactions, noting differences between the parties' proposals, attacking the other party's arguments, and asking for the other party's bottom line.[34]

CLAIMING VALUE

Negotiators use their power and sometimes hardball tactics to **claim value**, in other words, to get as much of the settlement range as possible. Claiming as much value as possible is the goal of distributive negotiation. Some of the behaviors negotiators use to claim value include defending their arguments to substantiate their position, making single-issue offers, suggesting creative solutions to meet their own interests, making threats, and referring to the bottom line and their power.[35] The tactics used however are not the only determinant of success in claiming value. The opening offers and target and resistance points a negotiator establishes before beginning a negotiation have a significant impact on the final outcome.

It is to a negotiator's advantage to be optimistic about what she can obtain in a negotiation. Research has found that bargainers who were more optimistic in their perceptions of the bargaining zone were more profitable in distributive bargaining and experienced no increase in impasse or damage to the relationship.[36] In negotiation, the old adage that "you get what you expect" seems to hold true. When a negotiator is more optimistic, she will establish targets that are more favorable to her, which may lead to greater persistence in negotiating.[37] Conversely, when a negotiator is more pessimistic, she typically sets less aggressive targets, making her more likely to agree to an offer that is close to her target, but less favorable than she might have otherwise been able to negotiate. Because optimistic bargainers are more persistent, negotiations take longer, and they may be perceived as less friendly and tougher.[38] Of course negotiators can err by being either overly optimistic or overly pessimistic; however, it seems best to err on the side of optimism. Research has found that optimistic errors are to some extent self-correcting (i.e., you learn as the negotiation progresses that you may not get everything you want), while pessimistic errors are self-fulfilling and self-defeating and thus a more serious error.[39]

CONCESSIONS

Concessions are what you give up and are expected in any negotiation. Negotiators establish opening offers with the expectation that it is unlikely that their counterpart will agree to their first offer. If a negotiator's first offer is immediately accepted, he is often left feeling like he could have done better[40] a condition referred to as the "**winner's curse.**" Making concessions goes hand in hand with claiming value and is usually a case of reciprocity in action—giving something with the expectation of getting something in return. Knowing how to manage the reciprocity so as to sustain your negotiation strategy, regardless of the other party's approach, is an important negotiation skill.[41] In the chapter scenario, if the salesman were to relent a bit and offer Sally a free one-year warranty with a retail price of $750 on the used car if she buys it today, she might be more willing to concede a slightly higher monthly payment in return for this gesture.

The pattern of concessions can signal where things are and where they are headed. Often negotiators begin with small concessions early in a negotiation to see if the other party will reciprocate. If the other party reciprocates, they may offer a larger concession in hopes that it too will be reciprocated. This continues and the parties work up to larger concessions until the parties near their reservation points, when the concessions get smaller. Conversely, if a negotiator has been making relatively small concessions and then makes a larger one, it may signal that he is giving up the remainder of what he has and that he can go no further on the issue.

Concession making can also involve the tactic known as **logrolling**; the exchange of support or favors. When you are logrolling, you make concessions on issues that have a low priority to you in return for gains on issues on which you place a higher priority. One example is when a buyer agrees to a slightly higher price if the seller agrees to deliver and install the product at no additional charge. An example in labor negotiations is when an employer agrees to raise the pay of employees if the employees agree to pay part of the cost of their medical insurance. Research has shown that logrolling offers yield higher profit for the initiator, and higher combined profits for both parties than purely distributive offers.[42]

COMMITMENT

The final step in any negotiation is obtaining commitment from the parties on all issues involved in the negotiation. In a single-issue negotiation, this is fairly straightforward; the parties either come to agreement or they don't. In multi-issue negotiations it becomes more complex. The parties typically agree on certain issues as the negotiation progresses and continue until agreement is reached on all issues. Needless to say it is important to document all agreed upon issues as the negotiation progresses. In contract negotiations, the term **tentative agreement** or **TA** is often used to indicate that the parties agree on a particular issue in anticipation of reaching an agreement on all issues involved. If that does not happen, the parties are not bound by any agreements on individual issues because they were tentative. It is important to note, however, that even though the agreements on individual issues are tentative, it is generally considered bargaining in bad faith to renege on an issue on which there is a TA. Thus, from a practical standpoint, tentative agreements are only tentative if a complete agreement is not reached.

Needless to say it is easier to obtain commitment on some issues than on others. In multi-issue negotiations the parties often start with smaller or less controversial issues and work their way up to the bigger, more contentious ones. In effect they use the small issues to build momentum for the larger ones. In labor contract negotiations the parties typically begin with any changes to the current contract language to provide clarity to all parties and work their way up to the more difficult, and inherently more distributive, issues of compensation and benefits. Not surprisingly, in negotiations that involve payment for goods or services, cost is typically the last issue upon which the parties agree. For example, if you are buying furniture, you should address the issue of delivery before agreeing to the price since you might be willing to pay a bit more if there is no charge for delivery.

There are several things a negotiator can do to keep the process moving and encourage commitment. A negotiator may suggest moving on to other issues, mutual trade-offs, or voting on proposals that represent a potential resolution on all or a subset of the issues.[43] It is also often helpful to establish a deadline for agreement. In negotiating modifications to an existing contract, the built-in deadline is the expiration date of the current agreement. The same holds true for the negotiation of local, state, or federal budgets where there is the potential of government services being halted due to lack of funding if agreement is not reached. In other cases, a party may present what is often referred to as an "exploding" offer where the offer is good only for a limited period of time. The idea is that if one party does not accept the offer, the opportunity is lost. This tactic is also used in sales to encourage people to buy products that they might not otherwise buy right away. In all of these examples, the party making the offer provides time checks[44] as the deadline nears to remind the other party that there is a deadline and to encourage the other party to accept the offer.

A tactic to encourage commitment is to note the similarities between the parties and their needs[45] and reinforce the benefits of coming to agreement. In a positive light, this might include promises made to the other party that will provide him value. In a labor-management setting, it might involve a promise of a better working relationship if agreement is reached. If you are negotiating to purchase a new bed, the salesperson might remind you of the benefits of a good night's sleep. At the other end of the spectrum, reinforcement might include threats of negative things that will happen if there isn't agreement. A union might reiterate their threat to strike or a customer might point out that the salesperson could lose the sale.

When the only thing preventing agreement is the money involved and the parties are fairly close, the parties may agree to split the difference. In this case, each party gives a little more to get an agreement. From a psychological standpoint, neither party is left feeling like she simply gave in. Allowing the other party to save face is especially important if she has to report back to constituents or others concerned with the negotiation. Another possibility is that one party may sweeten the deal by adding additional benefits to the other party at no additional cost. Common examples include free delivery and set-up of large items, free gift wrapping, free shipping, and free removal and disposal of the old item.

Once you get commitment from the other party, there is still the possibility that he will not follow through and do as he promised. In some cases there is greater concern than in others. Figure 3.3 provides a summary of the considerations that might indicate whether a negotiator is likely to keep his commitments.

There are several things you can do to increase the likelihood that the other party will keep his commitments. This is especially important if your experience with the other party suggests otherwise. People are usually more likely to follow through on commitments that have been made in public. Such public pronouncements are used everywhere from Weight Watchers to international politics. An extension of this in purchase agreements is getting the buyer to make a down payment. This is standard with big-ticket items such as furniture, cars, real estate, or special-order items. Often there is a stipulation that if the buyer backs out, she forfeits the down payment. While verbal public pronouncements are helpful, they are no substitute for a written

FIGURE 3.3 Indicators a Commitment will be Kept[46]

Consistency. Has the other party been consistent in what she has told you?
Honesty. Consistency. Has she lied about anything?
Authority. Does she have the authority to make decisions?
Respect. Did she treat you with respect?
Agenda. Did she follow the agreed-upon agenda?
Reputation. If she does not have a good reputation, have you built in safeguards?

agreement. Putting a negotiated agreement in writing can make it a legally enforceable contract.

Occasionally the other party makes a commitment to do something that you don't want him to do, such as breaking off negotiations. In this case you might simply ignore the threat or try to restate the position in softer, more favorable terms. Again, you should always try to find ways for the other party to save face. If the other party is embarrassed or, worse yet, humiliated, it increases the possibility that he will try to get even with you in the future. Similarly, you may find the need to back out of something. Perhaps you got caught up in the heat of the moment and made statements that you now regret. You may get lucky and have the other party ignore you, but if that doesn't work you could try making light of your statements. You might say something like "you really got me going with that" to indicate that whatever you said was only due to getting caught up in the heat of the moment. However, be sure that that at the end of the negotiation, both parties' commitments are clear. Hints and suggestions may be interpreted differently than intended; final clarification helps reduce the likelihood of broken commitments.

IMPASSE

Generally when negotiating, the parties start with their opening offers and then make a series of concessions. In a perfect world this give and take continues until the parties reach agreement. If it doesn't, the parties are said to come to **impasse**. The significance of this depends on what you are negotiating and with whom. In labor contract negotiations, the employer and the union are legally required to negotiate to impasse before the union can strike or the employer can lockout the employees. If you are negotiating to buy or sell something and you come to impasse, you might simply walk away from the negotiation and find someone else with whom to do business.

If the situation isn't one that you can or are willing to simply walk away from, you can always seek a third party to help resolve the conflict. This might involve appealing to a higher authority to settle the dispute. For young siblings it might mean having a parent decide the outcome. For coworkers it would likely involve taking the dispute to the boss and having her decide. In other cases it might mean taking the other party to court to have a judge decide the outcome. However, more parties today are turning to various forms of **Alternative Dispute Resolution (ADR)**, which is any means of settling disputes outside of the courtroom. ADR is increasingly used in disputes involving employment, consumer, technology, health care, bankruptcy, and civil disputes. The most common forms of ADR are arbitration and mediation. Both are faster and less expensive than litigation. In some states, courts order the parties to try mediation or arbitration before pursuing a lawsuit. While third-party intervention is always an option, it is better not to bring in the third party prematurely.[47] Both arbitration and mediation are covered in detail as part of our discussion of conflict resolution in Chapter 5.

Summary

In this chapter we discussed the various aspects of distributive negotiations. After identifying the characteristics of distributive bargaining, we explored the concept of mixed-motive bargaining. Next we addressed power in negotiation and the use of power tactics, including reason, friendliness, coalition building, bargaining, assertiveness, appealing to a higher authority, and imposing sanctions. We identified a number of common hardball tactics including highball/lowball, bluffing, bogey, the nibble, and good cop/bad cop, and offered strategies for responding if your counterpart in a negotiation is using them. The process of claiming value was discussed as was the role of concessions and commitment. Finally, we addressed the possibility of reaching an impasse.

Summary: The Big Picture

Distributive negotiation	Focus on the distribution of outcomes. Assumes finite resources, a zero-sum game. Adversarial relationship. Competitive strategies, to obtain as much of the settlement range as possible. Appropriate in some situations. Strategy depends on the parties and situation involved.
Mixed-motive bargaining	Distributive components in most negotiations. For a mixed strategy to be effective there must be an ongoing relationship and multiple issues. Social motives influence effectiveness. Cooperative approach to create value. Competitive approach to claim value.
Leverage/power	The higher the value of what you can offer and the better your BATNA, the greater the leverage.
Power tactics	Use depends on the type of negotiation, personalities of the negotiators, and characteristics of the situation. Rationality, ingratiation, coalition building, exchange, assertiveness, upward appeal, imposing sanctions.
Tactics to change power	Improve your BATNA, decrease the other party's BATNA, decrease the value of the other party's contribution, and increase the value of your contribution.
Hardball tactics	Highball/lowball, bluffing, intimidation, bogey, nibble, overwhelming the other party with information, good cop/bad cop.
Responses to hardball tactics	Prevent, ignore, discuss the behavior, and respond in kind.
Information sharing	Limited in distributive negotiations.
Claiming value	Goal is to obtain as much as possible.
Concessions	Often a signal to the other party.
Commitment	May tentatively agree on individual issues. Begin with small and work toward larger issues.
Impasse	When parties cease to make progress toward settlement.

Key Terms and Concepts

Alternative Dispute Resolution (ADR)   Any means of settling disputes outside of the courtroom.

Assertiveness   A power tactic that involves using a direct and forceful approach to push your own agenda and/or attack the other party's position.

Bluffing/chicken   A hardball tactic that involves going head to head with the other party to see who will back down first.

Claiming value   To obtain as much of the settlement range as possible.

Coalition building   A power tactic that involves obtaining the support of and forming an alliance with others.

Concessions   What you give up in a negotiation.

Distributive negotiation   An approach to negotiation where the focus is on the distribution of outcomes.

Exchange/quid pro quo bargaining   A power tactic that involves offering something to the other party in exchange for something in return.

Good cop/bad cop   A hardball tactic that requires two negotiators, one acting very tough and the other acting reasonably to gain the cooperation of the other party.

Highball/lowball   A hardball tactic where one party makes an extreme opening offer in an attempt to throw the other party off balance and get him to believe that he is not being realistic with his opening offer.

Impasse   When the parties to a negotiation cease to make progress toward a settlement.

Imposing sanctions   A power tactic that involves the use of coercive power to achieve the desired results.

Ingratiation   A power tactic that involves being friendly to the other party to get him to like you.

Intimidation   A hardball tactic that involves engaging in aggressive behavior.

Leverage   The amount of power a negotiator has in a negotiation.

Logrolling   Making concessions on issues that have a low priority to you in return for gains on issues that have a higher priority.

Mixed-motive bargaining   A situation when the negotiating agenda has "significant elements of conflict and considerable potential for integration."

Nibble   A hardball tactic that involves asking for additional small things after negotiation has begun or even reached tentative agreement on the main issues.

Overwhelming the other party with information/snow job/blizzard   A hardball tactic that involves providing the other party with so much information that she is left feeling distracted and overwhelmed so she will agree to what you want just to avoid wading through all the information.

Rationality   A power tactic that involves the use of reason and the logical presentation of facts or data.

Tentative agreement/TA   An indication that the parties agree on a particular issue in anticipation of reaching an agreement on all issues involved.

Upward appeal   A power tactic that involves obtaining support for your position from people in higher positions of authority.

Winner's curse   The feeling that you could have done better in a negotiation.

Discussion Questions

1. Describe the characteristics of distributive bargaining.
2. Compare and contrast the use of various power tactics in a negotiation.
3. Describe how you might respond to someone who is attempting to use hardball tactics against you in a negotiation.
4. Explain the influence of opening offers, and target and resistance points on claiming value in a negotiation.

5. Discuss the role of concessions in negotiations.
6. Describe the role of commitment in negotiation and identify ways by which you might obtain the commitment of another party in a negotiation.

Ethical Dilemma: International Gas Services (IGS)

Donna has recently begun handling the affairs for her ninety-year-old aunt who has Alzheimer's disease and is on a fixed income. As Donna was paying the bills for her aunt, she discovered that auntie was getting her natural gas for heating her home through IGS, a third-party provider, and paying 46% more per cubic foot than the regular utility provider was currently charging. Donna was outraged that the company was still charging such exorbitant rates when gas prices had fallen over the last couple of years. She called to cancel the third-party arrangement and ask for a credit for the difference in rates for the current bill. She explained the situation to the customer service representative who said IGS can't give credit, but suggested she speak to a supervisor. When Donna spoke with the supervisor, Mike, he said it was up to the customer to check the rates because IGS does not give credits, and that auntie had a contract so there was nothing he could do. Donna explained that since her aunt has Alzheimer's, she wouldn't have understood what she was agreeing to and certainly wouldn't be able to stay on top of current rates for natural gas. Mike said he was sorry, but there was nothing he could do.

Donna then calmly told him that she was going to write letters to the state attorney general and the public utility commission, as well as letters to the editors of every major newspaper in the state exposing how IGS operates and warning people to check their bills. Mike asked that she hold off on the letter writing until he could check and see if there was anything that he could do. He said he would call her back with an answer within twenty-four hours. Within twenty minutes, he called her back saying IGS would be issuing a refund check for the difference of $263.34 within four to six weeks. Donna was happy with the refund but wondered if she should still write a letter to the editor to warn others that they should check their utility bills.

Questions:

1. What distributive tactics were used by Donna and Mike?
2. Was the use of distributive tactics appropriate in this situation? Explain.
3. What might Donna have done to keep from threatening IGS to publicize the situation?
4. Should Donna write the letter to the editor to warn others or does she have an obligation to remain silent since they gave her a refund?

Endnotes

1. Fells, R. E. "Overcoming the Dilemmas in Walton and McKersie's Mixed Bargaining Strategy." *Relations Industrielles* 53 (2) (1998): 300–325.

2. Kersten, Gregory E. "Modeling Distributive and Integrative Negotiations. Review and Revised Characterization." *Group Decision and Negotiation* 10 (6) (2001): 493.

3. Weingart, L. R., L. Thompson, M. H. Bazerman, and J. S. Carroll. "Tactics in Integrative Negotiations." *Academy of Management Best Papers Proceedings* (1987): 285–289.

4. Fells, R. E. "Overcoming the Dilemmas in Walton and McKersie's Mixed Bargaining Strategy." *Relations Industrielles* 53 (2) (1998): 300–325.

5. Lytle, A. L., J. M. Brett, and D. L. Shapiro. "The Strategic Use of Interests, Rights, and Power to Resolve Disputes." *Negotiation Journal* 15 (1) (1999): 31–52.

6. Walton, R. E., J. E. Cutcher-Gershenfeld, and R. B. McKersie. *Strategic Negotiations*. Boston, Mass.: Harvard University Press, 1994.

7. De Dreu, C. K. W., L. R. Weingart, and S. Kwon. "Influence of Social Motives on Integrative Negotiation: A Meta-Analytic Review and Test of Two Theories." *Journal of Personality and Social Psychology* 78 (5) (2000): 889–905.

8. Lytle, A. L., J. M. Brett, and D. L. Shapiro. "The Strategic Use of Interests, Rights, and Power to Resolve Disputes." *Negotiation Journal* 15 (1) (1999): 31–52.

9. Kersten, G. E. "Modeling Distributive and Integrative Negotiations. Review and Revised Characterization." *Group Decision and Negotiation* 10 (6) (2001): 493.

10. Mumpower, J. L., J. Sheffield, T. A. Darling, and R. G. Miller. "The Accuracy of Post-Negotiation Estimates of the Other Negotiator's Payoff." *Group Decision and Negotiation* 13 (3) (2004): 259.

11. *Ibid.*

12. Kersten, G. E. "Modeling Distributive and Integrative Negotiations. Review and Revised Characterization." *Group Decision and Negotiation* 10 (6) (2001): 493.

13. http://www.ebayinc.com/who

14. Kersten, G. E. "Modeling Distributive and Integrative Negotiations. Review and Revised Characterization." *Group Decision and Negotiation* 10 (6) (2001): 493.

15. Walton, R. E., and R. B. McKersie. *A Behavioral Theory of Labor Negotiation*. New York: McGraw-Hill, 1965, pp. 161–162; and Walton, R. E., and R. B. McKersie. "Behavioral Dilemmas in Mixed-Motive Decision Making." *Behavioral Science* 11 (1966): 370–384.

16. Fells, R. E. "Overcoming the Dilemmas in Walton and McKersie's Mixed Bargaining Strategy." *Relations Industrielles* 53 (2) (1998): 300–325; and Gershenfeld, J. E. "The Impact on Economic Performance of a Transformation in Workplace Relations." *Industrial and Labor Relations Review* 44 (1991): 241–260.

17. Fells, R. E. "Overcoming the Dilemmas in Walton and McKersie's Mixed Bargaining Strategy." *Relations Industrielles* 53 (2) (1998): 300–325.

18. *Ibid.*

19. Kern, Mary C., Jeanne M. Brett, and Laurie R. Weingart. "Getting the Floor: Motive-Consistent Strategy and Individual Outcomes in Multi-Party Negotiations." *Group Decision and Negotiation* 14 (1) (2005): 21–41.

20. Cutcher-Gershenfeld, J. E. "Bargaining over How to Bargain in Labor-Management Negotiations." *Negotiation Journal* 10 (1994): 323–335.

21. Kim, P. H., R. L. Pinkley, and A. R. Fragale. "Power Dynamics in Negotiation." *Academy of Management Review* 30(4) (2005): 799–822.

22. Weingart, L. R., L. Thompson, M. H. Bazerman, and J. S. Carroll. "Tactics in Integrative Negotiations." *Academy of Management Best Papers Proceedings* (1987): 285–289.

23. Gelfand, M. J., V. S. Major, J. L. Raver, L. H. Nishii, and K. O'Brien. "Negotiating Relationally: The Dynamics of the Relational Self in Negotiations." *Academy of Management Review* 31 (2) (2006): 427–451.

24. Amanatullah, E. T. "Negotiating Gender Stereotypes: Other-Advocacy Reduces Social Constraints on Women in Negotiations." *Academy of Management Proceedings* (2008): 1–6.

25. Brass, D. J., and M. E. Burkhardt. "Potential Power and Power Use: An Investigation of Structure and Behavior." *Academy of Management Journal* 36 (3) (1993): 441–470.

26. *Ibid.*

27. *Ibid.*

28. Bacharach, S. B., and E. J. Lawler. *Power and Politics in Organizations*. San Francisco: Jossey-Bass, 1980; and Pfeffer, J., and G. R. Salancik. *The External Control of Organizations: A Resource Dependence Perspective*. New York: Harper & Row, 1978.

29. Lytle, A. L., J. M. Brett, and D. L. Shapiro. "The Strategic Use of Interests, Rights, and Power to Resolve Disputes." *Negotiation Journal* 15 (1) (1999): 31–52.

30. Amanatullah, E. T. Negotiating Gender Stereotypes: Other-Advocacy Reduces Social Constraints on Women in Negotiations. *Academy of Management Proceedings* (2008): 1–6.

31. Fisher, R., W. Ury, and B. Patton. *Getting to yes* (2nd ed.). Boston: Houghton-Mifflin, 1991.

32. Lytle, A. L., J. M. Brett, and D. L. Shapiro. "The Strategic Use of Interests, Rights, and Power to Resolve Disputes." *Negotiation Journal* 15 (1) (1999): 31–52.

33. Kern, M. C., J. M. Brett, and L. R. Weingart. "Getting the Floor: Motive-Consistent Strategy and Individual Outcomes in Multi-Party Negotiations." *Group Decision and Negotiation* 14 (1) (2005): 21–41.

34. *Ibid.*

35. *Ibid.*

36. Bottom, W. P., and P. W. Paese. "Judgment Accuracy and the Asymmetric Cost of Errors in Distributive Bargaining." *Group Decision and Negotiation* 8 (4) (1999): 349–364.

37. *Ibid.*

38. *Ibid.*

39. *Ibid.*

40. Galinsky, A. D., V. L. Seiden, P. H. Kim, and V. H. Medvec. "The Dissatisfaction of Having Your First Offer Accepted: The role of Counterfactual Thinking in Negotiations." *Personality and Social Psychology Bulletin* 28 (2) (2002): 271–283.

41. Lytle, A. L., J. M. Brett, and D. L. Shapiro. "The Strategic Use of Interests, Rights, and Power to Resolve Disputes." *Negotiation Journal* 15 (1) (1999): 31–52.

42. Moran, S., and I. Ritov. "Initial Perceptions in Negotiations: Evaluation and Response to 'Logrolling' Offers." *Journal of Behavioral Decision Making* 15 (2) (2002): 101.

43. Kern, M. C., J. M. Brett, and L. R. Weingart. "Getting the Floor: Motive-Consistent Strategy and Individual Outcomes in Multi Party Negotiations." *Group Decision and Negotiation* 14 (1) (2005): 21–41.

44. *Ibid.*

45. *Ibid.*

46. Cohen, Steven. *Negotiating Skills for Managers.* New York: McGraw-Hill, 2002.

47. Conlon, D. E., and P. M. Fasolo. "Influence of Speed of Third-Party Intervention and Outcome on Negotiator and Constituent Fairness Judgments." *Academy of Management Journal* 33 (4) (1990): 833.

Exercise 3.1   Characteristics of Famous Negotiators

For this exercise you will compare the characteristics and approaches of two famous negotiators. The individuals you choose can be currently in the news or from history. Using the following worksheet, identify each person's background (e.g., educational background, family background, significant life events), his or her approach to negotiations (e.g., focus on outcomes and/or relationships, unique characteristics related to negotiating), and what makes that person successful or unsuccessful. After describing the background and approach of the negotiators, identify as many similarities and differences in the negotiators as you can.

Worksheet: Exercise 3.1 Characteristics of Famous Negotiators

Negotiator #1: _____

Background: _____

_____

_____

_____

_____

Approach to negotiations: _____

_____

_____

_____

_____

Negotiator #2: _____

Background: _____

_____

_____

_____

_____

Approach to negotiations: _____

_____

_____

_____

_____

Similarities: _____

_____

_____

Differences: _____

_____

_____

_____

Exercise 3.2   Using the Internet in Negotiation
By Sharon E. Bell

The Internet is a great place for businesses to purchase major pieces of equipment. If you are located in a small town, the selection that is available over the Internet generally dwarfs local availability, and pricing can be very competitive. However, doing your homework is essential, as you cannot rely on the local reputation of a business, service can be much more difficult, and returns may be expensive. When you buy on the Internet, careful research, not only on the product but also on the seller, is even more important than when you buy locally.

This exercise will have you research the purchase of a security surveillance system for a small business. The central component of most systems is a digital video recorder (DVR). Necessary peripheral equipment includes indoor and outdoor cameras, special lighting, external and internal hard drives, and wiring.

Understanding the technology is the first step in the purchasing decision. Enter "DVR security system education" into an Internet search engine. Read at least three different consumer education sites. What features do you find for these systems? In the table below, list the features of a DVR that you find important to consider in selection of a DVR for a business. Using eBay, an Internet store, and a local store, compare and provide the supplier name, price, and features of a specific four-channel DVR.

Sellers: \ Features:	eBay-1 _____	eBay-2 _____	Internet _____	Local _____
Price				
Manufacturer & model				

It is also important to purchase the peripheral equipment. Purchasing it from the same supplier can ensure compatibility of equipment and save money on shipping. In the table below, supply the price of the peripheral equipment that each supplier has available. Also list any needed equipment that is not listed and the price of each item.

Sellers: / Peripherals:	eBay-1	eBay-2	Internet	Local
Wireless cameras				
Wired cameras				
Hidden cameras				
Outdoor cameras				
Internal hard drives				
External hard drives				
Special lighting				
Wiring				
Other:				

Selection of the supplier is very important. Some suppliers provide more service than others; some are more reliable than others. In the following table, provide available information about each supplier's attributes.

Sellers: / Attribute:	eBay-1	eBay-2	Internet	Local
Customer rating:				
Location				
Services provided				
Years in business				
Years on Internet				
Other:				

Having done your research, it is now time to select and negotiate with a supplier. Which supplier would you approach with an offer? What would you offer to buy? What services would you want as part of the package? What would be your initial offer?

Exercise 3.3   Power in Reel Life: The Movies

In this exercise you will be identifying examples of as many of the various power tactics as you can and providing possible responses to them. Find short movie clips or videos that demonstrate the use of each of the power tactics discussed in the chapter, such as the example of *The Fifth Element* noted in the beginning of the chapter, and complete the following worksheet.

Worksheet: Exercise 3.3 Power in Reel Life: The Movies

Power tactic:	
Movie:	
Description:	
Possible responses:	

Power tactic:	
Movie:	
Description:	
Possible responses:	

Power tactic:	
Movie:	
Description:	
Possible responses:	

Power tactic:	
Movie:	
Description:	
Possible responses:	

Power tactic:	
Movie:	
Description:	
Possible responses:	

Power tactic:	
Movie:	
Description:	
Possible responses:	

Exercise 3.4   Power in Real Life: Personal Experience

For this exercise you need to think of times in your life when others have attempted to use power tactics to get their way with you or someone you know, either successfully or unsuccessfully. The examples can be from work, school, or your personal life. For each example, try to remember as many details as possible—the who, what, where, when, and how of the situation. How have your responses been effective or ineffective? What was the effect on your relationship with the other party? To organize the examples for further analysis, complete the following worksheet.

After you have recorded the details of each example, identify commonalities in the situations. For example, are there particular people who are more likely to use power tactics than others? Which ones are more or less successful? Is there any response that seems more or less effective?

Worksheet: Exercise 3.4 Power in Real Life: Personal Experience

Power tactic:	
Used by:	
Description:	
Outcome:	
Alternative responses:	

Power tactic:	
Used by:	
Description:	
Outcome:	
Alternative responses:	

Power tactic:	
Used by:	
Description:	
Outcome:	
Alternative responses:	

Power tactic:	
Used by:	
Description:	
Outcome:	
Alternative responses:	

Power tactic:	
Used by:	
Description:	
Outcome:	
Alternative responses:	

Exercise 3.5   My Distributive Negotiation Experience

For this exercise you will need to think of a distributive negotiation in which you or someone you know was a participant and write a brief paper on the experience. In writing your paper, be sure to address:

Background

Who were the participants?

What was the subject of the negotiation?

What was the history, if any, between the parties?

The Negotiation

What were the opening positions of each party?

What power and/or hardball tactics were used by each party?

How did the other party respond to the power tactics?

What was the substantive outcome of the negotiation?

What was the relationship outcome of the negotiation?

Analysis

What was the turning point in the negotiation?

Were any power tactics used inappropriately?

Could either party have used power tactics more effectively?

Exercise 3.6   Just Make a Decision!

Instructions

In this exercise you will be assigned the role of Paul, Lisa, or observer. Your instructor will provide you with confidential role sheets based on your assigned role. Read all information provided, complete the worksheet, and prepare for the negotiation based on your knowledge of the situation.

Overview

Three weeks ago Paul, a buyer for General Manufacturing, issued a request for a proposal for five electric motors to three suppliers, one of which was Electronic Distributors. Lisa, the new salesperson for Electronic Distributors, immediately prepared a bid and sent it to Paul. She followed up with Paul last week and he assured her that he would have a decision soon. Lisa is in the area today and decided to stop at Electronic Distributors to follow up again. Paul comes out to greet Lisa and takes her back to his office.

Worksheet: Exercise 3.6: Just Make a Decision!

Buyer, Paul

Interests: _____

_____

Issue	Opening Demand	Target	Resistance

Salesperson, Lisa

Interests: _____

_____

Issue	Opening Demand	Target	Resistance

CHAPTER 4

Integrative Negotiations

Chapter Objectives

After studying this chapter and completing the exercises you should be able to:

- Develop strategies for integrative negotiations.
- Evaluate the importance of separating the people from the problem when negotiating.
- Analyze the interests of all parties in a negotiation.
- Generate options that create value in a variety of negotiation situations.
- Utilize various standards to evaluate options in a negotiation.
- Assess the dilemmas of trust and honesty.

In Chapter 3 we discussed the process of distributive bargaining, the traditional, often hard-line, approach to negotiations. We now turn our focus to integrative negotiations. One might assume that integrative negotiation is the opposite of distributive negotiation, but that is not the case. If distributive negotiation is "hard," where the parties are adversaries who do whatever is necessary to get their way, the opposite would be "soft" negotiation, where the parties are friends who agree to anything to maintain the relationship—whether or not the outcome satisfies the needs of the parties. In both cases, the parties are bargaining based on their positions. Instead, researchers at the Harvard Negotiation Project, most notably Roger Fisher and William Ury, developed an alternative called "principled negotiation" or "negotiation on the merits."[1] Over time this has become synonymous with the term "integrative negotiation." It is another technique to keep ready in your negotiating tool kit, since distributive and integrative approaches are each appropriate in certain circumstances.[2]

Chapter Scenario, Part I

Ken and Jamal were both mid-level managers at a medium-sized company. Both were doing well by objective standards but wanted to do something different with their careers. Ken was highly skilled in sales and marketing, but not as good with the financial aspects of business. Jamal was very good with accounting and finance, but lacking when it came to sales and marketing. After many discussions of their hopes and dreams, the two decided to start their own business where Ken focused on building sales and dealing with customers and Jamal focused on the daily operation of the business. By pooling their resources, both financial and human, they both ended up with a better outcome than either would have had if he had chosen to go it alone.

INTEGRATIVE NEGOTIATION

Integrative negotiation is sometimes referred to as **interest-based bargaining** because the focus is on the interests of each party as opposed to the distribution of a fixed resource.[3] It is a collaborative approach used when both your outcome and the relationship with the other party are important. It typically involves creating synergy—one of the reasons people form partnerships. The assumption is that resources are not finite, in other words, the pie is not fixed. It is a win-win approach, sometimes referred to as a non-zero-sum game, because the parties concentrate on finding ways to make the pie bigger so that everyone can get more. There are four basic components of integrative negotiation as identified by Fisher and Ury: separate the people from the problem, focus on interests not positions, generate a variety of alternatives that provide mutual gain, and evaluate the alternatives based on objective criteria.[4]

Separate the People from the Problem

The first component involves depersonalizing the problem so the focus is on the actual problem and not the individuals involved. In negotiation, you are dealing with other human beings with their unique characteristics, strengths, and weaknesses. Some people are by nature more agreeable than others. There are some people with whom we just click and are able to work things out. Unfortunately, this does not happen with everyone; at some point we will all be in the situation of having to negotiate with people with whom we don't mesh. A successful negotiator is able to recognize these situations and focus on the problem at hand instead of the person or people involved.

Even when the other party is someone with whom we would otherwise get along, in distributive bargaining, people often become emotionally attached to their positions in their effort to win the negotiation. When emotions run high, people may say or do things at which the other party takes great offense. Our feelings may be hurt; we may feel threatened, offended, and angry, which can lead us to become defensive or even hostile. This often sets in motion a downward spiral of contentious behaviors that are reciprocated without much consideration for the impact it will have on the negotiation.[5] Typically this begins with miscommunication, making it critical to be aware not only of what we say and how we say it, but of how the other party is reacting to our words. While initially this may take a very conscious effort, as you gain experience with integrative negotiations, your performance will improve.[6]

Having an ongoing relationship with the other party may also complicate the situation because the parties enter the negotiation with a history. Any past difficulties between the parties can impact the negotiation even if you are not fully conscious of it. In the chapter scenario, Ken and Jamal had a good working relationship developed over fifteen years of working together, which made negotiating the details of forming and running the business easier. Unfortunately, we don't always have a good history with the other party, yet still have to work together. Jack and Carol worked together at a small non-profit. Carol usually went home for lunch but one day had decided to stay in. Coincidentally, that same day Jack brought in lunch for the manager and himself. Carol saw them eating together and was hurt and offended that Jack hadn't invited her to join them. Jack had simply assumed that Carol wouldn't be there, so he didn't bring anything for her. It was an awkward situation for all involved and one that Carol remembered several weeks later when Jack asked for her help with a special project. Instead of agreeing to help her coworker, she found an excuse as to why she couldn't and Jack was left to do it on his own.

Whether or not Carol was being petty about the lack of a lunch invitation is irrelevant because it still impacted the relationship and future interactions with Jack. This situation could have been better handled if they would have dealt directly with the relationship issues. If Carol had let Jack know that she was hurt when she wasn't included, Jack would have had an opportunity to explain to Carol that it was not his intention to offend her but that he just assumed she wouldn't be there. By clearing up the misunderstanding they would have neutralized its impact on their future interactions. We will explore the role of interpersonal problems in more detail in our discussion of conflict resolution in Chapter 5.

Points to Ponder

1. What are the characteristics of people with whom you find it easy to work?
2. What are the characteristics of people with whom you find it difficult to work?
3. What new approaches might you try when dealing with difficult people?

Focus on Interests

The second tenet of integrative negotiation is to focus on the parties' interests, which are their needs, desires, concerns, and fears. This is in contrast to positions, which are the stances a negotiator takes during the course of a negotiation. In integrative negotiation, it is important that the parties' interests be the center of attention to make it possible to find solutions that meet the needs of both parties, while positions focus on the needs of only one party. Fisher and colleagues maintain that every negotiator has two types of interests—substantive and relationship;[7] other experts include dealing with the process and the principles involved as interests.[8]

Substantive interests are the needs that a negotiator has that relate to the material outcomes of the negotiation. In negotiating the purchase of an item, the substantive interests would include the characteristics of the item (e.g., a basic model versus one with additional options/features), the purchase price, and possibly the payment and delivery terms. The substantive interests of Ken and Jamal in the chapter scenario would have included how they would finance and run the business. Would they each be responsible for 50% of the financing or did one have greater financial resources than the other and be willing to contribute more? Would they each work the same number of hours? Would they be on the same schedule or would they work different schedules to allow the business to be open for additional hours? How much would each be paid? What would their job titles be?

Relationship interests deal with the ongoing relationship between the parties. While in some cases you may never have to deal with the other party again, that is typically not the norm. Even if you are unsure, there is benefit to be gained by staying on good terms with the other party. In workplace negotiations, you will almost always need to continue working with the other party. In a neighborhood setting, you need to be able to co-exist peacefully. If you are negotiating with a customer, you don't want him to speak ill of you or your company to other current or potential customers. For Ken and Jamal, it was important to have a good working relationship to ensure the smooth operation of the business, as well as to maintain their fifteen-year friendship which they both valued.

Process interests have to do with a party's interests in the negotiation or dispute resolution process itself. People want to be heard and taken seriously, and want their contributions to be recognized and valued. When these things are lacking, people become frustrated and may lash out. When this happens, it is sometimes helpful for people to vent their frustrations; after having done so, the parties are potentially more amenable to reaching an agreement. For Ken and Jamal, it was important to negotiate a process for resolving issues that would arise during the course of operating the business. For example, what if one or more of their children wanted to work in the business? What if they disagreed on how a particular situation (e.g., customer complaint, new advertising venue) should be handled? How would these and other disputes be resolved?

Interests in the principles involved include the parties' concerns about what is ethical and just. Many people have strongly held beliefs about what is right or proper in certain circumstances and have a very difficult time agreeing to something that goes against those beliefs. In some cases, one or both parties may not want to set precedence for the future. For example, an employer may not want to allow a particular employee to set her own work schedule because he is concerned that other employees may expect the same arrangement. Because Ken and Jamal both believed that everyone should earn his own way, they agreed that the financial returns of each partner should be proportionate to his contribution. They also agreed that any of their children would be employed by the company only if the child could make a real contribution, and compensation would be strictly based on performance.

Whatever the other party's interests may be in the substantive or relationship outcomes, or the process or principles involved, it is important that you understand what she really needs. Research has shown that taking into consideration the other party's perspective is beneficial, improves integrative performance and outcomes, and is a key to successful negotiation.[9] You have a better chance of having the other party agree to what you want if her needs are being met as well. Asking open-ended questions like those shown in Figure 4.1 can help identify those needs.

When identifying interests it is important to look forward, not back, especially when there have been prior problems. Looking back and rehashing old differences is likely to lead to trying to assess or assign blame, taking attention away from the current situation, and hindering the parties from moving forward and reaching an agreement. When there have been past problems, it is often helpful if the parties can explicitly agree to put the past behind them and look to the future. This requires directly addressing past problems; assuming or hinting is not sufficient. If the other party subsequently reverts to talking about the past, you can remind him that you agreed to start fresh and redirect the conversation to what each party needs.

As you are discussing needs, it is advantageous to focus on what you have in common with the other party as opposed to differences. Identifying common ground helps identify things upon which you can agree and sets a more positive tone for the negotiation. Essentially, this turns the discussion from "this is why we won't agree" to "here are the things upon which we can agree." When the parties can see the areas where they can both gain from the negotiation, they usually become more flexible about making concessions.

While being attentive to the other party's non-verbal communication is important throughout a negotiation, it may be even more so when you are trying to identify her interests. The manner in which she communicates—including the body language used—can provide important clues about the importance of her interests. Does the tone of her voice change or does she become more passionate when speaking about certain things? Does she seem to be more reluctant to discuss some things than others? Is the language used with some topics stronger than that used with others? Does her body

FIGURE 4.1 Open-Ended Questions for Identifying Interests

What would you like to accomplish?
Why do you want ...?
Help me understand ....
What features are most important?
Could you tell me more about that?
Are there any other concerns that you would like to discuss?

language provide an indication of the importance of particular interests? Generally speaking, others typically provide us with information about the relative importance of the bargaining mix without specifically stating "this is the most important issue" or "I really don't care about . . ." Good negotiators pay attention to nonverbal cues and use them to help achieve more favorable outcomes.

It is important to note that one's interests can change over time. The person who wanted a sporty car to bolster her image as a single woman may be looking for safety and practicality in a vehicle when she is married with children. Similarly, when a person is just entering the workforce he will likely be more concerned about opportunities for advancement than retirement benefits, while the opposite is true for someone who has been in the workforce for many years. Whatever the other party's interests may be, taking them into consideration can help you identify and combine options that will meet his needs as well as yours. If you first help to create value, there will be more value to be claimed later on.[10]

Generating Options for Mutual Gain/Creating Value

In its most basic form, **generating options** involves looking for possible solutions to the problem at hand. For example, if Joe needs to acquire a previously owned car, he could visit local car dealerships to see what is available. After identifying what is currently in stock, he would pick the one that best meets his needs. Whether or not his needs would be fully met would depend in large part on the timing of his search. If he happened to be looking at a time when there were many cars on the lot, he would be more likely to find one that had more of the features that he wanted than if he happened to look at a time when inventories were low.

In integrative negotiation, the goal is to go beyond the obvious alternatives by working together to develop alternatives that create additional value. This requires creativity and patience on the part of the negotiators. For example, Joe might work with the salesperson to see about locating a car that has more, if not all, of the options he wants. Often dealerships have someone who attends car auctions to buy cars that may have been part of a corporate fleet or leased cars. Joe and the salesperson could work together to see if the dealership could find a more suitable car at one of the auctions. The salesperson might also keep an eye out for a car that is being traded in to the dealership by someone purchasing a new car. Of course this takes time, but assuming Joe doesn't have to have a different car immediately, he would likely end up with one that better meets his needs and the salesperson would have a more satisfied customer.

While creativity is a trait that comes more naturally to some than to others, it is something that people can cultivate and develop over time. Being able to invent options is one of the most useful skills a negotiator can have.[11] As with identifying interests, it is helpful to ask open-ended questions to stimulate discussion and help the parties to begin the process of identifying alternatives. Figure 4.2 contains a number of generic questions that can be used as a starting point in a variety of situations.

A commonly used technique for generating options is brainstorming. Brainstorming involves having the parties identify and record any and all ideas that come to mind. The goal is to identify as many alternatives as possible without concern for their practicality. Unusual ideas are welcomed and the parties are encouraged to build upon others' ideas. There is no criticism or discussion involved until

FIGURE 4.2   Open-Ended Questions for Generating Alternatives

In a perfect world, what would you like to see happen?
Can you think of any other way to meet your needs?
How might we work this out?
If you were to have your needs met, what would you be able to do for me/us?
Can we combine any of these ideas?
Can we look at this from any other perspective?
Are there ways that we can expand our resources?

Chapter Scenario, Part II

While Ken and Jamal both had successful careers, they wanted something different. They wanted to build a business that would reflect their values and be able to operate it as they saw fit. Ultimately, they wanted a legacy they could pass on to their children. Once they identified their common interests, they began searching for alternative ways to meet their objectives. They investigated a variety of options ranging from purchasing an existing business to building one from the ground up. They considered everything from manufacturing products to providing a service. Throughout the process, they kept an open mind to all possibilities. In the end, they decided on a franchise where they would provide computer sales and service to regional customers. The end result was a successful business that has now been in operation for over twenty-five years.

the evaluation stage so as to help the parties feel more comfortable in suggesting ideas that might be less traditional. Brainstorming can be done in person or electronically, which is especially helpful when the problem is complex, as it allows time for the parties to ponder other possibilities.

Whether or not you are formally using brainstorming to generate options, there are other things that you can do to aid in the process. Some of the more commonly cited integrative behaviors include making positive comments, noting similarities and differences in general terms, suggesting compromises and tradeoffs, showing insight, suggesting the use of other processes, and making multi-issue offers.[12] People are more likely to relax and open up when they are in a warm and friendly environment, which positive comments can go a long way to create. For example, you might express optimism about the negotiation process and likelihood of reaching agreement to help set the expectation that a mutually satisfying agreement will be reached. You might also let the other party know that you want to come to an agreement that meets his needs as well as yours. Not surprisingly, research has shown that happy negotiators behave more cooperatively and identify greater mutual gain.[13] Similarly, demonstrating positive affect toward the other party reduces the use of contentious tactics[14] and is a significant predictor of joint gain.[15] It is also beneficial to focus on shared interests as you generate options, as they provide a focal point and impetus for finding a solution.

Indicating that you are interested in developing a relationship for future transactions lets the other party know that there is more to be gained in the long term, shifting the focus from a one-time interaction to a long-term relationship. Consider the case of Juanita, who after buying her first house needed to find a contractor to complete some renovations. While she didn't have the financial resources to immediately complete all of the home improvements that she envisioned, she knew that in time, she would have all of the work done. The first project was to have the roof replaced and she solicited bids from several contractors. When she spoke with each contractor, she let him know that this was only the first of a number of projects, which let the contractors know that doing a good job at a reasonable cost could lead to more business over time. When Juanita received the bids from the contractors, she considered how willing each was to work with her to complete the work to her standards in a timely manner, instead of focusing strictly on the lowest-cost bid. Ultimately she contracted with Mike, who was new to the area, because he listened to what she wanted and explained things without talking down to her. While his was not the lowest bid, it was competitive.

We can see from this example that differences in interests may also lead to a solution if each party wants different, but not mutually exclusive things. Juanita wanted to find a reliable contractor whom she could trust to work on her house. Because this was her first house, she didn't have a lot of experience with household renovations, making her need to be able to trust her contractor extremely important. Since Mike was new to the area, it was important to him to build his customer base for the long term.

In addition, it is beneficial to look for things the other party might value that you could provide without incurring a large cost, and vice versa. In the case of Mike and Juanita, Juanita had lived in the area all of her life and was very active in the community.

Since Mike was new to the area, he didn't know people and needed to get the word out about his quality work. Since Juanita knew many people, she was in a good position to let others know about the new contractor in town. She would also be a good reference for Mike when future customers asked for one. Thus, Juanita could help Mike build his business at no cost to her and Mike could help Juanita gain knowledge about maintaining her house. But there are other examples.

Sometimes a realtor who has a client who has found a house to purchase but has been unable to sell his house will guarantee the sale of the house within a certain period of time or buy the house herself at a lower price. In this example, the realtor assumes the risk of selling the buyer's house, but gains a sure sale. In the same vein, furniture stores may offer free delivery on purchases over a certain dollar amount. Essentially they are trading the use of their delivery trucks and people for higher-value sales. Since they already have the trucks and the employees, the additional cost to them is minimal, but delivery can be of great value to customers who might otherwise have to hire a third party to pick up their furniture.

Similarly, neighbors might join together to have a contractor come to the neighborhood to perform services such as landscaping, trimming trees, and so on. It is not uncommon to have a contractor, who comes to your house to perform work, include a separate or built-in cost for what amounts to a delivery, set-up, or house-call fee. By expending extra energy to arrange for the work to be performed at your home as well as for some neighbors, the total cost would be less than if each neighbor hired the contractor separately, since the contractor would have to come out only once. Moreover, the contractor would benefit from having more work to do. Even if your neighbors aren't interested in joining forces, you can still benefit from this principle by having more work done at once. For example, if you need to hire an electrician to replace a broken light fixture, you might also have him install an outside outlet for a fountain that you have always wanted to put in your garden. Even if you haven't found the fountain of your dreams, having the outlet installed while other work is being done allows it to be done at less cost.

Points to Ponder

1. How easy is it for you to think of creative solutions to problems?
2. What kinds of things have you done in the past to stimulate creative thinking?
3. What new approaches might you try to generate creative alternatives?

OBSTACLES TO CREATING VALUE So why don't we always work together and plan ahead to identify creative alternatives that provide the maximum possible value for all involved? Fisher and colleagues identify four major obstacles: making premature judgments (could be due to time pressure), searching for a single answer, believing the pie is fixed, and assuming the other party should meet his own goals.[16] We often make premature judgments when we feel rushed. Perhaps you need to purchase a vehicle because the one you had has broken down and would cost more to repair than it is worth. Perhaps you accept the first job you are offered because you have graduated and will have to start making payments on your student loans. You may have a fear that the other party will simply reject an unusual idea, so to avoid possible embarrassment, you opt not to share a potential solution with the other party. Similarly, you might be reluctant to prolong a negotiation by pressing for other alternatives if the other party holds more power, as is often the case when negotiating with a superior.

People often assume there is one best answer—essentially a magic bullet. If you find the magic bullet, everything will be perfect. In class we want to know the "right" answer, even when there are multiple acceptable answers. We search for the perfect job in the perfect company and the perfect house in the perfect neighborhood. We become so focused on finding the "right" answer that we fail to consider alternatives that would provide equal or even greater value. People also have a tendency to see things as black or white and assume that giving the other party what she wants will take away from anything we get. This **fixed-pie perception** is the belief that people's interests are fundamentally opposed, such that a gain for one must result in a loss for the other.[17] Finally, people are often self-centered when it comes to getting their needs met. They care only about their own needs and fail to see that if the other party gets what she needs, she will be more willing to meet their needs. Instead of saying "What's in this for me?" skilled negotiators often begin with "What can I do for you?"

To help combat these problems it is helpful to take a step back and ask yourself if you are taking enough time to explore the possibilities. Is there a power imbalance that is affecting your willingness to voice your ideas? Are you afraid of being embarrassed? Do you have an open mind to all possibilities, even those that are unusual? Do you understand the mutual interests? Are you looking for ways to meet the other party's needs? By double checking yourself, you can help ensure that you don't "leave money on the table" and end up with a suboptimum agreement.

Integrative negotiation calls for generating a number of alternatives, which may lead to including more issues in the negotiation than you initially planned. Obviously, this is beneficial if it helps everyone meet more of his needs. Ironically, research has found that individuals who negotiated the most issues felt worse about their outcome, likely because dealing with more issues generates more counterfactual thoughts, which lead to negotiators imagining even better possible outcomes.[18]

Evaluating Alternatives and Claiming Value

The final step in the integrative negotiation process is evaluating the options and claiming value. No matter how much creative problem solving enlarges the pie, it must still be divided; the value that has been created must be claimed.[19] Fisher and colleagues maintain that you should always insist on using objective criteria to evaluate alternatives.[20] This takes evaluating alternatives and claiming value from a test of the wills of the parties to a decision based on objective, accepted standards and helps to keep the negotiation from deteriorating into a win-lose situation. Decisions that are made based on accepted standards are less likely to be criticized later. Using objective criteria also depersonalizes the decision and helps preserve the relationship between the parties.

Of course, there may be multiple criteria that you could use depending on the situation. In some cases, there will be standards you can use that have been created by a third party. For example, if you are negotiating your salary, you might use salary survey data to determine a fair amount. But which salary survey should you use? A national average for a particular position may be high or low depending on where you live in the country, since salaries tend to be higher in large cities than in rural areas. If you are negotiating the price of a pre-owned car, you might use one of the websites that offer information on the value of vehicles; however, there are typically differences in the value each website places on a particular vehicle. In this case, you might agree to use an average from several sources. It is often helpful to engage in a joint search for a fair standard that is acceptable to all involved.

Depending on what you are negotiating, there may be no outside standards. When this is the case, there may be other commonly used approaches to making decisions. A classic example is two children who are sharing a piece of cake. One cuts the piece in two and the other gets to choose which piece will be his providing the motivation for the first child to divide it fairly. Alternatively, you might take turns selecting what you want. This is often done when dividing belongings when settling an estate or when couples divorce. Friends may also use this approach when deciding where to eat or what movie to see. Whatever method is used, evaluating proposals objectively according to their merits helps to avoid **reactive devaluation**,[21] which occurs when negotiators perceive that concessions made by the other party are made to benefit the other party.[22]

Once you have agreed upon which standard will be used, the next step is to make and evaluate proposals. When there are multiple issues, it is best to begin with the easy ones. Easy issues are generally nonemotional issues of mutual concern where the likely remedy is not burdensome. By starting with the less contentious issues upon which you are likely to agree, you get the ball rolling and set the stage for agreement on more difficult issues, gaining momentum with each subsequent agreement. It has also been suggested that combining offers, known as logrolling, may lead to more integrative agreements.[23] By including something the other party wants in your proposal, you make it easier for her to agree.

An effective way to encourage agreement is to highlight the interdependence between the parties. For example, in a labor negotiation, the union would point out that the employer needs skilled workers to run the business, while the employer would note that the employees need the jobs the employer provides. In a commercial purchasing transaction, a supplier would remind the customer of his good record of service and the customer might mention that his sales are increasing, which will lead to more business for the supplier.

Appealing to generally accepted principles helps to get the other party to agree to your proposals. In negotiating wages, a union may point out that the workers need a raise that is at least equal to the increase in the cost of living to avoid losing purchasing power. This puts the employer in the position of either agreeing to raise wages by the rate of inflation or acknowledging that the workers will be losing ground financially. Similarly, a contractor who is negotiating to remodel your house might explain that it is customary for a homeowner to make a down payment of half of the total price. If the homeowner didn't want to put half down, she would need to make a case for deviating from an industry standard.

Good negotiators sometimes use silence to encourage the other party to suggest movement. In the United States in particular, people tend to be uncomfortable with silence and seek to fill it.[24] In the claiming value stage of a negotiation, remaining silent after the other party has made an offer gives her the opportunity to add even more to her offer and provides signals that you are not in a rush to come to agreement. Conversely, if the negotiation seems to be stalling, you can use time constraints as an external source of pressure to reach settlement. In labor contract negotiations, the expiration of an existing contract frequently creates a sense of urgency in obtaining a final settlement.

Whatever the situation, you should not yield to pressure from the other party. Although power is typically viewed as the ability to influence others, research suggests that power can also protect people from influence.[25] Remember that your BATNA (Best Alternative to a Negotiated Agreement) is a source of power,[26] in that it makes you less dependent on the other party to meet your needs. When you have an attractive BATNA you can always simply walk away from the negotiation if the other party is not willing or able to meet your needs. Indeed, research has shown that negotiators who wish to maximize personal as well as joint outcomes should try to combine a power advantage in terms of exit options with a shared prosocial orientation.[27] In other words, you should first cultivate a good BATNA and then work cooperatively with the other party to create value and be firm in your efforts to claim it. While it might seem like people would be better at one than they are at the other, research has shown that people tend to see themselves as having relative strengths in both creating and claiming value—or if they felt that they were weak in one, they also saw themselves as weak in the other.[28] Similarly, another study found that people who believe they can become better negotiators do in fact achieve better results in both creating and claiming value.[29]

Many negotiations result in a written agreement. Whether the final agreement is written or verbal, whatever it entails should be understandable, appealing, and precise. Obviously, the parties need to be able to fully understand the terms of the agreement. Remember the example of Juanita and Mike? Juanita would need to understand exactly what Mike would be doing to her roof. What kind of materials would he use? Would he be removing the old roof or adding another layer on top? What would be included in the guarantee? Any agreement that they reach should be appealing in that both Juanita's and Mike's needs are being met. Finally, the agreement needs to be precise. How and when will payment be made? When will the work begin? How long is it expected to take? The more specific an agreement, the less likely there will be problems with it in the future. The time spent crafting an agreement that is very specific is time well spent. As they say, an ounce of prevention is worth a pound of cure.

While the process of integrative negotiation is relatively straightforward, there are two dilemmas that must always be faced by every negotiator: the dilemma of trust and the dilemma of honesty.[30] This occurs because engaging in a completely cooperative approach to negotiating leaves one vulnerable to last-minute power plays by the other party.[31]

THE DILEMMA OF TRUST

The **dilemma of trust** is essentially how much you believe you can rely on the other party to be truthful with you. In other words, how much of what the other party says should you believe? If the salesperson tells you that the used car you are considering buying has never had any problems and is in great shape, do you believe him? Do you simply trust that it isn't a car that was salvaged from a flooded area after hurricane Katrina? The answer is that how much you should trust any other person is a judgment call that depends on whether or not you have experience with her and have found her to be trustworthy, her reputation, and safeguards that you build into the final agreement. The more powerful party sets the tone of the negotiation as either positive and trusting or competitive and suspicious.[32]

As we know from the study of psychology, the best predictor of future behavior is past behavior. If you have had direct personal experience with the other party, you will have an indication of how he typically behaves. If you have negotiated with him before, was he generally cooperative and forthcoming or did he withhold information that would have led to a more integrative agreement? Even if you have not actually negotiated with him, observing his behavior in other situations can provide valuable information. Is he generally truthful? If he says he is going to do something, does he follow through on his commitment? Interestingly, one study demonstrated that simply liking the other party predicted negotiators' trust for each other and whether they reached an integrative agreement.[33]

In the absence of personal experience with the other party, you must rely on other sources of information. Depending on the situation, you can check references, talk with others who know the person, or check the Better Business Bureau, PayPal, or even eBay ratings. When using this type of information, more is better. If you are checking references, check several to get a more complete picture of what you can expect. Using multiple sources increases the reliability of the information. If you are talking to people who know the other party, choose those who have dealt with her in a variety of situations. Of course, none of this guarantees that the person will be trustworthy with you in this particular negotiation.

Fortunately, there are other things that you can do to ensure that you get what you were promised in a negotiation. You can put your agreement in writing with the signatures of all parties involved to make it a binding contract. Such agreements often spell out penalties for noncompliance. This is common with large or special-order purchases or rental agreements, where the seller requires the buyer to sign a sales/lease agreement and make a deposit, which is forfeited if the buyer doesn't live up to the terms of the agreement. Compliance is ensured in an employment setting when the employer requires applicants to sign a statement on the application form to attest to the truthfulness of the information provided. If it is later discovered that the applicant was not truthful, he can be terminated immediately. Ensuring compliance even happens in marriage with prenuptial and postnuptial agreements, or even with the relatively new covenant marriages, where the bride and groom make a commitment that goes beyond secular marriage. In the end, you have to decide on a case-by-case basis how much to trust the other party.

THE DILEMMA OF HONESTY

The second dilemma is the **dilemma of honesty**. Simply put, this dilemma involves how much about your position and motives you will disclose to the other party. It is essentially the flip side of the dilemma of trust. Research on the effects of being truthful in negotiations has produced mixed results. One study found that honest disclosure induces cooperation and can cause an opposing party to make less demanding offers and settle for less profit than she would in the absence of such disclosure.[34] Essentially, being open and honest with the other party leads her to be more cooperative. Conversely, another study found that negotiators who saw the other party as benevolent and trustworthy were more likely to use deceptive tactics.[35] Such negotiators engage in opportunistic betrayal, that is, they are deceptive because they believe they can get away with it or face minimal consequences if their deception is detected.

The extent to which you will be forthcoming with the other party is influenced by your personality, value system, the situation, and your relationship with the other party. Some people are more private while others are more open. Indeed, there are some who are so open that afterward they find themselves wondering why they just told their life story to a complete stranger. Similarly, people have different value systems when it comes to being truthful. One person selling her used car might adopt the attitude "let the buyer beware," while others simply wouldn't feel right if they didn't disclose every potential mechanical difficulty, no matter how insignificant. The situation may also have an impact; for instance, you might be more open if you are selling your used car to an individual versus trading it in to a car dealership. Likewise, you may disclose more if you are selling your car to a close friend or relative than if you were dealing with a total stranger.

The downside of disclosing too much information is that the other party may use the information to take unfair advantage of you.[36] Consider the story of Helen, a trusting young woman getting ready to purchase a car on her own for the very first time. She walks into Sample's Used Car Sales and is immediately greeted by Hal, the top salesman. Hal asks Helen what she is looking for and Helen replies that she needs a car but her budget is tight and she can't spend any more than $7,000. Hal immediately shows her a car with a price tag of $6,995. When Helen wants to look at other cars, he directs her to cars on the lot with sticker prices ranging from $6,500 to $6,999 even though there are cars available with a sticker price of $7,000 to $7,500 that might reasonably be sold for less than $7,000. Did Helen disclose too much information when she told Hal that the most she could spend was $7,000? Did that weaken her position in the negotiation? Maybe, maybe not; it all depends on how trustworthy Hal is.

In the end, how much you should trust the other party and how much you should disclose to the other party depends a lot on your perceptions of the other party and the situation. To an extent you have to learn to trust your instincts with people. If something doesn't seem right, it probably isn't. Your choices at that point are to not negotiate with the other party, or at a minimum, make sure you have an iron-clad contract. If all this seems like a matter of pure chance, rest assured that with experience you will become much more astute in reading people and making good decisions about trust and disclosure when negotiating.

Points to Ponder

1. To what extent do you consider yourself a trusting person?
2. To what extent do you feel comfortable opening up to others?
3. How has your life experience influenced your propensity to trust and be open with others?

Summary

In this chapter we identified the characteristics and four steps in the integrative negotiation process. First is to separate the people from the problem. By focusing on the problem instead of the people who are involved, a negotiator can move beyond any negative history the parties may have that may impede negotiating an agreement that provides for the maximum mutual gain. The second step is to identify the interests of all parties. Here we stressed the wisdom in seeking to meet the other party's needs so as to increase the likelihood of him helping to meet your needs. Next, we explored options for creating value to increase the size of what will later be divided. The fourth step of claiming value involves dividing the value that has been created in order to obtain the maximum value for all parties. Finally, we addressed the common dilemmas faced by all negotiators. The dilemma of honesty deals with how much information one should share with the other party. The dilemma of trust involves how much of what the other party says that you should believe.

Summary: The Big Picture

Integrative negotiation characteristics	Also interest-based bargaining. Win-win approach. Focus on both outcomes and the relationship. Assumes infinite resources, a non-zero-sum game. Cooperative relationship. Collaborative strategies, maximize total value.
Components of integrative negotiation	Separate the people from the problem. Focus on interests not positions. Generate alternatives that provide mutual gain. Evaluate alternatives based on objective criteria.
Types of interests	Substantive, relationship, process, and principles.
Identifying interests	Look toward the future, focusing on common ground. Look for non-verbal cues. Interests may change over time.
Generating options	Seek those that create mutual value, even if they are unusual. Consider brainstorming if needed.
Obstacles to creating value	Making premature judgments, searching for a single answer, fixed-pie perception, assumption that others should meet their own goals.
Evaluating alternatives and claiming value	Use objective/standard criteria, standard approaches, and generally accepted principles.
Dilemma of trust	How much to trust the other party depends on direct and indirect experience with him or sanctions for non-compliance built into the final agreement.
Dilemma of honesty	How much to share with the other party depends on your personality, value system, the situation, and your relationship with the other party.

Key Terms and Concepts

Dilemma of honesty.   How much about your position and motives you will disclose to the other party.

Dilemma of trust   The extent to which you believe you can rely on the other party to be truthful with you.

Fixed-pie perception   The belief that people's interests are fundamentally opposed, such that a gain for one must result in a loss for the other.

Generating options   Looking for possible solutions to the problem at hand.

Integrative negotiation/interest-based bargaining   An approach to negotiation where the focus is on the interests of each party as opposed to the distribution of a fixed resource.

Interests in the principles   The needs that a negotiator has that have to do with concerns about what is ethical and just.

Process interests   The needs that a negotiator has that have to do with a party's interests in the negotiation or dispute resolution process itself.

Reactive devaluation   When negotiators perceive that that concessions made by the other party are made to benefit the other party.

Relationship interests   The needs that a negotiator has that deal with the ongoing relationship between the parties.

Substantive interests   The needs that a negotiator has that relate to the material outcomes of the negotiation.

Discussion Questions

1. Evaluate the differences between distributive and integrative negotiation.
2. Discuss the importance of separating the people from the problem when negotiating.
3. Describe the four types of interests and provide examples of each.

4. Discuss the approaches to creating value in the integrative negotiation process.
5. Describe the methods of evaluating alternatives.
6. Assess the impact of the dilemmas of honesty and trust in integrative negotiation.

Ethical Dilemma: Having a [Not-So] Private Party

Summerville is a lakeshore community in the Midwest. In its heyday, the town relied heavily on the automotive industry for its tax base and jobs for its residents. As the automotive industry declined, many of the local manufacturing plants closed, leaving high rates of unemployment and a devastated tax base in its wake. Community leaders have tried to capitalize on Summerville's location on the shore of Lake Michigan to rebuild the community around tourism. In the process, they have tried to be business friendly, offering incentives and generally trying to accommodate the needs of businesses. Recently, an increasing number of bars and restaurants have applied for a license that allows them to provide outdoor food and beverage service on decks, patios, and rooftops. City officials have been supportive of the efforts to draw more tourists to the community. Many of these establishments border residential areas and offer live entertainment several nights per week. A longtime city ordinance states that music must not be heard from more than fifty feet away between 11:00 p.m. and 7:00 a.m. Periodically, residents call the police to complain about the noise.

Questions

1. How would you balance the interests of the neighbors' right to live in peace and quiet with the interests of the businesses to attract and entertain customers?
2. To what extent, if any, does the fact that the community is trying to recover economically come into play?
3. Assume that you are a city official and a resident complains to you about the noise in her neighborhood. How might you respond to the resident?

Endnotes

1. Fisher, R., W. Ury, and B. Patton. *Getting to Yes* (2nd ed.). Boston: Houghton-Mifflin, 1991.
2. Walton, R. E., J. E. Cutcher-Gershenfeld, and R. B. McKersie. *Strategic Negotiations*. Boston, Mass.: Harvard University Press, 1994.
3. Fisher, R., W. Ury, and B. Patton. *Getting to Yes* (2nd ed.). Boston: Houghton-Mifflin, 1991.
4. *Ibid*.
5. Lytle, A. L., J. M. Brett, and D. L. Shapiro. "The Strategic Use of Interests, Rights, and Power to Resolve Disputes." *Negotiation Journal* 15(1) (1999): 31–52.
6. Thompson, L. "Negotiation Behavior: Effects of Task, Partner, and Structural Similarity." *Academy of Management Best Papers Proceedings* (1989): 376–380.
7. Fisher, R., W. Ury, and B. Patton. *Getting to Yes* (2nd ed.). Boston: Houghton-Mifflin, 1991.
8. Lax, D., and J. Sebenius. *The Manager as Negotiator: Bargaining for Cooperation and Competitive Gain*. New York: Free Press, 1986.
9. Moran, S., and I. Ritov. "Experience in Integrative Negotiations: What Needs to Be Learned?" *Journal of Experimental Social Psychology* 43(1) (2007): 77–90.
10. Lax, D., and J. Sebenius. *The Manager as Negotiator: Bargaining for Cooperation and Competitive Gain*. New York: Free Press, 1986.
11. Fisher, R., W. Ury, and B. Patton. *Getting to Yes* (2nd ed.). Boston: Houghton-Mifflin, 1991.
12. Kern, Mary C., Jeanne M. Brett, and Laurie R. Weingart. "Getting the Floor: Motive-Consistent Strategy and Individual Outcomes in Multi-Party Negotiations." *Group Decision and Negotiation*, 14(1) (2005): 21–41.
13. Forgas, J. P. "On Being Happy but Mistaken: Mood Effects on the Fundamental Attribution Error." *Journal of Personality and Social Psychology*, 75 (1998): 318–331.
14. Peter J. D. Carnevale, and Alice M. Isen. "The Influence of Positive Affect and Visual Access on the Discovery of Integrative Solutions in Bilateral Negotiations." *Organizational Behavior and Human Decision Processes*, 37(1) (1986): 1–13.
15. Anderson, Cameron, and Leigh L. Thompson. "Affect from the Top Down: How Powerful Individuals' Positive Affect Shapes Negotiations." *Organizational Behavior and Human Decision Processes*, 95(2) (2004): 125–139.
16. Fisher, R., W. Ury, and B. Patton. *Getting to Yes* (2nd ed.). Boston: Houghton-Mifflin, 1991.
17. *Ibid*.
18. Naquin, Charles E. "The Agony of Opportunity in Negotiation: Number of Negotiable Issues, Counterfactual Thinking, and Feelings of Satisfaction." *Organizational Behavior and Human Decision Processes*, 91(1) (2003): 97–107.
19. Lax, D., and J. Sebenius, J. *The Manager as Negotiator: Bargaining for Cooperation and Competitive Gain*. New York: Free Press 1986, p. 33.
20. Fisher, R., W. Ury, and B. Patton. *Getting to Yes* (2nd ed.). Boston: Houghton-Mifflin, 1991.
21. Thompson, L., and G. J. Leonardelli. "The Big Bang: The Evolution of Negotiation Research." *Academy of Management Executive* 18(3) (2004): 113–117.
22. Ross. L., and C. Stillinger. "Barriers to Conflict Resolution." *Negotiation Journal* 7 (4) (1991): 389–404.
23. Moran, S., and I. Ritov. "Initial Perceptions in Negotiations: Evaluation and Response to 'Logrolling' Offers." *Journal of Behavioral Decision Making* 15(2) (2002): 101.
24. Adler, N. J. *International Dimensions of Organizational Behavior* (3rd ed.) Cincinnati, OH: Southwestern College Publishing, 1997, p 214.
25. Galinsky, A. D., J. C. Magee, D. H. Gruenfeld, J. A. Whitson, and K. A. Lijenquist. "Power Reduces the Press of the Situation: Implications for Creativity, Conformity, and Dissonance." *Journal of Personality and Social Psychology* 95(6) (2008): 1450–1466.
26. Thompson, L., and G. J. Leonardelli. "The Big Bang: The Evolution of Negotiation Research." *Academy of Management Executive* 18(3) (2004): 113–117.
27. Giebels, E., C. K. W. De Dreu, E. Van De Vliert. "Interdependence in Negotiation: Effects of Exit Options and Social Motive on Distributive and Integrative Negotiation." *European Journal of Social Psychology* 30(2) (2000): 255–272.
28. Nelson, D., and M. Wheeler. "Rocks and Hard Places: Managing Two Tensions in Negotiation." *Negotiation Journal* 20(1) (2004): 113–128.

29. Kray, L. J., and M. P. Haselhuhn. "Implicit Negotiation Beliefs and Performance: Experimental and Longitudinal Evidence." *Journal of Personality and Social Psychology* 93(1) (2007): 49–64.

30. Kelley, H. H. "A Classroom Study of the Dilemmas in Interpersonal Negotiation." In K. Archibald (ed.), *Strategic Interaction and Conflict: Original Papers and Discussion.* Berkeley, CA: Institute of International Studies, 1966, pp. 49–73.

31. Cutcher-Gershenfeld, J. E. "Bargaining over How to Bargain in Labor-Management Negotiations." *Negotiation Journal* 10 (1994): 323–335.

32. Anderson, C., and L. L. Thompson. "Affect from the Top Down: How Powerful Individuals' Positive Affect Shapes Negotiations." *Organizational Behavior and Human Decision Processes* 95(2) (2004): 125–139.

33. *Ibid.*

34. Paese, P. W., A. M. Schreiber, and A. W. Taylor. "Caught Telling the Truth: Effects of Honesty and Communication Media in Distributive Negotiations." *Group Decision and Negotiation* 12(6) (2003): 537–566.

35. Olekalns, M., and P. L. Smith. "Loose with the Truth: Predicting Deception in Negotiation." *Journal of Business Ethics* 76 (2006): 225–238.

36. Walton, R. E., and R. B. McKersie. *A Behavioral Theory of Labor Negotiation.* New York: McGraw-Hill, 1965.

Exercise 4.1   Negotiations in the News: It's Your Turn

For this exercise you (or your instructor) will identify a current or recent negotiation that has been reported in the media. Using the following worksheet, identify the interests (substantive, relationship, process, and principle) of all parties involved, identify alternatives that meet those needs, identify criteria for evaluating the alternatives, and then evaluate the options against the criteria.

Worksheet: Exercise 4.1 Negotiations in the News: It's Your Turn

Party: _____

    Substantive interests: _____

    Relationship interests: _____

    Process interests: _____

    Principle interests: _____

Party: _____

    Substantive interests: _____

    Relationship interests: _____

    Process interests: _____

    Principle interests: _____

Alternatives: _____

_____

_____

_____

Criteria: _____

_____

_____

Best alternative: _____

_____

_____

Exercise 4.2   Home for the Holidays

Instructions:

This exercise gives you an opportunity to identify and evaluate alternatives for assigning employees to work over the holidays (e.g., Thanksgiving, Christmas, New Years). For each of the industry examples below, identify alternatives and the advantages and disadvantages of each. Identify the best alternative and be prepared to discuss the rationale for your recommendations. Be sure to consider the nature of the work involved and the particular situation.

Industry: Retail

You are responsible for scheduling employees at a major grocery store located in a small college town. There are a few employees who live in the area year round but most are college students who are not from the area. The store is open 365 days per year—the only one in the area that is open every day, and customers have come to rely on it for their last-minute holiday needs. All employees, and you, want time off to be with their families. Your store director has asked you to consider alternatives for meeting the staffing needs for the upcoming holiday season and make a recommendation that is fair to all employees. You need to develop a proposal that works for everyone and prepare to present it to the store director.

Alternatives	Advantages	Disadvantages

Recommendation: _____

_____

_____

_____

Rationale: _____

_____

_____

_____

Industry: Hospitality

You are the assistant general manager for one of three restaurants in a hotel. The hotel is open every day and needs to provide food service for its guests. Historically, Thanksgiving, Christmas Day, and New Year's Day have been slow days; however, New Year's Eve is very busy. Most of the employees are young and often travel to spend time with their families over the holidays. The general manager has asked you to develop a staffing plan for the upcoming holidays that meets the needs of the hotel while being fair to all the employees.

Alternatives	Advantages	Disadvantages

Recommendation: _____

_____

_____

_____

Rationale: _____

_____

_____

_____

Industry: Hospital

You are the charge nurse in a critical care unit of a hospital. One of your responsibilities is to schedule RNs, LPNs, and nurses aides to provide care for patients 24-7. In general everyone tries to avoid scheduling major surgeries that require the patient to spend postoperative time in the critical care unit just before the holidays. Unfortunately emergencies are quite unpredictable and sometimes the patient load becomes unexpectedly heavy, which requires you to schedule some people to work a normal shift and others to be on call in case there is an unplanned need. While most employees live nearby, a number of them have families out of town and like to travel to see them over the holidays. Identify alternatives for meeting the staffing needs and prepare to make a recommendation to the director of nursing.

Alternatives	Advantages	Disadvantages

Recommendation: _____

_____

_____

_____

Rationale: _____

_____

_____

_____

Exercise 4.3   Exploring the Dilemma of Trust

For this exercise you need to think of three people you trust and three people you do not trust. The individuals might be family members, friends, coworkers, or casual acquaintances. On the worksheet provided, rate the level of trust you have for each person on a scale of 1 through 5, where 1 is a complete lack of trust and 5 is a very high level of trust. For each person, think about what makes you trust or distrust him or her. For example, is the person generally outgoing or secretive? To what extent does the person follow through on commitments? Next, think of experiences, good or bad, you have had with each person that have influenced your level of trust. Try to remember as much detail as possible—the who, what, where, why, and when of the situation(s).

After you have recorded the details for each person, identify commonalities in the characteristics and experiences that have influenced your level of trust. For example, are you generally more or less trusting when dealing with family members or friends? Are you more or less trusting in particular situations (e.g., work versus social)?

Worksheet: 4.3 Exploring the Dilemma of Trust

Person #1: _____ Trust rating: _____

Characteristics: _____

_____

_____

_____

Situation(s): _____

_____

_____

_____

Person #2: _____ Trust rating: _____

Characteristics: _____

_____

_____

_____

Situation(s): _____

_____

_____

_____

Person #3: _____ Trust rating: _____

Characteristics: _____

_____

_____

_____

Situation(s): _____

_____

_____

_____

Person #4: _____ Trust rating: _____

Characteristics: _____

_____

_____

_____

Situation(s): _____

_____

_____

_____

Person #5: _____ Trust rating: _____

Characteristics: _____

_____

_____

_____

Situation(s): _____

_____

_____

_____

Person #6: _____ Trust rating: _____

Characteristics: _____

_____

_____

_____

Situation(s): _____

_____

_____

_____

Considering the examples you have identified, complete the following paragraphs.

In general I tend to trust people who are _____

_____

_____

_____

In general I tend to distrust people who are _____

_____

_____

_____

_____

I am usually more trusting in situations that _____

_____

_____

_____

_____

I am usually less trusting in situations that _____

_____

_____

_____

_____

Exercise 4.4   Full Disclosure ... or Not?

In this exercise you need to think about your general level of comfort with discussing sometimes sensitive subjects (e.g., your finances/financial problems, health issues, difficulties at work, difficulties with a significant other/spouse) with various people in your life (e.g., parents, siblings, friends, supervisors, coworkers). For example, would you be comfortable discussing your financial problems with your family? How comfortable would you be discussing your health issues with your supervisor? Provide specific examples.

    After you have recorded your responses on the worksheet provided, write a paragraph summarizing your responses.

Worksheet: Exercise 4.4 Full Disclosure ... or Not?

Subjects I am comfortable discussing with my parents: _____

_____

_____

_____

Subjects I am not comfortable discussing with my parents: _____

_____

_____

_____

Subjects I am comfortable discussing with my sibling(s): _____

_____

_____

_____

Subjects I am not comfortable discussing with my sibling(s): _____

_____

_____

_____

Subjects I am comfortable discussing with my friend(s): _____

_____

_____

_____

Subjects I am not comfortable discussing with my friend(s): _____

_____

_____

_____

Summary: _____

_____

_____

_____

_____

Exercise 4.5   Negotiating a Change in a Work Schedule

Instructions

In this exercise you will be assigned the role of the HR associate, HR manager, or observer. Your instructor will provide you with confidential role sheets based on your assigned role. Read all the information provided and complete the worksheet based on your knowledge of the situation.

Overview

Kersman Medical Appliances (KMA) has been providing prosthetics and other assorted medical products since 1959. Abdi Oldschool has been with KMA for thirty years and has an associate's degree in office administration. He worked his way up the ladder from secretary and is currently the human resource manager.

Ed U. Kaitme is an HR associate at KMA. Ed has a bachelor's degree in HR with a minor in education. While he doesn't officially hold the title of trainer, he does virtually all of the training for KMA and is quite good at it. Lately Ed has been talking about pursuing a graduate degree but the program he is interested in offers classes only during normal business hours.

Worksheet

Employee: Ed U. Kaitme

Interests: _____

Issue	Opening Demand	Target	Resistance

Manager: Abdi Oldschool

Interests: _____

Issue	Opening Demand	Target	Resistance

Exercise 4.6 Doing Business in the Neighborhood: I Need Your Suppport for My Zoning Variance

Instructions

Read the overview provided and complete Part 1 of the worksheet below, identifying the likely interests of the parties involved based on your knowledge of the situation. While the information provided in the overview is quite limited, it represents what the general public might know about such a situation. After you have completed Part 1 of the worksheet, you will be assigned the role of Sub Station owner Pete, a neighbor (Dee, Jane, or Bob), a zoning commission member (Janet, Carter, or Shawn), or an observer. Your instructor will provide you with a confidential role sheet based on your assigned role. Use this additional information to complete Part 2 of the worksheet for your assigned part and prepare what you would like to say at the zoning commission meeting.

Overview

The Sub Station is a sub shop located on a corner lot that borders on a residential neighborhood. Originally it was a family-owned neighborhood grocery store, but when the large chain stores moved in, the neighborhood grocery was no longer able to compete. Pete, the grandson of the original owner, took over the grocery business fifteen years ago and turned the grocery stores into sandwich shops offering both eat in and take out service. The Sub Station is very popular with high school and middle school students. When they have half days at school, large groups of students make their way to the Sub Station for lunch and serious socialization. Pete wants to put in a drive-through window, which requires a special-use permit. Some of the neighbors are quite concerned about students trespassing on their property, vandalism, and increased traffic spilling out onto the road. The city officials want to support business, but also need to honor the wishes of the neighbors.

The setting is the monthly zoning commission meeting, which is open to the public. Janet, the zoning commission chair, is ready to call the meeting to order. The first item on the agenda is the Sub Station's request for a special-use permit. The owner, Pete, will present his request and those in attendance will have an opportunity to voice their support of or opposition to the request. Members of the zoning commission will have an opportunity to share their concerns and ask questions of all parties.

Worksheet: Doing Business in the Neighborhood

Part 1: Likely Interests

Sub Station owner Pete: _____

_____

_____

Neighbors: _____

_____

_____

Zoning commission members: _____

_____

_____

Part 2: Preparation for Meeting

Your role: _____

Your interests: _____

_____

_____

What you plan to say at the meeting: _____

_____

_____

_____

_____

_____

_____

Exercise 4.7 Personal Negotiation Project (PNP)

This assignment involves a real-life negotiation. You will plan and execute an actual negotiation for something of personal value, write a paper on it, and share the results with the class. Potential subjects for negotiation include, but are not limited to resolving a conflict with a roommate, spouse, parent, or friend; negotiating a new job assignment, salary, or working conditions with an employer; or the purchase of an automobile, house, furniture, and so on. Be creative! An outline which follows the format below must be submitted for approval. You are encouraged to discuss potential topics with your professor prior to submitting your outline. The paper should cover the specifics of the actual negotiation and follow the format below. You will also have the opportunity to share your experience with the class.

PNP Proposal Format:

Topic: descriptive title of the project

Parties: with whom you plan to negotiate

Likely interests: the interests of all parties who will be involved in the negotiation

Expected issues: all issues you anticipate negotiating with opening demands, target, and resistance points for each

Planned approach: how you will approach the negotiation

PNP Paper Format:

Overview:

Topic: descriptive title of the project

Parties: name, title, phone number, email address

Date, time, and location of negotiation

Interests: the interests of all parties to the negotiation

Issues negotiated: all issues actually negotiated with opening demands, target, resistance, and settlement points for each party. Cite any sources used for determining opening demands, target, and resistance points.

Execution/results: description of the negotiation.

Post hoc analysis: evaluation of what worked and didn't work in the negotiation, and what you would do the same and what you would do differently in future negotiations integrating appropriate concepts.

Conflict and Dispute Resolution

Chapter Objectives

After studying this chapter and completing the exercises you should be able to:

- Identify the types and causes of conflict.

- Assess whether statements made during a dispute are based on interests, rights, or power strategies.

- Develop effective strategies for resolving disputes.

- Identify the advantages and disadvantages of one-on-one dispute resolution, mediation, arbitration, and litigation when disputes arise.

- Evaluate the effectiveness of a specific apology.

- Recommend an appropriate dispute resolution method based on the characteristics of the dispute.

Copilot Jeffery Skiles was handling the controls when US Airways Flight 1549 took off from New York's LaGuardia Airport and hit a large flock of birds, disabling both of its engines. Captain Chesley "Sully" Sullenberger said simply "My aircraft" to Skiles, who replied "Your aircraft." In a few seconds and a mere four words, the two had determined who was to handle the controls in what easily could have been a catastrophic situation. Sully proceeded to guide the plane safely to a remarkable water landing in the Hudson River, saving the lives of all 155 people on board. This 2009 event, dubbed "the miracle on the Hudson," was in the news for weeks. Sullenberger and Skiles followed procedures and were in complete agreement as to who would decide the best course of action; there was no conflict. Unfortunately, not everyone follows the rules and not all negotiations result in such quick agreement between the parties . . . and happy endings.

Chapter Scenario, Part I

You are in court waiting for the judge to issue her ruling on your case. You are thinking about the time and energy you have put into fighting with your neighbor. You have owned your lakeside home for more than thirty years. Originally you used it as a weekend cottage, but over the years, you made many improvements to the property and had planned on making it your year-round residence when you retire. You now wonder whether this would ever be possible given the current situation with your neighbors, the Smiths, who bought the cottage next door seven years ago. Initially your relationship with them was cordial, but they have a very different lifestyle than yours. This has continued to create problems and the situation has gotten completely out of hand. Three years ago you were so frustrated that you hired an attorney and took legal action. This has cost you many sleepless nights and a tremendous amount of money ... so much that you are certain that your case has made a substantial contribution to the college education of your attorney's children. How did it all get to this point? What could have been done differently to avoid getting into this situation?

Situations like this, while fairly common, don't happen instantaneously. What often starts out as a small irritation between the parties can escalate over time until it deteriorates into an all-out war. In retrospect, we may see things that we could have done differently along the way, but once it has escalated, we often don't see a way to turn the situation around. Fortunately, there are constructive ways to ameliorate most conflicts and prevent them from getting out of control. In this chapter, we explore methods of dispute resolution.

CONFLICT

As we noted in Chapter 1, the dictionary defines "conflict" as a fight, battle, or struggle; a controversy or quarrel; discord of action, feeling, or effect; or incompatibility or interference.[1] As the definition suggests, conflict can range from something minor and easily resolved to something much more intense, even violent. In some cases, the conflict is based on true differences between the parties. In negotiation, this occurs when there is no overlap between the parties' resistance points. Let's say that IKR Manufacturing wants to hire a consultant to help the organization "go green," but is unwilling to pay more than $1,000 per day. SBL & Associates is the premier consultant in the field, but charges a minimum of $1,500 per day. The owner of IKR, Isaac Rosen, met with SBL principal, Steven Lister, to discuss the possibility of contracting with them. Rosen was impressed with SBL's expertise and SBL would have liked to take on the assignment; however, when the discussion turned to the cost, it soon became clear that there were real and significant differences.

In other cases, the conflict may simply be the result of a difference in perceptions. Fisher and his colleagues maintain that "Conflict lies not in objective reality, but in people's heads."[2] In other words, people's perceptions are *their* realities or truths, and they will operate and act within—and according to—that "truth," compelling us to offer the following alternative definition: "a process that begins when one party perceives that another party has negatively affected, or is about to negatively affect, something that the first party cares about."[3] Let's revisit the IKR and SBL example, only this time, let's suppose that Lister states their standard rate is $1,500 per day. Rosen replies that they were hoping to pay no more than $1,000 per day. Initially, the parties might perceive that there is a conflict and simply end the discussion, but if they were willing to dig deeper, they would find that Rosen's resistance point is actually $1,300 and Lister's is $1,200, giving them a positive bargaining range of $100. And that is without even exploring other more creative and integrative solutions. An even better result would be that they continue to discuss the possibilities and discover that Lister believes that his company could make a significant impact at IKR and would like to use their success at IKR in future advertising in exchange for accepting a lower fee. Rosen is amenable to that idea and they agree to work together for the good of both organizations.

Unfortunately, resolving conflicts like these may be more complicated than our example suggests.

The conflict we experience can be a result of differences related to substantive or interpersonal issues. **Substantive conflict** may arise over desired outcomes or processes. In our first example, the conflict between IKR and SBL centered on the cost per day of consulting time—a substantive issue. From an organizational standpoint, small amounts of this type of conflict can be functional as they can lead to increased creativity and help avoid complacency. If we never challenge or question what is (e.g., if it isn't broken, don't fix it), we continue doing what we've always done and remain where we've always been. In our example, the difference over the daily charge led to the consideration of the more creative solution involving future advertising. Even though this type of conflict can be valuable in organizations, it must still be managed so that it doesn't spiral out of control.

In some instances, substantive conflict is inherent in the roles of the individuals involved. For example, people who work in quality assurance seek to ensure that an organization's products are of the highest quality possible, while those responsible for purchasing the raw materials and component parts seek to minimize costs. These differences are often reinforced in the performance appraisal and compensation systems. While conflicts may arise, it is important to note that these differences can be beneficial as embedded checks and balances in the organization; those in quality assurance ensure that the products meet quality standards, while those in purchasing ensure that the company is not incurring excessive costs.

In contrast to substantive conflict that can be functional, **relationship conflict**, which is based on interpersonal differences, is almost always dysfunctional.[4] We all find ourselves at odds with others from time to time. We interact with a diverse set of people on a daily basis, from employees who work in other departments to fellow volunteers in community projects to a variety of service providers to the family that lives next door. The relationships we have with these people run the gamut from those for whom we have a great deal of respect and admiration to those we barely tolerate. Sometimes, we are able to avoid the latter, while in many other cases, for a variety of reasons, we have to be able to coexist with intolerable others—sometimes for a short while and other times indefinitely.

Conflict in relationships can be the result of inaccurate perceptions, emotions, and poor communication,[5] which may all interact in a negative way. If you perceive that the person with whom you are negotiating is trying to take advantage of you, you are more likely to dig in your heels and engage in distributive bargaining. The more emotional you become, the more likely you are to lose your composure and lash out at the other party. When there are breakdowns in communication, the parties are more likely to tune each other out. Even when one has been trained in integrative negotiations, defending oneself through reciprocation is a dominant, perhaps even instinctual response.[6]

At the heart of many relationship conflicts is a lack of trust. It has been suggested that mistrust is characterized by a reciprocal relationship that escalates with each interaction between the parties.[7] In other words, if I don't trust you, my behaviors will cause you not to trust me either. When trust has been broken, disputes become more difficult to resolve as the parties become more defensive. They may fear that the steps they take to repair the relationship (e.g., an apology) may be used against them later. Even when the stakes are high, the parties may respond in kind and become drawn into a downward spiral of contentious behaviors without much forethought about the impact it is likely to have on the negotiation.[8]

Relationships may be strained simply because the parties are incompatible. Have you ever met someone who immediately irritates you? If you meet someone whom a trusted friend or colleague "warns you about," do you automatically expect them to be irritating, untrustworthy, or difficult? A relationship may also be strained due to a previous negative history between the parties (the idiom "tigers never change their stripes" applies here). Let's revisit Rosen and Lister one more time. This time let's imagine that Rosen and Lister have known each other since their college days when they were in the same fraternity. Initially they were friends and had a number of classes together. They studied together and socialized together. That all ended in their senior year when they had a falling out. Both had applied for a highly sought-after internship, which was awarded to Rosen. Based on comments from a couple of fraternity brothers, Lister came to believe that he lost the internship because Rosen had spoken ill of him during his interview. Even though Lister had become very successful as a consultant, he still resented losing the internship and didn't really trust Rosen. When Rosen indicated that the company couldn't afford to spend $1,500 per day on a consultant, Lister didn't believe him and thought he was merely using it as a ploy to get a lower rate.

> **Points to Ponder**
>
> 1. Think of people you dislike. What about them do you find most offensive?
> 2. What types of behaviors cause you to mistrust another person?
> 3. What might another person do to regain your trust?

CONFLICT RESOLUTION STRATEGIES AND TACTICS

Whether a conflict is real or perceived, and rooted in substantive or relationship issues, it is usually best for everyone if it can be resolved. In Chapter 2 we introduced you to the Thomas-Kilmann model that depicts an individual's inherent approach to conflict along the dimensions of cooperativeness and assertiveness.[9] Those whose predominant approach to conflict is low on both dimensions have a natural inclination to avoid conflict. People who are high on cooperativeness and low on assertiveness are more apt to accommodate the other party. Conversely, those who are low on cooperativeness and high on assertiveness, have a propensity to approach a conflict as a competition. Those who are moderately cooperative and assertive will typically try to find a compromise, while those who are high on both dimensions are more likely to take a collaborative approach.

While we all have our natural tendencies toward dealing with conflict, we may deviate from those tendencies depending on the parties involved, their underlying interests, and the specifics of the situation.[10] For example, even if you are naturally competitive, you may be more inclined to accommodate your coworkers when you begin a new job. On the other hand, if you are normally a very cooperative person you may adopt a more competitive approach if the conflict involves something about which you are very passionate. Thus, we need to understand and be able to effectively apply a variety of approaches to resolving conflict.

In every negotiation, the parties have interests in both the substantive outcomes of the negotiation and the relationship with the other party, either of which can result in conflict. If the conflict is substantive you will be best served by adopting an integrative approach and engaging in joint problem solving. In doing so you are more likely to create additional value so that both parties can obtain more value from the negotiation. Unfortunately, resolving a substantive conflict by using an integrative approach is not always that straightforward. In the dispute resolution context, which is often ugly and difficult, the use of integrative strategies may be neither easy nor effective.[11] Often the people involved are a source of the problem. Fisher and colleagues maintain that if the conflict is interpersonal, you need to work on the relationship and do what you can to separate the people from the problem.[12]

Simone and Victor had known each other for many years. They had worked together in the past and never really got along. Both were involved in the local chamber of commerce and had recently been appointed to a committee to investigate alternatives for promoting the community to new businesses. At the first committee meeting, Victor made several remarks at which Simone took great offense. After the meeting, Simone approached Victor, but instead of berating him for his comments, she acknowledged their past differences and indicated that she would like to get beyond them and work together to do the best job possible for the chamber. Victor agreed that the committee work was important and indicated that he would do his best to work with Simone. By focusing on their common interest of helping the chamber, Simone and Victor were able to put aside their interpersonal differences so they could focus on accomplishing their shared goals. Unfortunately, the parties may not always have such an obvious shared interest.

When there are both substantive and interpersonal differences, it is important to deal with the relationship issues directly and not try to solve them with concessions on substantive issues.[13] Making needless concessions only serves to reduce the value that you might otherwise gain from negotiating. Instead, focus on the source of the problem. If the problem is a result of incorrect perceptions on the part of the other party, work to correct the misperception. If the other party has become very emotional about the situation, it is generally helpful to let her vent her frustrations and wait to deal with the conflict when both parties are composed. If there are misunderstandings due to poor communication, you should work to clarify the issues.

Ultimately, if attempts to separate the people from the problem are unsuccessful, it may be best to change the players. Consider the case of Pat, who had just moved into a new house with her ten-year-old German Shorthaired Pointer, Baron. At their previous house, Baron had a fenced-in yard in which to run. Pat was anxious to erect a fence at the new house and went to the city building department to see what the regulations were for fencing a yard. When Pat arrived, Carl, one of the building inspectors, came out to answer her questions, but instead of discussing the building code for fences, he proceeded to advise Pat that she should take her dog to obedience classes so she wouldn't need a fence. Pat was not interested in taking her dog to obedience school and was clearly annoyed that Carl would make such a suggestion. As their voices became louder, Justin, another building inspector emerged with a printed copy of the city ordinance for residential fences. Pat was relieved to be dealing with someone who would provide the information she needed without providing unsolicited advice on how she should handle her dog.

Another way of viewing dispute resolution is with the interests, rights, and power framework developed by Ury, Brett, and Goldberg.[14] This framework holds that the parties in a dispute use tactics that focus on their underlying interests, rights, or power:

- A **power-based approach** involves using one's authority or other strengths to coerce the other party to make concessions. One example of this is a customer who threatens to take his business elsewhere if a supplier doesn't lower her price. Another example is a labor dispute where the union threatens to go on strike or the employer threatens to close the business if their respective demands aren't met. Power approaches may be more contentious if there is direct interaction between the parties and may create new disputes or result in one or both parties attempting to get revenge.[15] As you would expect, this approach leads to distributive agreements or worse, failed negotiations.
- A **rights-based approach** seeks to apply a standard of fairness, contract, or law to resolve the dispute. This is the approach used in lawsuits and the legal system in general. Examples include a supplier who threatens to take a customer to court if she doesn't pay her delinquent bill or a landlord who threatens a tenant with eviction if he does not abide by the terms and conditions of the lease. While this approach also typically leads to distributive agreements, it may be somewhat less damaging to the relationship if the dispute is taken out of the parties' control and decided by a court or a third party.[16]
- An **interest-based approach** focuses on the parties' common concerns, priorities, and preferences and is more likely to achieve an integrative agreement that is beneficial to all parties. This is the only approach that addresses why the dispute happened in the first place and is more likely to result in a better relationship between the parties than either power or rights strategies. For example, a local school district that needs to reduce expenses due to a serious budget shortfall might try to work with the union representing the district's bus drivers to see if there is a way that they could reduce transportation costs without having to resort to outsourcing the district's bus services. By working together, they may be able to find an alternative that would reduce the costs to the district while saving the jobs of the bus drivers.

While power, rights, and interests are three distinct approaches, they are not mutually exclusive.

A study by Lytle, Brett, and Shapiro found that the parties moved frequently between interests, rights, and power tactics in the same negotiation and also combined approaches.[17] Good negotiators are conscious of what they are saying and anticipate the responses their words are likely to evoke from the other party. We know that people are typically inclined to reciprocate the other party's behaviors, but reciprocity needs to be managed strategically to avoid conflict spirals.[18] So how should you respond when the other party is using a power or rights approach against you? Ideally, you should not reciprocate with tactics based on rights and power. You should also not simply concede. You need to be able to neutralize their tactics and refocus the negotiation on interests. One way to do this is to ask an interest-based question. For example, if the other party is demanding a particular concession, you might ask why that particular issue is so important or if there are other ways to meet her needs. Another tactic is to simply label the other party's behavior. If the other party is threatening to walk out of the negotiation, you might say something like "I feel that by threatening to leave, you are trying to intimidate me into agreeing with your proposal when we haven't explored any other options." Notice that the speaker takes ownership in this statement ("I feel") and refrains from blaming, causing defensiveness, or escalating the conflict.

In some cases you might combine a rights or power statement with one that offers an interest-based alternative to help shift the focus away from rights or power. For example a statement like, "I doubt that either one of us wants to end up in court over this, so why don't we try to come up with a solution that meets both our needs," provides the other party with the opportunity to shift to a more integrative approach and save face. By doing so, you decrease the likelihood that the other party feels backed into a corner and reacts with additional negative tactics.

Is it ever appropriate to use rights or power tactics? In some cases, yes, if the other party refuses to come to the table, or if repeated attempts at an integrative approach clearly aren't working to the point that negotiations have broken down and you are at an impasse.[19] In these extreme cases it may be a last ditch effort. One way to do this is to state a specific, detailed demand with a deadline, followed by a specific, detailed credible threat that harms other party's underlying interests, and ends with a specific detailed, positive consequence that will follow if the demand is met by the deadline.[20] For example, "We must receive your payment in full by the end of the month or we will turn your account over to a collections agency, which will negatively affect your credit rating. You can avoid this action by paying the balance on your account by the end of the month." We must caution, however, that this approach should only be used as a last resort. If you offer a threat you must be prepared to follow through on it or lose all credibility. Further, once you implement a threat it no longer gives you power over the other party because they have already suffered the threatened consequence. Thus, it is crucial that you leave them a legitimate way to avoid the threatened consequences. If the threat is carried out, the other party may feel as if he has nothing left to lose and retaliate in ways that may be very harmful to you.

ALTERNATIVES FOR RESOLVING DISPUTES: AN OVERVIEW

Conflict can arise in any relationship. When this happens, there are several methods of resolving the dispute, as shown in Figure 5.1. The methods vary in terms of the degree of formality and the time and cost involved. At one extreme is acquiescence, an informal strategy where you simply give in to the other party. Since it is an individual approach, it is relatively fast and there are no costs or fees involved. At the other end of the continuum is litigation, either in civil or small-claims court. If the dispute ends up in

FIGURE 5.1 **Dispute Resolution Approaches**

Informal				Formal
Acquiescence	One-on-One	Mediation	Arbitration	Litigation

civil court, the costs can be in the tens of thousands of dollars and sometimes take years to resolve. Between these endpoints are one-on-one dispute resolution, mediation, and arbitration, each increasing in terms of formality. Acquiescence and one-on-one dispute resolution are individual approaches that you can pursue on your own, while mediation, arbitration, and litigation require the involvement of a third party. Which approach you should use depends on the situation, but generally speaking, the less formal the approach the faster and less expensive it is. We discuss each of the alternatives in detail in the following pages.

Acquiescence and the Power of an Apology

Acquiescence is to simply give in to the other party and comply with his demands. The Thomas-Kilmann model[21] suggests that this strategy would be appropriate if you don't care about either the issue or the relationship and wish to avoid the conflict, or if you care more about the other party than the issue and would rather accommodate the other party. In some cases you may not like it, but may decide to live with it because it may not be worth expending effort to change the outcome. Ury, Brett, and Goldberg use the term "lump it"[22] from the phrase "like it or lump it" for this. While it leads to quick resolution of the issue at hand, we must caution that unilateral concessions may encourage the other party to continue the use of power or rights tactics and not stop a conflict spiral.[23] In other words, if you just capitulate, the other party may decide to try for even more—now and in the future. As the old adage warns, give them an inch and they'll take a mile.

In some cases it's not enough to merely agree to the other party's demands. If you have caused harm to the other person, you may need to apologize. It is one thing to say "I'm sorry" or "excuse me" if you accidentally bump into a stranger. Most people do this automatically without even thinking about it. It is a different issue, however, when you did something that you know you shouldn't have done, and it wasn't an accident. You may be embarrassed by what you did or you may fear that admitting your mistake could result in negative repercussions. In the legal system, defendants in criminal cases are even given the option of pleading nolo contendere or no contest instead of pleading guilty. The courts treat such a plea the same as they would a guilty plea when administering punishment, but technically speaking, the defendant is not admitting guilt so it can't be used against him later in a civil case.

That said, a sincere apology can go a long way toward deescalating conflict and repairing a relationship. It's been said that "an apology may be one of the least costly and most rewarding investments you can make."[24] Consider the example where someone is chastising you over and over because they were hurt by something you did. If you defend your behavior without acknowledging the harm that it caused, the other party is likely to keep reminding you of how deeply they were hurt. If on the other hand, you acknowledge that your actions harmed the other person and offer a sincere apology, there is not much the other person can say. You are in effect agreeing with them. If they continue to chastise you after you have apologized, they become the unreasonable party.

In the last few years, we've had the opportunity to witness a number of public apologies from executives (e.g., Toyota President Akio Toyoda and JetBlue Airways CEO David Neeleman), politicians (e.g., Bill Clinton and John Edwards), and sports and entertainment figures (e.g., Tiger Woods, Mark McGwire, and Don Imus). So what is the difference between a good and a not-so-good apology? Most would agree that a poor apology is one that seems insincere (e.g., "my bad"), doesn't accept responsibility (e.g., "I'm sorry that you were offended"), or tries to convince the victim the action wasn't hurtful (e.g., "I do that all the time with my friends and they don't have a problem with it"). Not surprisingly, research has shown that a partial apology is worse than saying nothing at all.[25] Beverly Engle identifies the Three R's—Regret, Responsibility, and Remedy—as components of an effective apology.[26] The person seeking forgiveness needs to express regret for causing the hurt or damage, accept responsibility for his actions, and express a willingness to take action to remedy the situation.

One public apology that has been cited as a perfect example was issued in February 2007 by David Neeleman, CEO of JetBlue Airways, after a major snow storm hit New York's JFK airport (See Figure 5.2.). JetBlue customers were stuck on an airplane for over eight hours and flights were delayed/canceled for five days, which led to public outcry and a tremendous amount of negative publicity.

FIGURE 5.2 • Analysis of the JetBlue Apology

Salutation	Dear JetBlue Customers,
This short statement at the top of the page expresses humility and remorse. It also sets the tone in this sample apology letter.	We are sorry and embarrassed. But most of all, we are deeply sorry.
This paragraph gives a specific and detailed account of the incident and takes full responsibility for the situation. It is worth noting that although the catalyst was a winter storm, NO blame is placed on it—full responsibility is taken by the company.	Last week was the worst operational week in JetBlue's seven year history. Following the severe winter ice storm in the Northeast, we subjected our customers to unacceptable delays, flight cancellations, lost baggage, and other major inconveniences. The storm disrupted the movement of aircraft, and, more importantly, disrupted the movement of JetBlue's pilot and inflight crewmembers who were depending on those planes to get them to the airports where they were scheduled to serve you. With the busy President's Day weekend upon us, rebooking opportunities were scarce and hold times at 1-800-JETBLUE were unacceptably long or not even available, further hindering our recovery efforts.
Here, we see that they recognize their role in the situation and acknowledge the hurt and damage done.	Words cannot express how truly sorry we are for the anxiety, frustration, and inconvenience that we caused. This is especially saddening because JetBlue was founded on the promise of bringing humanity back to air travel and making the experience of flying happier and easier for everyone who chooses to fly with us. We know we failed to deliver on this promise last week.
This paragraph details their commitment to change and shows customers the preventive measures being taken to ensure that this type of situation will not happen again.	We are committed to you, our valued customers, and are taking immediate corrective steps to regain your confidence in us. We have begun putting a comprehensive plan in place to provide better and more timely information to you, more tools and resources for our crewmembers, and improved procedures for handling operational difficulties in the future. We are confident, as a result of these actions, that JetBlue will emerge as a more reliable and even more customer responsive airline than ever before.
The company now offers the recipients of the letter a form of restitution and compensation. This cleverly crafted commitment to change (through a Customer Bill of Rights) will shed a positive light on the company from both existing and future customers and the public at large. JetBlue also understands the Art of Apologizing by providing a link on their website to a video message from the CEO and author of the letter. This unique approach is what makes this a perfect sample apology letter.	Most importantly, we have published the JetBlue Airways Customer Bill of Rights—our official commitment to you of how we will handle operational interruptions going forward—including details of compensation. I* have a video message to share with you about this industry leading action. *Note how this is the first and only time in the letter where they use the word 'I' as opposed to 'we'. This underscores the personal connection that the founder and CEO of the company is trying to establish with his customers.
This statement expresses regret and lets customers know that the company is hoping to continue the relationship.	You* deserved better—a lot better—from us last week. Nothing is more important than regaining your trust and all of us here hope you will give us the opportunity to welcome you onboard again soon and provide you the positive JetBlue Experience you have come to expect from us. *Note how the last paragraph is "You" focused. They "humbly" give the customer back all the power.
Closing	Sincerely,
	David Neeleman Founder and CEO JetBlue Airways

Source: Perfect Apology, http://www.perfectapology.com/sample-apology-letter.html Used with permission.

One-On-One Dispute Resolution

Often conflict begins as a simple misunderstanding resulting from ineffective or inaccurate communication. **Informal dispute resolution** is generally most effective in the early stages of conflict before the parties have become entrenched in their positions. It begins with a unilateral action by one of the parties (e.g., one person makes the first move and approaches the other party about discussing the situation) at which point the process begins.

The first step is to identify and define the problem. Although people often assume they know what the problem is—the other party's unreasonable behavior—the behavior is only a symptom of the underlying issues. Especially when the conflict has become intense, it may be tempting to open with a power strategy. While there is a slim possibility that the other party will capitulate, he is much more likely to reciprocate with a power tactic of his own.[27] Similarly, people often believe that they should prevail in a conflict because they are acting within their legal or civil rights, which may entice them to open by asserting those perceived rights. Although this can be a strong offensive opening, it will likely be reciprocated and is not likely to move the conversation toward a collaborative end.[28] Instead, consider using an interest-based approach, where you focus on the other party's interests, ask questions, and provide some information while identifying the relevant facts. Doing so is a low-risk strategy that works very well, especially if you believe the other party will be cooperative and there are common interests.

Discussing the facts helps to outline what is and is not in dispute, and identifies any areas on which the parties already agree.[29] You must use care, however, because what one party considers a "fact" may only be her perception. Take for instance a dispute between neighbors over a property line. One party may "know for a fact" where the line is; however, without a proper survey to prove it, his assertion may or may not be correct. After defining the problem, you should work with the other party to identify and evaluate possible solutions. When one or both parties seem intent on a single solution, it is often helpful to engage in brainstorming to identify as many alternatives as possible, regardless of what each party thinks is actually viable.

Once the alternatives are identified, they must be evaluated to determine the extent to which they satisfy the interests of everyone involved. The parties should jointly select the solution that best meets their collective needs. If this is difficult to do, the parties can select their top two or three interests separately and then see if there is overlap on the two priority lists. Once a solution is selected, the parties should identify very specifically how the solution will be implemented. Continuing with the example of the

Chapter Scenario, Part II

As you are sitting in court you think back to when you decided to take legal action three years ago. You really didn't want to do it, but you were at the end of your rope. After a relatively quiet winter, the Smiths opened their pool for yet another summer of parties with loud music and screaming children. You had hoped they would have gotten past the novelty of having a new pool and that as their children got older they would outgrow the screaming stage and you would no longer have to listen to the constant shrieks and screams. Over time though you came to realize that it wasn't just the children; the parents were very loud too. It seemed like they couldn't speak in a normal voice, they were constantly screaming. At the time you had thought about trying to talk with them one-on-one, but were fairly confident that it would get you nowhere. Out of desperation, you had even screamed in their direction to quiet down on a couple of occasions, but your words fell on deaf ears.

You imagine that you had talked with them and explained that you enjoyed your quiet time as much as they enjoyed their parties. In your fantasy, they understood where you were coming from and offered a sincere apology. They promised that they would respect your need for peace and quiet and behave accordingly in the future. As you are imagining a tremendous sense of relief at having the problem resolved, you are jarred back into reality by the sound of the judge's gavel calling for order in the court. As the sound of the gavel echoes for the last time, the judge calls your case, but instead of instructing your attorney to begin his opening statement, the judge explains that she thinks your case would be appropriate for mediation.

neighbors with the dispute over the property line, let's say they decide they need to erect a fence. Issues of who will be responsible for performing various tasks, how and when they will be done, and who will pay the costs are all important issues to discuss. The more detailed their plan, the less likely there will be future disputes involving this situation. Ideally, the parties will evaluate the results to determine whether their solution resolved all of the issues, and if not, discuss the necessary next steps. Unfortunately, this step is often bypassed as the parties move on with their lives, while the likelihood of future conflict over the issue slowly increases over time.

Points to Ponder

1. How might you have approached the Smiths in this situation before resorting to legal action?
2. What could the Smiths have said to help resolve the situation to your satisfaction so that you wouldn't have felt the need to hire an attorney?

Third-Party Involvement

If the parties are unable to resolve a dispute informally on their own, they always have the option of bringing in another person or persons to help them resolve the dispute. When a dispute becomes protracted and the parties are hostile, bringing in a third party may be the only way to resolve it. We must note however that while third-party intervention is generally very effective, it is best not to bring in a third party prematurely. When a third party becomes involved too quickly, disputants are likely to perceive a lower level of control over the decision.[30] They may feel like they did not have sufficient opportunity to work things out on their own or even that they were somehow forced into turning their dispute over to a third party. In contrast, interventions that occur later in the process result in parties reporting higher levels of satisfaction and perceiving the intervention as more appropriate.[31] Third-party interventions include informal and formal mediation, arbitration, and litigation.

In its simplest form a third-party intervention involves asking someone you trust to intervene. Depending on the situation, the third party might be a supervisor, colleague, friend, or relative. The techniques used by such a person are essentially the same as those we discussed for the one-on-one approach. However, the advantage of third-party intervention is that the person asked to intervene is presumed to be more objective because she is not directly involved in the dispute. People sometimes refer to this type of third-party intervention as "mediation." While it is mediation in the sense that the third party intercedes in an attempt to reconcile the parties' dispute, it is important to note that this is a very informal process, such as when a manager resolves a dispute between subordinates by listening to both parties and encouraging them to work out their own solution.

There are a number of books and seminars available on this type of mediation, with some proclaiming there are no special skills or training required to be a mediator. A program offered by the Mediation Training Institute maintains that resolution will happen naturally if you can just get the parties to commit to spending a predetermined amount of time working out their differences and not putting each other down.[32] We think this oversimplifies the mediation process and trivializes the training and continuing education of mediators. You should give serious consideration before attempting to mediate a dispute informally. If you're not careful, you might end up with both parties upset with you!

That said, you may be asked at some point to help resolve a dispute between others. You should attempt to take on this role only when you are ready, willing, and able to do it. You must be comfortable with the process and have both the time and the patience required. Managers are often accustomed to making quick decisions about how things should be done, but having a supervisor make a unilateral decision with which the subordinates must live is not what the parties are typically seeking when they ask you to mediate. Mediation, even when it is informal, is about voluntary agreements crafted by the parties with the assistance of the mediator, which takes a great deal more time than a unilateral decision. You must be willing to spend the time listening to each side and be patient as they work to resolve the problem—even when you have other things to do. You must want to help the parties reach their own agreement and be willing to give up control over the outcome. You must also be able to remain neutral even though you know the parties and may have an opinion on the situation. If the final agreement is to truly be voluntary, the parties must not feel pressured or coerced. If not, there will be little motivation on the part of the disputants to abide by the agreement. When the mediator is a superior, there are naturally power differences, and one or more of the parties may feel compelled to agree to conditions she otherwise wouldn't.

If you don't have the time or patience or you feel it would be difficult to be impartial, you should seek outside assistance. If there are legal issues involved, such as disputes covered by a union contract or various discrimination laws (e.g., obligations under the Americans with Disabilities Act), you should seek the assistance of a mediator who has been trained in the formal process.

Mediation

Formal **mediation** is a common type of **Alternative Dispute Resolution (ADR)**. In a formal mediation, a neutral third party, the mediator, helps those involved in the dispute work through the issues and come to a mutually agreeable solution. Mediators are trained in the general mediation process and may have additional training in special topic areas. Depending on the type of mediation involved, mediators may also be required to engage in continuing education to maintain their certification. Mediation is voluntary in that the parties are not required to agree to anything; however, some judges require the parties to attempt mediation before they will hear a case. During mediation, the mediator controls the process, even if the parties have attorneys and they are present for the mediation. The parties, however, maintain control of the outcome in that they decide the terms and conditions of the agreement. In essence, mediation is a way of helping the parties fashion their own agreement.

Typically, mediations are confidential and mediators cannot be subpoenaed to testify in court. However, if something comes out in the mediation that causes the mediator to suspect abuse or neglect of another person, the mediator is legally bound to report it to the proper authorities in the same way that school teachers or social workers are required to make a report. Mediators don't force the parties to resolve the dispute and the parties determine the content of any agreement reached. Mediation is integrative in nature. Because the parties work together to resolve their dispute, there is a greater opportunity for creativity and a better chance of finding an optimal solution. Thus, it is no surprise that some have concluded that "mediation produces better organizational outcomes than either no intervention or an adjudicatory one like arbitration."[33] Another advantage of mediation is that it allows the parties to face each other and share their views on the situation, allowing for clearing up of any miscommunication that has contributed to the dispute.

There are two basic approaches in mediation: repairing the relationship and focusing on the benefits of negotiating a resolution.[34] Some mediators maintain that if the relationship is not repaired, there won't be an agreement. Others acknowledge that not all relationships can be repaired; instead, focusing on helping the parties understand it is in their best interest to negotiate an agreement. Still others assert that the mediator must do both to achieve a successful agreement.[35]

Mediation follows a set process that begins with an explanation of the ground rules and putting the parties at ease. Each party then has an opportunity to present his or her side of the situation, without interruption, to voice concerns, and explain his or her position. Each party needs to be heard and may be allowed an opportunity to vent. Providing the opportunity for the parties to speak freely without being cut off by a judge is one advantage of mediation over litigation, as judges typically have neither the time nor the patience to allow the parties to verbalize all of their feelings about the case. People who feel like they are being heard often retreat from hard-line positions and become much more cooperative; moreover, allowing the parties to vent their emotions helps to deescalate tensions and gradually build trust.[36] Thus, most mediators allow the parties to wrangle with each other for a while knowing that adequate uninterrupted time makes disputants more amenable to third-party suggestions.[37] At the same time, saving face can be an interest of one or both parties in mediation and may emerge as an issue during mediation. If it is not addressed and resolved, it can stop progress on resolving other issues.[38]

After the opening statements, interests and issues are identified with a focus on common interests. The mediator helps the parties work together to identify alternatives and creativity is encouraged. As the process continues, the parties come to point-by-point agreement on how the dispute should be resolved. This generally begins with smaller items on which the parties easily agree and progresses to larger, more difficult issues. When there is agreement on all issues, the agreement is put in writing and the parties sign it. Once signed, the agreement is enforceable in court. The mediation should end on a positive note and follow-up should be scheduled to ensure the agreement is working.

If you are looking for a mediator, there are three sources: the Federal Mediation and Conciliation Service (FMCS), private practice mediators, and community dispute resolution programs. Both federal and private practice mediators provide their services for a fee typically based on the amount of time involved in the case. Community mediation programs offer a wide variety of mediation services, often at a low or even no cost.

COMMUNITY MEDIATION **Community mediation** is a method for resolving a variety of disputes that arise within a community. Several large cities began experimenting with these programs in the early 1970s. They were very successful, and today, most states have some type of a community dispute resolution program, typically administered by the state's Supreme Court Administrative Office. It is most often defined as a form of ADR; however, in New Jersey the term **Complementary Dispute Resolution (CDR)** is often used instead because it puts mediation and arbitration in parity with litigation.[39] Regardless of the nomenclature used the basic premise is the same.

In general, the programs train and approve people to serve as mediators in a variety of disputes that include breach of contract, neighborhood disputes, divorce or postdivorce issues, guardianship, and special education. In the aftermath of hurricanes Katrina and Rita in 2005, Louisiana and Mississippi both adopted state-mandated mediation programs to more quickly resolve disputed insurance claims by people affected by the hurricanes. In addition, many states have restorative justice programs that bring victims and offenders together in an attempt to repair the harm caused by criminal behavior. In some cases, these are diversion programs to help keep first-time and juvenile offenders out of the court system; in other cases, mediation is done after the case has been to court to determine restitution and help the parties heal.

Most state court-approved mediation programs require forty hours of training and completion of a supervised internship. Internship requirements vary, but typically new mediators must observe actual mediations conducted by, co-mediate with, and be observed by, trained mediators before being permitted to mediate on their own. Some states also require mediators to engage in continuing education. These advanced training sessions typically cover topics ranging from neutrality and standards of conduct for mediators to agreement writing. Certain types of mediation programs require additional training and continuing education for a person to qualify as a mediator.

The volunteer mediators, under the supervision of a public or nonprofit agency, help clients, regardless of their ability to pay, identify issues, improve communications, explore possible solutions, and ideally, reach a mutually agreeable resolution to the dispute. The majority of cases heard by volunteer mediators are those involving neighbors or family members or others who have a fairly close relationship. They range from noise complaints, landlord-tenant and consumer-merchant disputes, to assaults, threats, and harassment problems.[40] Many of these cases are referred by the court systems in an attempt to resolve the dispute before it goes to trial; doing so generally saves time and money for all involved. While steps in the mediation process can vary a bit from state to state, in general, they follow the same basic process used in Michigan shown in Figure 5.3.

FIGURE 5.3 BADGER: The Michigan Model for Mediation[45]

In Michigan, the acronym for the mediation process is "BADGER," which stands for Begin, Accumulate information, Develop the agenda, Generate options/movement, Escape to caucus, and Resolve the dispute.

Begin. The mediation begins with the mediator greeting the participants and escorting them to the mediation room where she introduces herself as a neutral third party who has been trained in the mediation process. The mediator then explains the mediation process and the ground rules, and asks everyone in the room to sign a confidentiality agreement.

Accumulate Information. The mediation begins with each party having an opportunity to present his or her side of the situation without interruption. During this time the other party has an opportunity to take notes to help them remember questions when it is their turn to speak. After all parties have had an opportunity to make their opening statements, there is an opportunity for the mediator and parties to ask for clarification where needed. Throughout, the mediator listens attentively to the parties, takes notes, and takes note of the parties' nonverbal communication.

Develop the Agenda. In this stage the mediator paraphrases the parties' statements and helps them to identify and prioritize issues. The mediator then summarizes the areas of agreement and disagreement.

Generate Options/Movement. The mediator solicits the parties' suggestions for resolution of the dispute. Often the mediator will pose the question to each party "In a perfect world what would you like to see happen as a result of this mediation?" Phrasing the question in this way helps to avoid responses like "I would like ... but I know the other party won't agree." In some cases the mediator may suggest other alternatives. Once the alternatives have been identified, the mediator restates them and identifies common interests. If the parties are reluctant to move from their original positions, the mediator may direct the conversation to the consequences of not reaching an agreement (e.g., protracted court battle, etc.).

Escape to Caucus. In some cases, the mediator may determine that it would be helpful to meet with each party privately in what is known as a caucus. A caucus provides an opportunity for the mediator to conduct a reality check with each party, explore hidden agenda items, review the court agenda, or even have the participants engage in role reversal. Anything discussed in caucus is confidential unless the party gives the mediator permission to share particular item(s) with the other party. It is also important for the mediator to be aware of the time spent in caucus with each party to avoid the impression that the mediator favors one party.

Resolve the Dispute. The final step in the mediation process is to put the agreement in writing, which is then signed by all parties. The agreement must be very specific, stating exactly what each party agrees to do and what happens if one does not live up to the terms of the agreement. If the agreement involves payment of money, it should state when and how (check, money order, etc., via mail or in person) the payment(s) will be made, as well as the consequences for late or nonpayment. All parties are provided with a copy of the agreement, and if the mediation was court ordered, a copy of the signed agreement is also sent to the court. Many mediations involve a single mediator; however, in some cases, there are two co-mediators. If this is the case, the co-mediators "debrief" after the parties leave, which provides them the opportunity to discuss the mediation process and identify things that were done particularly well, things that might have been done differently, and any turning points in the mediation. Debriefing with a co-mediator is a continuous quality improvement practice that helps mediators hone their mediation skills.

In addition to general community mediation, there are other specialized types of mediation. One example is known as **Restorative Justice (RJ)**. RJ brings victims and offenders together to discuss a crime and can be used to determine restitution. From the victims' perspective, it provides an opportunity to ask questions and tell the offender the harm they have caused. For offenders, it can help them see the harm they have done to another human being, offer an apology, and begin to reconnect with the community. Other examples of specialized mediation include the REDRESS® program of The United States Postal Service (USPS) described in Figure 5.4 and Civil Rights mediation.

CIVIL RIGHTS MEDIATION[41] Since 1999, the U.S. Equal Employment Opportunity Commission (EEOC) has offered mediation as an alternative to litigation in resolving discrimination complaints nationwide in cases where the EEOC has determined there is probable cause and the employee has followed all reporting requirements. Mediation is completely voluntary and both parties must agree before it can be used. If the parties opt for mediation, the EEOC complaint is put on hold for a reasonable time so mediation can

FIGURE 5.4 Mediation in Practice: U.S. Postal Service REDRESS® Program[46]

The mediation we have discussed thus far is technically known as facilitative mediation, the oldest and most commonly used form of mediation. The USPS uses a different type of mediation in its award winning REDRESS®—which stands for Resolve Employment Disputes, Reach Equitable Solutions Swiftly—program for resolving EEOC complaints filed by postal service employees. Instead of facilitative mediation, the postal program requires the use of a type of mediation known as "transformative mediation."[i] Transformative mediation views conflict as a crisis in a relationship and focuses on the relationship between the parties as opposed to a focus on the specific conflict. The belief is that if the relationship is healed, the conflict will be resolved in the process. Given the focus on the relationship, transformative mediation works particularly well when the dispute is rooted in relationship conflict as is often the case in employment disputes.

[i]Bush, B., and J. Folger. *The Promise of Mediation*. Jossey-Bass: San Francisco, 1994.

take place. If the mediation is successful, the charge is either settled or withdrawn. If it is not successful, the complaint is then processed through normal channels. As with all mediation, the process is confidential and information from the mediation has no effect on the investigation or future court cases. These types of mediation agreements are no-fault settlements. When a written agreement is reached in mediation, there is no admission of fault or violation of the law. Like the postal program, the EEOC mediation program is proving to be very successful.

Chapter Scenario, Part III

You are leaving the mediation of your case against the Smiths and you are both happy and relieved. At first you were nervous, but the mediator explained the process and put you at ease. You had the opportunity to explain to the Smiths that you had a great deal of stress in your life as a result of working in a high-stress job and taking care of your elderly parents. You explained your need to decompress and that your house was a sanctuary where you could do just that. You told them you would like to get along and be respectful of one another. The Smiths explained that they encouraged their children to invite friends over to their house so they would always know what their children were doing and who they were with. They acknowledged that while they were trying to be good parents, they lost sight of the impact it had on their neighbors. They expressed their regret for the inconvenience they caused and seemed genuinely sincere. Upon discussing the situation, you all came to an agreement that they would end their parties by 10 p.m. and keep the noise at an acceptable level. You also agreed to phone them if the noise was bothering you at any point. You came away from the mediation seeing the Smiths in a different light and optimistic that things would be different in your neighborhood from now on.

Arbitration

Arbitration is another form of ADR. Unlike mediators, arbitrators act as judges to hear and decide the case. The process is simple—the disputing parties present their case and the arbitrator makes a decision. Thus, arbitration is distributive in nature with the arbitrator controlling the final outcome. The parties control the process, in that they choose to agree to arbitration, but give up control over the outcome to the arbitrator.

A specific form of arbitration, known as **rights arbitration**, has been used extensively in unionized organizations where virtually all labor contracts contain a provision for the handling of **grievances**—a complaint about the interpretation or application of the union contract. Grievances are initially addressed through a series of meetings with union and company representatives, but if a grievance can't be resolved, the dispute is submitted to arbitration. The arbitrator hears each side and renders a decision that, except in rare cases, can't be appealed to the court system.

In the United States, the use of arbitration to settle disputes in unionized organizations dates back to the Taft-Hartley Act of 1947,[42] which identified arbitration as a primary method of resolving employment disputes that arose during the life of a collective bargaining (i.e., union) agreement. Labor arbitration was further legitimized by the U. S. Supreme Court in 1960 in a series of three cases, commonly known as the Steelworkers Trilogy.[43] In those cases, the court ruled that if there is an agreement to arbitrate in the labor contract, the parties must use it to resolve disputes and arbitrators' decisions are typically not subject to judicial review. Most labor arbitrators are affiliated with either the FMCS or the American Arbitration Association (AAA).

While arbitration of employment disputes was historically limited to union settings, many nonunion employers today are using arbitration to settle disputes and avoid costly lawsuits. These employers typically require employees to sign an agreement to arbitrate as a condition of employment. Often these disputes involve claims of discrimination on the basis of age, sex, or race, or sexual harassment.

In addition to employment arbitration, there are an increasing number of companies that require consumers to arbitrate disputes over product or service quality. Typically this is stated and the procedure is spelled out in the contract or product packaging and the courts have generally upheld the requirement to arbitrate. There is, however, considerable variation in how this is handled. You may have input in the selection of an arbitrator, the arbitrator may come from an independent agency, there may or may not be a cost involved, the decision may or may not be binding, and the proceedings may or may not be confidential. The procedures can vary considerably from state to state and industry to industry. For example, arbitration in the construction industry is well established and has its own traditions, while arbitration of disputes in health care is relatively new, but becoming widespread. If you have been admitted to a hospital within the last few years (and paid attention to all the forms they ask you to sign), you have probably signed an arbitration agreement.

Litigation: Civil/Small-Claims Court

The most formal type of dispute resolution is litigation, which can take place either in civil or small-claims court. It is important to note that with either civil or small-claims cases, the judge may still refer them to mediation for possible resolution before proceeding to trial. Civil court has very formal rules and procedures and almost always involves hiring an attorney to represent you. Thus, it can be very costly and time consuming. For example, the National Floor Safety Institute estimates that the average cost to defend against a slip-and-fall lawsuit is $50,000, and if the plaintiff prevails in a trial, the average judgment awarded is $100,000.[44] Obviously, it makes good financial sense to resolve disputes before they become lawsuits. Because you would have legal representation throughout the process, we will not go into detail about the specifics here. Instead, we focus on the type of litigation where you would be completely in charge of your own case—small-claims court.

Small-claims court involves private disputes under a certain dollar limit, typically $3,000–$10,000 depending on the state. The time you have to file a case and whether or not the decision can be appealed also varies by state. Typical cases might involve the failure to pay a bill, repay a loan, complete work as agreed (e.g., car or house repairs), or property damage. Small-claims cases for landlord/tenant disputes might involve the return of a security deposit or the eviction of a tenant.

Procedures in small-claims cases are simplified to expedite the process. Parties don't have legal representation—they represent themselves. Practically speaking, given the dollar amounts involved, it's not worth the cost of hiring an attorney. The key to winning is presenting clear, convincing evidence. The judge doesn't know the parties, so without evidence, the case consists of one party's word against the other. The courts do not function as collection agencies, so even if you "win" your case, you may have difficulty collecting any money you are owed. The other party may simply not have the money to pay you or may attempt to delay or avoid payment altogether. The court's judgment will stay on the other party's record until it is paid in full. This affects his or her credit rating, but some people are less concerned about their credit score than they are about avoiding payment.

Finally, we must note that television shows such as *Judge Judy* and *Judge Joe Brown* are not really courts, even though they give appearance of such. In reality, they are forms of arbitration where the parties agree to let the arbitrator (i.e., judge) decide their case. One might guess however that the television ratings might not be as high if the shows were titled "*Arbitrator Judy*" or "*Arbitrator Joe Brown*."

Points to Ponder

1. To what extent are you comfortable with resolving disputes informally with another person?
2. How would the type of dispute influence your preferred method of dispute resolution?

Summary

Conflict can be rooted in real or perceptual differences and can be functional or dysfunctional. Functional conflict is associated with differences over substantive issues related to desired outcomes or processes, or is inherent in the roles of the individuals. Relationship conflict is dysfunctional and may be a result of inaccurate perceptions, emotions, miscommunication, or mistrust. When disputes arise, we may attempt to resolve them informally with the other party or formally through mediation, arbitration, or litigation. If we need to offer an apology, we should express regret, accept responsibility, and offer a remedy.

Summary: The Big Picture

Conflict	Can be related to substantive or relationship issues; inherent in roles; related to the task, process, or relationship.
	Often involves lack of trust and miscommunication.
	May spiral out of control.
Conflict resolution strategies & tactics	Basic tendencies: avoid, accommodate, compete, compromise, and collaborate.
	Strategies may focus on interests, rights, power, or a combination.
Acquiescence	Give in to the other party.
Apologies	Should express regret, accept responsibility, and express a willingness to remedy the situation.
One-on-one	Begins with unilateral action by one party, best to focus on interests.
Mediation	Trained mediator helps parties work through a formal process to reach their voluntary agreement.
	Various types of mediation include community mediation, postal, and civil rights.
Arbitration	Arbitrator hears a case and renders a decision. Includes labor and commercial arbitration.
Litigation	Civil and small-claims cases.

Key Terms and Concepts

Acquiescence An approach to dispute resolution that involves giving in to the other party and complying with his or her demands.

Alternative Dispute Resolution (ADR) A means of resolving disputes outside the state or federal judicial system.

Arbitration A type of Alternative Dispute Resolution (ADR) where a neutral third party, the arbitrator, acts as a judge to hear and decide the case.

Civil Rights mediation Mediation offered through the U.S. Equal Employment Opportunity Commission (EEOC) to resolve employment disputes.

Community mediation A method for resolving a variety of disputes that arise within a community.

Complementary Dispute Resolution (CDR) Another name for Alternative Dispute Resolution.

Grievance A complaint about the interpretation or application of a union contract.

Interest-based approach An approach to dispute resolution that focuses on the parties' common concerns, priorities, and preferences and seeks to achieve an integrative agreement that is beneficial to all parties.

Mediation A type of Alternative Dispute Resolution (ADR) where a neutral third party, the mediator, helps those involved in the dispute work through the issues and come to a mutually agreeable solution.

One-on-One/Informal dispute resolution   An approach to dispute resolution that involves approaching the other party to discuss the situation.

Power-based approach   An approach to dispute resolution that involves using one's authority or other strengths to coerce the other party to make concessions.

Relationship conflict   Conflict that is based on interpersonal differences.

Restorative Justice (RJ)   A method of dealing with criminals that encourages them to accept responsibility for their crimes and make restitution to their victims/their community.

Rights arbitration   A specific form of arbitration used to resolve a dispute about the interpretation or application of a union contract.

Rights-based approach   An approach to dispute resolution that seeks to apply a standard of fairness, contract, or law to resolve the dispute.

Small-claims court   A method of resolving private disputes under a certain dollar limit where the parties represent themselves and a judge decides the outcome of the case.

Substantive conflict   Conflict that arises over desired outcomes or processes.

Discussion Questions

1. Discuss the types and causes of conflict and provide examples of each.
2. Evaluate the use of interests, rights, or power strategies in dispute resolution and supply examples of each.
3. Describe a conflict with which you are familiar that was the result of real differences between the parties. What strategies were employed? What has been done to more effectively resolve the differences?
4. Describe a situation you have encountered where perceptual differences have led to conflict. What strategies were employed? What might have been done to more effectively resolve the conflict?
5. Evaluate the advantages and disadvantages of resolving disputes informally or through mediation or litigation.
6. Describe an apology that you have given or received and assess the extent to which it expressed regret, accepted responsibility, and offered a remedy.

Ethical Dilemma: When Opportunity Knocks . . .

Aaron is an accountant who specializes in corporate taxes at Anderson & Westerhouse, a large accounting firm. Aaron has worked at A&W for five years and is hoping to be named a partner next year. His coworker Anne, who was hired at the same time as Aaron, also seeks to be named a partner, but it is not likely that A&W would name two new partners in the same year. Aaron and Anne have been in competition since they were both hired and have never cared for each other. About a year ago, Anne found an error in a report that Aaron had prepared and seized the opportunity to publicly embarrass Aaron in front of the senior partners. Aaron nearly lost his job as a result of

Anne's actions and has never forgotten it. Now the tables have turned and Aaron has found an error in Anne's work. He sees this as a perfect opportunity to get revenge on Anne and help ensure that he is named the next partner.

Questions

1. What might Aaron do? What would you do?
2. What are the possible ramifications of Aaron exposing Anne's error?
3. How might Aaron resolve the conflict with Anne?

Endnotes

1. *The American Heritage® Dictionary of the English Language, Fourth Edition.* Retrieved June 8, 2009, from Dictionary. com website: http://dictionary.reference.com/browse/conflict
2. Fisher, R., W. Ury, and B. Patton. *Getting to Yes* (2nd ed.). Boston: Houghton-Mifflin, 1991, p 2.
3. Thomas, K. W. (1992). Conflict and negotiation processes in organizations. In M.D. Dunnette & L. M. Hough (Eds.), *Handbook of Industrial and Organizational Psychology*, (2nd ed., Vol. 3, pp. 651–717.) Palo Alto, CA: Consulting Psychologists Press.
4. Yang, J., and K. W. Mossholder. "Decoupling Task and Relationship Conflict: The Role of Intragroup Emotional Processing." *Journal of Organizational Behavior* 25(5) (2004): 589–605.
5. Fisher, R., W. Ury, and B. Patton. *Getting to Yes* (2nd ed.). Boston: Houghton-Mifflin, 1991.
6. Brett, J. M., D. L., Shapiro, and A. L., Lytle. "Breaking the Bonds of Reciprocity in Negotiations." *Academy of Management Journal* 41(4) (1998): 410–424.
7. Butler, J. K., Jr. "Behaviors, Trust, and Goal Achievement in a Win-Win Negotiating Role-Play." *Group & Organization Management* 20(4) (1995): 486–501.
8. Lytle, A. L., J. M. Brett, and D. L. Shapiro. "The Strategic Use of Interests, Rights, and Power to Resolve Disputes." *Negotiation Journal* 15(1) (1999): 31–52.

9. Thomas, K. W., and R. H. Kilmann. *Thomas-Kilmann conflict mode survey.* Tuxedo, NY: Xicom, 1974.

10. *Ibid.*

11. Lytle, A. L., J. M. Brett, and D. L. Shapiro. "The Strategic Use of Interests, Rights, and Power to Resolve Disputes." *Negotiation Journal* 15(1) (1999): 31–52.

12. Fisher, R., W. Ury, and B. Patton. *Getting to Yes* (2nd ed.). Boston: Houghton-Mifflin, 1991.

13. *Ibid.*

14. Ury, Q.L., J. M. Brett, and S. B. Goldberg. *Getting Disputes Resolved* (2nd ed.). San Francisco: Jossey-Bass, 1993.

15. Lytle, A. L., J. M. Brett, and D. L. Shapiro. "The Strategic Use of Interests, Rights, and Power to Resolve Disputes." *Negotiation Journal* 15(1) (1999): 31–52

16. *Ibid.*

17. *Ibid.*

18. Brett, J. M., D. L. Shapiro, and A. L. Lytle. "Breaking the Bonds of Reciprocity in Negotiations." *Academy of Management Journal* 41(4) (1998): 410–424

19. Lytle, A. L., J. M. Brett, and D. L. Shapiro. "The Strategic Use of Interests, Rights, and Power to Resolve Disputes." *Negotiation Journal* 15(1) (1999): 31–52

20. *Ibid.*

21. Thomas, K. W., and R. H. Kilmann. *Thomas-Kilmann conflict mode survey.* Tuxedo, NY: Xicom, 1974.

22. Ury, Q. L., J. M. Brett, and S. B. Goldberg. *Getting Disputes Resolved* (2nd ed.). San Francisco: Jossey-Bass, 1993.

23. Lytle, A. L., J. M. Brett, and D. L. Shapiro. "The Strategic Use of Interests, Rights, and Power to Resolve Disputes." *Negotiation Journal* 15(1) (1999): 31–52

24. Fisher, R., W. Ury, and B. Patton. *Getting to yes* (2nd ed.). Boston: Houghton-Mifflin, 1991, p. 32.

25. Robbenolt, J. (2003). *Apologies and Legal Settlement: An Empirical Examination.* 102 Michigan Law Review, 460–497.

26. Engle, B. (2007). *The Power of an Apology.* John Wiley & Sons, pp 66–68.

27. Lytle, A. L., J. M. Brett, and D. L. Shapiro. "The Strategic Use of Interests, Rights, and Power to Resolve Disputes." *Negotiation Journal* 15(1) (1999): 31–52.

28. *Ibid.*

29. *Ibid.*

30. Conlon, D. E., and P. M. Fasolo. "Influence of Speed of Third-Party Intervention and Outcome on Negotiator and Constituent Fairness Judgments." *Academy of Management Journal* 33(4) (1990): 833.

31. *Ibid.*

32. For more information on their programs see http://www.mediationworks.com/

33. Bingham, L. D. "Employment dispute resolution: The case for mediation." *Conflict Resolution Quarterly* 22(1,2) (2004/2005): 145.

34. Poitras, J., R. E. Bowen, and S. Byrne. "Bringing Horses to Water? Overcoming Bad Relationships in the Pre-Negotiating Stage of Consensus Building." *Negotiation Journal* 19(3) (2003): 251–263.

35. *Ibid.*

36. *Ibid.*

37. Conlon, D. E., and P. M. Fasolo. "Influence of Speed of Third-Party Intervention and Outcome on Negotiator and Constituent Fairness Judgments." *Academy of Management Journal* 33(4) (1990): 833.

38. van Ginkel, E. "The Mediator as Face-Giver." *Negotiation Journal* 20(4) (2004): 475–487.

39. Greenbaum, R. S. "Dispute Resolution and Counsel: Changing Perceptions, Changing Responsibilities." *Dispute Resolution Journal* 55(2) (2000): 40–44.

40. http://www.nafcm.org/pg5.cfm, accessed 2 February 2010.

41. For more information on this program see http://www.eeoc.gov/mediate/index.html

42. Cihon, P. J., and J. O. Castagnera. *Employment and Labor Law* (3rd ed.). Cincinnati, OH: West Educational Publishing Company, 1999.

43. *Ibid.*

44. http://www.costhelper.com/cost/finance/slip-fall-lawsuit.html

45. Michigan Supreme Court (2003). *Mediator Training Manual Community Dispute Resolution Program* (2nd ed.).

46. For more information on this program see http://www.usps.com/redress/

Exercise 5.1   Your Customers Are Using My Parking Lot!

You own a hardware store that is located in a strip mall. Three months ago an Italian restaurant opened next door. Parking is limited and each respective business in the strip mall has a designated number of parking spaces in front. This is generally not a problem because your store has more customers during the day, while the restaurant is busier at night. The problem is on Friday and Saturday nights when your store is open later and the restaurant is busier. You are concerned because business at the restaurant has been increasing as the restaurant becomes more well known.

Instructions: Identify the advantages and disadvantages of each dispute resolution method as it applies to this situation and recommend a strategy, including advance preparation, for resolving the dispute.

Approach	Advantages	Disadvantages
One-on-one		
Mediation		
Litigation		

Recommendation: _____

_____

_____

_____

_____

_____

_____

Exercise 5.2 Ready to Rumble

You are the Manager of Heronswood, a luxury condominium complex. Most of the 450 units are detached and residents can personalize their space within certain limitations. Some condo owners have installed fountains or statuary. For the last three years, Heronswood has contracted with Lou's Landscape Service (LLS) to maintain the landscape in the complex. The contract specifies that LLS is responsible for mowing lawns, fertilizing, trimming trees and shrubs, and snow removal. In the course of completing this work, occasionally there is some incidental damage to sprinklers or landscaping. The contract specifies that LLS is responsible for repairing any damage caused.

Initially LLS was quite responsive when damage was incurred, but lately a number of condo owners have been complaining about damage that has not been repaired. You have contacted LLS, speaking directly with Lou on several occasions in an attempt to have the damage repaired. You even stopped by their office to speak with Lou in person, which did not help at all. Lou, who is a large and intimidating man said, "I'll get to the repairs when I feel like it!" and "If you know what is good for you, you better not make me mad!" You were very intimidated and left LLS immediately wondering if Lou might physically harm you. You went back to Heronswood wondering what you should do to resolve this without placing yourself at risk of being hurt.

Instructions: Identify the advantages and disadvantages of each dispute resolution method as it applies to this situation and recommend a strategy, including advance preparation, for resolving the dispute.

Approach	Advantages	Disadvantages
One-on-one		
Mediation		
Litigation		

Recommendation: _____

_____

_____

_____

_____

_____

_____

_____

Exercise 5.3   I Just Want My Car Fixed!

Eight years ago you bought a new car that has served you very well and required very few repairs in spite of your long commute to work. You really like the car and would like to keep it as long as you can. Three weeks ago you began having problems with the transmission and didn't want to find yourself stranded on the highway. You took the car to the dealership and they recommended putting in a whole new transmission. You didn't want to spend a lot of money given the car's age and mileage, so you took the car to Rick's Transmission Shop. Rick said he could repair the transmission and assured you the repair would be complete within one week, so you rented a car to use while yours was in the shop. As it was nearing the end of the week, Rick called to say that he was having trouble getting the proper parts and that it would be another week before the repairs would be complete. You weren't happy about it, but still didn't want to spend a lot of money to replace the transmission.

Another week passed and there was another call from Rick. This time he explained that the part that he replaced didn't correct the problem, he would have to replace another part, and it would take another week. Your patience was fading fast. You had already paid to rent a car for two weeks and now he was telling you it was going to be yet another week. He explained that the transmission in your car had been used by the manufacturer for only a couple of months because it had problems; thus, the difficulty in getting parts. Once again, he assured you that it would be fixed in a week. You didn't know what else to do so you agreed to give him one more week. At the end of the third week, it still wasn't fixed and Rick said he didn't know what else to do. You have paid to rent a car for three weeks, your car still isn't fixed, and Rick just handed you a hefty bill for his time and the parts he replaced.

Instructions: Identify the advantages and disadvantages of each dispute resolution method as it applies to this situation and recommend a strategy, including advance preparation, for resolving the dispute.

Approach	Advantages	Disadvantages
One-on-one		
Mediation		
Litigation		

Recommendation: _____

_____

_____

_____

_____

_____

_____

_____

Exercise 5.4   Apologies: The Good, the Bad, and the Insincere

In this exercise you will be evaluating the effectiveness of a public apology. Your instructor will either assign an apology for you to evaluate or allow you to find your own example. Use the following worksheet for your evaluation.

Worksheet: Exercise 5.4 Apologies: The Good, the Bad, and the Insincere

Person making the apology and the reason for the apology:

_____

_____

_____

_____

To what extent was regret expressed for causing the hurt or damage?

_____

_____

_____

_____

To what extent did the person accept responsibility for his or her actions?

_____

_____

_____

_____

_____

To what extent did the person express a willingness to take action to remedy the situation?

_____

_____

_____

_____

What could have made this a better apology?

_____

_____

_____

_____

_____

Exercise 5.5   A Loaf of Bread, a Jug of Wine …

Instructions

In this exercise you will be assigned the role of Vive la Vino! owner Giada, Healthy Kneads proprietor Ramona, or an observer. Your instructor will provide you with confidential role sheets based on your assigned role. Read all information provided and complete the worksheet based on your knowledge of the situation.

Overview

Vive la Vino! is a wine shop owned by Giada Lombardi located in Oakdale. Giada opened Vive la Vino! fifteen years ago after her husband suddenly passed away. She started out in a small storefront and built the business from the ground up. She worked long hours, six days a week. In the early days she had help from her two teenage children, but ultimately they went off to college, got married, and began families of their own. Giada had hoped that they would return to Oakdale to help her with the business, but both of them opted to follow different career paths. Giada respected their need to live their own lives, but missed having them nearby. Two years ago Vive la Vino! had outgrown the original location and Giada decided to take a leap of faith. She purchased and renovated an old building in the heart of the city. For many years, there had been talk of revitalizing the downtown area and Giada wanted to be part of that and give back to the community that had rallied around her after her husband died. The new building was large and to help cover the expenses, Giada decided to rent out part of the building to Healthy Kneads, a boutique bakery.

Healthy Kneads is owned by Ramona Riuz who started the bakery in her home three years ago. She soon found that trying to build the business from her home kitchen was problematic. She needed more space to make the variety of breads and other baked goods that her customers wanted. She thought that her prayers had been answered when Giada moved into her new building and had extra space available for rent. Initially it worked well; Ramona had the space she needed and was able to cover all of her expenses. In the past year it became increasingly difficult for her to pay her bills after the local economy took yet another hit when its largest employer announced they were moving their operations out of the country. Both Vive la Vino! and Healthy Kneads typically see a decrease in business during the winter months, but this year has been especially tough with the high unemployment rate in the county. The bakery was particularly hard hit and is now three months behind in rent. Giada has threatened to begin the process to evict Ramona so she can rent the space to someone else.

Worksheet: Exercise 5.5   A Loaf of Bread, a Jug of Wine . . .

Vive la Vino! owner, Giada Lombardi

Interests: _____

_____

Issue	Opening Demand	Target	Resistance

Healthy Kneads proprietor, Ramona Ruiz

Interests: _____

_____

_____

Issue	Opening Demand	Target	Resistance

Exercise 5.6 The Warring Coworkers

Instructions

In this exercise you will be assigned the role of Ari, Frankie, Marty, or an observer. Your instructor will provide you with confidential role sheets based on your assigned role. Read all the information provided and complete the worksheet based on your knowledge of the situation.

Overview

Ari Cirious and Frankie Funlover have worked together at WCI for many years. They haven't gotten along for at least the last five years, but in the past year they have become very vocal and hostile toward each other. This is especially evident in department meetings where they openly snipe at each other. The manager of the department, Phil, is well liked by all, but he doesn't like to deal with conflict. He seems to ignore the coworkers' behavior despite the disruption in the workplace and the negative impact on morale. Marty Middleton has been in the same department as Ari and Frankie for the last two years. She gets along with everyone in the department and generally tries to ignore the hostility; however, this has become increasingly difficult.

Worksheet: Exercise 5.6 The Warring Coworkers

Employee #1: Ari Cirious

Interests: _____

_____

_____

Issue	Opening Demand	Target	Resistance

Employee #2: Frankie Funlover

Interests: _____

_____

_____

Issue	Opening Demand	Target	Resistance

Employee #3: Marty Middleton

Interests: _____

_____

_____

Issue	Opening Demand	Target	Resistance

Interpersonal/Contextual Characteristics

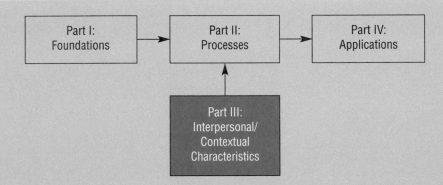

CHAPTER 6

Understanding Yourself and How That Impacts Negotiation

Chapter Objectives

After studying this chapter and completing the exercises you should be able to:

- Identify and assess personality attributes that influence your approach to negotiation and behavior during negotiations.

- Describe the role of locus of control and self-monitoring in negotiation and dispute resolution.

- Evaluate the extent to which you have an internal or external locus of control and how it impacts you in negotiations.

- Assess your tendencies toward self-monitoring and the impact it has in your negotiations.

- Assess and effectively utilize knowledge of your data-gathering and decision-making preferences in preparing for and executing a negotiation.

- Assess your degree of masculinity and femininity and utilize this knowledge in negotiation processes.

- Compare advantages and disadvantages of the various communication styles as it relates to negotiating and resolving conflicts.

- Evaluate your and others' communication style (passive, aggressive, or assertive) and utilize this knowledge in planning and executing a negotiation.

A s you now know, individuals negotiate often and in many different contexts. How successful you are in negotiation depends on a number of factors. In this chapter, we discuss the importance of understanding yourself and how your preferences, tendencies, and style influence your approach to and behaviors during negotiation. By exploring what makes you unique, and how these dimensions influence your and others' negotiation behaviors, you will enhance your negotiation knowledge, capability, and confidence.

Imagine someone picks a fight with you. Assuming there's no escaping the impending battle, one of the first things you'd do after sizing up your opponent is to take stock of your assets and liabilities. In what aspects would you have an advantage that you can exploit, and under what conditions might you have a weakness that might need disguising or shoring up?

In a test of physical strength, sizing up your strengths and liabilities would be a fairly straightforward task, assuming you are honest and accurate in your assessment. When the test is an intellectual one, such as negotiation, the task is more complicated. This chapter is designed to increase your awareness of how your unique characteristics may impact how you plan for and behave during a negotiation. This **self-awareness** will enable you to recognize how these characteristics facilitate or hinder your effectiveness in the negotiation process. For example, if you have a natural

Chapter Scenario

Micah and his twin brother Sam just started attending college at a medium-sized regional school in their town. Over their eighteen years, the boys always had a good relationship, and their choice to attend the same school came as no surprise to family and friends. They became even closer a year ago, following their dad's unexpected and untimely heart attack and death at the age of 49. The boy's college fund covers the tuition, but the cost of books, fees, and living expenses—especially now that their mom is the sole breadwinner—has created some tough choices.

Micah, the more adventurous of the two, wants to live in an apartment near campus. Sam prefers to stay home, and drive forty-five minutes each way to campus. Micah argues that college is an opportunity to be independent, and besides, there are loans that could be obtained and deferred until after graduating and getting a good-paying job. Sam prefers not taking on debt and is happy to stay close to his mom. Micah really wants Sam to share an apartment with him, as this would help with the transition to college, defray Micah's apartment costs, and be more fun. Micah has been pushing hard on Sam, and Sam feels torn choosing between his brother and mother . . . not to mention the additional expenses. Sam, who tends to shy away from confrontation, wishes Micah would just drop the subject and live at home, at least for the first year.

tendency to be passive and avoid confrontation, when you find yourself in such a situation, your awareness enables you to recognize this tendency and consciously choose another, albeit less comfortable, approach. Gaining this self-awareness will help you train yourself to take a mental time-out to assess the situation and purposely choose the most appropriate style or approach for the situation—even if it's not your typical or natural style.

There are a number of dimensions which speak to your uniqueness that have a particular relevance in negotiation, as demonstrated in past research.[1] The following three are discussed in this chapter:

- Personality attributes
- Gender
- Communication style

PERSONALITY ATTRIBUTES

The study of personality traits—enduring characteristics that describe an individual's attitude, cognitive processes, and behaviors[2]—has yielded much valuable information about individual characteristics such as aggression, shyness, helpfulness, adaptability, and independence. Most of these traits, which explain how people tend to approach and respond to others and their environment, have been found to be quite stable over time.[3] This means a person who is cold and uncaring in one situation is likely to behave similarly in other situations. Clearly, there is much value in understanding our tendencies—and being able to read others'—when it comes to negotiation. Knowing that the person with whom you will negotiate acts aggressively or rarely budges from his or her position will help in how you prepare, and enable you to choose strategies and tactics that fit best with the upcoming negotiation.

Over the last few decades, negotiation researchers have assumed that individual differences (i.e., personality) impact negotiation processes and outcomes; however, empirical support for these assumptions has been inconclusive.[4] Some of the earliest research in this area focused on personality traits such as authoritarianism (being dictator-like) and Machiavellianism (doing whatever it takes to win or get what one wants); however, as reported by scholars Bruce Barry and Raymond Friedman, findings from one study were not replicated in—or some cases, were opposite in—subsequent studies.[5] Barry and Friedman provide explanations as to why these inconsistencies may have existed (including measurement and sampling issues) and conclude that "individual differences are important in understanding how individuals manage conflict [and negotiation]."[6] While there is still much more to be learned about the many personality dimensions that have the potential to influence your and others' approach to and behavior in negotiations, we will examine the following four dimensions:

- Locus of control
- Self-monitoring
- Data-gathering/thinking preferences
- Decision-making/doing preferences

In addition, we provide end-of-chapter exercises to help you determine your personal style or preferences that influence your approach to and behavior in negotiations.

Locus of Control

Originally developed by Rotter in the 1950s, locus of control is a personality trait that describes individuals' beliefs about the cause of or control over situations and events. Individuals can possess an *external* or an *internal* locus of control. Everyone knows people who tend to blame their failures on bad luck or other people, or those who would remark, "I would have gotten an A if my big brother didn't forget to wake me up early to study." These individuals are said to possess an *external* locus of control because they view environmental causes and situational factors as being more important than those which are internally controlled. **Externals** tend to view fate or luck rather than personal effort as the cause of their successes or failures. They are also likely to view themselves as the victim in any given situation.[7]

Individuals with an *internal* locus of control see themselves as responsible for the outcomes of their own actions. **Internals** believe that they have control over their actions—both positive and negative—and their destiny. You might hear an internal say something like, "I know if I put my mind to it, I can quit smoking." An external might view the same situation as "Why bother trying to quit? My parents both smoke, some of my friends smoke . . . the deck is stacked against me." A review of past research suggests that internals, who spend more time doing homework and studying, tend to outperform their external counterparts in educational or vocational realms.[8]

Past research has demonstrated relationships between locus of control and other variables. For example, early research found that externals are more alienated from the work environment than internals,[9] and that internals have higher job satisfaction than externals.[10] Another study found that internals show more cooperativeness and a greater ability to work with others than externals.[11] Other studies demonstrated that internal managers had a stronger task orientation[12] and did better in stressful situations than externals.[13] For example, internal top managers were more likely to innovate and pursue new markets, while externals tended to stick with established practices and markets.[14] This finding echoes Rotter's early research (in 1966), which found that as a group, entrepreneurs had the lowest (most internal) scores among the general population. A later study (in 1982)[15] examining locus of control and strategy making among thirty-three Canadian firms representing a variety of industries found that the more internal the top executives, the more innovative the firm. In terms of the impact of locus of control on attitudes toward negotiation, two studies published by Bigoness are informative. In his earlier (1976) study of eighty student negotiating dyads participating in a simulated collecting bargaining game, Bigoness found that external pairs demanded smaller total opening bids, conceded a greater amount, and left fewer issues unresolved than internal dyads or mixed dyads.[16] Similar findings emerged in his 1978 study, which showed that faculty members (at a university without a union—nor drives for creating one) who were external were more favorably disposed toward the role of collective bargaining than internals.[17] Bigoness explained that because externals perceive their fate in the hands of others and beyond their control, they felt a greater need for a union than did internals who expect that their higher performance leads to greater rewards.

It's important to remember that having an internal or external locus of control isn't necessarily good or bad. Rather, this trait describes whether individuals see outcomes of their actions as contingent on internal actions/control or external events, people, or situations. Because of its impact on individuals' motivation, expectations, self-esteem, and risk-taking behavior, locus of control has implications for our expectations of, approaches to, and behaviors during a negotiation. For an internal, preparation is key. Spending time researching options, developing contingency plans, and devising mutually beneficial options are all part of ensuring that there are few surprises. Success requires adequate preparation and planning, and internals are willing to do this because they see a connection between their efforts and the rewards such efforts bring. Externals might be less likely to prepare . . . or to prepare fully. After all, externals may believe that because of the strong role that fate plays in their lives, things don't always turn out as planned,[18] and they may believe that preparation guarantees neither success nor failure. By clarifying negotiation goals, quantifying them based on relevant research and data gathering, and role playing the negotiation before the actual event, externals might be able to more clearly see the connection between their negotiation preparation and outcomes.

During a negotiation, this attribute may present itself in terms of confidence, self-efficacy, and approach to risk. Believing in their preparation and ability to succeed when efforts are invested, internals approach the negotiation with confidence and, as shown in prior research, make larger opening demands and smaller concessions. When negotiating with an external, internals would be wise to demonstrate support for their opinions and beliefs with hard data and logic, and then solicit externals' input on what would work best and why, thus building on what's comfortable as opposed to starting from a fresh—and thus untried—approach. Similarly, externals should prepare and ask their internal counterparts questions that require explanation of the data and objective criteria used in arriving at the opening demands and other values. (See Exercise 6.1 to determine your locus of control.)

Points to Ponder

1. What if you are an external and your negotiation opponent is an internal? What challenges will you likely face?
2. If you are an external, what steps could you take to approach the negotiation proactively, that is, assume that you can impact the outcome and prepare/take action accordingly?
3. If you are an internal, what blind spots might your predisposition create for you when it comes to preparing for and completing a negotiation? How would you overcome these?

Self-Monitoring

Self-monitoring is the tendency to adjust our behavior relative to the changing demands of social situations.[19] According to self-monitoring theory, people vary in how likely they are to pay attention to and control what they say and do in public situations.[20] High self-monitors are those who seem preoccupied with what others think and are motivated to behave in ways that matches others' expectations. For example, a high self-monitoring female working in a male-dominated organization is likely to publicly downplay her emotions in a meeting to ensure that her male colleagues take her seriously. Low self-monitors seem uninterested in others' opinions, and may behave or speak without concern for others' approval or acceptance. Because of this, they are more consistent in their behavior, e.g., displaying their feelings and communicating their opinions, regardless of the situation or who is watching them.[21] While being a high or low self-monitor isn't necessarily good or bad, it is important to know our self-monitoring tendencies and their advantages and disadvantages in organizational settings. By being aware of our natural tendency to self-monitor, we can assess our own behaviors and attitudes, acknowledge the elements we are satisfied with, and develop plans for addressing those aspects we want to change.

Researchers have studied how one's tendency to self-monitor impacts one's behavior in organizational settings and the resulting outcomes. Self-monitoring is related to cooperation, communication, and relationship building.[22] Because they observe social cues and adjust their behavior accordingly, high self-monitors are generally rewarded in terms of greater interview success, job performance, promotions, and position in their networks.[23] It is easy to see how self-monitoring is related to both the process and outcomes of negotiation. High self-monitors are more likely to engage in pre-negotiation planning, and thus, more likely to achieve the goals they set for a particular negotiation.[24] This is consistent with the idea that high self-monitors are concerned with behaving as expected; they take time to gather relevant information and establish strategies and contingency plans to ensure they can perform effectively and adapt as needed in the negotiation. On the down side, however, high self-monitors may hide their true feelings and concerns in an effort to conform to others' expectations. This tendency may show up as an agreement on paper, but which lacks complete commitment to the principle behind it. Knowing this about yourself or your negotiating partner can help you make the necessary adjustments or allowances. For example, you might ask to delay the final signing of a contract to allow both parties ample time to review decisions made.

One of the advantages of being or negotiating with a low self-monitor is their behavioral transparency and consistency. You know how they feel and what they want, even when communicating those feelings or needs may be unwise or socially unacceptable. There may be no need to beat around the bush. For example, in the 2007 movie *Charlie Wilson's War*, Tom Hanks plays Congressman Charlie Wilson, who makes no bones about his desire for alcohol, women, and trading his vote for whatever is important to him. Questions are asked and answered; deals are requested and made. If he doesn't like what is offered, he bluntly refuses. His behavior helps him achieve his goals expeditiously, though he insults some influential individuals along the way and becomes an easy a target for news scandals. Unchecked, people who refuse or are unable to adjust their behavior relative to the audience or situation may experience serious impediments to personal and professional success. "Letting it all hang out" can be freeing, but it can also appear as an unwillingness to collaborate or compromise in negotiations with others who possess different personal and cultural values and expectations. Low self-monitors may also have a difficult time keeping a poker face during a multi-issue negotiation, and lose the ability to effectively trade off low-priority issues for high-priority ones.

It is important to note that gender and cultural differences play a role in the tendency toward—and negotiation outcomes of—self-monitoring. Research findings regarding whether women or men are more likely to engage in self-monitoring behavior are mixed; however, a recent study suggests that whether gender's influence on self-monitoring is positive or negative on outcomes depends on the situation.[25] In addition, because of their collectivistic nature, people from China and Japan are more likely to conform to expected behavior and are less likely to openly disagree than those from the United States. Knowing—and being able to adjust—your self-monitoring tendencies, and awareness of this trait in others, can help in negotiations and in life. (See Exercise 6.2 to determine whether you are a high or low self-monitor.)

Points to Ponder

1. Considering individuals in your personal and professional network, is there a pattern among those who are the most successful; that is, do they self-monitor more or less in personal vs. professional situations? What insights could be gained from this evaluation?
2. If you have traveled abroad, what patterns of self-monitoring and conformity have you noticed among people of different nations?

Two personality differences that impact how we prepare for and behave in negotiations relate to our **data-gathering (thinking)** and **decision-making (doing) preferences**. Building on the early work of Isabel Myers (who built her Myers-Briggs Type Indicator based upon the work of psychologist Carl Jung), David Keirsey developed the Temperament Sorter to help people understand that differences among individuals are normal, expected, and not necessarily bad.[26]

The Temperament Sorter reflects four temperaments—artisans, guardians, rationals, and idealists—that are derived from individual responses to four scales that indicate preferences relative to characteristic attitudes, values, and talents and patterns of behavior and communication.[27] They are described below:

Artisans (similar to Myers-Briggs Sensing-Perceiving) prefer jobs where they can troubleshoot, respond to crises, and negotiate. They also enjoy identifying and responding to opportunities, particularly since they are adaptable, competitive, and enjoy seeking out adventure. They pride themselves on being unconventional, bold, and spontaneous.

Guardians (similar to Myers-Briggs Sensing-Judging) prefer jobs that demand responsibility. Because they tend to focus on tradition and schedules, they enjoy improving the efficiency of processes and setting up standardized procedures. They are cautious about change (must look carefully before leaping) and tend to follow rules and cooperate with others.

Rationals (similar to Myers-Briggs iNtuitive-Thinking) enjoy jobs that demand a high level of expertise and high standards of competence. They pride themselves on being independent and strong willed, caring little about political correctness and customary procedure if it wastes time and resources. They enjoy designing and understanding systems and will work tirelessly on any project they set their mind to.

Idealists (similar to Myers-Briggs iNtuitive-Feeling) enjoy jobs that allow them to support and encourage others. Their tendency to be enthusiastic can energize and improve the morale of others. Conflict and confrontation are not welcome to idealists as it gets in the way of creating harmonious, caring relationships. Instead, they are trusting and nurturing, and work to help others fulfill their potential.

Data-Gathering or *Thinking* Preferences

By understanding how we go about gathering and mentally sorting through data helps us understand how we—and those with whom we negotiate—tend to approach negotiation. In terms of what we say or how we think, Keirsey notes that there are two ends of a continuum: abstract (similar to Myers-Briggs's intuition dimension) and concrete (aligns with Myers-Briggs's sensing dimension). Some people—the abstracts—tend to talk more about ideas, theories, beliefs, philosophies, often asking if, why, what if, what might be. The Idealists and Rationals prefer to brainstorm all the possible reasons for and solutions to issues. Others—the concretes—tend to talk more about everyday reality, such as facts and figures . . . discussing who, what, when, where, and how. They (Guardians and Artisans) prefer to gather the necessary facts and figures, deal with the known, and develop a step by step plan to find THE solution. In a negotiation between these two types, it's easy to see how either type would become frustrated with the other: the concrete's impatience with the abstract's seeming unwillingness to efficiently consider the known variables, arrive at a single solution, and develop a specific action plan, and the abstract's bewilderment over the concrete's inflexibility and inability to consider multiple options that might resolve the issue, and in general, valuing efficiency over effectiveness.

Decision-Making or *Doing* Preferences

The other dimension supporting the four temperaments concerns our decisions and actions. On this continuum, Keirsey suggests the existence of two extremes: the Utilitarians (Rationals and Artisans) and Cooperatives (Idealists and Guardians). **Utilitarians** are concerned with logic and structure and tend to ignore feelings and neglect relationship building, while **Cooperatives** focus on harmony and values, often giving in to others' wishes to keep the peace. Utilitarians can be found doing what works best or is most practical to achieve their goals. They might "do first, ask for forgiveness later." When cooperatives set out to achieve their goals, they first determine what is right or socially/morally accepted . . . even if it is not the most efficient way of approaching a task.

During a negotiation, utilitarians may be seen as competitive—pursuing their goals even if it means angering their negotiating partner. In fact, their behavior may be perceived as fighting over a fixed pie (distributive), an approach opposite of the more integrative or relationship-building, pie-enhancing approach. Cooperatives, on the other hand, tend to be more concerned about the relationship and doing "the right thing" even if that means giving up power, backing down on their position, or re-evaluating their interests if doing so will preserve the relationship and keep the peace.

What are your thinking and doing preferences? How do they influence your approach to persuasion? How do others see these preferences? Complete Exercise 6.3 and find out.

GENDER AND NEGOTIATION

Traditionally, if you were to ask individuals to visualize a successful negotiator—a CEO acquiring another company, a hard-driving salesperson, a newly minted MBA attempting to maximize the initial job offer—most would visualize a male. Given the stereotype of men being more aggressive, competitive, and direct than women in their communication style, this traditional image makes sense. However, in the current work environment, you are almost as likely to be negotiating with—and against—women. As of 2009, women comprise 46.8% of the total U.S. labor force, the majority of whom work in management, professional, and related occupations (40%) and in sales and office occupations (32%).[28] In addition, over the last fifteen to twenty years, the number of women-owned businesses have grown steadily (currently about 7 million in the United States), and in some industries, growth rates over the 1997–2006 period have reached 130% in industries such as service, retail trade, and real estate/rental/leasing.[29] Understanding the potential gender-based differences in communication styles, related traits, and negotiating approach can allow members of both sexes to effectively utilize their strengths and weaknesses in different types of negotiation situations.

Exactly how are men and women different, and how does that affect negotiation? First, we must clarify that, according to renowned gender researcher Sandra Bem, the terms *masculine* and *feminine* are NOT the same as *male* and *female*. *Masculine* and

TABLE 6.1	Traits Associated with Gender Stereotypes[37]
Male-Associated Adjectives	**Female-Associated Adjectives**
Aggressive	Affectionate
Autocratic	Complaining
Capable	Cooperative
Competitive	Emotional
Coarse	Easily Influenced
Decisive	Forgiving
Humorous	Indecisive
Individualistic	Illogical
Loud	Mild
Objective	Passive
Opportunistic	Sensitive
Reckless	Subjective
Tough minded	Tactful
Unemotional	Weak

feminine describe traits and ways of behaving that have come to be associated with men and women; Table 6.1 provides a summary of these traits. However, according to Bem, healthy functioning in society requires individuals to utilize a combination of both styles—depending on the situation—and not overrely on one or the other.[30] Her advice will become clearer once you understand how these differences play out in communication and bargaining processes.

Masculine and feminine ways of communicating have been studied by researchers such as Kathleen Reardon, Alice Eagly, and Deborah Tannen. Realizing that not all women are seen as feminine nor all men are perceived as masculine, it is important to be aware of communication differences, their origin, and their impact on others' perceptions. In general, research demonstrates that women tend to use communication to connect with others; they express feelings, empathize, and build relationships, and in so doing, tend to speak in ways that are indirect, vague, and even apologetic.[31] In contrast, men tend to use communication to assert their status and request action; in doing so, they tend to use more direct, succinct language and can be seen as even putting others (women in particular) in a one-down position.[32] This language pattern, e.g., "If you have time, perhaps you could prepare this chart," demonstrates how women pay deference to others but may be viewed as "unleaderlike" or even ineffective due to their perceived unwillingness to assert their authority even when their organizational standing warrants it.

In negotiations, this stereotype of women negotiators as passive, cooperative, and relationship oriented suggests that women (or feminine negotiators) would not fare well in distributive situations, whereas the style and traits of men (or masculine negotiators) are designed for success in distributive negotiations.[33] In fact, recent research by Barron showed male students who had nearly completed MBA degrees outperforming their female counterparts in mock job interviews. In this setting, each student was offered a $61,000 salary by a manager for a fictitious company; however, men made significantly larger salary requests than women—$68,556 versus $67,000 for the same job.[34] Following the mock interviews, Barron asked the students, most of whom were engaged in real job searches of their own, to report on their negotiations. Their qualitative responses suggested that women felt uncomfortable—even incapable—of valuing themselves in dollars, while men did not. She also noted that men tended to try to prove themselves in the interview by citing experience and proven capabilities, whereas women said they would prove themselves on the job.[35] Although these findings are from only one study, they seem to support the existence of gender stereotypes: men see salary negotiation as an opportunity to advance their own interests (i.e., more distributive in nature), whereas women feared that pushing hard for a higher salary would damage their reputation or relationships (i.e., more integrative in nature).

In sum, it appears that women (or feminine negotiators) may have the edge in integrative negotiations that focus on building long-term collaborative relationships among negotiators, while men (or masculine negotiators) may have the edge in distributive negotiations, and may be seen as too competitive and unsympathetic to build collaborative relationships.[36] It bears repeating, however, that all men and women may not act in ways consistent with the gender stereotypes listed in Table 6.1. It would be unwise to look across the negotiating table and assume that a male negotiator would only be interested in a distributive outcome or that a woman would easily concede her goals and interests when other negotiators strongly assert their position or goals. Of course, the more exposure and knowledge we gain through working with diverse others in professional and social settings, the better able we are to understand and adjust to them. (Exercise 6.5 provides an opportunity to learn about your gender-role behavior.)

COMMUNICATION STYLE

As we will discuss in greater detail in Chapter 7, communication is the primary mechanism by which negotiators endeavor to resolve their differences in negotiation. It is how we let others know what we want and learn what others want. Beyond principles of effective negotiation, it is important to know how our communication tendencies affect whether and how we approach negotiation or conflict situations. Our natural communication patterns can explain whether we ask for or get what we want in life and in negotiations. Some people tend to avoid confrontation, while others deal with it head on either by asserting their own wishes or bullying others in an effort to get their own way. How you tend to communicate—whether passive, aggressive, or assertive—will influence what you ask for and get in a negotiation. It will also influence how others respond to you in negotiation.

Passive

People whose communication patterns are primarily passive, like the character in Figure 6.1, are more likely to be indirect, to avoid conflict, be easily persuaded/bullied, and be overly concerned about pleasing others. You might recall Sam from the opening scenario—the brother who felt torn between staying with his mother and sharing an apartment with his brother following the death of their father. Sam's passive communication style and discomfort with confrontation may result in having Micah make the decision for him. Because they fear being seen as pushy, difficult, or insubordinate, passive communicators tend to screen or withhold their thoughts and feelings to the extent that the persons with whom they interact have no idea of their real opinions on the matter being addressed. They also tend to apologize and use disclaimers in their speech (e.g., "I'm not sure if this idea will work, but . . . ") and hesitate or straddle the fence when directly asked about their opinions or desires, frequently allowing others to decide for them.

In general, passive communicators avoid confrontation at all costs, though they will frown, whisper under their breath, or simply say nothing because they fear losing someone's affection or have low self-esteem. While there are times when passive may be the most appropriate response (such as when another person threatens you with a weapon or is high on drugs, if you are waiting for an emotionally charged situation to calm, or if you have decided that the issue isn't worth taking a stand), it is usually not recommended in the workplace, as it seldom results in getting what you really want. Also, realize that culture plays a role. For example, some Asians will choose not to assert themselves—particularly toward authority figures—as a sign of deference and respect, and out of a desire to maintain face and harmony. In many cultures, women are expected to speak only when spoken to and are certainly not to initiate confrontation. While we don't recommend speaking in ways that anger those in your family or cultural circle, we do suggest that all individuals—regardless of gender and national origin—realize that situations may arise in which assertive behavior will protect them and others.

Aggressive

This style of communication includes exerting control over others, humiliating others, dominating, being pushy, always needing to be right, using absolute terms, and blaming others.[38] People who tend to communicate aggressively want to be in control, are

FIGURE 6.1 Dilbert Cartoon "I Ask For So Little . . . "

FIGURE 6.2 "The Salary is Negotiable . . . "

Source: © Original Artist: Reproduction rights obtainable from www.CartoonStock.com

insecure, are afraid, don't value the opinions of others, or have unresolved anger. They use this style—verbally and nonverbally—to win or dominate, proving they are right while others are wrong. Aggressive communicators, like the character in Figure 6.2, often give commands (e.g., "Don't ask why. Just do it.") and show little regard for the feelings and rights of others.

In negotiation, this style of win-lose communication may help the aggressive communicator get what he wants, but at a cost. The yelling, insults, and dominating style may force compliance—out of fear of what would happen otherwise—coupled with resentment. As persuasion expert Kathleen Reardon notes, whereas persuasion accomplishes a long-term behavior change on the part of the person being persuaded, coercion builds at best, short-term acquiescence, and may develop into sabotage over time.[39] While aggressive communication is usually not recommended, it can be appropriate if you are in an extreme situation that dictates the need for an aggressive response, such as responding to a situational crisis or physical attack.

Assertive

This style of communication is characterized by fairness, directness, honesty, tact, and sensitivity, and involves speaking up for your rights and taking into account the rights and feelings of others.[40] Assertive communicators keep contact lines open and show respect for others while affirming their beliefs and preferences. Have you ever had a colleague who consistently asked for favors or asked you to cover for her? A boss who wouldn't give you a much-deserved raise? How did you handle this? If you avoided the colleague or the boss, your behavior was passive. Unfortunately, many people feel uncomfortable being assertive; some falsely equate assertiveness with aggressiveness and instead use passive styles of communication.[41] Even saying "no" to a colleague is difficult when doing so might result in others thinking you're not a team player. In fact, by passively agreeing to extra work, you set up the expectation that you'll always do it, since saying nothing is akin to saying it's okay (e.g., "I don't mind being taken advantage of."). Being firm about your needs while still being kind and tactful is essential in the workplace and, especially, in negotiation.

While few people use only one communication style, and as mentioned, there are times when each style can be appropriate, assertive communication will be the most effective communication style to use in the majority of situations.[42] People who communicate assertively pass on information accurately and intelligently in order to accomplish objectives while demonstrating respect for others and not making them feel put down.[43] Do you know the style you most often use when communicating? Do you typically get what you want or are you the perennial nice guy/gal who "takes one for the team?" Exercises 6.7 and 6.8 will help you find out.

Points to Ponder

1. Considering your track record in negotiations, to what degree does your typical style of communication facilitate or impede achieving goals you've set for the negotiation?
2. When during a negotiation would it be ideal to communicate aggressively, passively, and assertively? What are the pros and cons of each style within a negotiation?
3. Will a passive communicator always lose to an aggressive communicator?
4. How can you practice being assertive if this style is less familiar or comfortable to you? What benefits would be realized if you were to communicate more assertively in negotiation, and in life?

Summary

If you have a high degree of self-awareness, you'll be able to capitalize on your strengths and tendencies and develop plans for improving or compensating for your limitations when involved in a negotiation. Knowing the unique ways of how you view situations; tend to think, speak, and act; and feel about conflict are all pertinent in negotiation situations. If you know your tendencies, you will have a better chance of adapting, should adaptation be necessary or helpful. Put another way, if you don't know where you begin, how will you know if you have reached the finish line?

Summary: The Big Picture

Self-awareness	Ability to recognize one's strengths, weaknesses, tendencies, and annoyances. Knowing oneself is key to planning and implementing the negotiation strategy to maximize strengths, minimizing weaknesses, and find common ground among the parties.
Locus of Control	Degree to which individuals believe they have control over situations and events. Individuals with an internal locus of control believe they control their destiny. Individuals with an external locus of control believe what happens is a matter of chance.
Self-monitoring	Degree to which individuals are aware of their surroundings and adjust their behavior relative to the demands of social situations.
Thinking and doing preferences	Psychological traits assessed in the Keirsey Temperament Sorter that help individuals understand others' and their preferences in how data is gathered and decisions are made.
Masculinity and femininity	Describes styles of communication and behavior that fit stereotypes of male and female behaviors that may or may not align with one's biological gender (i.e., sex).
Communication style	Three types: passive, aggressive, and assertive. While each has its advantages and disadvantages, assertiveness—expressing one's wishes clearly and directly without bullying or avoiding confrontation.

Key Terms and Concepts

Aggressive   People whose communication patterns involve being pushy; always needing to be right; using absolute terms; and exerting control over, humiliating, dominating, and blaming others.

Assertive   People whose communication is characterized by fairness, directness, honesty, tact, and sensitivity, and speak up for their rights taking into account the rights and feelings of others.

Cooperatives   People who focus on harmony and values, often giving in to others' wishes to keep the peace.

Data-gathering (thinking) preferences   An individual's natural approach for collecting information.

Decision-making (doing) preferences   An individual's natural approach for choosing between alternatives.

Externals   People who view fate or luck as the cause of their successes or failures.

Internals   People who believe that they have control over their actions and destiny.

Locus of Control   The degree to which individuals believe they have control over situations and events; internal or external.

Passive   People whose communication patterns are primarily indirect, and who avoid conflict, are easily persuaded/bullied, and overly concerned about pleasing others.

Self-awareness   Ability to recognize one's strengths, weaknesses, tendencies, and annoyances.

Self-monitoring   The degree to which individuals adjust their behavior relative to the changing demands of social situations; high or low.

Utilitarians   People who are concerned with logic and structure and tend to ignore feelings and neglect relationship building.

Discussion Questions

1. In what ways does your locus of control influence how you prepare for and perform in negotiations?
2. In what ways do your self-monitoring tendencies influence how you prepare for and perform in negotiations? What might you pay attention to in your next important negotiation?
3. What has your experience been regarding the degree to which gender differences have impacted your negotiations?

   What adjustments might you make when negotiating with someone of a different gender?
4. What are the advantages and disadvantages of the various communication styles when it comes to negotiation?
5. Based on what you learned in this chapter, what advice would you give Micah and Sam to more effectively negotiate with each other?

Ethical Dilemma: And I Trusted You???

Marco owns a small business that manufactures several auto accessories. In business for about five years, Marco has managed to keep the company afloat, though he's still waiting to pay himself a salary, opting instead to reinvest the revenues into advertising and new product development. (He is able to do this because his wife has a job that pays enough to support them.)

Recently, Marco hired a woman—recommended highly by a colleague and the two references Marco called—to be his office/sales manager. Initially, he was impressed with Sharon's skill set and go-getter attitude. She not only tended to the administrative tasks that Marco preferred not to do, but she also spent time trying to establish new contacts and retailers to carry Marco's products. The more they worked together, the more Marco grew to trust her and her ability, and the more responsibility Marco gave her. At some point, Sharon became the one responsible for calculating and printing out her paycheck, which she did twice per month, and then gave it to Marco to sign. Busy traveling to industry shows and meeting with reps responsible for selling his products, Marco had little time or interest in double-checking Sharon's calculations and just signed her

checks without asking for documentation that she conveniently didn't provide. Yet her pay seemed to rise with each paycheck. The amounts were noticeable but not enough to cause great alarm at first. But over the seven months Sharon had been working, the additional funds amounted to approximately $8,000 . . . about 50% more than her salary. Marco, easy-going and understanding, needed to confront the more aggressive Sharon, but was afraid of losing his only employee and person capable of "holding down the fort" during Marco's increasingly frequent business trips. One day, while checking the books, Marco noticed that Sharon had been paying herself overtime, even though, in Marco's mind, Sharon was clearly a salaried employee.

Questions

1. Since Marco signed the checks, he basically approved Sharon's pay. Do you agree? Why or why not?
2. In her mind, because Sharon frequently worked more than 40 hours per week, she felt she was entitled to overtime. She assumed Marco agreed, after all, he signed her checks.

She didn't feel she did anything wrong. Do you agree? Why or why not?

3. Marco assumed Sharon was a salaried employee; to be sure, Marco called the Department of Labor to confirm Sharon's status and eligibility for overtime pay. Because of her title, responsibilities, and pay level, Sharon's status ("salaried, exempt") meant she was ineligible for overtime pay. Marco felt Sharon—a former paralegal who should have known the law in this case—intentionally took advantage of him and his easy-going nature. What would you have done if you were Marco? If you were Sharon?

4. What role did Marco and Sharon's individual differences play in this situation?

Endnotes

1. W. C. Hamner, (1980). The influence of structural, individual, and strategic differences. In D. L. Harnett & L. L. Cummings (Eds.) *Bargaining Behavior* (pp. 21–80). Houston, TX: Dame Publications.

2. Buss, A. H. "Personality as Traits." *American Psychologist* November 1989, pp. 1378–1388.

3. Staw, B. M., N. E. Bell, and J. A. Clausen. "The Dispositional Approach to Job Attitudes: A Lifetime Longitudinal Test." *Administrative Science Quarterly* 31: 56–77.

4. Neale, M. A., and Northcraft, G. B. (1991). Behavioral negotiation theory: A framework for conceptualizing dyadic bargaining. In L.L. Cummings & B. M. Staw (Eds.), *Research in Organizational Behavior* (Vol. 13, pp. 147–190). Greenwich, C'12. JAI Press.

5. Barry, B., and R. A. Friedman. "Bargainer Characteristics in Distributive and Integrative Negotiation." *Journal of Personality and Social Psychology* 74 (1998): 345–359.

6. *Ibid*, p. 346.

7. Rotter, J. B. "Generalized Expectancies for Internal versus External Control of Reinforcement." *Psychological Monographs* 80 (1966).

8. M. J. Findley and Harris M. Cooper (1983) Locus of Control and Academic Achievement: A Literature Review. *Journal of Personality and Social Psychology*, 44(2), February 1983, 419–427.

9. Mitchell, T. R. Expectancy Models of Job Satisfaction, Occupational Preference and Effort: A Theoretical, Methodological and Empirical Appraisal. *Psychological Bulletin*, 81 (1975): 1053–1077; Seeman, M. On the Personal Consequences of Alienation in Work. *American Sociological Review*, 1967, 32, 973–977; Wolfe, R. N. Effects of economic threat on autonomy and perceived locus of control. *The Journal of Social Psychology*, 1972, 86, 233–240.

10. Organ, D. W., & Greene, C. N. Role ambiguity, locus of control and work satisfaction. *Journal of Applied Psychology*, 1974, 59, 101–102; Pryer, M. W., & Distefano, M. K., Jr. Perception of leadership behavior, job satisfaction and internal–external control across three nursing levels. *Nursing Research*, 20 (1971): 534–537.

11. Tseng, M. S. "Locus of control as a determinant of job proficiency, employ-ability, and training satisfaction of vocational rehabilitation clients." *Journal of Counseling Psychology* 57 (1970): 49–54.

12. Sceman, M. "Alienation and social learning in a reformatory." *American Journal of Sociology* 69 (1964): 270–284.

13. Anderson, 77; Anderson Hellriegel & Slocum, 77

14. Miller, D., M. F. R. Kets De Vries, and J.-M. Toulouse. "Top Executive Locus of Control and Its Relationship to Strategy-Making, Structure, and Environment." *Academy of Management Journal* 25(2) (1982): 237–253.

15. *Ibid.*

16. Bigoness, W. J. "Effects of Locus of Control and Style of Third Party Intervention upon Bargaining Behavior." *Journal of Applied Psychology* 61(3) (1976): 305–312.

17. Bigoness, W. J. "Correlates of Faculty Attitudes toward Collective Bargaining." *Journal of Applied Psychology* 63(2) (1978): 228–233.

18. Bigoness, 1976.

19. Snyder, M. *Public Appearances/Private Realities: The Psychology of Self-Monitoring.* New York: Freeman, 1987.

20. Gangestad, S., and M. Snyder. "Self-monitoring: Appraisal and reappraisal." *Psychological Bulletin* 126 (2000): 530–555.

21. *Ibid.*

22. See Gangestad & Snyder, 2000, for a review.

23. Flynn, F. J., and D. R. Ames. "What's Good for the Goose May Not Be as Good for the Gander: The Benefits of Self-Monitoring for Men and Women in Task Groups and Dyadic Conflicts." *Journal of Applied Psychology* 91(2) (2006): 272–281.

24. Jordan, J. M., and M. E. Roloff. "Planning skills and negotiator goal accomplishment." *Communication Research* 24(1) (1997): 31–63.

25. Flynn & Ames. (2006).

26. Keirsey, D. *Please Understand Me II: Temperament, Character, Intelligence.* Del Mar, CA: Prometheus Nemesis Book Co, 1998.

27. *Ibid.*

28. U.S. Department of Labor, Bureau of Labor Statistics, *Employment and Earnings, 2009 Annual Averages and the Monthly Labor Review*, November 2009.

29. Lahle Wolf About.com: Women in Business. http://womeninbusiness.about.com/od/wibtrendsandstatistics/a/statswibindustr.htm, accessed June 16, 2009.

30. Bem, S. L. (1976) Yes: Probing the Promise of Androgyny. In M. R. Walsh (ed.), *The Psychology of Women: Ongoing Debates.* New Haven, CT.: Yale University Press.

31. Tannen, D. "I'm Sorry I'm Not Apologizing." *Executive Female* (1991): 21–24.

32. Reardon, K. K. *They don't get it do they? Communication in the Workplace - Closing the Gap Between Women and Men.* Boston, MA: Little Brown & Co., 1996.

33. Kray, L., L. Thompson, and A. Galinsky. "Battle of the sexes: Gender stereotypes and reactance in negotiations." *Journal of Personality and Social Psychology* 80 (2001): 942–58.

34. Barron, L. "Gender Differences in Negotiators' Beliefs and Requests for a Higher Salary." *Human Relations*, June 2003.

35. Barron, 2003.

36. de Janasz, S., K. Dowd, and B. Schneider. *Interpersonal Skills in Organizations (3/e).* Burr Ridge, IL: Irwin-McGraw Hill, 2009.

37. Portions from J. E. Williams and D. L. Best, Cross-Cultural Views of Women and Men, in *Psychology and Culture* (p. 193). Boston: Allyn and Bacon, 1994.

38. Robbins S., and P. Hunsaker. *Training in Interpersonal Skills.* Upper Saddle River, NJ: Prentice Hall, 1996.

39. Kathleen Reardon, 1991. *Persuasion in Practice* (2/e), Thousand Oaks, CA: Sage.

40. McKay, M., M. Davis, and P. Fanning. *Messages: The Communication Skills Book, Second Ed.* Oakland, CA: Harbinger Publications, Inc., 1995.

41. Albert, R. E., and M. L. Emmons. *Your Perfect Right: A Guide to Assertive Behavior.* San Luis Obispo, CA: Impact Publishers, Inc., 1974.

42. Raudsepp, E. "Are You Properly Assertive?" *Supervision* (1992): 17.

43. Fleishman, A. "Going Back a Little Bit." *St. Louis Business Journal* (2000): 29.

44. Snyder, M., and Gangestad, S. "On the nature of self monitoring." *Journal of Personality and Social Psychology* 51(1) 1986.

45. Bem, 1976.

46. Gambrill, E. D., and C. A. Richey. "An assertion inventory for use in assessment and research." *Behavior Therapy* 6 (1975): 550–61. All Rights Reserved.

Exercise 6.1 Locus of Control

Visit the website below to complete and score a twenty-item Locus of Control assessment.
http://www.mcgrawhill.ca/college/feldmanPower/ch01/locus.mhtml

In case there are difficulties with the website, the survey is reproduced below. Your instructor has information about scoring.

1. I usually get what I want in life.
☐ True ☐ False

2. I need to be kept informed about news events.
☐ True ☐ False

3. I never know where I stand with other people.
☐ True ☐ False

4. I do not really believe in luck or chance.
☐ True ☐ False

5. I think that I could easily win a lottery.
☐ True ☐ False

6. If I do not succeed on a task, I tend to give up.
☐ True ☐ False

7. I usually convince others to do things my way.
☐ True ☐ False

8. People make a difference in controlling crime.
☐ True ☐ False

9. The success I have is largely a matter of chance.
☐ True ☐ False

10. Marriage is largely a gamble for most people.
☐ True ☐ False

11. People must be the master of their own fate.
☐ True ☐ False

12. It is not important for me to vote.
☐ True ☐ False

13. My life seems like a series of random events.
☐ True ☐ False

14. I never try anything that I am not sure of.
☐ True ☐ False

15. I earn the respect and honors I receive.
☐ True ☐ False

16. A person can get rich by taking risks.
☐ True ☐ False

17. Leaders are successful when they work hard.
☐ True ☐ False

18. Persistence and hard work usually lead to success.
☐ True ☐ False

19. It is difficult to know who my real friends are.
☐ True ☐ False

20. Other people usually control my life.
☐ True ☐ False

Exercise 6.2 Self-Monitoring Assessment[44]

The statements below concern your personal reactions to several different situations. If a statement is TRUE or MOSTLY TRUE as it applies to you, circle "T." If a statement is FALSE or MOSTLY FALSE as it applies to you, circle "F." Answer honestly.

T F **1.** I find it hard to imitate the behavior of other people.

T F **2.** At parties and social gatherings, I do not attempt to do or say things that others will like.

T F **3.** I can only argue for ideas that I already believe.

T F **4.** I can make impromptu speeches even on topics about which I have almost no information.

T F **5.** I guess I put on a show to impress or entertain others.

T F **6.** I would probably make a good actor.

T F **7.** In a group of people, I am rarely the center of attention.

T F **8.** In different situations and with different people, I often act like very different persons.

T F **9.** I am not particularly good at making other people like me.

T F **10.** I am not always the person I appear to be.

T F **11.** I would not change my opinion (or the way I do things) in order to please someone.

T F **12.** I have considered being an entertainer.

T F **13.** I have never been good at games like charades or improvisational acting.

T F **14.** I have trouble changing my behavior to suit different people and different situations.

T F **15.** At a party, I let others keep the jokes and stories going.

T F **16.** I feel a bit awkward in public and do not show up quite as well as I should.

T F **17.** I can look anyone in the eye and tell a lie with a straight face (if for a right end).

T F **18.** I may deceive people by being friendly when I really dislike them.

Your instructor has information about scoring this assessment.

Exercise 6.3   Keirsey Temperament Sorter

Go to http://www.advisorteam.org/instruments/ and complete the Keirsey Temperament Sorter II (the test and results are free). It is similar to the Myers Briggs Type personality type indicator. The four temperaments, which derive from individual responses to four scales that indicate preferences relative to characteristic attitudes, values, and talents and patterns of behavior and communication, include Artisans, Guardians, Rationals, and Idealists.

1. According to the instrument, which style are you? How well does that match how you see yourself?

2. What are Artisans' strengths and challenges in preparing for and operating during negotiations?

3. What are Guardians' strengths and challenges in preparing for and operating during negotiations?

4. What are Rationals' strengths and challenges in preparing for and operating during negotiations?

5. What are Idealists' strengths and challenges in preparing for and operating during negotiations?

6. By focusing on the negotiation strengths and challenges of each type, you have a clearer sense of yourself as well as how that fits (or not) with other types. Which of the preceding types represents the most challenging or different to you? Why?

7. What three things can you focus on to improve your effectiveness when negotiating with someone who fits this type?

Exercise 6.4   Observation Exercise: Applying the Temperament Sorter

As discussed in the Keirsey website, there are two primary dimensions of human behavior: what we say and what we do. By taking a closer look at these dimensions, you'll be able to identify these differences and effectively manage those differences in a variety of situations, including negotiations.

What we say (words):
Abstract (Idealist and Rational) vs. Concrete (Guardian and Artisan)

What we do (deeds):
Utilitarian (Rational and Artisan) vs. Cooperative (Idealist and Guardian)

Watch a favorite TV show and identify the data-gathering and decision-making preferences of each of the main characters by listing specific examples of what she or he said or did in particular situations.

1. What is the name of the show?

    _____

    _____

2. Which of these characters has a style that is most like yours? Cite evidence to support your answer.

    _____

    _____

    _____

    _____

    _____

    _____

    _____

    _____

3. Which of these characters has a style that is least like yours? Cite evidence to support your answer.

    _____

    _____

    _____

    _____

    _____

    _____

    _____

    _____

Exercise 6.5   Bem Sex Role Inventory[45]

Rate yourself, on each item, on a scale from 1 (never or almost never true) to 7 (almost always true).

rating (1-7)		rating (1-7)		rating (1-7)	
1. self reliant		2. yielding		3. helpful	
4. defends own beliefs		5. cheerful		6. moody	
7. independent		8. shy		9. conscientious	
10. athletic		11. affectionate		12. theatrical	
13. assertive		14. flatterable		15. happy	
16. strong personality		17. loyal		18. unpredictable	
19. forceful		20. feminine		21. reliable	
22. analytical		23. sympathetic		24. jealous	
25. leadership ability		26. sensitive to other's needs		27. truthful	
28. willing to take risks		29. understanding		30. secretive	
31. makes decisions easily		32. compassionate		33. sincere	
34. self-sufficient		35. eager to soothe hurt feelings		36. conceited	
37. dominant		38. soft spoken		39. likable	
40. masculine		41. warm		42. solemn	
43. willing to take a stand		44. tender		45. friendly	
46. aggressive		47. gullible		48. inefficient	
49. acts as a leader		50. childlike		51. adaptable	
52. individualistic		53. does not use harsh language		54. unsystematic	
55. competitive		56. loves children		57. tactful	
58. ambitious		59. gentle		60. conventional	
Column Total:		**Column Total:**		**Column Total:**	
Column Average:		**Column Average:**		**Column Average:**	

- Add up your ratings in column 1 and divide the total by 20.
- Add up your ratings in column 2 and divide the total by 20.
- Add up your ratings in column 3 and divide the total by 20.

Your instructor has more information about scoring this inventory.

Exercise 6.6   Implications of the Sex Role Inventory

According to the instrument, what is your:

Feminine score? _____

What does this mean in terms of your strengths and weaknesses in distributive negotiations? Integrative negotiations?

_____

_____

_____

_____

_____

_____

_____

Masculine score? _____

What does this mean in terms of your strengths and weaknesses in distributive negotiations? Integrative negotiations?

_____

_____

_____

_____

_____

_____

_____

Androgynous score? _____

What does this mean in terms of your strengths and weaknesses in distributive negotiations? Integrative negotiations?

_____

_____

_____

_____

_____

_____

_____

Exercise 6.7   The Assertion Inventory[46]

This exercise is completed in two passes. First, using the scale below, indicate your **degree of discomfort** or anxiety related to each situation presented. Even if you have never been in a particular situation, imagine what it would feel like and indicate your degree of discomfort.

1. None
2. A little
3. A fair amount
4. Much
5. Very much

Next, concealing the answers you just gave, go over the list a second time and indicate the probability or likelihood of your displaying the behavior if actually presented with the situation. For example, if you rarely apologize when you are at fault, you would mark a "4" after that item. Utilize the following scale to indicate **response probability**:

1. Always do it
2. Usually do it
3. Do it about half the time
4. Rarely do it
5. Never do it

Situation	Degree of Discomfort	Response Probability
1. Turn down a request to borrow your car		
2. Compliment a friend		
3. Ask a favor of someone		
4. Resist sales pressure		
5. Apologize when you are at fault		
6. Turn down a request for a meeting or date		
7. Admit fear and request consideration		
8. Tell a person you are intimately involved with when he/she says or does something that bothers you		
9. Ask for a raise		
10. Admit ignorance in some areas		
11. Turn down a request to borrow money		
12. Ask personal questions		
13. Turn off a talkative friend		
14. Ask for constructive criticism		
15. Initiate a conversation with a stranger		
16. Compliment a person you are romantically involved with or interested in		
17. Request a meeting or a date with a person		
18. Ask for a meeting when your initial request was turned down		
19. Admit confusion about a point under discussion and ask for clarification		
20. Apply for a job		
21. Ask whether you have offended someone		
22. Tell someone that you like them		
23. Request expected service when such is not forthcoming, for example, in a restaurant		
24. Discuss openly with the person his/her criticism of your behavior		
25. Return defective items, for example, in a store or restaurant		
26. Express an opinion that differs from that of the person you are talking to		

(Continued)

Situation	Degree of Discomfort	Response Probability
27. Resist sexual overtures when you are not interested		
28. Tell the person when you feel he/she has done something that is unfair to you		
29. Accept a date		
30. Tell someone good news about yourself		
31. Resist pressure to drink		
32. Resist a significant person's unfair demands		
33. Quit a job		
34. Resist pressure to do drugs		
35. Discuss openly with the person his/her criticism of your work		
36. Request the return of a borrowed item		
37. Receive compliments		
38. Continue to converse with someone who disagrees with you		
39. Tell a friend or someone with whom you work when he/she says or does something that bothers you		
40. Ask a person who is annoying you in a public situation to stop		
TOTAL:		

Last, please indicate the situations you would like to handle more assertively by placing a circle around the item number.

Assertion Inventory Scoring Grid

	Response Probability Low (105+)	Response Probability High (40–104)
Degree of Discomfort High (96+)	Unassertive/Passive	Anxious performer
Degree of Discomfort Low (40–95)	Don't care	Assertive

Source: Gambrill, E. & Richey, C. (1975) An Assertion Inventory for Use in Assessment and Research, *Behavior Therapy*, Vol. 6, pp. 550-561. Copyright 1975 by the Association for Behavioral and Cognitive Therapies. Reprinted by permission of the publisher and author.

Exercise 6.8   Observation Exercise: Communication Style

Watch a favorite TV show, and identify the communication mode (passive, aggressive, assertive) that each of the main characters typically uses by writing specific examples of what each character said or did (includes nonverbal communication).

1. Which of these characters would you most like to model your communication style after? Why?

_____

_____

_____

_____

_____

_____

_____

_____

_____

2. Which of these characters would you least like to model your communication style after? Why?

_____

_____

_____

_____

_____

_____

_____

_____

_____

_____

CHAPTER 7

Communication in Negotiation

Chapter Objectives

After studying this chapter and completing the exercises you should be able to:

- Improve your ability to send clear messages.
- Identify and reduce barriers associated with ineffective communication.
- Send messages that directly express and address your wants, needs, and opinions.
- Use behaviors that demonstrate that you are a good listener during negotiations.
- Ensure that your verbal and nonverbal messages are congruent.
- Accurately interpret others' nonverbal messages.

From our first breath on, we communicate. We communicate because we want something to happen or we want to satisfy a need. In the same way a newborn shares information about her wants and needs, negotiators share information about what they want and why, albeit in slightly more discernible ways. Communication, or the process of sending and receiving verbal and nonverbal messages, is the basis upon which negotiation processes occur. Negotiators communicate opening offers, interests, counteroffers, goals, and ideas for generating solutions in an effort to resolve conflicts or differences between them.

What we communicate is as important as how we communicate. In fact, many times, the inability of negotiators to reach a mutually beneficial or agreeable solution can be explained as much by differing goals as it can by differences in how we directly and indirectly share and interpret the messages within the negotiation process. In this chapter, we explore the basic process of communication, discuss the benefits of and challenges to sending and receiving accurate messages, explore the role and importance of listening and nonverbal communication, and offer strategies and tactics for improving both what and how you communicate in negotiation. We also discuss communication in virtual negotiation.

Chapter Scenario, Part I

Sadie and Olivia have been co-workers for the last three years. They became friends when both went through their company's orientation program at the same time. During the last project—the two of them are internal consultants in their defense electronics firm and often deliver employee effectiveness workshops together—Sadie fell through on a promise she made to the internal client, a manager of the printed circuit board group. Sadie didn't think it was too big a deal not sending the plan for the four-hour workshop to the manager several days before the workshop occurred; after all, it went well and the employees seemed to get a lot out of it. Olivia, however, was incensed. She told Sadie—in no uncertain terms—how unprofessional she thought Sadie had been and how it reflected poorly on Olivia and their department. Sadie sat there feeling scolded and unable to respond and thought to herself, "Do I have to take this? She's my co-worker, not my boss." Later that afternoon, when Sadie passed by Olivia's office, she purposely looked at the floor and clenched her teeth as she made her way back from the copy machine . . .

THE COMMUNICATION PROCESS: MORE COMPLICATED THAN IT SEEMS . . .

Have you ever walked away from a conversation feeling confident that the message you sent was clear and understood . . . only to find out later that such was not the case? Perhaps you communicated a request or delegated a task, and at the agreed-upon follow-up time, the request was not fulfilled or the task was not completed. Sound familiar? This happens more than you might imagine. In what might seem like a simple exchange of words, the reality is a far more complex situation—one which is rife with potential distortion, as depicted in Figure 7.1.

Part of this distortion comes from the noise or interference that impedes the transmission process. However, the larger part of the distortion comes from the fact that the words that are communicated, e.g., "I need this report as soon as possible," comprise only 7% of communication that is transmitted. The remaining 93% of what is communicated is transmitted through body language (55%) and tone of voice (38%).[1] The speaker believes he clearly communicated the task, while the listener may have sensed a relaxed body posture (e.g., "hmmm . . . maybe 'as soon as possible' means he needs it within a week or two") and tentative tone (e.g., the inflection suggested a question as opposed to a command). Moreover, the sender's and receiver's values, beliefs, expectations, and

FIGURE 7.1 The Communication Model[42]

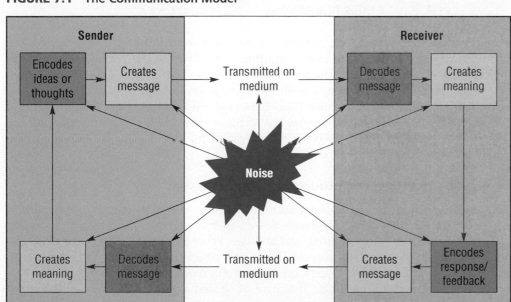

recent (and not-so-recent) experiences impact how they consciously and subconsciously transmit and interpret the messages sent and received. Let's look at the following dialog between subordinate (Keith) and supervisor (Sarah):

> KEITH: "I think I deserve a raise."
>
> SARAH: "Hmmm . . . I don't think I can do that . . . not now, anyway."

However, the message that Keith is sending likely differs from what he intended, and Sarah's message in response—which is based on what she hears and infers from the initial message—likely differs from what she intended. What really might be happening is this:

> KEITH (THINKING): (Ever since one-third of the employees in the department were laid off, I've been working longer hours in an effort to complete my tasks and those that were completed by my former co-workers. I've been doing this for four months now, and I'm exhausted. The extra work has taken a toll on me and my family, and I'm not being rewarded for all of this extra effort. In fact, the extra hours have cost me more in terms of meals out, babysitters, and paying others to do things like mowing the lawn that I no longer have time to do. If I don't get a raise of at least 5%, I'm going to start looking elsewhere for a company that appreciates my skills, experience, and dedication to the organization. I'm going to ask Sarah for a raise, and because she knows just how dedicated I am to her and the company, she will give it to me.) To Sarah, he says, "I think I deserve a raise."
>
> SARAH (THINKING): (Wow . . . I was afraid he'd ask. I know that ever since we had those layoffs, Keith has been working late and coming in early . . . and I've told him before how much I appreciate his dedication. But everyone is stretched, including me! Half the time, I'm not sure whether I'm coming or going! I haven't gotten a raise in 18 months, and now Keith is asking me to give him one? At this point, our division is lucky to not be on the latest list of targets for additional cutbacks. How do I respond to his request? To Keith, Sarah responds, "Hmmm . . . I don't think I can do that . . . not now, anyway."

This is just an illustration, but one not too far from what happens frequently in communication exchanges. The words communicated, that is, the verbal message, was fairly clear. Keith, while neither assertive nor verbose in his request, wanted and asked for a raise. Sarah, similarly stingy with her words, responded to his request. Asked (though not in the form of a question) and answered. End of story, right? Obviously not. As you will see, there are many factors that explain why and how communication can break down. They include the sender, receiver, and the communication environment. We will analyze each of these next.

Barriers to Effective Communication: Sender Issues

As can be seen from Figure 7.1, the communication process begins when a communicator (the *sender*) decides that a message needs to be sent and **encodes** this message according to her own perceptions, experiences, and abilities. What impact do these individual differences have on the encoding process? The impact could be substantial and could mean the difference between being understood and not. For example, if a sender perceives that the receiver is "on the same page" because of shared experiences, the sender might choose to send only a skeletal message, assuming that the receiver will "fill in the blanks."

Sometimes, this approach may be effective. Have you ever had a conversation with a close friend that consisted primarily of winks and nods? However, this is the exception and not the rule of effective communication. The sender's assumptions may be inaccurate, his memory of the shared experiences with the receiver may vary greatly from that of the receiver, and his ability to translate his thoughts into words may be below average.

Next, the sender determines which **communication channel**—the method or medium—is most appropriate to use to convey the message. Should he send an email, letter, or text message; place a call; or take a short walk to the receiver's cubicle to have a face-to-face conversation? That depends on the sender's habits, but ideally, that choice should be dictated by the content and nature of the message itself. Each medium has its advantages and disadvantages. We've all heard of the employee who gets a layoff notice in the interoffice mail—not a very effective means of communicating that particular message; however, given many managers' fear of confrontation and feedback, this situation is neither surprising nor uncommon.[2] The encoded message travels across the chosen communication channel and is then decoded (by the *receiver*) who interprets (**decodes**) the message according to his own perceptions, abilities, and experiences. That is, of course, assuming that there were no technical difficulties, postal strikes, or downed phone lines.

In a face-to-face negotiation, the choice of medium is likely face-to-face; however, that doesn't mean that misunderstandings will not arise. While this medium facilitates the opportunity for immediate clarification and feedback, negotiators who are more shy and passive might choose not to question or confront, whereas they might do so in a virtual negotiation or in the emailed conversations that precede and follow a face-to-face negotiation. Early research on computer-mediated communication suggested that in the absence of social cues, communicators are less inhibited.[3] More recently, it has been found that electronic communication reduces interpersonal skill differences between negotiations because individuals have time and opportunity to think about others' messages and compose and revise their own.[4]

Barriers to Effective Communication: Receiver Issues

As human beings, we have the ability to process only a finite amount of information. The sheer volume and constancy of incoming information from various media is increasing faster than we can reasonably absorb it. **Information overload** occurs when the volume of information a person receives exceeds his capacity to process it.[5] In fact, one study demonstrated that having more information doesn't necessarily lead to better negotiation outcomes.[6] To ensure that the receiver effectively receives the message, tailor your message to the receiver. This requires that you review the key points you want to make and practice presenting them concisely and compellingly; use jargon sparingly, if at all; consider using visuals to back up your points and for presenting complex data; and check for understanding and pause frequently, giving the person time to formulate clarifying questions and indicate to you that she understands what you are saying. If no questions are forthcoming, ask the receiver if she would like anything clarified, and allow time for doing so.

Another issue relates to the receiver's readiness to receive the message being sent. Think about it; someone approaches you to ask your opinion or for a favor. This "someone" has likely thought about what she wanted to communicate—both what to say and how to say it. She is ready, whereas the listener may not be; after all he didn't initiate the conversation. He may be preoccupied by tasks or emotions that limit his ability to focus clearly on the message being sent. Additionally, because of his previous interactions with the sender, he may give little credence to her and thus the message; or, he might have "heard" two or three words and "assumed" the rest.

Barriers to Effective Communication: Environmental Issues

Another key set of challenges to effective communication relates to noise and environmental issues. **Noise** is any distortion factor that blocks, disrupts, or distorts the message sent to the receiver, interfering with the communication process.[7] Some of these distortion factors are tangible barriers in the physical negotiation environment, such as computers or phones that are not working as intended (e.g., computer turned off, email system down, phone battery dead), and barriers which challenge the senses (e.g., loud background noise, telephone static, or poor room logistics or acoustics that make it difficult to hear). Other distortion factors relate to individual differences in communication. For example, using slang (e.g., "cool," "bad," "hot") or misinterpreting gestures when discussing the features of a new product design to a foreign counterpart could lead to a distortion of the interpreter's meaning, which would constitute noise.

LISTENING AND NONVERBAL COMMUNICATION IN NEGOTIATION

Listening, a critical component of the negotiation process, goes beyond merely hearing what another person is saying to constructing meaning from all the verbal and nonverbal signals the speaker is sending. As previously mentioned, words often comprise only a small part of a message being sent.[8] To obtain the complete message you must listen with your ears, eyes, and heart.[9] Effective listening has three dimensions: sensing, processing and evaluating, and responding. Sensing involves hearing the words and receiving the nonverbal signals such as body language and facial expressions. Processing and evaluating involves understanding the meaning, interpreting the implications, evaluating the nonverbal cues, and remembering the message. Responding involves the listener sending the speaker verbal or nonverbal signals that he is being heard.[10] Listening is an essential skill for success in negotiation . . . and in life!

Many confuse the ability to hear or simply recognize sound with the skill of listening or the ability to comprehend what is heard. Hearing is an unconscious, physiological process, making it a passive activity. Listening—truly listening—demands attention, concentration, and effort.

There are several different types of listening:[11]

Passive listening   occurs when one is trying to absorb as much of the information presented as possible. The listener acts as a sponge, taking in the information with no or little attempt to process or enhance the message(s) being sent by the speaker.

Attentive listening   occurs when one is genuinely interested in the speaker's point of view. The listener is aware something can be learned and gained from the interaction. In attentive listening, the listener will make assumptions about the messages being relayed by the speaker and fill in gaps with assumptions based on what the listener wants to hear rather than on what the speaker is actually saying. At this level of listening, the listener doesn't check to see whether what she heard is what the speaker intended to say.

Active or empathetic listening   is the most powerful level of listening and requires the greatest amount of work on the part of the listener. In active listening, communication is a vibrant, two-way process that involves high levels of attentiveness, clarification, and message processing. In active listening, the listener not only hears and reacts to the words being spoken but also paraphrases, clarifies, and gives feedback to the speaker about the messages being received. Think about the offer-counteroffer process in a negotiation. Both parties are trying to influence each other, which is aided by the ability to determine common ground, and in the process, the parties are able to narrow the bargaining range (or create value with innovative approaches to increasing the pie) and move the discussion toward a mutually agreeable resolution. Without active listening, resolution may take additional time and energy . . . if it happens at all.

The Importance of Active Listening in Negotiation

As summarized in Figure 7.2, active listening provides negotiators with a number of benefits, beginning with showing the speaker that you are concerned. By paying full attention to the speaker, the listener is able to focus on the key elements of the

FIGURE 7.2   How Active Listening Improves Success in Negotiation

- Shows the speaker that you are concerned and leads to getting more and better information
- Can calm someone who has become upset or emotional; makes them feel like they've been heard
- Invites the other party to listen to you; because you listened to them, they will respond in kind
- Leads to better cooperation and problem solving by uncovering unspoken goals and alternatives
- Builds better relationships, in particular, across geographical borders

message being sent, ask questions to clarify meanings, and offer statements that enhance both the speaker's and the listener's understanding of what is being said. Active listening leads to getting more and better information—key in negotiations. By asking clarifying questions, the listener motivates the speaker to be more precise when explaining the nuances of a situation, enabling the listener to obtain details that otherwise might not have surfaced. Imagine a mother asking her teenage son how his day went. If she accepts his one-word answer ("fine"), she limits her understanding of his situation and might communicate that she really doesn't care to know more. Similarly, if a negotiator is asked why a particular position is so critical and responds, "It just is," there is an obvious need for further communication.

Let's return to Keith and Sarah's exchange. While Keith's initial message— "I think I deserve a raise"—lacked assertiveness, Sarah's response—"Hmmm . . . I don't think I can do that . . . not now, anyway"—effectively ended the conversation for Keith. He missed an opportunity to actively listen. He could have said, "Sarah, you said that you don't think you can do that. Could you say more about that? On what are you basing this view?" Or, "Sarah, as you know, I've worked really hard to pick up the slack since the last round of layoffs but I don't feel as though my efforts are being rewarded at the moment. You said 'not now.' Could you elaborate on why now is not a good time and when you think the time would be better?" Notice that both of these choices were attempts to continue the conversation. Keith didn't get angry or cause Sarah to become defensive . . . but he did demonstrate his listening (by paraphrasing parts of Sarah's message) and ask for additional information. In the absence of this step, there would be little chance for Keith and Sarah to understand where each is coming from or determine common ground for a future resolution.

Another benefit of active listening is that it can sometimes calm someone who has become upset or emotional, which can happen when we negotiate with loved ones or over something we fear being taken away from us. Think for a moment about airline ticket agents and how calm most of them are when confronted by an aggressive, frustrated, or tired passenger. Most airline ticket agents have received customer service training that emphasizes the importance of listening to the customer. While an agent can seldom do anything that would directly respond to the passenger's needs, such as change the weather or get the flight to leave on time, the best agents are skilled at focusing their attention on passengers in distress, hearing them out, and calmly working with them to discover acceptable alternatives to situations in which they find themselves. These agents use listening skills to make the passenger feel heard and understood. They listen, ask clarifying questions, empathize, and offer potential solutions for consideration by the passenger—all in a way that is intended to relax the distressed passenger. Similarly, in a negotiation that has become heated, taking a moment to listen to both the words and emotion behind the words and show appropriate empathy can pay huge dividends, and can even keep a negotiation from completely derailing.

Active listening invites others to listen to you. By listening actively, you set a good example for others and remind them that listening is a valuable skill that they can also use. People who have been listened to actively are more likely to reciprocate. This benefit of active listening is echoed in one of the habits in Stephen Covey's bestseller *The Seven Habits of Highly Effective People*: seek first to understand and then to be

Chapter Scenario, Part II

Olivia, noticing that Sadie avoided eye contact when she passed by Olivia's office, called out to Sadie. Sadie stopped, turned around, and slowly walked back to Olivia's office. "You called me?" Olivia responded, "Yes, I did. Do you have a couple of minutes?" Sadie wanted to decline, but the few hours that passed since Olivia's browbeating seemed to soften Sadie a bit. "Sure," Sadie responded, and walked into Olivia's office. Olivia started, "Listen. I know I was a bit hard on you earlier, and I hope that you understand where I was coming from. We are a team, and we were a team when we delivered that training session. And while I agree that it went well, I was upset because you not keeping your promise to let the manager know ahead of time what we were going to do reflected poorly on both of us and the department.

I take my word—or in this case, our word—very seriously. It's all about credibility . . . you know, do what you say and say what you do. I need this job, and hope that someday soon I will move up in the company. From what I've seen, credibility is really important. Does that make sense?" Sadie shrugged and responded, "I guess so." Olivia continued, "We're on the same team, and I want us to help each other perform at our best and project a positive image for the department. What do you think?" Sadie asked a few questions, and finally, she apologized to Olivia. "It was an oversight. I intended to send the manager our plan, but I got caught up in two other projects. I'm sorry." Olivia was relieved. "That's OK. We're in this together. How do you want to handle the training for the finance folks next month?"

Points to Ponder:

1. What role did active listening play in this conversation?
2. In what way did this exchange resolve the earlier issue between Sadie and Olivia?
3. In what way did this exchange set the stage for future conversations and collaborations between Sadie and Olivia?
4. How would you have handled the situation if you were Sadie? If you were Olivia?

---

understood.[12] Typically, when two people disagree, one is likely to say something like, "OK, we don't agree. Let me tell you why you're wrong and how my way is superior." Perhaps that statement is a bit exaggerated, but it demonstrates the need many of us have to be right and have our say—first and foremost. Imagine how this exchange would differ if it sounded like this: "OK, we don't agree. Why don't you tell me your idea and why you think it will work." When we actively listen to other people, chances are very high that they'll do the same in return. In a negotiation process, this is essential.

Active listening leads to better cooperation and problem solving. We're all human and it's easy to make mistakes when we think we understand what someone is trying to say. By listening actively, asking questions, and probing for understanding, together the listener and speaker are generally able to understand the spoken and unspoken goals and needs and develop more creative solutions than if the listener had remained passive, not offering any insight or support.

Finally, listening skills are increasingly critical in the global society in which we live and work. A recent study of 409 expatriates (working in 51 different countries) from American and Canadian multinational firms sought to determine success factors for facilitating relationships across borders.[13] Of the nine factors identified, good listening topped the list. This is especially important as American managers are characterized as poor listeners and overly direct, blunt, and competitive.[14] Improving your listening skills is key for successful negotiation anywhere and with anyone. It is important not only to actively listen, but to also demonstrate these behaviors in a negotiation. Doing so signals your sincere interest in the other party and his interests. Figure 7.3 summarizes several behaviors that will help you practice and demonstrate listening skills.

FIGURE 7.3   Strategies for Improving and Demonstrating Listening Skills[43]

- *Ask questions if you don't understand completely.* Ask for clarification on points of contention ("Did he say that we would need to lay off employees or just cut costs?") as well as follow-up questions ("When will she have to start this process?").
- *Avoid distractions.* Avoid doing two (or more) things at once. Give your full attention to the speaker, making her feel like she is the most important person in the world. Do not check your email, take a phone call, or focus on a document while other negotiators are speaking.
- *Do not interrupt.* When you do, you communicate to the speaker that you don't value what she is saying. To quote the American etiquette expert, Letitia Baldridge, "Good listeners don't interrupt—ever—unless the building's on fire." Pause and take a breath to make sure the speaker has completed her statement before you start.
- *Evaluate the message after hearing all the facts.* This is a corollary to the preceding point and a common habit of listeners: forming a response before the speaker is finished. Avoid judgments by allowing the individual to complete the entire message before assessing the content and merit of the statements.
- *Read both the verbal and nonverbal messages.* Good listening technique involves good detective work. Take the time and energy needed to understand the whole message and not just what is being spoken.
- *Be empathetic.* Recognize and acknowledge the other person's feelings and emotions. If they're distressed, cracking a joke or making light of the situation might be interpreted as not caring about the speaker. Instead, say what you are sensing and check your perception: "It seems that you are upset about the deal that's on the table. Am I right? Which component concerns you most and why?"
- *Paraphrase to correct misinterpretations, reflect the literal message, and improve retention.* Repeat statements for clarification. Say, "If I heard you correctly . . ." or "So what you are saying is . . ." This method also reduces the "beating a dead horse" phenomenon—where parties agree yet rehash and rehash.
- *Concentrate on the message as well as the messenger.* Focus on the delivery as well as the content of the message itself, but be sure to check your potential biases about the messenger before you start the listening process. Are you making assumptions because of the speaker's accent, appearance, choice of words that you would not have made if the speaker were more similar to you? While it may not be possible to remove your biases, it's important to be aware of them.
- *Give feedback to check accuracy, express your perspective, and broaden the interaction.* For example, you might say, "So you want us to get back to you on this proposal by noon Friday?" or "It sounds like we disagree; are there any elements of the plan on which we can both agree?"
- *Don't talk too much!* If you know you have tendencies toward verbosity, be on guard.

Nonverbal Communication

The communication process involves much more than just the spoken word. In any interpersonal interaction—whether a friendly conversation or a business negotiation—we form our impressions about others based on many factors, including any and all direct and indirect information available to us. As noted earlier, 93% of communication is transmitted through physiology (body language) and through the tone of voice (a component of verbal communication) and only 7% through words alone.[15] These statistics reinforce the need for sending verbal and nonverbal messages congruently. Negotiators must carefully consider the potential message being sent nonverbally through gestures and body language. The nonverbals must reinforce the message, not contradict it. You may be misunderstood if you are rolling your eyes when you are confirming your acceptance of a suggestion. Not only does eye rolling convey sarcasm, but it also reduces the trust that the receiver has in your following through on said suggestion. If you are not happy with the suggestion or alternative on the table, you must say so—clearly and convincingly—with a message that is congruent verbally and nonverbally. Better still, explain why you're uncomfortable with the suggestion and offer to resume brainstorming to find other, more acceptable solutions.

The goal of negotiation is to identify common ground and mutually agreeable solutions; one way to do this is to make your messages clear and not send mixed signals. We discuss nonverbal negotiation next, but be aware that nonverbal behavior and its meaning vary with culture, gender, and even generational differences.[16] In fact, we address some of these cross-cultural differences in Chapter 10. As you read what follows, remember that the only thing that is certain about nonverbal behavior is that nonverbal behavior is neither consistently nor universally interpreted accurately. One expert suggests that people who consciously read body language are right about 50% of the time.[17] If you are unsure about what you've witnessed, ask.

The nonverbal component of communication comes in many forms. Some messages we send nonverbally are deliberate and conscious; other times, like the eye-rolling example, we may send messages that are neither intentional nor add value in the negotiation. For example, in Western society, making eye contact while trying to persuade someone or when receiving similar messages is important.[18] However, continuous, penetrating eye contact should be avoided as it might be perceived as staring and lead to perceptions of suspicion instead of trust.[19] Similarly, having one's hands near one's mouth or nose could suggest that the speaker is trying to cover something up.[20] If a negotiator wants to convey trust and a sincere message, he should look attentively at his target, with momentary glances away, especially when searching for a particular word or detail.[21] Likewise, the party to whom the negotiator is speaking should also make eye contact to show that she is attending to the speaker's message.

Our posture also communicates interest in the speaker and her message. If the listener is slouching, turning away from the table, or appearing overly relaxed, he may indicate a lack of respect for the speaker. If the listener rolls his eyes, crosses his arms over his chest, or furrows his brow, he may be indicating his disapproval of the message. These indications may be intentional, for example, the speaker is long-winded and domineering and the listener's body language is an attempt to send a nonverbal message when it is difficult to send a verbal one. Or, these indications may be unintentional. Remember, however, that because of the challenges inherent in the communication process—including message encoding, decoding, and the potential for noise—messages we intend may be interpreted differently. Our desire to work collaboratively and build a win-win solution might actually be interpreted quite differently because of the nonverbal messages we unconsciously send.

We also use gestures in negotiation. Sometimes we use gestures to let the speaker know that we are interested and to encourage him to continue. Nodding, smiling, gesturing with an upturned hand to signal "go on" and muttering a soft "uh-huh" are indications—in Western culture—of interest and approval. By contrast, a listener signals her disapproval of the message when she frowns, scowls, rolls her eyes, or holds up a hand vertically as if to "stop" the speaker. Or, she may be fidgeting in her chair, indicating that she might be impatient with the process and wants to leave. Be careful about how you interpret these gestures, however. For example, while the hand signal for OK (thumb and forefinger joined in a circle with the remaining fingers extended) may seem like a clear agreement (e.g., "sounds good to me"), the same gesture to a French person reads "that proposal is a zero." Similarly, a male negotiator meeting his female counterpart for the first time may opt to soften his handshake grip so as to demonstrate his respect to a woman. She might interpret his soft grip as a lack of confidence or comfort with the situation.

Many workplaces are comprised of people from multiple countries. Just because the negotiation occurs between representatives from two firms (or neighborhoods) located in the same town doesn't guarantee that gestures used will be interpreted in the same way. Be aware of these conscious differences, as well as any unconscious gestures you use. A trusted co-worker can provide you with feedback your nonverbal behaviors or habits that might present a potential problem in the negotiation.

The physical distance we keep while communicating and even how we seat ourselves in a negotiation are additional dimensions of nonverbal communication in negotiation. **Proxemics** is the study of what you communicate by the way you use interpersonal space. According to anthropologist Edward T. Hall, we unconsciously use different distances or zones to communicate and interact with others.[22] You may notice

FIGURE 7.4   How does where you sit affect communication in negotiation?

Typically, when negotiators enter the negotiating room, the two parties tend to sit across from one another at the table, literally taking sides. With one side positioned against the other, and with a physical barrier between them, it's no wonder that negotiations are seen as opportunities to compete and win. The Japanese take a different approach. They prefer to have all the negotiators sit along the same side of the table, and they tackle the problem together. It's the negotiators against the problem, and not one party against the other.

 If this doesn't seem like something you can implement at your next negotiation, try to at least alternate the parties, for example:

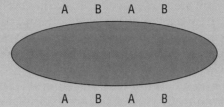

Doing so will increase the likelihood of parties seeing themselves as working with as opposed to against one another.

that when talking to a close friend, you stand very near—perhaps a foot or less away. Conversely, when you go to the beach, you are more likely to look for a spot that is at least 10 feet from the next occupied space. How closely we stand to others with whom we communicate has a powerful effect on how we regard others and how we respond to them. (See Figure 7.4.) For example, Americans prefer a "safe zone" when interacting with others, a space of a couple of feet or more. By contrast, many people in Latin American countries stand quite close and often touch those with whom they speak—in personal and even professional conversations.

 In Chapter 6, we provided an instrument that enables you to discern your dominant style of communication. We also discussed how important it is to communicate clearly and assertively. What happens when you don't? Can you recover from such a situation? Better still, we recommend that once you realize how important it is to communicate clearly and assertively, you identify, practice, and increase your comfort using appropriate behaviors and strategies.

 Consider the following scenario, which is a wife's attempt to negotiate not attending her husband's company's annual picnic later that day:

WIFE (IRONING A DRESS WHILE LOOKING
        IN HER HUSBAND'S DIRECTION):   "Do we *have* to go to the picnic?"

HUSBAND (NOT LOSING EYE CONTACT
        WITH THE LIVE BROADCAST OF
        A BALL GAME IN ACTION):   "Yup."

Let's analyze what went wrong by examining the factors that contributed to this failed negotiation. We will begin with the sender, the wife, and the history leading up to this occasion. Remember, this is an annual company picnic. For how many years has the wife not enjoyed accompanying her husband at this event? Why? Did something happen at the first one that made her uncomfortable or unhappy? If so, did she say anything to her husband? Probably not. And so, the wife's choice to say nothing—essentially saying that she had no issues with the picnic—set a pattern in motion: each year the date is set and they attend.

 The next key sender error is indirectness. Reading between the lines, it's clear that she didn't want to go to the picnic. Then why didn't she say so? Perhaps she was afraid of how her husband might respond, so she took the subtle or passive approach. Worse still, she asked a closed question and received a one-word answer, effectively ending the conversation. Remember, in negotiation, you don't get what you don't ask for.

She hoped to imply that she had concerns about attending the picnic; the implication was inferred as a benign query—one to which the husband quickly responded. At that point, there was little opportunity for clarifying her interests, finding common ground with his interests, and determining a mutually beneficial solution. Imagine trying to make the case for a salary increase or promotion with this approach: "Gee, boss, is this year's budget as tight as last year's?"

We're not through with her yet. Remember the dress she was ironing? What nonverbal message did that behavior send? *I'm getting ready for the picnic.* Combine that message with the indirect verbal one and you have a recipe for disaster. Similarly, don't expect to get what you want if you attempt to ask your boss for a raise or promotion, while your eyes are fixed on your feet and your posture approximates slouching or cowering. Our verbal and nonverbal messages must be congruent if we are to appear credible, and thus, persuasive.

What about the timing of her request? Have you ever approached someone whose attention you really needed but accepted that despite their eyes on the TV, newspaper, laptop or Blackberry, they heard you? Sometimes, they do. More likely, however, they were only partially (if at all) listening. If you have something important to say or ask someone, be sure that you have that person's full attention, even if that person is your boss, client, or a dignitary. Don't accept "I'm listening" when the nonverbals suggest anything but that. How can you ensure this? Start by stating what you need directly, for example, "I have something to ask that requires your full attention; is this a good time?" or "I need five minutes of your time; is now good or should I come back after lunch?" Instant gratification is desirable, but full attention is optimal, especially when you need all parties to commit fully to the request or outcome.

How did the husband rate in this exchange? He answered a question he was asked. However, as indicated by the wife's tone (i.e., the italicized *have*) in her question, she had some concerns about attending the picnic. A good negotiator (and husband) would have read into this inflection and responded along the lines of, "Hmmm, I get the sense that you're not particularly thrilled about going to the picnic. Am I right? What are your concerns?" By stating—and offering her the opportunity to validate—his perception, he keeps the conversation going, which is necessary in order for negotiating parties to find common ground. The husband may feel strongly about attending; that is his position. The wife may feel strongly about not attending; that is another position. Without uncovering the interests behind their positions—whether in professional or personal situations—it would be quite difficult to find a solution that both parties feel good about.

Points to Ponder

1. Have you ever had (or witnessed) a conversation like the one above?
2. What keeps you and others from directly stating the desired goal or outcome?
3. How does the nature of the relationship (e.g., family, friend, colleague) impact your willingness and comfort to be direct, in general, and in challenging situations in particular?
4. What actions can you take to increase the likelihood that the messages you send in a negotiation process are clearly understood?

COMMUNICATION IN VIRTUAL NEGOTIATIONS

Without a doubt, we are a wired society. Each year well over four trillion emails are sent worldwide from more than half a trillion mailboxes,[23] and the number of mailboxes worldwide is expected to increase by 138% each year.[24] As opportunities for virtual communication have increased, so too have opportunities for carrying out all or part of a negotiation. The ability to negotiate virtually—via phone, fax, email, synchronous chat and teleconferencing—brings with it benefits and challenges. One of the obvious benefits of utilizing electronic methods of communication, instead of or in concert with face-to-face methods, is the cost savings. For example, Lockheed Martin has assembled a team of engineers and designers from around the world to design and build a new stealth fighter plane to be used in military operations.[25] Imagine how having a global team meet virtually instead of face-to-face would reduce the costs of travel, lodging, and meeting space, not to mention employee time. Lockheed Martin calculated this savings. Over the course of the ten-year, $225 billion project, the company expects that meeting virtually instead of in person will save over $250 million.[26] Such benefits don't come without a cost. Reductions in communication bandwidth—varied by the particular electronic communication channel chosen—will impact both the process (e.g., norms of behavior, accuracy of communication interpretation) and outcomes of a virtual negotiation.[27]

Early research on the impact of computer-mediated communication on interaction amongst members of a virtual group suggested that anonymity and lack of social cues could incite more aggressive communication behavior.[28] However, the communication among the 500 members of an online community of ham radio enthusiasts is not easily compared with the communication among a team of employees working toward a common goal, such as the design team described above, or a team of employees negotiating the purchase of several fighter planes from said supplier. Not unlike the research on virtual teams, which is unequivocal on the importance of an initial face-to-face meeting to build trust critical to the success of a team,[29] research on interacting negotiating parties suggests that personal rapport is more easily developed in face-to-face communication than with other channels.[30] In addition, because it is easier to hide behind one's computer, parties in face-to-face negotiations are more likely to disclose information truthfully.[31] Because building rapport and trust is so important to the success of negotiations, parties about to engage in a virtual negotiation should insist on an initial face-to-face meeting, or failing that, a teleconference or videoconference meeting. Doing so helps improve trust, cooperation, and optimism about negotiating a resolution now and in the future among the parties.[32]

In addition, once the negotiation moves from face-to-face to virtual channels, the parties benefit from the ability to take the time to gather necessary data and think through their responses, unlike the irresistible urge to respond immediately in a face-to-face negotiation to avoid silence.[33] While the asynchronicity of communication likely lengthens the time that elapses over the course of a negotiation, the quality and quantity of information shared appears to be greater in a virtual setting.[34] Communicating virtually reduces the impact of nonverbal behavior, which can be an advantage as well as a disadvantage. Virtual negotiators may miss the inflection and emphasis that comes from tone and gestures; however, this can be helpful when one party perceives power differences or maintains a bias against some observable characteristic of the other party. One example is the case of divorced parents who were finally able to communicate effectively via teleconference because the mother was no longer intimidated by the father's nonverbal cues.[35]

Interestingly, the increase in popularity of virtual negotiations has spawned an industry designed to provide access to dispute resolution processes in an online environment, called ODR or online dispute resolution. While these tools are established by and typically staff professionally trained resolution experts, some can be used or modified for use by parties attempting to negotiate virtually without a third party. The platforms available, such as electroniccourthouse.com, smartsettle.com, and resolvemydispute.com[36] comprise synchronous (e.g., live chat) and asynchronous communication (e.g., posting a document that can be modified by all parties, streaming a video of a witness's testimony).

When negotiating virtually, remember that while some of these channels can be extremely fast, accurate, and efficient, they still require judgment, discretion, and "people skills" to be used correctly. One of the first rules of using electronic communication in negotiation is to "remember the human." Do not lose sight that on the other end of the quick response to an email is another human being who will interpret the message.[37] Our online actions and messages affect people.[38] Following this advice, along with that in Figure 7.5, will help you succeed in negotiations that occur in—or are augmented by—electronic means.

FIGURE 7.5 **Top Ten Rules for Virtual Negotiations**

1. Try to meet face-to-face at least once before or early in the negotiation.
2. Clarify the process or procedure to be followed in the negotiation.
3. Ensure everyone is introduced and their roles are clarified.
4. Select the communication channel that is most likely to facilitate achieving full consideration of information offered and needed by all parties.
5. Don't use computer jargon, acronyms, or emoticons that may not be universally understood.
6. Ensure everyone has a turn and speak up if someone is being left out.
7. Check assumptions and ask questions about what is and isn't said (i.e., nonverbal communication such as gestures, inflection, tone, and the use of silence).
8. In an email or synchronous chat-based negotiation, carefully review any real or implied promises . . . particularly those that cannot be kept, because everything that is communicated is retained.
9. When face-to-face communication is limited, the temptation to engage in unethical behavior may increase. Be wary of this.
10. As with any new tool, your comfort and ability using it may be limited at first. Realize this, and allow yourself more time (and patience) with the process and your role in it.

Summary

Communication is the backbone of negotiation. As such, it is imperative that we communicate effectively, which sounds simple but is far more complex. Effective communication involves encoding messages that are likely to be interpreted as intended, choosing a channel most appropriate for transmitting the messages, listening actively to both verbal and nonverbal messages, and asking for feedback to ensure the message is received accurately. In the negotiation process, our goal is to find common ground and collaboratively seek one or more solutions that will maximize the value and satisfaction received by both parties. Without effective communication, it will be difficult to achieve this goal. In this chapter, we explored barriers to effective communication, the importance of listening and nonverbal communication in negotiation, and discussed the impact of electronic and computer-mediated communication on negotiations. The better the communicator you are, the better the negotiator you will be.

Summary: The Big Picture

Communication process	Shows the steps, media, and potential interference inherent when a sender encodes and a receiver decodes messages.
Barriers to communication	There are sender, receiver, and environmental barriers to the communication process.
Listening behavior	Three types or levels include passive, attentive, and the one requiring the most energy and attention—active or empathic listening. Active listening is crucial for effective negotiations for a variety of reasons.
Nonverbal behavior	Messages conveyed beyond the actual words, this includes voice tone/inflection, body language and gestures, posture, and proxemics (use of interpersonal space).
Virtual communications in negotiation	This involves the use of electronic or computer-mediated communication to carry out the negotiation process. Although time and money are saved when negotiating virtually, there are several challenges to overcome.

Key Terms and Concepts

Active/empathetic listening When the listener not only hears and reacts to the words being spoken but also paraphrases, clarifies, and gives feedback to the speaker about the messages being received.

Attentive listening When the listener is genuinely interested in the speaker's point of view and makes assumptions about the messages and fills in gaps with assumptions based on what the listener wants to hear rather than on what the speaker is actually saying.

Communication channel The method or medium used to convey a message.

Decode   To interpret a message according to your perceptions, experiences, and abilities.

Encode   To put thoughts into a message according to your own perceptions, experiences, and abilities.

Information overload   When the volume of information a person receives exceeds his capacity to process it.

Listening   A critical component of the negotiation process that goes beyond merely hearing what another person is saying to constructing meaning from all the verbal and nonverbal signals the speaker is sending.

Noise   Any distortion factor that blocks, disrupts, or distorts the message sent to the receiver, interfering with the communication process.

Nonverbal communication   Any means of conveying information to another that does not involve the use of words.

Passive listening   When the listener acts as a sponge, taking in the information with no or little attempt to process or enhance the message(s) being sent by the speaker.

Virtual negotiation   Any negotiation that occurs via phone, fax, email, synchronous chat, or teleconferencing.

Discussion Questions

1. Describe the communication process in negotiation.
2. Evaluate the impact of the barriers to communication on negotiation.
3. Describe the types of listening and how you might improve your listening skills.
4. Discuss the importance of nonverbal communication in negotiation.
5. Discuss the challenges involved in virtual negotiation.

Ethical Dilemma: A Change for the Better?

Margaret and her husband, Rupert, both in their mid-sixties, have been working with Anil, their investment counselor, for the last ten years. Recently, Rupert was diagnosed with Alzheimer's disease. At the moment, he is lucid more often than not, but the doctors suggest that within a few months, things will take a turn for the worse.

Concerned about how Rupert's condition will impact their financial situation in the short term (e.g., additional co-pays, out-of-pocket expenses) as well as the growing (and sad) likelihood that Margaret will have to deal with more (and soon all) of the financial duties relating to their estate, Margaret makes an appointment to see Anil. She shares with him the situation, and tells Anil that some changes need to be made in their portfolio. Anil asks Margaret a few questions, but becomes convinced that she is overreacting, and that he needs to keep things the way they've been to maximize her returns. Anil explains his logic, and Margaret—not accustomed to playing a key role in such discussions—hesitatingly agrees.

However, after pondering her conversation with Anil and chatting with a few friends, Margaret has second thoughts. She calls and leaves a message for Anil. Hours later, there is no response, so Margaret calls again, and transfers to the operator. She asks to speak to Anil's manager, Melinda. Melinda offers to have Margaret work with a different investment counselor, but now Margaret feels bad; after all, as far as she knows, Anil has performed well to this point. But Margaret can't help but think that Anil really didn't listen to her. Now Margaret doesn't know what to do . . .

Questions

1. What issues are at play in this situation?
2. How effectively did Margaret communicate in this scenario? Explain.
3. How effectively did Anil communicate in this scenario? Explain.
4. What would you do if you were Melinda? Why?
5. What would you do if you were Margaret? Why?
6. What would you do if you were Anil? Why?

Endnotes

1. Mehrabian, A., and M. Weiner. "Decoding of Inconsistent Communication." *Journal of Personality and Social Psychology* (1967): 109.
2. Jackman, J. M. "Fear of Feedback." *Harvard Business Review* (2003): 54–63.
3. Sproull, L., and S. Kiesler "Computers, Networks, and Work." *Scientific American* 265(3) (1999): 116–123.
4. Croson, R. T. A. "Look At Me When You Say That: An Electronic Negotiation Simulation." *Simulation & Gaming* 30 (1999): 23–37.
5. Thomas, G. F., and C. L. King. "Reconceptualizing E-Mail Overload." *Journal of Business and Technical Communication* 20(3) (2006): 255.
6. O'Conner, K. M. "Motives and Cognitions in Negotiation: A Theoretical Integration and an Empirical Test." *International Journal of Conflict Management* 8 (1997): 114–131.
7. Kelly, D. "Using Vision to Improve Organisational Communication." *Leadership & Organization Development Journal* 21(1/2) (2000): 93.

8. Mehrabian, A., and M. Weiner. "Decoding of Inconsistent Communication." *Journal of Personality and Social Psychology* (1967): 109.

9. Kaye, S. "Attitude Adjustments." *Quality Progress* 32(3) (1999): 30.

10. Drollinger, T., L. B. Comer, and P. T. Warrington. "Development and Validation of the Active Empathetic Listening Scale." *Psychology & Marketing* 23(2) (2006): 160–164.

11. Robbins, S., and P. Hunsaker. *Training in Interpersonal Skills.* Upper Saddle River, NJ: Prentice Hall, 2005.

12. Covey, S. R. *Seven Habits of Highly Effective People.* New York: Simon and Schuster, 2004.

13. Tung, R. L. "American Expatriates Abroad: From Neophytes to Cosmopolitans," *Journal of World Business* Summer (1998): 124–144.

14. Kinicki, A. and R. Kreitner. *Organizational Behavior: Key Concepts, Skills and Best Practices* (2nd ed.). Burr Ridge, IL: McGraw-Hill/Irwin, 2006.

15. Fatt, J. P. T. "Nonverbal Communication and Business Success." *Management Research News* 21(4/5) (1998): p. 7; and Mehrabian A., and Weiner, M. "Decoding of Inconsistent Communication." *Journal of Personality and Social Psychology* (June 1967): 109.

16. Puccinelli, N. M., L. Tickle-Degnan, and R. Rosenthal. "Effect of Dyadic Context on Judgments of Rapport: Dyad Task and Partner Presence." *Journal of Nonverbal Behavior* 27 (2003): 211–236.

17. Bowden, M. *Winning Body Language.* Burr Ridge, IL: McGraw Hill, 2010.

18. Burgoon, J. K., D. A. Coker, and R. A. Coker. "Communication of Gaze Behavior: A Test of Two Contrasting Explanations." *Human Communication Research* 12 (1986): 495–524 and Kellerman, J. L., J. Lewis, and J. D. Laird. Looking and Loving: The Effects of Mutual Gaze on Feelings of Romantic Love. *Journal of Research in Personality* 23 (1989): 145–161.

19. Lewicki, R. J., B. Barry, and D. M. Saunders. *Negotiation,* (6th ed.). Burr Ridge, IL: McGraw Hill/Irwin, 2010, p. 171.

20. Bowden, M. *Winning Body Language.* McGraw Hill, 2010.

21. Ibid.

22. Hall, E. T. *The Hidden Dimension.* New York: Doubleday, 1990.

23. Sussan, A. P., and A. Recascino. "The Impact of E-Mail Utilization on Job Satisfaction: The Case of Multi Locations." *The Business Review* 6(10) (2006): 25.

24. Hewitt, P. "Electronic Mail and Internal Communication: A Three-Factor Model," *Corporate Communications* 11(1) (2006): 79.

25. Robbins, S. P., and T. A. Judge. *Essentials of Organizational Behavior* (9th ed.). Upper Saddle River, NJ: Pearson Prentice Hall, 2008, p. 145.

26. S. Crock, "Collaboration: Lockheed Martin," *BusinessWeek* (November 24), 2003, p. 85.

27. Bazerman, M. H., J. R. Curhan, D. A. Moore, and K. L. Valley. "Negotiation." *Annual Review of Psychology,* 51 (2000): 279–314.; and Lewicki, R. J. and B. R. Dineen. "Negotiating in Virtual Organizations. In Heneman, R. & Greenberger, D. (Eds.), *Human Resources Management in Virtual Organizations.* New York, John Wiley and Sons, 2002.

28. Sproull and Kiesler, 1986.

29. For a review, see Martins, L. L., L. L. Gilson, and M. T. Maynard. "Virtual Teams: What Do We Know and Where Do We Go from Here?" *Journal of Management* 30(6) (2004): 805–835.

30. Drolet, A. L. and M. W. Morris. "Rapport in Conflict Resolution: Accounting for How Face-to-Face Contact Fosters Mutual Cooperation in Mixed-Motive Conflicts. *Journal of Experimental Social Psychology,* 36 (2002), 26–50.

31. Valley, K. L., J. Moag, and M. H. Bazerman. "A Matter of Trust: Effects of Communication on the Efficiency and Distribution of Outcomes." *Journal of Economic Behavior and Organization,* 34 (1998) pp. 237–247.

32. Morris, M., J. Nadler, T. Kurtzberg, and L. Thompson. "Schmooze or Lose : Social Friction and Lubrication in E-mail Negotiations." *Group Dynamics-Theory Research and Practice,* 6 (2000), pp. 89–100.

33. Coltri, L. *Alternative Dispute Resolution: A Conflict Diagnosis Approach.* Upper Saddle River, NJ, Prentice Hall, 2010, p. 223.

34. Coltri, 2010, p. 223.

35. Springer, 1991, as quoted in Coltri, 2010, p. 223

36. Coltri, 2010, p. 221.

37. Sturges, P. "Remember the Human: The First Rule of Netiquette, Librarians and the Internet." *Online Information Review* 26(3) (2002): 209.

38. See Richard Gan Kon Guan et al. "The Impact of the Internet on the Managers' Working Life." *Singapore Management Review* 24(2) (2002): 77, and Spinks et al. "Netiquette." p. 145.

39. Exercise is adapted from Laurie Coltri, 2010, p. 53.

40. This case study was contributed by Kristine L. Krueger, Ph.D., Manager, Training & Support Services, Duke University Health System, July 2007.

41. Exercise is adapted from Kinicki, A., and R. Kreitner. *Organizational Behavior: Key Concepts, Skills and Best Practices* (2nd ed.). Burr Ridge, IL: McGraw-Hill/Irwin, 2006, p. 290.

42. Kinicki, A. *Organizational Behavior: Core Concepts.* Burr Ridge, IL: McGraw Hill, 2007, p. 133

43. Adapted from de Janasz, S., Dowd, K. and Schneider, B. *Interpersonal Skills in Organizations* (3rd. ed.). Burr Ridge, IL, McGraw Hill, 2009.

Exercise 7.1   Checking Perceptions[39]

Part A: Imagine yourself in the following situation:

You are driving north on the highway. You enter an intersection at a green light to turn left. You wait, since there are oncoming cars. The light turns yellow, then red, and you start your left turn to clear the intersection . . . but the oncoming car fails to stop at the red light. It comes right for you; thanks to your quick reflexes, you manage to miss colliding with the car by a few inches.

Do not read part B yet. Instead, use the lines below to jot down your attitudes and feelings about the driver of the car who nearly hit you.

Part B: Read the following paragraph which describes what is going on in the mind of the driver of the car that nearly hit you.

I am driving home from the hospital. Three days ago, my fiancé of three years and I were coming back from our wedding rehearsal dinner with our families. We are deeply religious and do not drink. On the way home, our car was struck by a drunk driver. The car hit us on the driver's side. I was shaken but not seriously hurt. My fiancé, however, was thrown against the windshield. While the doctors seem to have repaired his broken tibia and bandaged up the surface wounds effectively, they do not know why he hasn't regained consciousness. He breathes through a tube and is fed through an IV. I am by his side nearly every moment . . . talking with him and telling him how much I love him. But this morning, the doctors said that the latest MRI looked bad and that his chances of ever waking up are increasingly slim. I am in shock. He is the love of my life, and without him, I have no life.

In the lines below, describe how, if at all, this new information has revised your views about what caused the driver to nearly hit you. Does this new information change the way you think about the person?

Finally, what conclusions do you draw about the impact of perceptions—accurate and inaccurate—on how you interpret the words and actions of others during a negotiation process? What can you do to manage your own words and behavior in response to your perceptions of others?

Exercise 7.2   Out of Sight, Out of Mind: An Active Listening Role Play

You are a department manager of a software development firm. This morning, you received from a group of your subordinates (three programmers and an administrative assistant) a formal suggestion regarding the adoption of telecommuting in your department. While the idea has merit, and is in line with the organization's vision of being "green," you're concerned about your department's ability to achieve its goals, maintain its customer relationships, and move forward on new projects if your employees have different schedules. Furthermore, the logistics and planning required to keep track of the employees will put a strain on your already overworked secretary. In short, you don't know what to do . . .

The roles: (your instructor will distribute these)

Group of four employees, represented by Tashi Yakimoto, the senior programmer of the group

The department manager

An observer (possibly the department secretary)

All role players should take a few moments to prepare the critical elements of their arguments to increase their ability to be persuasive. In addition, the role players should identify their goals and interests, make an educated guess about the goals and interests of the other party, and brainstorm potential solutions that will meet the needs of both parties. The observer should observe the conversation, take notes using the observation grid below, and be ready to provide his or her findings.

Observation Grid:

How well did the parties:	Group of employees (list examples of what you heard or said during the role play)	Department Manager (list examples of what you heard or said during the role play)
paraphrase or summarize the other party's arguments?		
utilize nonverbal gestures that demonstrate listening (e.g., leaned in, nodded head, muttered "uh-huh")?		
utilize eye contact as a way to communicate interest, sincerity, etc.?		
refrain from interrupting the other party?		
provide potential solutions that incorporate both parties' interests?		
ask clarifying questions to ensure the message sent was understood?		
provide feedback to demonstrate that the message was received as intended?		

Exercise 7.3   Customer Service . . . At What Price?

You work at the customer service desk of a home improvement store (e.g., Lowes or Home Depot) in your suburban town. It's mid-September and in walks a man who firmly but politely presents his receipt and insists on returning the barbecue he bought in mid-June for a full refund. He explains that "it doesn't work as well as it should." For your part, it's clear that this man bought the barbecue to enjoy summertime grilling, and now that the summer is over, he no longer needs the barbecue—at least until next summer. Your company's return policy is to take back any product within 90 days of purchase with a receipt and within one year if the product is defective. It's been exactly 90 days (according to the store computer), and by the look of the barbecue, it's been used a fair amount during the last three months.

On the one hand, you think this man's request is unethical. Sure, the policy suggests that you take back the barbecue and refund the customer nearly $300. But refunding this money would give the customer "permission" to buy a snowblower in a few months and return it within 90 days, and on and on. And, what if he shares his strategy with friends and neighbors? Profit margins at the store are more squeezed than ever.

Questions

1. What is your immediate reaction to the scenario? How does your perception of the customer and his actions influence how you interpret this situation and its relation to the store policy?
2. Given your reaction to the situation, what is your goal in the message you will convey to the customer in response to his request? Exactly what would you say to him, and how does it serve the goal?
3. As an employee, would you get anyone else involved in this situation? Why or why not?
4. How could this situation have been avoided?

Exercise 7.4   What about Bob?[40]

You are leading a meeting whose purpose is to decide whether or not your company should bid for a new piece of business. All the right people are there and are prepared to contribute. You have introduced the participants and have discussed why each of them is at the meeting. You have reviewed the agenda, established operating guidelines, and are leading a discussion of the first agenda item, which is how the new piece of business could fit into the company's strategic plan. You notice that Bob, the Director of Sales, is not making eye contact with anyone, is occasionally drawing stick figures on his note paper, and just softly commented "Who cares how this fits our strategy; our strategy is completely off the mark." You look at your watch. Of the time you have allocated for this discussion, there are three minutes remaining for this agenda item.

Questions

1. What is your interpretation of Bob's nonverbal and verbal communication? Explain.
2. If you were the speaker and meeting leader, what can you say to Bob to check your interpretation? If your interpretation is accurate, what would you say or do next and why, given the time constraint?
3. What could have been done before or at the start of the meeting to ensure that all the participants are on the same page? Why would this strategy or approach be effective (or not) in your view?

Exercise 7.5   Responding with Empathy

Rico is a newly minted MBA. Upon graduation from Yale, Rico received several offers (including signing bonuses!) from top consulting firms. He chose to stay in Connecticut, accepting a position from a smaller, boutique consulting firm in Stamford—partly because he'd heard that in the big four firms, it would take at least a year before Rico would be able to work directly with the client as opposed to functioning as one of several analysts on a consulting team. At Townsend and Associates, where Rico replaced a consultant who just retired, he was given three clients for whom he was lead consultant, as well as being asked to serve on two other project teams for larger, long-standing projects.

From his first few months at Townsend, Rico impressed management with his business acumen and no-nonsense attitude. The work got done, the clients were pleased, and word of mouth was picking up steam. However, some of his co-workers—teammates on project teams—are beginning to resent Rico's competitive nature. His high standards—for himself and his teammates—has contributed to some members feeling like Rico is something of a drill sergeant. On Friday, Rico read Lester the riot act for coming late to the meeting. Lester said nothing at the moment, but after the meeting ended, he walked into Rico's office and said:

> Why are you giving me such a hard time about being five minutes late for our team meeting? Give me a break! You know that I have responsibilities at home and it is hard for me to get here on time. I'm 40 and I have a wife and two small sons at home. Do you have to deal with sick kids? Do you have to arrange an emergency babysitter so you can get to class on time? Do you have to fight traffic to get here after working a full day? You would be much more understanding if you weren't just a kid with no responsibilities!

Questions

1. If you were Rico, what would be the goal of your response to Lester's complaint?
2. How would you word your response to meet this goal? Explain.
3. Because you are teammates, you will need to show empathy and trust. Further damage to your relationship with Lester will not only impact his productivity, but that of the team as well. In what ways does your response in #2 communicate empathy and trust? Explain.

Exercise 7.6   To Email or Not to Email . . . That Is the Question

Remember Sadie and Olivia from the opening scenario? Well, Sadie was still fuming when she got home from work after being scolded by Olivia. She was so upset, she couldn't concentrate on making dinner, and decided to check her email and Facebook instead. After about 15 minutes, she noticed that Olivia posted a picture on a mutual friend's Facebook profile. Sadie saw this and thought to herself, "I need to let her know how I feel. We're peers . . . she's not my mother and doesn't get to scold me." So she begins a note that she plans to upload to Olivia's Facebook inbox:

> Dear Olivia:
>
> We've been friends for some time now, but to be honest, I'm not feeling too friendly about our conversation earlier today. OK, I admit I didn't fulfill my promise of sending an advance copy of the workshop plan to the manager before our workshop, but it went really well! But you didn't have to scold me as if I were a small child! I mean, YOU'RE NOT MY BOSS. We are friends and co-workers, and there are other ways that we could have discussed what happened. I think you owe me an apology. Until that happens, I'm not sure I'll be able to team up with you in a way that represents our department in the most positive light. In fact, at the moment, I'm having trouble just thinking about working together on future projects when all I see when I look at you is the face of my mother.
>
> Fondly,
> Sadie

Questions

1. Evaluate Sadie's response.
   a. What is effective about this response, and why?
   b. In what ways is it ineffective?
   c. What do you think the outcome will be?
2. Would you send Olivia an email if you were in Sadie's shoes? Why or why not?
3. If you were to choose the same medium as Sadie, how would you rewrite the letter? Or, if you were to choose a different medium for your message, what would your message include and how would you send it?

Exercise 7.7   My Way or the Highway[41]

Hasso Plattner, cofounder and chairman of the German software company SAP, believes in obtaining consensus among his lieutenants; however, his method for doing so irritates people along the way. His confrontational style is deliberate. Wolfgang Kenna, CEO of SAP America, notes that Plattner "creates stressful situations. He fuels the discussions with provocative statements. Sometimes he's rigid, even rude. But it's about getting people engaged so they can be creative."

What do you think?

1. Does an aggressive, confrontational style of communication facilitate creativity? Why or why not? Are there some environments or situations in which this style is effective?
2. What impact does this style likely have on Plattner's lieutenants' willingness and ability to negotiate changes in the workplace? Explain.
3. If you were to approach Plattner about a change in internal work processes, such as how work gets done, or decisions get made, how would you prepare for such a negotiation? What would you say or do to start the conversation? How would you like to end it? What other communication strategies would you utilize to facilitate the desired changes?

CHAPTER 8

The Role and Importance of Persuasion in Negotiation

Chapter Objectives

After studying this chapter and completing the exercises you should be able to:

- Define persuasion and contrast that with manipulation, coercion, and threats.

- Identify and discuss six steps that can be used—separately or in combination—in persuasion efforts.

- Identify options for strengthening your credibility and thus your ability to persuade.

- Discuss and compare three theoretical frameworks that underpin persuasion, including cognitive dissonance theory, inoculation theory, and the ACE Theory.

- Compare various strategies and tactics for persuading others to adopt a point of view or behavior different from current views or behaviors.

- Evaluate a variety of persuasion situations that raise ethical concerns and discuss approaches for avoiding or resolving these situations.

About 2,300 years ago, Aristotle defined persuasion as the *ability* to convince others to adopt your ideas. More specifically, he wrote that to be persuasive, you have to "win over minds with logic, win over hearts with emotion, and manage yourself." His ideas are just as if not even more relevant in today's business environment. Managers, as well as employees who lack positional authority, are tasked with getting work done with and by others who expect to be treated with respect and involved in decisions that affect them. Persuasion does not involve commanding others to do what you want. Instead, it involves presenting information and engaging in a process of dialogue with the ultimate goal of others adopting the behavior, belief, or attitude you desire. In so doing, employees, teammates, and loved ones cooperate with an effective persuader because they want to, not because they have to.

Chapter Scenario

When she was hired, Monica accepted a salary that was 5% lower than that in her previous job. She rationalized accepting a lower salary for two reasons. First, the twenty-minute commute was about half that of her previous job, saving her time and money. Second, her boss told her that in ninety days, her performance would be evaluated and "an adjustment to her salary would be made." Over the last four months, Monica's performance has been excellent. Even her boss has told her so . . . on several occasions. The problem is that it's been more than a month past the promised performance evaluation and Monica has yet to sit down with her boss beyond a couple minutes here and there. He's been traveling quite a bit, and under great pressure to "make the numbers," especially since the company's recent acquisition by a larger firm. Monica knows she deserves that salary adjustment, and has gently—and sometimes, jokingly—reminded her boss of his promise. Unfortunately, it seems like everything else has a higher priority for him. Monica fears that the more time that passes, the greater inequity and unmotivated she will feel about working for less than she's worth. The time never seems to be right, as all her hints and reminders go unheeded. What can Monica do to get her boss to act and make good on his promise?

A form of influence, **persuasion** involves careful preparation and proper presentation of arguments and supporting evidence in an appropriate and compelling emotional climate.[1] By doing so, your goal is for the persuadee to choose to adopt this new behavior or belief. Notice that there's a choice. Persuasion is something you do *with* another and not *to* another.[2] For persuasion to be truly effective, it must not rely on deceit, force, manipulation, or coercion as these tactics remove the persuadee's choice and could lead to several undesirable effects, which we'll discuss later.

More recently, in his work on emotional intelligence, Daniel Goleman tells us that leaders are most effective in persuading others to buy into their ideas when they are democratic in their approach and show that they respect and care about others' beliefs and needs, regardless of their position or status.[3] Put simply, by helping others achieve their goals, we can achieve our own.

Points to Ponder

1. Is it really possible to get what we want by first focusing on helping others achieve what they want?
2. Aside from her boss being busy and occasionally absent, what might explain Monica's lack of persuasion success so far?
3. Have you been in a situation similar to the one in the opening scenario? How did you resolve the situation?
4. How can you get a peer or even superior to do something for or with you when your organizational position doesn't provide the authority to do so?

PERSUASION CAN BE POWERFUL

This idea may make sense on a conceptual level, but in practice, getting others to willingly buy into your ideas because you help them achieve *their* goals is harder than it looks. Typically, we decide what we want and then work hard trying to convince others to give it to us, sometimes digging in our heels and achieving more frustration than success. Instead, if you take the counterintuitive path and approach your goal by first figuring out what the other party wants—what makes him or her tick—then you can present your point in a way that helps others achieve what they want while simultaneously getting what you want. Some time ago, I was sitting in the office of a car salesman purchasing a new vehicle. A newly minted MBA at the time, I knew what I wanted to pay, and I wasn't prepared to pay more than that (especially given the mountain of student debt I had amassed!). After haggling unsuccessfully with my salesman for about ten minutes, I paused and noticed several salesman-of-the-month awards adorning the walls of his cubicle. So I changed tactics. "I noticed that you've been salesman of the month several times in the last year. That's pretty impressive. With only a few days left in this month, I'm guessing that getting my sale will help you achieve this award again.

Is that true?" He responded affirmatively. "By giving me the car at this price, you increase your chances of receiving the award, the dealership gets credit for—and perhaps additional dealer rebates for—the sale, and I get a good car at a fair price." The sale was completed about twenty minutes later and for the price I wanted!

A PROCESS FOR EFFECTIVE PERSUASION

We all know people who have an innate ability to persuade. What makes them successful? Based on a review of research in psychology, sociology, communication, and business, we've come up with six critical steps. They are listed in Figure 8.1 and then described in detail in this chapter.

Understand Others' Motivations and Needs

In his best seller *Seven Habits of Highly Effective People,* Stephen Covey tells us that if we want others to listen to us, we must first listen to them.[4] When two people disagree, the typical response is "I disagree. Let me tell you why and you'll see why my way is better." How would you respond to such a statement? If you're like most, you would listen—but minimally. Your attention is less on what the speaker is saying and more on how you'll rebut his argument. What if, instead, someone said to you, "We disagree. Tell me again why you think your approach will work . . ." In this situation, you are given the floor and an open invitation to share your views. Assuming the speaker demonstrates that he has truly heard and understood the views you shared, your natural inclination would be to respond in kind, e.g., "Why don't you tell me why you think your approach will work?" By giving space for and really listening to what the persuadee wants or needs, you will be better equipped to frame what you want in those terms.

To really understand others' needs, you need several skills:

Listen actively—To not only the specific words said but also the feelings behind them. In other words, try to stand in the speaker's shoes to truly understand what is being communicated. To do this, you'll need to pay close attention to the speaker's verbal and nonverbal communication (e.g., tone, inflection, gestures). Someone who offers a meek "okay" but doesn't make eye contact with you is likely not to fully support the proposal under discussion. Accepting the "okay" response may be efficient, but it will be ineffective in the long run. Along these lines is the oft-misunderstood silence. "So, we're all in agreement" may seem like a great way to check if there's consensus, but statements like these—which are leading, and do not facilitate further discussion—may result in little or no response. For the speaker who believes that silence means agreement, this result may be a welcome end to a long discussion. This leads to the necessity of the following skill.

Check for understanding—This involves sharing your perceptions and soliciting feedback. For example, "When I asked if we were all in agreement, no one spoke up. Does this mean everyone supports the proposal and will do their part? What do you think, Bob?" Directing a question to a specific person is particularly important when

FIGURE 8.1   Six Critical Steps for Effective Persuasion

- **Understand others' motivations and needs**
- **Establish credibility**
- **Frame for common ground**
- **Engage in joint problem solving**
- **Support preferred outcome with logic and reasoning**
- **Reinforce with appeal to emotions and basic instincts**

there are more than two people involved in the interaction, due to the dynamics at play in group settings. Doing so will communicate to Bob, for example, that his opinion is being specifically solicited.

Read people—Learning what makes others tick may involve direct (active) and indirect (passive) means.[5] Asking open-ended questions is a fairly direct approach, and will often bring about the information you need. You might also learn this through your interactions with and observations of this person on and off the job. How does she dress (e.g., to impress, for comfort)? How does he spend his free time? What sort of personal items (e.g., photos, knickknacks, a mug with the company logo) are in her office? How well organized is his office? Where did she go to school? No one clue will tell you everything, but the more you understand and the more you ask, the more you'll know, assuming you can maintain your objectivity when processing your observations.[6]

Establish Credibility

Imagine you are walking down a busy street and you notice a disheveled, dirty man running around proclaiming that "a spaceship has landed and aliens have come to take us away." Chances are, you'll laugh to yourself and think "what a crazy man." Because of his appearance and the words he is speaking, you will not take him seriously, as neither he nor his speech is credible. An exaggerated example, perhaps, but it is illustrative. Management guru Jay Conger believes that for persuaders to be effective, they must be perceived as credible.[7] You will be considered credible to the degree you demonstrate the following four personal characteristics: appearance, expertise, trustworthiness, and composure.[8]

> *Positive impression or appearance*—Perhaps the first thing that others notice about you is your appearance. We're not talking about attractiveness, though recent research shows that physical attractiveness can positively influence negotiation outcomes through an increase in one's referent power.[9] How we look and dress communicates how we feel about ourselves and our situation and influences how others see us. Have you ever been in court (remember that speeding ticket you tried to fight?) and noticed that the attire of those in attendance (lawyers excluded) varies widely, from crumpled, dirty, ill-fitting to clean, pressed, tailored suits? Have you also noticed that the judge is more lenient to the latter group? The plaintiff who doesn't bother to shave or wear clean, conservative clothing is telling the court that he doesn't respect himself or the judge, so why should the judge respect him? The same is true when dressing for a job interview, yet we've all heard of (or seen) examples of outlandish or inappropriate attire in those situations, usually resulting in quick, dismissive interviews. If you want to persuade others that what you have to say is important, you have to dress the part. You have to act the part as well, and this includes displaying appropriate gestures (handshake, posture) and behaviors (manners, business etiquette, remembering others' names), and may also include the possession of credentials (appropriate title, education).

While first impressions are important, so too are the sum total of your interactions with others. Others' historical impressions of you (and your reputation) can work to your advantage or disadvantage. A history of positive interactions and appropriate appearances will likely overshadow one atypical moment. In the 2007 movie "The Pursuit of Happyness," actor Will Smith plays a tenacious single father trying desperately to succeed despite the many challenges he faces. After several well-presented and groomed meetings with the HR director of a stock brokerage, Smith finally gets the interview he covets. Unfortunately, circumstances leave him showing up at the designated time wearing only a paint-splattered undershirt and pull-on pants, along with a casual zippered jacket. Knowing how bad he looks, Smith's character earnestly explains the situation in a way that evokes both humor and empathy. Because all of his previous interactions were positive and professional, the interviewers overlook the momentary lapse of credibility and offer him the job. Conversely, if your previous encounters have been negative or inconsistent, others are likely to question and search for faults in your reasoning, creating an uphill battle for your current persuasion attempt.

Expertise—To be effective, the persuader must be very knowledgeable about the subject matter (e.g., the product or service you are offering) and be able to present it in such a way that the listener(s) can be compelled to adopt the point of view being presented. You must demonstrate this knowledge by presenting appropriate information (e.g., product specifications), reliable data (e.g., independent studies, verifiable outcomes), and a passion for the subject. Do not exaggerate claims or otherwise manipulate the facts. Moreover, you must be able to respond positively and nondefensively to questions or criticism. As you've probably seen, a good salesperson will know her product, how it compares to competitors' products or services, and will also expect—and have responses for—what would be considered typical objections. The same is true for an effective persuader. One word of caution. Never invent answers when you really don't have any. When the correct answer is later revealed, the damage to the relationship may be difficult to reverse.

Trustworthiness—Trustworthiness is acquired over time through personal and professional relationships in which others perceive you—directly or through others' opinions of you, i.e., your reputation—as consistent, reliable, and conscientious. People who keep their promises, say what they mean and mean what they say, and display strong emotional and moral character tend to be seen as worthy of others' trust. They also listen without judgment or criticism. After all, such criticism may be interpreted as personal rejection and can set up a wall of defensive behavior. When you trust others, you feel comfortable disclosing your needs, as well as your fears or concerns, without worrying that this information will later be used against you. Typically, this trust is then reciprocated,[10] enabling an open, honest dialog that can facilitate the building of mutually beneficial solutions. In new relationships, trustworthiness can be demonstrated by actively and empathically listening to others, communicating directly and unambiguously (e.g., your body language is in sync with your verbal language, being humble, willing to admit you are wrong or don't have an answer), and looking out for the other's best interest. Another way to build trust is to show how you share commonalities in where you're from or what's important to you. For example, you might realize that you and the party with whom you are negotiating went to the same school (e.g., noticing the school ring or bumper sticker), grew up in the same town, or have friends or acquaintances in common. Mentioning this commonality may invoke some instant trust, as you suddenly go from stranger to fellow alumni or network member. Because people have identities with which they identify (e.g., engineer, Buckeye, single mother, Texan), the newly established link connects you with a common identity and can be helpful in building your credibility. "Surely another Texan would be honest about. . . ."

A recent study by Anderson and Shirako suggests that actual interactions are not the only means by which opinions about one's trustworthiness and cooperativeness are formed. Individuals who are socially connected—share common networks—and are talked or gossiped about have reputations that precede them.[11] Their study suggested that the reputations of such individuals are not necessarily positive; in fact, social connectedness is a double-edged sword due to its effect of increasing scrutiny on individuals' positive qualities and achievements as well as their negative qualities and failures.[12] When parties enter into a negotiation, actual and perceived (i.e., reputational) behaviors will lead to expectations of behaviors such as cooperativeness, trustworthiness, and even competitiveness and dishonesty.

Composure—When you are composed, you are solid and self-assured, even under pressure. The phrase, "Never let them see you sweat" describes the importance of composure in establishing credibility. How do you appear composed? First, you must have a plan, which means knowing what to say and when. Remember the first time you had to make an important presentation? You probably prepared note cards with key points and then practiced making your speech in front of a mirror. Even with all that preparation, you might have been nervous and lost your place or fell apart. Now imagine not having prepared at all!!! Such a situation would make even the strongest person perspire! Flying by the seat of your pants is not recommended for any important presentation, nor is it recommended when you are trying to be persuasive in a negotiation. When you have outlined what you want to say, practiced making your pitch, and feel confident enough to answer any questions, you will demonstrate that you are confident, composed, and thus, credible.

Points to Ponder

1. Does what you wear really matter that much? Have you gotten a different level of service in a store relative to how you were dressed? Why does this matter?
2. How typical is the opening scenario, where one party is being persuaded, as compared with situations where both parties engage in persuasion tactics? How would this influence your preparation?
3. In what ways can practicing an upcoming negotiation by role playing with a friend or colleague increase your credibility for the actual negotiation?

Frame for Common Ground

Once you understand what makes others tick and are able to project credibility, you need to present a framework, or a plan for how to proceed, that involves describing your position in ways that identify common ground. As we discussed in Chapter 2, framing is used in negotiation to establish a perspective or context within which negotiation goals (e.g., conflict resolution, a contract) are sought. Moreover, these frames—positive, negative, or neutral—will impact the outcome.[13] When the frame used is seen as establishing a common ground, it sets a collaborative tone and attains the following three interrelated objectives:[14]

1. It provides a perspective we would like the other party to consider. Sometimes, it's all in how we package the message. For example, if you need to introduce a new computer system to your company, you could present the technology as something new and exciting *or* something that can free up time to be spent on more important tasks. Chances are the latter approach will be more effective. Doing this successfully requires knowing what motivates the person you are trying to persuade.
2. It provides an open-minded way for alternatives and ideas to be compared and contrasted. For example, "We need a solution for this problem. I've jotted down some benefits these improvements will likely bring and a few ideas for consideration. How do you think we can arrive at a solution?" In this common ground, the speakers can unite and work together to compete against the shared problem—talking through differences—as opposed to competing against one another.
3. It creates a logical structure by which decisions can be made. This structure might also include a joint articulation of the constraints or limits within which a decision or solution must fit. Clarifying the rules up front reduces the appearance of arbitrariness and manipulation down the line (e.g., one day this, the next day that).[15] By planning and communicating a framework ahead of time, you provide a clear and fair process by which you and others can collaborate in the problem solving that follows.

Engage in Joint Problem Solving

Involving the other party in the search for a solution is one of the best ways to get him to commit to the solution. This notion is analogous to the use of empowerment in the workplace, where managers create an environment that has the potential to support the motivational power inherent in satisfying higher-level needs, like the need for self-esteem and self-actualization.[16] Rather than closely monitoring and prescribing employees' behaviors, effective managers provide increased autonomy, respect, power to make decisions, status, and freedom to grow and develop within the organization. Sharing power with, or empowering, workers helps managers address the needs of workers and results in satisfied workers.[17] In the same way, involving the persuadee in the search for solutions demonstrates that you are open to and interested in her ideas and increases the likelihood that she will fully support the solutions, which were jointly developed, compared, and contrasted. Furthermore, since two heads are better than one, collaborating may result in the development of new and different ideas, which when considered collectively, may bring about a more innovative and mutually beneficial solution than either party had previously conceived prior to the discussion.

Not all persuasion attempts come with the opportunity to create an entirely new solution. However, involvement can come in other forms. Even something as small as having the purchaser complete all or part of her own order or sales agreement can increase her commitment to complete the sale. Putting your commitment on a piece of paper ups the ante as most will do what they've agreed in writing to do. This public commitment/consistency principle has been applied successfully in the goal-setting arena, and has been shown to be especially effective when used with people with a high level of pride or public self-consciousness.[18]

Support Preferred Outcome with Logic and Reasoning

Presenting compelling evidence is extremely effective as a persuasion technique. Do you remember being told by a parent to do something and when you asked why, you got, "Because I said so?" Chances are that answer didn't sit well with you. While there are situations where people in powerful positions (a parent or boss) can use their power to make others comply, this may amount to coercion, and result in minimal (if any) commitment to the desired outcome. In fact, a study of the effectiveness of various influence behaviors across multiple cultures cites rational persuasion—the use of logic—as the most effective form of influence across all cultures tested and pressure tactics (consisting of demands and threats—which constitute coercion) as the least effective type of influence across all cultures.[19] Or perhaps, you may have been swayed by a significant other's impassioned plea (and accompanying tears). While emotion can facilitate influence, in most situations, it should not be your primary mechanism; instead, consider relying on facts and data to get your audience to support your argument.[20] Do your homework, and be ready to share illustrative charts or graphs and identify the sources for your data; others might ask. Any errors in your reasoning can give the listener reason to doubt you and your credibility.[21] This does not imply that you must say everything you know about the subject. Rather, select the information that you believe will have the greatest impact on your audience. For most people, this information will include a compelling and logically supported review of the projected benefits the persuadee can expect to receive by adopting the preferred view.

Points to Ponder

1. Can your persuasion attempt be too logical? In other words, can your pitch seem too good to be true?
2. While data (e.g., in charts, tables, graphs) can help persuade your audience, it can also hurt your case. How?
3. What is logical to one person may not be to another. How can you improve the likelihood that your arguments are deemed logical?

Reinforce with an Appeal to Emotions and Basic Instincts

While logic is essential, so too is appealing to people's feelings, fears, values, dreams, frustrations, egos, vanities, or desires.[22] Many charismatic leaders, such as John F. Kennedy, Martin Luther King, Jr., and Mother Teresa, inspired others to support or join their cause not only because of its importance, but also because of their contagious passion and conviction to the cause. By engaging yourself and your audience in the subject matter, everyone is vested in working together to find solutions to the problem at hand. In essence, by appealing to others' emotions, you can inspire them to "join the crusade."

Sociologist and scholar Robert Cialdini has written extensively on influence. In his book *Influence*, Cialdini talks about certain triggers that evoke an automatic response in humans. These "click-whirr" responses are instinctual shortcuts that save us time and effort when we need to make decisions.[23] By communicating and behaving in ways that trigger a "yes" response, you will be more likely to be influential. Three of these universal forms of influence that are particularly relevant in negotiation processes are included here.

Reciprocity/obligation—In general, people want to, or feel obligated to, repay favors and kindness. If you buy me a gift, however small, I feel obligated to respond in kind, lest I seem thoughtless, cheap, or ungrateful! Moreover, when I am given something, I'm anxious to restore the balance, e.g., I don't owe you and you don't owe me. Advertisers use this principal when they give away free samples. Of course, one goal is to get consumers to try the new product. However, another is the hope that after receiving some of the product for free, you will feel obliged to purchase the next "batch." Or how about the religious groups who hand out free pencils or calendars . . . but ask for your kind donation. You haven't paid for a calendar; instead you reciprocated a gift. Consider also the packaging, for example, "buy two, get one free." Not only are we getting a good deal, we are getting something for nothing.

There are several ways to use the reciprocity/obligation rule in persuasion:

- Give information, support, concessions, even gifts, and give first. While our tendency may be to hold our cards close to the vest and keep our aces up our sleeves, sharing information freely leads to others doing the same.

- Practice giving regularly and genuinely. If you give only when you want something from someone, your request will be seen as manipulative rather than consistent with your generous spirit.

- Consider the rejection-then-retreat approach. Ask someone to agree to a more costly proposal, but be ready to present a lower cost alternative. Because he turned down your first offer, he will view your second offer as a concession, and may feel inclined to respond with a concession of his own—complying with your second request.[24] A recent comic strip illustrates this point. A man asks his wife if he could have a mistress. When she says "no," he responds with, "Would you mind if I played golf with the guys on Saturday?"

A few words of wisdom about the reciprocity rule. When giving, be careful not to respond to others' acknowledgements with phrases like "it was nothing," or "no problem." Such phrases negate your contribution and thus the reciprocity norm. Also, remember that you get what you give. If you give help, you'll get help, but if you give trouble, you'll get trouble.

Scarcity—People are more motivated to go after that which they perceive is scarce. Consider the tactics of the various home shopping networks. In addition to the "Today, and today only, we have a limited supply . . ." introduction, viewers are able to see a continuously updated counter showing how much of the item is remaining. If you watch carefully during the typical two-minute segment, you'll notice that the greatest volume is sold in the remaining thirty to forty-five seconds. This is when the buyer fears he may be shut out of this once-in-a-lifetime opportunity. While it may be tempting to use the scarcity principle to entice consumers to buy a product or service, the information must be accurate. If it is later revealed out that there was in fact no shortage, the persuadee will feel manipulated and will lose trust in the persuader.

Consensus/social proof—People often decide what to do based on what they see others doing. Why else would most drivers drive at five or ten miles over the posted speed limit on a busy freeway, even when a traffic ticket could have multiple negative consequences? Or, why would all drivers stop to view an accident, further tying up an already stalled road? Cialdini explains that we "view a behavior as correct in a given situation to the degree that we see others performing it."[25] Advertisers are aware of this and persuade us to buy their products by telling us not necessarily how good a product is, but how strongly others think so (e.g., "number one selling," or "most popular model").[26] Conversely, we see no problem with what could be considered deviant behavior if everyone does it, as is the case in a parking garage that has been littered with unwanted flyers posted to unsuspecting drivers' cars. Currently, there has been a shadow of controversy over the high-fashion modeling industry because of the use of rail-thin models. The controversy is not about thin girls and women, per se, but about the purported effect this practice has had on girls and women who, believing that they are not attractive or likable unless they too are a size 0, struggle with dangerous eating disorders. As this example shows, not all models of behavior are positive or healthy, but an effective persuader can use this notion to:

- Show the persuadee that similar others (those the persuadee would identify with) are doing what you are asking them to do.
- Show that others have benefited as a result of saying "yes" to your request.
- Share testimonials of similar others and experts.

PERSUASION CONCEPTS AND APPLICATIONS

Some of the skills and techniques of persuasion are rooted in research in traditional and cognitive psychology. Back in the 1950s, psychologist Leon Festinger coined the term "**cognitive dissonance**" to explain the tension that exists when individuals' beliefs do not align with their behaviors. The dissonance results in tension or discomfort.[27] Because of her extensive preparation, an effective persuader will be aware of this dissonance, and employ a variety of tactics[28] to help restore consonance or alignment between the persuadee's espoused values or beliefs and his behaviors or actions. To illustrate, let's say that you are recently hired by a company that touts itself as "family-friendly," a fact that weighed heavily in your decision to accept the job. Several weeks into the job, your supervisor asks you to work on a Saturday in order to get ready for an upcoming client meeting. Unfortunately, you already have plans to attend your child's school play. Your supervisor seems pretty intent on having you come in, and being new on the job, you want to make a favorable impression. However, the commitment to your child is important to you, and, as you thought and hoped, consistent with the company's philosophy. How would you persuade your supervisor to happily accept your rejection of his request to work on Saturday? We've created an exercise (Exercise 8.6) to help you develop your approach to this situation.

Another theory that underpins the concept of persuasion is **inoculation theory.** Borrowing from the medical field, McGuire suggested that in the same way individuals receive a small injection of a disease-producing substance to strengthen the body's immunity against that disease, persuaders can be effective when they anticipate the objections of the persuadee and address those objections before they arise.[29] For example, a firm could distribute information showing lower-than-expected profits prior to announcing a decreased merit pool. Other strategies for countering objections include presenting all points (for and against) and demonstrating how what's being proposed is the right solution, and broaching controversial subjects gently and early, before your audience has the chance to raise an issue that could become contentious or divisive. By raising the objections before the persuadee has a chance to, you may take the wind out of her sails and leave her without a strong argument to counter your view. Doing so also suggests that you have the persuadee's interests and needs in mind.

A more recent model of persuasion effectiveness is Reardon's **ACE Theory.** She suggests that people use three criteria to determine whether to respond to a persuader's arguments: Appropriateness, Consistency, and Effectiveness.[30] By utilizing these criteria as you plan your persuasion approach, you can increase the likelihood of achieving the desired outcome. You might use one or more of these criteria, in combination, or separately.

> *Appropriateness*—The right thing to do, based on generally accepted standards or norms, or in some cases, rules of law or morality. Appropriateness appeals are geared to the persuadee's or audience's belief system and interests.
>
> *Consistency*—The degree to which the action or belief proposed compares to that of similar others or to their own past behaviors or espoused beliefs. Appeals to consistency demonstrate that the persuader understands the beliefs or past behaviors of similar others and presents arguments that make sense or track with these beliefs or behaviors.
>
> *Effectiveness*—The degree to which an action or idea leads to a desirable state or outcome. By knowing what the persuadee or audience wants or needs, a persuader can demonstrate how adoption of the proposed idea or action will help meet those needs.

Returning to our opening scenario, Monica could use the ACE Theory as a means to persuade her boss to keep his promise of performance evaluation and salary adjustment. After arranging a time to meet with her boss, Monica might say, "Mr. Copley, when you hired me four months ago, you said that after ninety days, you would evaluate my performance. I know you've been very busy since the acquisition, but I also know you are a man of your word." (Consistency appeal). "My performance has been excellent—as you have told me so on several occasions, such as the time I found a way to save the company thousands of dollars each month by renegotiating our company car leases. The 5% raise we discussed is miniscule compared to these and other savings I've brought the company. Not only was a raise promised, but it's the right thing to do as a reward for my performance." (Appropriateness appeal). "I know that my motivation and performance will rise to an even higher level if I feel I'm being paid what we both agreed I deserve." (Effectiveness appeal). Any one of these statements might work; Monica should begin with her strongest statement and determine which, if any, others need to be included to effectively persuade her boss to evaluate and adjust accordingly.

STRATEGIES FOR EFFECTIVE PERSUASION

Persuasion is a complex two-way communication process that is most effective when the persuader has taken into consideration several elements regarding himself, the audience, and the issue or object at hand. In addition to the concepts and applications already discussed, we offer a few more strategies or tactics to use when you want to persuade others.

> *Ask for a favor*—This strategy is particularly effective when you are one-up with your persuadee. That is, you've given, and given generously, and instead of directly asking him to pay his debt, you instead ask for a favor. The favor sometimes works because it is not a command, it involves a choice on the part of the persuadee, and, in the absence of previous "gifts," your request for a favor amounts to a voucher for a return favor. A co-worker might ask, "Would you mind finishing the report tonight? I stayed late last night and got most of it done, but tonight I really need to get home by 6 p.m. because it's my wife's birthday and I promised to take her to her favorite restaurant."

Push for stereotyped response—Every language has its share of proverbs and idioms. Whether true or perceived to be true, these responses often come without a need to expend extensive cognitive energy. For example, many believe that you "get what you pay for." In short, cheaper isn't necessarily better, and the more you pay for a product (to a point), the higher its perceived quality. The word *cheap* refers to the cost as well as the quality of a product. A salesman might promise, "You can buy a cheaper version of the original, but you'll pay more in the long run when you have to replace it. Ours comes with a lifetime warranty."

Consider the effect of the context—Many people will pay more for the same or similar item depending on where they purchase it. When at a drug store or mass merchandiser, I might spend ten minutes or more comparing and debating the purchase of several brands and types of mascara, which cost between five and seven dollars. However, when shopping at the cosmetics counters of a department store, I don't think twice about plunking down fifteen to twenty dollars for a single tube of mascara. I know that a number of studies have shown these products to be of similar quality—in fact, some brand name manufacturers private label their brand for companies selling their products through drugstores. Yet, I expect to pay more in a department store, and willingly do.

Consider the effect of timing—It's been found that when men purchase accessories for a suit (e.g., matching tie, vest) before purchasing the suit, they spend less than when they buy the suit first. The reason for this is that once they make the big purchase, say $300 for a suit, the cost of a $30 tie—by contrast—doesn't seem so steep.[31]

THE DARK SIDE OF PERSUASION

By following the guidelines we've discussed, persuasion efforts are likely to be effective, resulting in positive outcomes for both the persuader and persuadee, both in the short term and long term. Those who are unskilled in persuasion, or have ulterior motives, may resort to tactics that are less than savory. At best, such tactics may be viewed as **manipulation** or **coercion**—convincing people to agree to something that is not in their best interest or anything they would ever do without the influence of the persuader. For example, imagine a boss telling a new hire that "everyone who wants to advance works for at least an hour after he punches out." It doesn't seem fair, and in fact, such an act is illegal, though not all companies comply with the law. The boss's comments come across as a threat, that is, if you don't work "off the clock"—in essence, provide free labor—your chances of advancing are slim. Because you want to make a positive impression, perhaps you adhere to this practice. However, you probably feel you had no choice, and are therefore complying out of fear. Clearly, from your perspective, this situation doesn't feel good, nor does it engender positive feelings toward your boss or the organization. The good news is that there are some ways to respond to situations like these; Figure 8.2 describes a few.

From the boss's perspective, the threat—even indirect—was successful. She got what she wanted, and quite easily, leading her to use this tactic even more frequently. She may overlook the employees grumbling over the practice, particularly if she was able to get what she wanted, which also helped make her department's numbers look good to her supervisors. However, as time passes, employee discontent increases, and other requests or commands are met with resistance, compliance (however minimal), or perhaps, sabotage. In the long run, coercive tactics like these do not work or bring about the desired change in behavior or belief. Within a negotiation, using these tactics tends to damage the quality of the agreement; they also damage the relationship.[32]

How do you know whether you or the person with whom you are interacting is using persuasion or manipulation tactics? Answer these questions:[33]

- Who is really benefiting as a result of this act?
- Is the information being presented accurately?
- Does this interaction feel like a test of wills—a competitive game—or is it a healthy and positive debate—a two-way interchange?

FIGURE 8.2   Smart Alternatives to Lying[34]

Harvard Business School Professor, Deepak Malhotra, offers practical advice on how all parties in a negotiation can avoid lying and being lied to.

- Don't succumb to time pressures—be prepared and allow sufficient time. Also consider the cross-cultural differences in one's approach to allocating for and spending time in negotiations.
- Refuse to answer certain questions—reframe or defer until you have more info or are "allowed" to answer. For example, if you are asked to grant a discount but do not have the authority to do so, don't answer, "sure, we can do that" just to get the contract. Instead, you might answer, "I don't have the ability to lower the price, but I will check and get back to you in 24 hours."
- Adopt the logic of exchange—take turns sharing. If you are put on the spot, respond with what you know and can share and then ask another question.
- Eliminate the lie by making it true—reshape the facts to make the truth easier to share.
- Observe the shadow of the future—realize the value of the relationship in the long term and reframe or respond accordingly.

Warning signals of manipulation include the persuader having more to gain from the exchange than the persuadee, discrepancies in the facts being presented as part of the argument, a war of words that heavily favors just one side, and a larger role for self-interest than public interest. If any or all of these conditions are present in an interaction, it's best to disengage and either discontinue or agree to resume the interaction when you can gain a more equal footing. To defend yourself against manipulation:

Be clear on your convictions and why you hold them.   Avoid being a victim of unscrupulous manipulators by being smart when interacting with them. Ask plenty of questions to ensure you understand clearly all sides of an issue. Analyze their intent and evaluate their argument before accepting what's being said, especially if your opinion is based primarily on the person's likeability or reputation.

Think substance, not appearance.   Base your acceptance of a persuader on the strength of his reasoning, not simply because he has connected with you or the audience emotionally.

Doubt the truth of what's being said.   Do ask questions of speakers before being convinced by the power of their words that they are right. Most of the time you will encounter presenters and persuaders who are truthful and honest. But it's a good strategy to be aware of the tactics that can be utilized by some whose self-interests override their interest in others.

Know the source.   Increasingly, people rely on the web for information and expertise. Yet much of the material readily available can't be attributed to a specific author, organization, or date. Out-of-context information is unreliable. Know the source before using content in personal or professional decision making.

Consider the needs of others besides yourself.   When being courted by a persuader, consider not just your interests but those of others who may be affected by the action or perspective being advocated.[34] Is the action of benefit to the greater common good? Or will it benefit only a select few?

Summary

Your ability to persuade and influence others is more critical than ever before. No longer is one's position or sheer power enough. We work with and for others who expect to exercise their rights to think, make decisions, and participate in situations that affect them. Commanding their compliance within negotiation will result not only in little, if any, commitment to a solution, but will also damage the relationship. By following the guidelines presented, you can increase your confidence in and ability to persuade others to adopt a view or behavior that will benefit all parties involved in a negotiation.

Summary: The Big Picture

Persuasion	What we do with others to get them to adopt a new behavior or belief. It does not include manipulation, deceit, coercion, or force.
Credibility	Required for persuasion, it includes a positive impression, expertise, trustworthiness, and composure
Framing for common ground	Involves identifying and presenting a plan or framework for the negotiating context that comprises common interest and facilitates collaborative decision making.
Using logic and reasoning	Presenting compelling and error-free evidence (facts, data, charts, or graphs) that support your arguments.
Appealing to basic instincts	Communicating and behaving in ways that evoke an automatic (click-whirr) response; these include reciprocity/obligation, scarcity, and consensus/social proof.
Cognitive dissonance	Tension that exists when individuals' beliefs do not align with their behaviors; the persuader's goal is to suggest approaches or solutions that will reduce this tension.
Unethical persuasion tactics	These arise out of a lack of skill, ulterior motives, and needs to "win at all costs," and can damage the trust and relationship between the parties.

Key Terms and Concepts

ACE Theory   A theory in persuasion that holds that people use three criteria (appropriateness, consistency, and effectiveness) to determine whether to respond to a persuader's arguments.

Appropriateness   The right thing to do, based on generally accepted standards or norms, or in some cases, rules of law or morality.

Cognitive dissonance   The tension that exists when individuals' beliefs do not align with their behaviors.

Consensus/social proof   A principle in persuasion that holds that people often decide what to do based on what they see others doing.

Consistency   The degree to which the action or belief proposed compares to that of similar others or to their own past behaviors or espoused beliefs.

Effectiveness   The degree to which an action or idea leads to a desirable state or outcome.

Frame for common ground   Identifying and presenting a plan or framework for the negotiating context that comprises common interest and facilitates collaborative decision making.

Inoculation theory   A theory in persuasion that holds that persuaders can be more effective when they anticipate potential objections and address them before they arise.

Manipulation/coercion   Convincing people to agree to something that is not in their best interest nor anything they would ever do without the influence of the persuader.

Persuasion   The presentation of arguments and supporting evidence to get others to adopt a new behavior or belief.

Scarcity   A principle in persuasion that holds that people will be motivated to obtain something they believe is in short supply.

Discussion Questions

1. Reflect on a time when you were successful in getting an individual or a group to do or believe in what you wanted. What did you do or say, and why was it effective?
2. Reflect on a time when you were not successful in persuading an individual or a group. What did you do or say? If you could replay the scenario, what would you do differently and how might the outcome differ?
3. What are your thoughts about the ways in which products and services are marketed to grab your attention and business? Are the practices employed ethical? Why or why not?
4. If you were to market one of your favorite products (e.g., soft drink or other beverage, tennis shoe, car), what three things would you be sure to include? Why? What impact would they have on potential buyers?

Ethical Dilemma: Power of the Professor?

Susan Jaymes is a professor at a mid-sized regional university. Dr. Jaymes has always been popular with the students, who frequently cite her enthusiastic style, hands-on approach, and excellent knowledge base as reasons for taking her class. Her popularity is even further boosted by teaching evaluation scores, which are gathered by the student council and published at the start of each semester. These same scores are also factored into all professors' yearly performance appraisals, and as appropriate, merit increases.

Lately, merit increases have become smaller, and the bar that seems to matter most in determining raises has become higher. In response to this, Dr. Jaymes has taken steps to *ensure* that her teaching evaluations are as high as possible. First, knowing that only the most serious students will attend, she hands out the evaluation during an optional exam review session. Second, she brings snacks and drinks to the session (something she never does during normally scheduled class sessions). Finally, after handing out the forms and before leaving the classroom, she reminds the students "how much your input counts on my remaining employed with the university and how important getting a raise—albeit tiny—is for me to be able to pay my huge monthly student loan payments, considering how little faculty here are paid."

Discussion Questions

1. Discuss how Dr. Jaymes is using persuasion to facilitate her goal. What methods or theories are being used?
2. Do you think these methods will be effective? Why or why not?
3. Do you think Dr. Jaymes' approach is ethical? Explain.
4. If you were her boss, in other words, the department chair, and you found out what she was doing, what, if anything would you do and why?
5. If you were a student thinking of taking Dr. Jaymes' class and a former student of hers told you about her practices, in what way would this information affect your decision?

Endnotes

1. de Janasz, S., K. Dowd, and B. Schneider. *Interpersonal Skills in Organizations* (3rd ed.). Burr Ridge, IL: McGraw Hill, 2009.
2. Reardon, K. K. *Persuasion in Practice.* Newbury Park, CA: Sage Publications, 1991, p. 2.
3. Goleman, D. *Emotional Intelligence: Why it can matter more than IQ.* New York: Bantam Books, 1995.
4. Covey, S. R. *Seven Habits of Highly Effective People.* New York, NY: Simon and Schuster, 1989.
5. Dimitrius, J.-E., and M. C. Mazzarella. *Reading People: How to Understand People and Predict Their Behavior.* New York, NY: Ballantine Books, 1999.
6. *Ibid.*
7. Conger, J. A. "The Necessary Art of Persuasion." *Harvard Business Review,* May–June 1998, p. 84.
8. Reardon, *Persuasion in Practice.*
9. Potgieter, J. "The Road to Becoming an Advanced Negotiator." *eZineArticles,* August 16, 2007, from http://EzineArticles.com/?expert=Jan_Potgieter, accessed September 2, 2007.
10. de Janasz et al., *Interpersonal Skills in Organizations.*
11. Anderson, C., and A. Shirako. "Are Individuals' Reputations Related to their History of Behavior?" *Journal of Personality and Social Psychology* 94(2) (2008): 320–333.
12. *Ibid.*
13. Bazerman, M. H. and M. A. Neale, "Negotiating Rationally: The Power and Impact of a Frame." *Academy of Management Executive 6(3),* 1992, pp. 42–51.
14. Sussman, L. "How to Frame a Message: The Art of Persuasion and Negotiation." *Business Horizons,* July–August 1999, p. 2.
15. Covey, S. R. "30 Methods of Influence." *Executive Excellence,* April 1991.
16. Maslow, A. H. *Motivation and Personality,* (2nd ed.). New York: Harper and Row, 1970.
17. Laschinger, H. K. S., J. E. Finegan, J. Shamian, and P. Wilk. "A Longitudinal Analysis of the Impact of Workplace Empowerment on Work Satisfaction." *Journal of Organizational Behavior* 25(4) (2004): 527–543.
18. Fenigstein, A., M. F. Scheier, and A. H. Buss. Public and private self-consciousness: Assessment and theory. *Journal of Consulting and Clinical Psychology* 43 (1975): 522–527.
19. Fu, P. P., G. Yukl, J. Kennedy, E. S. Srinivas, A. Cheosakul, T. K. Peng, and P. Tata. "Cross-cultural comparison of influence behavior: A preliminary report." *2001 Academy of Management Proceedings.*
20. Andrew, D. C. *Technical Communication in the Global Community.* Upper Saddle, NJ: Prentice Hall, 1998.
21. Tannen, D. *You Just Don't Understand: Women and Men in Conversation.* New York: Ballantine Books, 1991.
22. de Janasz et al., *Interpersonal Skills in Organizations.*
23. Cialdini, R. B. *Influence: Science and Practice.* Boston: Allyn and Bacon, 2001.
24. Cialdini, *Influence,* p. 38.
25. Cialdini, *Influence,* p. 100.
26. "In fact, this trend is even more pronounced when looking at the growing importance of one's online social networks on buying behavior. For example, among 18-24 year olds, purchase decisions are primarily influenced by Facebook friends, with a nearly invisible effect from reading respected, published reports of a car's safety, reliability or economy." "Social Networks and UGC" http://www.newmediatrend-watch.com/markets-by-country/17-usa/127-social-net-works-and-ugc , accessed August 30, 2011
27. Festinger, L. *A Theory of Cognitive Dissonance.* Stanford, CA: Stanford Univ. Press, 1957.
28. These include: increase the attractiveness of the chosen alternative, decrease the attractiveness of the unchosen alternative, create cognitive overlap, or revoke the decision. See Festinger for more information.
29. McGuire, W. J. "The Effectiveness of Supportive and Refutational Defenses in Immunizing and Restoring Beliefs against Persuasion." *Sociometry* 24 (1961): 184–197.
30. Reardon, *Persuasion in Practice.*
31. Whitney, R.A., T. Hubin, and J. D. Murphy. *The new psychology of persuasion and motivation in selling.* Englewood Cliffs, NJ: Prentice-Hall, 1965.
32. Fisher, R., and S. Brown. *Getting Together: Building Relationships as We Negotiate.* New York, New York: Penguin Books, 1988.
33. Pascarella, P. "Persuasion Skills Required for Success," *Management Review,* September 1998, p. 68.
34. Malhotra, D. "Smart Alternatives to Lying in Negotiation." *Negotiation* 7(5) (May 2004).
35. Nelson, R. A. "Ethics and Social Issues in Business: An Updated Communication Perspective." *Competitiveness Review* 13(1) (2003): 66.

Exercise 8.1 Assessing Your Influence Skills[*]

Respond to each of the following statements by marking the option closest to your experience. Be honest. If your answer is "never," circle 1; if "occasionally," circle 2; if "frequently," circle 3; and if "always," circle 4.

		Never	Occasionally	Frequently	Always
1	I look at other people's points of view before defining proposals.	1	2	3	4
2	I am clear about my goals before I arrive at a meeting.	1	2	3	4
3	I express my ideas with confidence and enthusiasm.	1	2	3	4
4	I stay calm and focused when presenting ideas to others.	1	2	3	4
5	I know my own strengths at work and use them to the fullest.	1	2	3	4
5	I choose my words with care, being careful not to offend anyone.	1	2	3	4
6	I listen carefully to what others say.	1	2	3	4
7	I treat setbacks as learning opportunities rather than problems.	1	2	3	4
8	I ensure that I am dressed appropriately, whatever the occasion.	1	2	3	4
9	I listen carefully to opposing views before summarizing them.	1	2	3	4
10	I keep abreast of developments within my industry.	1	2	3	4
11	I take the first step in introducing myself to new acquaintances.	1	2	3	4
12	I back up my ideas with logical reasons and evidence.	1	2	3	4
13	I seek the support of my superiors for my goals and plans.	1	2	3	4
14	I verbally acknowledge the needs and interests of others.	1	2	3	4
15	I rehearse my presentations thoroughly beforehand.	1	2	3	4
16	I faithfully keep my promises and commitments.	1	2	3	4
17	I use nonverbal behaviors (tone, gestures) to emphasize my points.	1	2	3	4
18	I offer support to others without waiting to be asked.	1	2	3	4
19	I listen for emotive words used by people I talk to.	1	2	3	4
20	I work through differences with others openly and honestly.	1	2	3	4
21	I make my proposals attractive by explaining their benefits.	1	2	3	4
22	I neutralize disputes by trying to understand the other party's position.	1	2	3	4
23	I am comfortable working with people who are more senior than me.	1	2	3	4
24	I listen without criticizing others' points of view.	1	2	3	4
25	I am specific about asking for what I want or need.	1	2	3	4
26	I find out what matters to the people I work with.	1	2	3	4
27	I check for understanding others' responses to my proposals.	1	2	3	4
28	I handle disagreements by looking for mutual interests.	1	2	3	4
29	I invite others to join me in searching for mutually beneficial solutions.	1	2	3	4
30	I keep an open mind when others present opposing points of view.	1	2	3	4
31	I assume that there can be a positive outcome to nearly every issue.	1	2	3	4
32	I can read people's wants and needs by observing their surroundings and actions.	1	2	3	4
	Total				

[*]Adapted from Roy Johnson and John Eaton. *Influencing People.* New York: Dorling Kindersley Limited, 2002, pp. 66–69. Used with permission.

Scoring guide:

Total up your points. If your score is:

32–63: You could be more influential. Focus on being proactive and finding common ground as opposed to being reactive to and critical of others' views.

64–95: You are influencing well and have built some good working relationships. Consider expanding your network and span of influence by winning over the hearts and minds of those around you.

96–128: You are a skilled influencer who relates to others well. Keep improving your abilities; you're on your way to achieving professional and personal success!

Exercise 8.2 Online Assessment: What Is Your Influence Quotient?

Earlier in the chapter, we referenced the influence research of Cialdini. On his website, www.influenceatwork.com, there is a wonderful (and challenging!) scenario-based quiz. Visitors to this website can register and take this 10-question quiz for free. Two sample questions are listed below:

Questions:

- If you want to influence someone to agree to a costly proposal (e.g., time, effort, money), should you present the most or least costly option first?
- Is it better to tell someone what she or he will gain from complying with your request or what she or he will lose if she or he doesn't?

Answers:

- More (reciprocity principle: rejection [now you owe me] then retreat [so buy/do this for me]).
- Lose (scarcity principle: People are more motivated to go after what's scarce)

Debrief:

1. How did you do?
2. Did any of the answers surprise you? Explain.

Exercise 8.3   Back to the Future

Your parents own a small print shop, one that had been passed down from one of their parents during the B.C. (before computers) period. Inventory and sales records are kept in notebooks or on cards filed in shoeboxes. Customers' names and numbers are listed on cards in a Rolodex file. The 350 annual Christmas cards are sent by one employee hand-addressing the envelopes. While technology has changed, things in the print shop have not.

You are home over winter break and wish to apply some of your technology-based knowledge and skill to improve things in the print shop. You know of several computer systems and software applications that can keep track of customers, sales, and inventory all at the touch of a button. Send a letter to only those customers in a particular city? A piece of cake almost anywhere else, but not at your parents' shop. You explain the value of computers to them, but they insist that all is well in the print shop. Besides, they tell you, "If it ain't broke, why fix it?"

To convince them to adopt (and use!) the kind of computer system you know will benefit them, you decide to apply the six steps of persuasion. Use the worksheet below to develop a script for what you'll say and do to address each of the six steps of persuasion.:

Understand others' motivations and needs

_____

_____

_____

Establish credibility

_____

_____

_____

Frame for common ground

_____

_____

_____

Engage in joint problem solving

_____

_____

_____

Support preferred outcome with logic and reasoning (and benefits)

_____

_____

_____

Reinforce with appeal to emotions and basic instincts

_____

_____

_____

Exercise 8.4 Applying the Six Persuasion Steps to Your Own Situation

Jot down a current situation in which you would like to persuade someone to do something that you think she is likely not to do in the absence of your persuasion attempt.

Current situation:

_____

_____

What I would like to see (ideal situation):

_____

_____

Now, complete the following worksheet as if you were preparing a script to use in this persuasion attempt:

Understand others' motivations and needs

_____

_____

_____

Establish credibility

_____

_____

_____

Frame for common ground

_____

_____

_____

Engage in joint problem solving

_____

_____

_____

Support preferred outcome with logic and reasoning (and benefits)

_____

_____

_____

Reinforce with appeal to emotions and basic instincts

_____

_____

_____

Exercise 8.5   Understanding the Power of Leveraging Basic Instincts

This chapter discussed three ways to use Cialdini's basic instincts to persuade others. They are listed below. Research current events in the workplace or the world and provide examples of each. Then explain why the persuasion attempt was successful.

	Example	Why it worked
Reciprocity/Obligation		
Scarcity		
Consensus/Social Proof		

Pick one of the instincts and apply it to an upcoming persuasion attempt in the space below. Describe which approach you would use and how you would use it. Be specific in describing exactly what you would do or say in employing this approach.

Upcoming Persuasion Attempt:

_____

_____

What I would say or do in employing the _____ instinct in this attempt:

_____

_____

_____

_____

Exercise 8.6 Creating Consonance Out of Dissonance

Earlier in the chapter, we shared the example of a newly hired employee (of a family-friendly company) who is being asked by her boss to work on a Saturday to get ready for an upcoming client meeting when she already has plans to attend her child's school play. Knowing of the company's family-friendly philosophy and the dissonance involved in this request, how would you advise her to persuade her supervisor to accept her refusal to work on Saturday?

Why is there dissonance? Explain.

_____

_____

How can she restore consonance? For example, Festinger advises that the persuader can show attractiveness of the chosen alternative, increasing it in the eyes of the persuadee. The persuader can also decrease the attractiveness of the unchosen alternative. Use the space below to create a script that demonstrates your application of Festinger's advice in this situation.

_____

_____

_____

_____

_____

_____

_____

_____

Exercise 8.7   Applying the ACE Theory

You work at an insurance firm with approximately 150 employees, most involved in desk work. You would like to convince the owner that an exercise/wellness program should be added to the workplace. The owner is a man in his mid 50s and is highly concerned with attendance and productivity. Use the worksheet to script out how the ACE Theory could help you in being successful in your persuasion attempt.

Appropriateness (What is typical, common, or accepted practice for similar others?)

_____

_____

_____

_____

Consistency (In what ways might developing an exercise/wellness program align with the owner's behaviors or beliefs?)

_____

_____

_____

_____

Effectiveness (How would developing an exercise/wellness program result in a positive outcome for the owner?)

_____

_____

_____

_____

Exercise 8.8   Persuasion in the Movies

The following movies (and starring actor) demonstrate persuasion in action.

Braveheart (Mel Gibson)

Charlie Wilson's War (Julia Roberts)

Erin Brokovich (Julia Roberts)

Falling Down (Michael Douglas)

Fatal Attraction (Glenn Close)

Five Easy Pieces (Jack Nicholson)

Harry Potter (Daniel Radcliffe)

Philadelphia (Tom Hanks)

The Pursuit of Happyness (Will Smith)

Scent of a Woman (Al Pacino)

Twelve Angry Men (Henry Fonda)

Wall Street (Charlie Sheen)

Some of the scenes depict persuasion: something done *with* another and not *to* another (e.g., *Pursuit of Happyness*) while others depict coercion or manipulation (e.g., *Falling Down*). Select one of these movies and:

1. Briefly describe two scenes which depict persuasion in action.

   _____

   _____

   _____

2. Explain the method or theory being utilized by the persuader (actor).

   _____

   _____

   _____

3. Discuss your view on the effectiveness of this method
   a. As shown in the scene (i.e., how the story plays out)

   _____

   _____

   _____

   b. If the same approach were used in an attempt to persuade you.

   _____

   _____

   _____

4. If you were the actor, how would your approach to persuasion be similar and different?

   _____

   _____

   _____

Exercise 8.9   Do I Want to Be Managed by This Guy?

One of the more maligned professions as it relates to persuasion is sales. In this scene (www.youtube.com/watch?v=y-AXTx4PcKI), taken from *Glengarry Glen Ross* (1992, directed by James Foley, based on a David Mamet play), Alec Baldwin's character is sent to one of the low-performing offices of a real-estate company to improve the salesmen's performance. After watching the scene, discuss:

How would you feel if you were one of these salesmen? Explain.

_____

_____

_____

_____

Would you expect Baldwin's character to be successful in his persuasion attempt? Explain.

_____

_____

_____

_____

_____

How would you approach this situation if you were Alec Baldwin's character? Why?

_____

_____

_____

_____

_____

Exercise 8.10 The Dark Side of Persuasion

As discussed, persuasion is done *with* another and not *to* another. When manipulation, fear (including threats), or deceit are involved, the target of the persuasion effort has little to no power to choose, or so it seems.

Consider a situation where you were the target of such efforts. Perhaps someone threatened you (if you don't do this, I will do that), deliberately deceived you (e.g., lied about the history or characteristics of a product or service she was selling), or used unfair or manipulative tactics (e.g., used guilt, aggressive behavior, overwhelmed with too much information). Use the worksheet below to analyze this situation:

What was the situation? (Who was involved? What was the history? What was at stake? What was the persuader's likely motivation for engaging in this behavior?)

_____

_____

_____

_____

How did you feel about the way you were being treated?

_____

_____

_____

What, if anything, did you try to do to counteract or respond to this treatment? What effect did your attempt/s have?

_____

_____

_____

If you could replay the situation now, what might you say or do differently in response to this situation, and how would the outcome have changed?

_____

_____

_____

What lessons can you apply about persuading others in both professional and personal situations?

_____

_____

_____

CHAPTER 9

The Nature of the Relationship in Negotiating and Resolving Disputes

Chapter Objectives

After studying this chapter and completing the exercises you should be able to:

- Assess the challenges of negotiating and resolving conflicts with others spanning the spectrum of distant (e.g., acquaintances, casual friends) to close (e.g., family) relationships.

- Evaluate various situations that call for negotiation with service providers and prepare for those negotiations.

- Appraise the impact of friendship when negotiating with a friend.

- Develop proactive and appropriate strategies for negotiating and resolving conflicts with family members and close friends.

- Assess the challenges of doing business with family and close friends.

- Evaluate the options for third-party involvement in resolving conflict in a family business.

W e negotiate with a wide variety of people on a daily basis, from assorted service providers to business associates to close friends and relatives. The relationships we have with these people fall on a continuum from those we barely know to those we know very well and from formal (e.g., contractors, landlords) to informal (e.g., friends, family). The more formal the relationship, the more likely our negotiations will result in written, legally binding contracts that contain sanctions for noncompliance. Among the people we know well, there will be some for whom we have a great deal of respect and admiration, and there will be others whom we simply tolerate. In some cases, we are able to avoid the latter type of people, but in many other cases, for a variety of reasons, we have to coexist, sometimes for a short period of time and other times indefinitely. The relationship we have with the other party influences our approach to negotiation and dispute resolution. In this chapter we explore the role of the relationship and its influence on negotiation and dispute resolution with a wide variety of people, including contractors, landlords, neighbors, acquaintances, friends, business partners, and family members.

Chapter Scenario, Part I

Anna Rose and Nikko have been best friends since their freshman year at Northern University. They were suitemates and active in a business fraternity. In their junior year, they cochaired the fraternity's annual fundraiser, a formal gala that had become one of the college town's best-known and best-attended events. It was simultaneously exciting and a bit overwhelming. There were so many details and they didn't want anything to slip through the cracks. They wanted to make sure this was the best gala in the history of the fraternity. As cochairs, they were responsible for negotiating all aspects of the event from the venue to the food and beverage service to the music. They were negotiating with people they had just met and wanted to make sure their agreements would be upheld.

NEGOTIATING WITH CONTRACTORS

A "**contractor**" is anyone you pay to provide goods or services at a certain price or rate. This could be a one-time arrangement (e.g., home or business renovations) or an ongoing relationship (e.g., landscape or snow removal services). You choose your contractors, but once you sign a contract, you have entered into a legal relationship that may be difficult and/or costly to break. Ensuring you are dealing with a reputable contractor and checking with the Better Business Bureau are important steps when you are preparing for these negotiations. If any type of construction is involved, be sure you also check with the local builders' association. Always check references and, when appropriate, make sure that the contractors are licensed and insured.

If you are negotiating a one-time project/arrangement (e.g., a major remodel, wedding photography), speak with former clients. If it is an ongoing service (e.g., cleaning services), talk with current clients. Ask questions about both the quality and timeliness of the contractor's work. If you are speaking with a former client, ask if she would hire the contractor again. Whenever possible, arrange to view examples of the contractor's work. The better your research up front, the better outcome you will likely have. This is especially important with any type of construction or special events.

When you are dealing with construction projects, there is typically a substantial amount of money involved, and if there are problems with the work, you can't simply return it for a refund as you can with other purchases. Depending on the nature of the project, substandard work can result in additional damage. For example, if your newly installed roof leaks, there could be damage to the contents of your home. Worse yet, a furnace that is not installed properly could result in the release of deadly carbon monoxide gas into the building. When you are contracting for services to be performed at a special event (e.g., wedding, bar mitzvah) you have only one opportunity for them to be done correctly. If the food provided by the caterer gives the guests food poisoning you don't have the opportunity to redo the catering since the event is over.

Typically, negotiations with contractors are more formal and legalistic than negotiations with people we know well. There is likely to be a signed agreement that specifies the terms and conditions of the arrangement (i.e., what is to be done, where, when, and how) and includes sanctions (as discussed in Chapter 3) for failure to live up to the agreement. Contractors usually require a down payment that is forfeited if the customer changes his mind about having the work done. While a down payment is customary, you should never pay in full before the work is completely done to your satisfaction. If you do, you will have no leverage in getting the contractor to correct problems or complete the work in a timely manner.

These negotiations also have a tendency to be more distributive because the parties don't have an established relationship. Getting to know the other party and building trust and a good working relationship facilitates integrative negotiations. Like most people, contractors are more apt to go the extra mile for people they like and with whom they have a good relationship. It is fairly common for delays and problems to crop up and you should be careful not to overreact when they happen. Instead, focus on how to get things back on track. Be flexible and open to creative, integrative agreements.

FIGURE 9.1 **Negotiating with Contractors: A Word of Caution**

While ideally you will have a good relationship with your contractors, it is important that you stay on top of things lest you fall victim to an unscrupulous contractor. We would be remiss if we didn't mention something known as a "**mechanic's lien**." If a contractor doesn't pay his suppliers or subcontractors (i.e., anyone who provides materials or does work) the suppliers or subcontractors could put a mechanic's lien on the property where the supplies were used or the work was performed. Generally speaking, some period of time is allowed to resolve the dispute between the contractor and the suppliers or subcontractors, usually sixty days to six months. If the dispute is not resolved, the supplier or subcontractor could force the sale of the property at auction to get the money he is owed. While these disputes are not typically taken to this extreme, the property owner is liable and often ends up paying the supplier or subcontractor and then suing her contractor for reimbursement. As you might guess, disputes with contractors can be very time consuming and costly and often end up in court or mediation.

Learn as much as you can about the nature of the goods or services for which you are contracting so you are better able to see the other party's perspective. For example, if you are contracting for any work that is done outdoors, you need to understand the impact the weather has on a contractor's work schedule. The contractor may have told you he would start work on your addition on the first of the month, but if it has rained for the previous two weeks, he will almost certainly be behind on prior job(s) and need to finish those before beginning yours. While the work is in progress, be sure to stay in close contact with the contractor to ensure the work is being completed as agreed. It is easier to negotiate solutions to any problems before the work is complete and you have paid the contractor in full. Figure 9.1 provides just one example of what could happen if you are not careful.

Points to Ponder

1. What types of contractors have you dealt with? What contractors are you likely to negotiate with in the next five years?
2. What might you do to educate yourself before negotiating with a contractor?
3. What specifics will you research before entering into a contract?

Chapter Scenario, Part II

In their senior year, Anna Rose and Nikko decided to live together off campus. They found a very nice second-floor apartment, but the landlord required two months rent as a security deposit. Anna Rose and Nikko were both very responsible but had been putting themselves through college and in their last year, their finances were very tight. They went to speak to the landlord and explain their situation. The landlord explained that in the past he required only one month's rent as a security deposit, but the last tenants caused so much damage that the security deposit didn't cover the cost of the damage, and he wanted to make sure that didn't happen again.

LANDLORD/TENANT RELATIONSHIPS

As with contractors, a relationship with a landlord is voluntary, but signing a lease agreement creates a legal relationship. A key interest of landlords is to rent/lease their property and minimize vacancies since theirs is essentially a perishable product. If a property is vacant, a landlord can never recoup the lost income. As we saw in the chapter scenario, another interest of landlords is to have tenants who will take care of the property and cause minimal damage. From a tenant perspective, a fundamental interest is to have suitable housing at a reasonable cost. Of course how someone defines "suitable housing" will vary from person to person. Most tenants seek a clean property in a safe location but beyond that the minimum requirements can vary dramatically and can include access to public transportation, good schools, and proximity to the beach, mountains, or a park.

Most landlords require a security deposit to cover the cost of any damage caused by the tenant(s). This provides both an incentive for the tenants to take care of the property and a sanction if they don't. Most states regulate when and how security deposits are returned. In general, a landlord has a specified period of time (fourteen to thirty days is common) to return the deposit or provide the tenant with an itemized list of the deductions from the deposit. Some states require that interest be paid on the deposit. To minimize the possibility of future disputes—and strengthen their position should there be one—when tenants move in, they should take photos of anything that is not in good condition and document the condition of the property using a checklist like the one shown in Figure 9.2.

Landlords have a legal obligation to maintain the property, and if that obligation is not met, a tenant has different options depending on the state in which the property is located. Some states allow a tenant to withhold some or even all of the rent, while in others, a tenant may have the right to have the repairs done and withhold the cost of the repairs from future rent payments. Depending on the nature of the problem, a tenant might also call the local building inspector and let her deal with the landlord. In some cases a tenant may have the legal right to move out, even in the middle of the lease, as was the case of a colleague who learned about the physical and health effects of mold that apparently wasn't noticed when the property was first inspected. She was later released from her lease. From a landlord's perspective, he has the right to terminate your lease and ultimately evict you for unpaid rent (though the time line varies by state), violations of the rental agreement, serious damage to the property, or involvement in illegal activity. Obviously, understanding your lease and careful research and preparation are critical in preventing or resolving these types of situations.

Withholding rent and eviction are extreme measures. At the heart of most landlord–tenant disputes is a difference in standards between the tenant and the landlord. What a tenant views as a major problem may be considered trivial by the landlord and vice versa. More often than not, it is most effective to build a good relationship and use an integrative approach. If you pay your rent on time and take good care of the property, the landlord will be more likely to be responsive when you have a problem than if you are chronically late with the rent and disrespect her property. Similarly, a landlord who corrects problems in a timely manner is more likely to have tenants who respect the property.

FIGURE 9.2   Checklist for Documenting the Condition of a Rental Property

- Furnace/air conditioner. Adjust the thermostat to make sure it works.
- Sink/tub faucets. Check each for leaks, proper drainage, and water temperature.
- Toilets. Flush and check for leaks.
- Ceilings and walls. Check for cracks, water stains, or other damage.
- Carpet/floor coverings. Check for stains or other damage.
- Windows. Are they secure? Are the latches in good working order? Are there storm windows and screens for each window?
- Water heater. Check for leaks.
- Door locks. Do they operate freely with each key provided?
- Light switches. Turn on each one to see if it works.
- Electrical outlets. Use a small portable light or hairdryer to ensure they work.
- Smoke detectors. Press test button to ensure they work.

Chapter Scenario, Part III

Ultimately, Anna Rose and Nikko were able to negotiate a lower security deposit by convincing the landlord that they were trustworthy young adults who would be responsible tenants and take care of the property, negating the need for a higher security deposit. They moved in and all was well until two months into their

(continued)

year-long lease when the neighbors downstairs got a new roommate, Dillon. Dillon liked to have parties and stay up late. Often the party-goers would take all the parking spaces available for the tenants. The parties kept Anna Rose and Nikko up at night and on several occasions they arrived home from work only to find nowhere to park. They were very angry. The situation had gotten out of hand and it needed to be resolved.

IN THE NEIGHBORHOOD

Neighbors, residential or commercial, are those who are geographically close. You don't choose them—they (or you) simply move in. You also can't fire them or force them to leave if you don't like or get along with them, and there are varying degrees of interdependence with your neighbors. Think of all the neighbors you have had in your lifetime and what it was like to be their neighbor. At one extreme, there may have been some that you were able to completely ignore, while at another you may have been best friends watching each other's house, pets, or even children when the other was away. In between the extremes the possibilities are endless. You might have had one neighbor whom you knew only by sight, but waved every time he passed your house. You might have had another who shared your love of gardening and with whom you traded plants and gardening tips. You might have had still another who hosted an annual neighborhood barbeque or one who wanted to prevent others from removing any trees. There may have been several neighbors who regularly got together for anything from a Bible study to a poker night. Understanding and appreciating their differences will go a long way in building positive—and if need be—collaborative relationships with future neighbors.

Sharing resources (e.g., a driveway, parking area) of any kind creates additional opportunities for disputes to arise and makes it very difficult to merely ignore the other party. You may also choose to work with your neighbors for the good of the community. In a residential neighborhood you may be part of a neighborhood association. In a commercial setting you might belong to a merchants' association. Both types of associations may establish a neighborhood watch to fight crime. These groups often arrange for presentations by the police to discuss neighbors' concerns and to share tips and techniques for keeping the neighborhood safe. Merchants' associations also work together to promote neighboring businesses. They may sponsor local events and fundraisers to draw people to the area in an effort to stimulate the local economy or pool their resources to advertise as a group.

Whatever the circumstances, it is usually beneficial if you take an integrative approach to negotiating and resolving disputes that may arise. If a neighbor is doing something of which we disapprove, we often remain silent until we reach a breaking point, at which point we engage more in venting than in problem solving. We almost always wish we had addressed the situation much earlier. In the chapter scenario, Anna Rose and Nikko should have shared their concerns with their neighbors when the parties first began.

Points to Ponder

1. Consider the relationships you have or have had with neighbors. What were the characteristics of the relationships you had with "good" neighbors? What were the characteristics of the relationships you had with "bad" neighbors?
2. What might you do to facilitate a good relationship with your neighbors?
3. In the Chapter Scenario, what might Anna Rose and Nikko do to resolve the situation with Dillon?

NEGOTIATING WITH ACQUAINTANCES

Another category of people with whom we have an ongoing relationship are **acquaintances**. We define acquaintances as people we know either professionally or personally, but whom we either don't know well enough or are not close enough to consider a friend. This includes coworkers and the people with whom we network professionally. Because Chapter 12 focuses on negotiating and resolving disputes in the workplace, our primary focus here is on your **professional network**. While you may not have regular contact with those in your professional network, they can be critical to your career success. Often these are people who can provide assistance with everything from helping to obtain a job to facilitating a meeting with someone who may be able to help further your career.

When you begin a job search you should alert those in your professional network as they may know of opportunities that could be of interest to you. Even if they aren't aware of any current openings, letting them know about your situation alerts them to keep their ears open and pass along news of any openings that may arise. Similarly, if you are selling a product or service to an organization where an acquaintance is employed, it is often helpful to contact her first. Even if she is not the person you need to approach, she may be able to help you connect with the right person and give you the inside track.

As you might guess, most negotiations with acquaintances involve obtaining or providing some type of assistance. When you need the help of others you must persuade them to help you. On the surface, it may appear one-sided; you are asking someone to do something for you without receiving much, if anything, in return. At the same time, others network with you because of the assistance you can provide. From a purely self-serving viewpoint, it is a bit illogical. Why would someone spend his time and effort doing something for you without negotiating to receive something in return? It takes time away from other activities, which likely provide him with some type of reward or pleasure. In some cases, the cost of providing the assistance is minimal, perhaps making a phone call to alert someone that you will be calling. In cases where more is involved, be conscious of what the assistance is costing the person in terms of time and resources, and consider how much time she has available to meet your request. Someone who is already very busy may receive your request differently than a person who has time available. The easier you can make it for the other party to meet your request, the more likely she is to agree to do it.

But even if you make it easy, why would the other person agree to your request? What does she receive in return for helping you? Think back to our discussion of reciprocity in Chapter 2. People sometimes do things because it helps to meet their need of being a "good" person. In other cases, people provide assistance because of the implied obligation it creates for you to help them in the future. Either way, you can help satisfy the other party's needs by thanking her and offering to help her in the future.

If a dispute arises between acquaintances, it is generally best to try to repair the relationship, because you never know when you might have to deal with the person again. Generally speaking, the less formal one-on-one approach discussed in Chapter 5 is the most effective. If you don't see repairing the relationship as possible or worthwhile, you have the option of ending the relationship and simply walking away. That is typically more difficult to do if the other party is your friend.

Points to Ponder

1. To what extent are you comfortable asking an acquaintance for assistance?
2. How would the type of assistance you are requesting influence your comfort level?

WHEN THE OTHER PARTY IS YOUR FRIEND

Negotiators may become friends as the parties get to know each other through a series of interactions over an extended period of time, as sometimes happens with attorneys and those who negotiate labor contracts. This is different however than negotiating when there is a long-term, pre-existing friendship.[1] Research has shown that when friends negotiate, they are more likely to rely on the kinds of integrative bargaining tactics that yield high-quality deals for both parties, including information sharing and trading concessions on low-priority issues.[2] The extent to which you like the other party influences your perception of him, expected movement from initial positions, and types of strategies prepared for the negotiation. Imagine having to negotiate a mutually agreeable work schedule with a coworker whom you consider a friend. You are more likely to enter the negotiation with the view that your coworker is friendly, easy to understand, and calm.[3] Of course he is; he's your friend! The better you know the other party, the more likely you are to perceive the situation as being conducive to agreement.[4] You understand his wants and needs, and he understands yours. You are better able to anticipate his reactions and counterproposals, and can tailor your approach accordingly. Not surprisingly, when friends negotiate, there is a higher level of trust than when negotiating with a stranger.[5]

The extent to which we like the other party also influences our initial positions and willingness to compromise on a variety of issues. The possibility of mutually supportive, trusting relationships can act as an incentive for maintaining constructive negotiations, even at the expense of short-term gains.[6] Research has found that affective trust between the parties prior to a negotiation predicts subsequent turning points in the negotiation.[7] Turning points are the point at which something changes direction. In a negotiation they can mean the difference between settlement and impasse. If we trust the other party because we are friends who have shared values and goals, we may be more willing to make a leap of faith that initiates a positive turning point.

Conversely, reduced liking or familiarity decreases one's willingness to reach compromise agreements.[8] If you don't care about maintaining the relationship, you have less to lose by taking a firm stand to attain your objectives. A study that investigated outcome preferences of roommates versus strangers when resources are scarce, found that roommates prefer equal allocations (each get the same) to maintain the relationship, with some even sacrificing their own benefit in order to maintain the relationship.[9] On the other hand, strangers focused on equity (i.e., fairness) in the allocation of rewards and preferred to meet the needs of the highest contributor.[10]

The Influence of Friendship on Strategy

We have maintained throughout the book that there is not one best approach to negotiations. Instead you must consider both the substantive and relationship outcomes desired and choose an appropriate strategy. This is consistent with the recommendations of experts who counsel managers to select a negotiation strategy based on the importance of relationship and substantive outcomes.[11] If neither the relationship nor the substantive issues are important, they advocate actively avoiding negotiating; if the relationship is important but the substantive issues aren't, they recommend open subordination; if the relationship is unimportant but the substantive issues are, they propose firm competition; and if both the relationship and the substantive issues are important, they advise one to "trustingly collaborate."[12] In all cases, both the relationship and the substantive issues are given equal consideration when selecting a strategy.

When the parties to a negotiation are concerned about the other party and her outcomes, they are more likely to select strategies that are relationship focused.[13] Strutton and Pelton maintain that one's negotiation strategy should be determined by the relationship sought with the other party.[14] They recommend an "open submission" strategy where you make concessions on all but the baseline issues to build the relationship when the opposing party is trusted and the relationship, or the potential for one, is valued.[15] The argument for adopting such a strategy is that building a favorable relationship will lead to greater rewards in the future. But is that always the case?

The Role of Scripts

There are certain norms or scripts for interacting with friends. We tend to be less formal and more trusting. When interacting with close friends there is a shared history, similarity of values, mutual respect, trust, and past affection for each other.[16] Similarly we have scripts for most events, including negotiating in a variety of settings. People typically negotiate with a salesperson in a car lot, but it is rare indeed for people to negotiate for funeral services for a loved one. From a purely economic standpoint, this makes little sense since both involve thousands of dollars.

Friendship scripts and **event scripts** interact[17] and clash.[18] When negotiating with a friend we almost always approach it differently than when negotiating with a stranger or casual acquaintance. With a friend, we are more likely to trust and be more concerned about the other person's needs being met. We may also pay more attention to behaviors and monitor words and actions for standards of trust and fairness.[19] Conversely, with strangers we don't expect to trust or be trusted or to look out for each other's best interests.[20] We are more likely to negotiate to get the best deal possible. When negotiating with strangers there is an endowment effect such that we believe things are more valuable just because they are ours. Friendship can moderate[21] and even reverse the endowment effect.[22]

Friendship scripts also typically call for generosity, but it is asymmetric in that the seller's offers to friends are generous but buyer's offers are not.[23] We don't want to be seen as greedy or taking advantage of a friend, especially if we are the one with the item. We already have, and presumably no longer want/need, what our friend wants/needs—how could we not be generous? As might be expected, research has shown that strong ties among negotiators can produce economically suboptimal agreements.[24]

Many people are quite uncomfortable negotiating with close friends and would prefer to avoid it completely. When negotiation is necessary, they want to complete it as soon as possible. They may agree on prices without discussion,[25] which is less likely when negotiating with strangers. A discussion that starts out being about price often leads to discussions about other considerations. If you don't talk about price, you run the risk of prematurely ending the negotiation before exploring other, possibly better, solutions on a variety of issues. As you would expect, negotiations among close friends produce fewer integrative solutions than negotiations among strangers.[26] This doesn't however have to be the case.

Integrative solutions between friends are possible if the parties are willing to put forth the effort. It is important to distinguish between norms of fairness and generosity.[27] Fairness implies that each party gives something and receives something. Generosity suggests that one person is giving to another without the expectation of additional remuneration. Ideally, generosity between friends is also fair over the long term. You can be very generous with your friends, but if it is rarely reciprocated, you will likely become resentful over time. Similarly, if you don't accept the generosity of your friends, you deny them the opportunity to feel generous and they may become resentful. While negotiations can be affected and damaged by relationships, relationships can also be affected and damaged by negotiations.[28]

The Importance of Maintaining the Relationship

Most research on the impact of relationships on negotiation has been with studies that look at developing, short-term, or casual relationships. In laboratory studies, this usually involves giving the subjects a scenario and then specifying whether the other party is a stranger or a friend, without qualifying the nature of the friendship. Yet the nature of the relationship has an influence on people's expectations regarding what they, as well as others with whom they imagine negotiating, would do.[29] People in long-term relationships may trade off issues over time without even thinking about it as negotiating.[30] Indeed, most couples take turns with everything from choosing a restaurant or a movie, to deciding who gets a new vehicle. These tradeoffs happen regularly and have little effect on the long-term relationship.

In order for a negotiation to affect an ongoing relationship, the negotiation has to be of some importance to the negotiators, either because the negotiation takes place over a long period of time or because the issues are particularly meaningful to the participants. In long-term relationships, people develop their own ways of dealing with each other.[31] Sometimes the approaches are healthy and sometimes they aren't. A couple who were friends of one of the authors never offered an apology to end a disagreement; one would simply say to the other "I forgive you." While most would not see this as a particularly good way of resolving conflict, it seemed to work for them, at least in terms of ending the immediate conflict.

While we typically have some desire to maintain all of our friendships, we are naturally more vested in maintaining those that are closest. It follows that the more the parties care about each other, the stronger their concern about potentially damaging the relationship through negotiation.[32] Yet tensions are a natural part of any relationship. When they are severe, we sometimes end the relationship; however, in most cases, we are willing to put more effort into maintaining the relationship, even at the expense of substantive outcomes.

Research has shown that dating couples used fewer pressure tactics and were less willing to push hard for their own interests than were mixed-sex stranger couples, and achieved considerably lower joint economic gain than strangers because they were concerned about the relationship.[33] While give and take is part of any healthy relationship, again, it must be balanced. Sometimes the relationship is so important to one of the parties that she always acquiesces to the wishes of the other. She may see this as a way to accumulate relational capital, even though it comes at the expense of economic capital. She may, however, become resentful over time.

A strong focus on maintaining the relationship isn't limited to relationships in our personal lives; it also occurs where there are close friendships in the workplace. Decisions in the workplace can be affected when scripts for interacting with friends become more salient than organizational policies.[34] From an organizational standpoint, this is problematic if managers negotiate based on what is best for their friends instead of what the organization's policies require. Many people in organizations have some experience with the "old boys" network, either as a member of the club who has benefited from special treatment or as an outsider who has witnessed the behavior. From an individual standpoint, whether the special treatment is viewed as just the way business is done or completely unfair likely depends on whether you are a participant or an observer.

The Challenges of Negotiating with Friends/Family

While some people feel more comfortable negotiating with people they know and like, there is some risk involved. When negotiating with friends and family, you will likely be more flexible and want to reach agreement to avoid conflict, and are more likely to use an integrative approach. In an ongoing relationship, the parties may not want to risk the appearance of greed, especially if the outcome is not critical to the individual.[35] If both parties hold the same views toward maintaining the friendship, they face the risk of premature closure[36] and a suboptimal agreement. When resources are scarce, parties may avoid the question of whose needs go unmet by making equal allocations.[37] The result is that neither party's needs are met, but they avoid conflict. They live happily ever after, albeit with unmet needs.

Chapter Scenario, Part IV

One weekend Anna Rose and Nikko were snowed in by a particularly strong blizzard. The weather had them trapped in their apartment and both were looking for something to make them feel better. Anna Rose, who was from California, decided she wanted to imagine it was summertime and make lemonade.

Nikko, raised in the Northeast, wanted something warm and comforting, and planned to make his grandmother's lemon poppy seed muffins. Each remembered there were three lemons in the refrigerator, went out to the kitchen, and reached for the lemons.

If Anna Rose and Nikko were both more concerned with the other's needs being met than their own, there is a good chance that they would simply split the lemons in half and make do with half the amount. The result would be that Anna Rose would end up with either half as much or half-strength lemonade, and Nikko's muffins would be more poppy seed than lemon. If however, one party places a very high priority on maintaining the friendship and being fair, and the other party doesn't, the increased flexibility may leave one more susceptible to being exploited by the other.[38] If Nikko was more concerned about the relationship than Anna Rose, he might let her use all of the lemons for her lemonade and forego making his muffins. In both of these examples, one or both parties' needs go unmet, consistent with research that has found friendship is not related to satisfaction with outcome of the negotiation.[39]

Think about a possible outcome if Anna Rose and Nikko focused equally on their respective needs and maintaining the relationship. They likely would spend more time exploring why each needed the lemons and looking for ways to satisfy the other's needs. Nikko would share that his recipe called for the zest (outer layer) of the lemon and Anna Rose would explain that she needed only the juice. Nikko would have all the zest he needed and Anna Rose would have sufficient juice to make a very tasty pitcher of lemonade. Thus, especially when negotiating with friends, it is wise to avoid premature closure if all parties' needs are not being met.

The Cost of Conflict When Negotiating with Friends/Family

While we encourage you to avoid suboptimal agreements when you are negotiating with friends and family, we must also point out that there is more at stake in those negotiations, which means the cost of conflict is higher. When negotiating with strangers or acquaintances, the costs can often be recouped if the negotiation fails. For example, if you are selling an automobile to a stranger and you fail to come to agreement, both parties simply walk away and find another alternative. If your friend is attempting to purchase your car and you are unable to agree on a fair price, you will both still have to find another alternative. In both cases there is some cost associated with the failed negotiation; however, in the negotiation with your friend, there may also be costs in terms of a damaged relationship. The potential cost to the relationship if the negotiation is unsuccessful is likely the reason people are more agreeable . . . and more prone to suboptimal agreements when negotiating with friends.

DOING BUSINESS WITH FRIENDS/FAMILY

Obviously we deal with close friends and family on a personal basis, but we may also deal with them in a financial or business context. We might purchase assets together such as cottages, vacation property, recreational vehicles, boats, etc. We may be asked to loan them money. We may work or even form a business together. In the case of a family business, we might not seek it out, we might inherit it. Indeed, more than 90% of businesses in the United States are family owned.[40] These businesses run the gamut from small mom-and-pop operations to multi-billion-dollar Fortune 500 corporations. As might be expected, when dealing with business and personal relationships simultaneously, negotiations are more complicated and the boundaries between what is personal and what is business are often blurred.

Chapter Scenario, Part V

After college, Anna Rose and Nikko got jobs at the same company in the same department. Both were good employees, but after several years, Anna Rose was promoted to manager of the department and became Nikko's boss. The relationship became rather awkward. Anna Rose was invited to social events with other managers and Nikko felt left behind.

Anna Rose valued the friendship, but felt it was important for her career to participate in events for managers. Nikko tried to compensate by regularly having lunch with Anna Rose and going out after work. Anna Rose was concerned about giving the appearance to other subordinates that she favored Nikko.

Points to Ponder

1. To what extent would you be comfortable loaning money to a close friend or family member? What if she didn't repay you?
2. What boundaries might be negotiated when working with close friends?
3. How would you broach the subject?

When Friends Become Business Partners

An extreme version of close friends working together is when they decide to go into business together. Consider the case of Ester and Camilla, two very good friends who shared a love of crafts. Camilla was the more sophisticated of the two, very outgoing with a great deal of self-confidence, especially in her business skills. What Ester lacked in business knowledge, she made up for with her knack for a variety of crafts. She had recently inherited some money from her aunt and wanted to invest this money in something that would provide an income for years to come. Ester and Camilla began talking about opening their own craft store and decided to go for it. Initially business was pretty good. They had a lot of traffic in the store and received good publicity in the community. Over time though business dropped off and they were struggling to pay the bills. From the beginning, Camilla was in charge of the financial end of the business. Ester felt that Camilla was secretive about the finances and as the business began to struggle, she became quite suspicious. As the business deteriorated, so did the friendship. Ultimately the business closed, Ester's money was gone, and the friendship was over, never to be resurrected.

The story of Camilla and Ester is more common than you might think. People are attracted by the allure of owning their own business and being their own boss. When there is another person to share the dream, the work, and the costs, it may seem less daunting than striking out on your own. While there will always be a certain amount of risk in starting a new business, you can negotiate agreements that reduce the risk and increase the probability of success.

Slowinski, Farris, and Jones suggest using phased relationships and offer guidelines for negotiating cooperative instead of competitive strategic partnerships.[41] While their work involves corporate partnerships, we believe their guidelines also apply on a smaller scale. The first phase is when a partnership is initially formed. In this stage the partners should clearly define their strategic, operational, and business goals; seek an accurate mutual understanding of each other's strengths and weaknesses; ensure that anyone working for them understands the importance of a cooperative relationship; formalize the expectations of all parties; and plan an exit strategy in case things don't work out.[42]

Once the partnership is operational, the focus turns to managing the ongoing relationship. During this stage the parties need to manage the partnership as a process as opposed to an event; understand the value of their relationship; effectively manage the addition of new employees; adapt to the each other's operating style; and keep key people (e.g., family members) in the loop to ensure their support in the long term.[43] While it is not possible to anticipate all potential interpersonal problems when forming a partnership, these guidelines provide good base upon which to build.

Points to Ponder

1. To what extent would you be comfortable going into business with a friend or family member?
2. Think about starting a business with your best friend. What might be some possible problems?
3. What agreements might you negotiate to prevent the problems?

The Family Business

Family firms are the most common form of business organization in the world.[44,45] Whether it is the Ford Motor Company in its early years or the family farm, whenever you are dealing with family members, family dynamics come into play, adding complexity to negotiations. Family binds naturally diverse people together.[46] We choose our friends, generally people who are like us, but when it comes to family, we don't have a choice. There may be sibling rivalry or long-standing family feuds involved. We may not particularly like certain family members, but they are still family. Nicholson argues that families generate a unique dynamic—a family climate—based on the individual differences of their members.[47] This can be an advantage or a disadvantage, depending on the situation and the individuals involved.

From an organizational standpoint, the typical advantages are that family members are more committed, satisfied, and loyal; more inclined to seek harmony; and less likely to turn over than nonfamily members,[48] all of which can facilitate negotiation and conflict resolution. On an individual level, there is the notion of **parental altruism**,[49] a trait that positively links a parent's welfare to that of their children and facilitates mutual trust, communication, and reciprocity. Parental altruism fosters a set of exchange practices including gifts, favors, respect, and love that directs each family member's interest toward the family's mutual welfare.[50] Again, this can support negotiation and conflict resolution.

For individual family members working in a family business, there are typically special advantages for getting ahead.[51] While special privileges are certainly an advantage for family members, this is not the case for employees who are not part of the family. Typically, one of the primary concerns of nonfamily members who work in a family business is that they will not enjoy the same perks or have the same opportunities to be promoted to top positions as family members. This often results in conflicts between the outsiders and the family members.

Family businesses are uniquely vulnerable to intra-family conflicts and their spillover into the business[52] and vice versa. Research has found that increased social interaction increases the extent of conflict[53] and that family business crises usually arise from the transfer of family dynamics into the business.[54] For many people, when there are problems at home, work can become a refuge, an escape from whatever is going on at home. Of course the opposite is also true—when there are problems at work, home is the place to get away from it all. But when you work with family, avoiding each other can be virtually impossible. Research has found that increased business tensions in a family business are related to lower levels of satisfaction and higher levels of destructive conflict with a spouse[55] supporting the suggestion that "trouble with the family and trouble for the individual may go together."[56]

A further complication is that there are often multiple parties, either directly or indirectly, involved in negotiations related to the family business. This includes immediate and extended family members who may be related by blood or marriage. The more people involved, the longer arguments generally last.[57] When additional parties are involved, they are also less likely to receive their information first hand. Research has shown that secondhand information may be more polarized or exaggerated (positively or negatively) than firsthand information, yet people regularly use it in their decision-making processes.[58] This is referred to as an amplification effect because the original information is magnified.

Divorce also can have an impact on a family business.[59] Often a couple that owns a family business has most of their assets tied up in the business. If they divorce, they typically don't want to continue to work together and at least one wants to liquidate his or her share of the business. Similarly, a death can lead to an upheaval in a family business. We watched this happen in the well-publicized case of Dale Earnhardt Inc. When Dale Sr. was killed in a tragic racing accident, his widow Teresa, who had worked side-by-side in the business with Dale Sr. for many years, was left in charge of the company. His son, Dale Earnhardt, Jr., also a NASCAR driver, thought he should run the company instead of his stepmother. Hostilities erupted, attempts to negotiate a settlement failed, and Dale Jr. ultimately left the organization.

It's not hard to imagine that Dale Sr. would have liked to see his wife and son continue the business he built. Most entrepreneurs would like to see the business they have built continue as their family legacy after they are no longer at the helm. In family businesses there are often conflicts over the issue of succession.[60] Statistics consistently show that only about 30% of family businesses successfully make it to the second generation, while the number drops to approximately 10% for those that are successfully able to move onward to the third generation.[61,62] A likely reason for this is conflict.

CONFLICT IN CLOSE RELATIONSHIPS

Research has found that family firms can be inundated by conflicts among family employees[63] and between family and nonfamily employees.[64] Conflict in family businesses also increases across generations.[65] There are two important dimensions of conflict within any ongoing relationship: the extent or intensity of the issues and the frequency of disagreements. The degree of conflict and cooperation depends on a combination of family structure and family climate.[66] In some families, conflict is rare, relatively mild, and short-lived, while in other families intense conflict is the norm. As discussed in Chapter 5, conflict can be either substantive or interpersonal. Naturally, substantive conflicts are easier to resolve. If you like someone, there is a greater chance that you can work together to come up with a solution that works for all parties than if you have a difficult time getting along with another person, regardless of the topic.

The potential for conflict may be exacerbated in family firms, which are notorious for the degree to which family members express emotions freely.[67] Of course this will be influenced by the personalities of the individuals involved. An aggressive style of resolving conflicts increases the severity of conflict, which in turn decreases the quality of life.[68] One study of conflict among best friends and romantic partners found that individuals who were less secure in their relationships had more difficulty managing conflict.[69] Presumably, family members working in family firms would feel more secure and be more likely to speak up than nonfamily members or people working in nonfamily businesses. More secure individuals are also more likely to use conflict management strategies involving emotional support (e.g., emotion sharing, affection, and disclosure) than avoidance and withdrawal.[70]

Another consideration is that the standards for fairness in families versus in business are typically quite different.[71] The norms of fairness within a family are based on equality and un-metered reciprocity, as opposed to the equity-based norms that govern relationships among unrelated people.[72] This is particularly visible in the distribution of assets (e.g., gift-giving, inheritance) in families versus business where rewards (e.g., merit pay, promotions) are based on performance. These differences in family and business cultures can lead to conflict.[73]

Family business founders working with their children is an environment ripe for conflict. The parents want to protect and direct their investment, while children working in the business increasingly wish to assert their autonomy.[74] Often the founder of the business has had to struggle to build the business and may feel that the children don't fully appreciate that fact. Thus, parents are motivated to exert more control and to do so for longer than their offspring are likely to tolerate.[75] At the same time, the children may feel that their parents don't recognize that they are adults and want to be treated as such or that the parents value the contribution they make or could make to the business. The children may also feel a sense of entitlement, leading them to demand unconditional benefits in greater amounts and for longer periods of time than parents are willing to provide.[76]

One study found that family arguments are more likely to end the longer they last, unlike wars and strikes, which are more likely to become entrenched.[77] This may be related to the fact that over time businesses tend to grow, resulting in the involvement of more people in running the business. Larger firms have more nonfamily managers who dilute the family culture and lead to more objective decision making that is less burdened by emotional family dynamics and the subsequent conflicts.[78]

Of course there are exceptions; sometimes the hostilities in families extend through generations. An example of this is the well-known Mondavi family. Whether or not your lips have ever made contact with a fine glass of Opus One, you probably recognize the Mondavi name as being associated with wine. What you may not realize is that the wine dynasty that spans four generations and over 100 years has been rife with conflict the entire time. Julia Flynn Siler's book chronicles the trials, tribulations, and deep-seated conflicts in the family.[79] When the company founder Cesare died, the conflict between his sons Robert and Peter escalated, and their mother Rosa banished Robert from the family business. Robert subsequently built his own company, making

Mondavi the "first name in American wine," ultimately turning it over to his own feuding sons, Michael and Timothy. After the company went public, the independent directors, with the support of sister Marcia Mondavi, took control away from Michael and the family, and began breaking up the billion dollar empire. This story and others like it lend support to Nicholson's contention that some families are better suited to cooperative enterprise than others, and some should not attempt to run a business at all.[80]

Points to Ponder

1. Think of families you know. Are there any you think would be good at operating a family business? Are there any that wouldn't be? Why?
2. Do you think members of your own family would work well together in a family business?

MANAGING CONFLICT/IMPROVING RELATIONSHIPS

In family firms there is codependence around the shared investment in power and wealth[81] making it more difficult for either party to simply walk away when there is conflict, assuming they would even want to. Thus, learning how to resolve conflicts becomes even more critical. Within any group of people, including family, there are going to be some people with whom we are very close. They are allies who support us in our endeavors and side with us when there is conflict. Conversely, there are some with whom we just don't get along. They oppose our initiatives and we view them as adversaries or even enemies. Negative relationships have a bigger impact than positive relationships,[82] commanding more of our attention. We may become suspicious and self-protective; our reactions can range from mild to almost paranoid.

Yet all relationships are contingency based; therefore, if you can change the contingencies, you can change the relationship.[83] Having more friends doesn't compensate for our negative relationships; so from a conflict management standpoint, it is important to focus on reducing specific negative relationships.[84] Instead of focusing on differences with your adversaries, seek out common ground. Of course this means you will have to communicate with the other party and seek to build trust.

Trust is a process. The question is not whether to trust or not, but whom, how much, and in what areas of responsibility should you trust another person.[85] Changing a relationship to turn an adversary into an ally takes time and effort to build trust and open the lines of communication. It is generally most effective to start with small issues and work your way up to larger ones. Of course this requires that you begin sharing information. In some cases this can require a leap of faith on your part, especially when the relationship has been particularly negative. With sufficient desire and effort from both parties, you will be able to work out your differences through negotiation. In turn, this can impact the affect, communication, and levels of trust between you and the other party.[86]

Third-Party Involvement

Of course there are no guarantees that any two individuals will be able to work out their differences on their own. In some cases it is beneficial to solicit the assistance of a third party. This could be another family member who is not involved in the business or someone outside the family. In some cases the third party acts as a **"trust catalyst,"** who inspires family members to trust each other,[87] which can go a long way in resolving conflicts.

Even when family members are not involved in the operation of the business, they still know the players and personalities involved, and are part of the family social group. They typically have a good understanding of the family dynamics, if not the business, and may be able to intervene when there are conflicts between family members who work in the business. Essentially they act as mediators. They have credibility as family members, yet are typically seen as more neutral when it comes to business conflicts because they are not directly involved. In fact, research has found that involving family members who don't work in the business can help reduce both the frequency and extent of conflict.[88]

Another option for third-party involvement is to bring in someone from outside the family and business to help resolve the conflict(s). There are consultants who specialize in working with family businesses, many of whom have a background in some branch of psychology or even family therapy. They recognize the role of family dynamics. They seek to understand the players and their roles and responsibilities in the decision-making process and help to clarify this for the family members themselves. Bringing clarity to the roles and responsibilities often assists in dissipating tension and allowing for resources to become focused on targeted and agreed-upon goals, rather than diverting those resources to competing goals.[89]

You must be cautious when dealing with third parties when they have a preexisting relationship with the person with whom you are trying to improve a relationship. Of course this would be the case when the third party is another family member. If the third party also has a conflict with the other party, it can influence your views toward that person and potentially draw you into their conflict.[90] Thus, it is important to be conscious of all the relationships involved and avoid being influenced by someone who is already in conflict with the other party.

Conflict and Fairness

The likelihood of conflict is diminished when everyone sees the system and procedures as fair and just. As noted earlier, the standards for fairness in the distribution of rewards in families (equality) and business (equity) are generally different and often lie at the heart of conflict in a family business.[91] The issue becomes one of reconciling the differences between the economics and the emotions. To that end, it is essential to define the processes for determining rewards and communicate the process to all involved. The basis for the rewards is less important than everyone understanding the system. Application of a fair process improves both economic performance of the organization and satisfaction and commitment of family and nonfamily members involved with it.[92]

But what constitutes a fair process? Van der Heyden and colleagues[93] identify five characteristics of fair processes in family firms:

- Communication and voice—all participants have the opportunity to be heard;
- Clarity of information, process, and expectations—everything is defined and communicated accurately and in a clear, understandable manner;
- Consistency—with stated values and as applied across people and over time;
- Changeability—a procedure to change course as necessary;
- Commitment to fairness—by all involved in decision making.

In addition to defined processes for distributing rewards, there should be processes for making major decisions and resolving conflicts. A system of family governance is needed to overcome weaknesses and protect from fractures, especially with nongenetic ties (i.e., in-laws, spouses, etc.) where problems may be more common.[94] Because there are often conflicts over who will carry on in the family business, succession planning is very important. When there are nonfamily managers and executives, care must be taken to protect them from family interference.[95]

Knowing Where to Draw the Line

Unfortunately it's not always possible to resolve conflict with another person. Most people have no problem walking away from a negotiation with a stranger. If we don't like the terms they are offering, we simply go elsewhere. This is not the case however when we are dealing with close friends or family members. While it may not be easy, it is possible and sometimes beneficial, to walk away from a family business, but not the family. Indeed, it's not uncommon for family members to work outside the family business for a time. This may happen before a person joins the family business or later if they just need a break. Working outside the family business provides an opportunity to learn other ways of doing business, develop skills, and build professional credibility.

In other cases, a person may walk away from close friends or family completely. Sometimes as much as we would like to preserve a relationship, it is best to walk away.

FIGURE 9.3   The Myths of Having a Minority Interest in a Business[96]

A number of myths exist about one's rights when owning a minority interest in a business, whether or not it is a family business. In general, most people believe a person with a minority stake in the ownership of a business:

- can always sell her interest for a "fair" price
- is entitled to a percentage of the business profits and other benefits equal to her share of ownership
- is entitled to know all the details of what is going on in the business
- is entitled to a voice in the operations of the business.

Unfortunately, unless you have negotiated a written agreement that specifically grants one or more of these rights, they simply don't exist. In the absence of such an agreement, a minority owner has no real power. At best all she can do is threaten to, or actually, cause trouble for the majority owner giving him an incentive to either acquiesce to some of the demands or buy the minority owner's share in the company.

This is especially true when the relationship is destructive, abusive, or very dysfunctional; yet even then, walking away can be very difficult. In some cases, we may not be willing to walk away without a fight. Typically, this involves taking some sort of legal action, usually filing a lawsuit, which can take years to work its way through the legal system. Obviously this can be very costly, taking both a financial and an emotional toll. Even then, there is no guarantee that you will prevail. Anyone contemplating such an action needs to be sure they are on very sound legal ground. Figure 9.3 illustrates some common misperceptions about the rights of a person who owns less than the majority interest in a business.

Cultural Differences

Clearly, there is no one-size-fits-all when it comes to negotiating and resolving conflicts in family businesses. In addition to typical differences from one family to another, there are significant differences in negotiation[97] and conflict resolution[98] in families from one culture to another. Our discussion of negotiation and conflict resolution has assumed an individualistic, typically Western, culture. When dealing with nonwestern values, more emphasis is usually placed on the concerns for relationships, family, interpersonal norms, and collective interests.[99] This can lead to very different outcomes for similar situations. For example, instead of dividing assets equally between children, which is the norm in western cultures, the norm in eastern cultures is to leave everything to one child, often the eldest male, who will bear full responsibility for carrying on the family legacy. Similarly, when dealing with conflict, people in western cultures are more likely to speak up and question authority, even within the family. In collectivistic cultures, the will of the individual is usually subordinated to the family[100] and conflict is to be avoided.

Summary

We negotiate a variety of situations with people ranging from contractors and landlords to neighbors and acquaintances to friends and family members. The less familiar we are with the other party, the more formal the relationship, and the greater likelihood our negotiations will result in formal written agreements with sanctions for noncompliance. Our relationship with the other party influences how we interact when we negotiate or attempt to resolve conflicts with them, especially in a business environment. Maintaining the relationship takes on additional importance when we are negotiating with those with whom we are very close. We have additional knowledge about the other party and his interests, suggesting the possibility of higher value agreements, but may be more inclined to agree to settlements that are expedient and perhaps less than optimal in order to maintain the relationship. This can make us more vulnerable to opportunistic behavior by the other party. Dealing with family in a business setting is much more difficult because the lines between business and family become blurred. There are steps we can take to prevent and manage conflict within a family business, which may involve third parties to serve as mediators. Unfortunately, not all conflicts can be resolved and in some cases it is simply best to walk away.

Summary: The Big Picture

Negotiating with contractors	May be one time or ongoing service. Agreements are more likely to be in writing with sanctions for noncompliance. Disputes often end up in mediation or court.
Landlord/tenant relationships	Most disputes are a result of a difference in standards between the parties. Building a good working relationship is important.
In the neighborhood	Best to address issues in the early stages before they escalate.
Negotiating with acquaintances	Usually involves obtaining assistance. Reciprocity is a key factor.
When the other party is your friend	Friendship influences the choice of strategy. Scripts are important. Desire to maintain the relationship may result in suboptimal agreements.
Doing business with friends or family	Boundaries between business and personal relationships are blurred. May benefit from third-party involvement.
Conflict and fairness	There are different standards of fairness in business than family relationships. May need to walk away.
Cultural differences	The role of the relationship in negotiations among family members varies among cultures.

Key Terms and Concepts

Acquaintances   People we know either professionally or personally, but whom we either don't know well enough or are not close enough to consider a friend.

Contractor   Anyone you pay to provide goods or services at a certain price or rate.

Event scripts   Norms for behavior in certain situations.

Friendship scripts   Norms for interacting with one's friends.

Mechanic's lien   A legal claim against one's property as a result of a contractor's failure to pay for materials or labor.

Parental altruism   A trait that positively links a parent's welfare to that of their children and facilitates mutual trust, communication, and reciprocity.

Professional network   Acquaintances who may provide assistance to further your career.

Trust catalyst   A third party that helps family members to trust each other.

Discussion Questions

1. Compare and contrast the unique characteristics and challenges of negotiating with contractors and landlords versus neighbors and acquaintances versus close friends and family.
2. Develop a plan for negotiating with a contractor to put an addition on your house.
3. Describe a negotiation that you have had with a friend and the impact the friendship had on the negotiation.
4. Discuss the special considerations of managing conflict with family and close friends.
5. Describe the challenges of doing business with family and close friends and develop a plan for addressing the challenges.
6. Compare and contrast the advantages and disadvantages of the options for third-party involvement in resolving conflict in a family business.

Ethical Dilemma: Loyalty Tested

In general your boss Dina has been good to you. Three years ago she set out to get approval for a special salary adjustment to bring your salary into line with other recent hires in the department. It wasn't an easy undertaking, but she was persistent and in the end got approval for a substantial adjustment to your salary. In return, you have been loyal to Dina, defending her to other employees who were very critical of her. You felt as if you owed her for working so hard for your salary adjustment, but lately you have begun to wonder if your coworkers are right about her. Dina regularly praises Charlotte, a person in your department who arrives late, leaves early, and generally doesn't do much when she is at work. You just don't understand how a manager could defend such behavior. The Human Resources department is housed in another building and it doesn't appear that they are aware of Charlotte's behavior. You have tried to talk to Dina about this situation, but she doesn't want to discuss it. You suspect that Dina is defending Charlotte because they have similar backgrounds. You are torn between defending a person who has been good to you in the past and voicing your concerns about the current situation.

Questions

1. What conflict needs to be resolved?
2. How might negotiation be used in this situation?
3. Do you have any obligation to Dina because she worked hard to gain approval for your salary adjustment three years ago?
4. Do you have an obligation to voice your concerns about Charlotte's transgressions?
5. What risks do you face if you do speak up?
6. Based on your value system, what would you do in this situation?

Ethical Dilemma: Sailing, Sailing . . . the Boat Partnership

Jane, who is married to Stuart, and Betty, a divorced single parent, had been best friends for more than ten years. They did many things together socially and their young children were friends. Stuart was an avid sailor who crewed for others in races whenever he could. Jane had no experience sailing and didn't have the opportunity to learn since they didn't own a boat. One summer Betty dated a sailor. While the relationship was brief, Betty fell in love with sailing. She also wanted something she and her children could do together as a family as they got older. Stuart had a friend that wanted to sell his boat and Betty and Stuart started talking about a partnership. Ultimately they agreed that Betty would buy the boat for $2,000 and Stuart would teach Betty how to sail. They would split the expenses (maintenance, slip fees, etc.) and after the first sailing season, they would be fifty-fifty partners. There was no written agreement; after all, they were good friends. Stuart had hoped that through Betty, Jane would become interested in sailing, but that didn't happen. One year later, it was sailing season again and the $1,000 slip fee was due. One night Jane went to Betty's house, handed her their boat file, and said "It's all yours." Jane said it was because they were short on money. Betty was shocked and miffed that there was no warning and no discussion. It was just dumped on her at the last minute when the bills were due. Betty knew they were giving $5,000 to Stuart's eldest daughter for her wedding and believed that Jane was using their finances as an excuse to walk away from the boat. The friendship was strained and they ceased getting together socially. Several months later, Betty and Stuart ran into each other and Stuart said Betty owed him money for his half of the boat.

Questions

1. Was Jane's behavior appropriate? Why or why not?
2. Should Betty pay Stuart? If so, how much?
3. What could have been done differently to avoid a rift in the relationship?

Endnotes

1. Kurtzberg, T., and V. H. Medvec. "Can We Negotiate and Still Be Friends?" *Negotiation Journal* 15(4) (2009): 355–361.
2. O'Connor, K. M., J. A. Arnold, and E. R. Burris. "Negotiators' Bargaining Histories and Their Effects on Future Negotiation Performance." *Journal of Applied Psychology* 90(2) (2005): 350–362.
3. Druckman, D., and B. J. Broome. "Value Differences and Conflict Resolution Familiarity Or Liking?" *The Journal Of Conflict Resolution* 35(4) (1991): 571–593.
4. *Ibid.*
5. Olk, P., and M. Elvira. "Friends and Strategic Agents: The Role of Friendship and Discretion in Negotiating Strategic Alliances." *Group & Organization Management* 26(2) (2001): 124–164.
6. Strutton, D., and L. E. Pelton. "Negotiation: Bringing More to the Table than Demands." *Marketing Health Services* 17(1) (1997): 52–58.
7. Olekalns, M., and P. L. Smith. "Moments in Time: Metacognition, Trust, and Outcomes in Dyadic Negotiations." *Personality & Social Psychology Bulletin* 31(12) (2005): 1696–1707.
8. Druckman, D., and B. J. Broome. "Value Differences and Conflict Resolution Familiarity Or Liking?" *The Journal Of Conflict Resolution* 35(4) (1991): 571–593.
9. Sondak, H., M. A. Neale, and R. L. Pinkley. "Relationship, Contribution, and Resource Constrains: Determinants of Distributive Justice in Individual Preferences and Negotiated Agreements." *Group Decision and Negotiation* 8(6) (1999): 489–510.
10. *Ibid.*
11. Savage, G. T., J. D. Blair, and R. L. Sorenson. "Consider Both Relationships And Substance When Negotiating." *The Academy of Management Executive* 3(1) (1989): 37–48.
12. *Ibid.*
13. Olekalns, M., and P. L Smith. "Social Value Orientations and Strategy Choices in Competitive Negotiations." *Personality & Social Psychology Bulletin* 25(6) (1999): 657–668.
14. Strutton, D., and L. E. Pelton. "Negotiation: Bringing More to the Table than Demands." *Marketing Health Services* 17(1) (1997): 52–58.
15. *Ibid.*
16. Halpern, J. J. "The Effect of Friendship on Personal Business Transactions." *The Journal of Conflict Resolution* 38(4) (1994): 647–664.
17. *Ibid.*
18. Kurtzberg, T., and V. H. Medvec. "Can We Negotiate and Still Be Friends?" *Negotiation Journal* 15(4) (2009): 355–361.
19. *Ibid.*
20. Halpern, J. J. "The Effect of Friendship on Personal Business Transactions." *The Journal of Conflict Resolution* 38(4) (1994): 647–664.
21. *Ibid.*
22. Mandel, D. R. "Economic Transactions Among Friends: Asymmetric Generosity But Not Agreement in Buyers' and Sellers' Offers." *The Journal of Conflict Resolution* 50(4) (2006): 584–606.
23. *Ibid.*
24. Tenbrunsel, A. E., K. A. Wade-Benzoni, J. Moag, and M. H. Bazerman. "The Negotiation Matching Process: Relationships and Partner Selection." *Organizational*

Behavior and Human Decision Processes 80 (1999): 252–283.

25. Halpern, J. J. "The Effect of Friendship on Personal Business Transactions." *The Journal of Conflict Resolution* 38(4) (1994): 647–664.

26. Thompson, L., E. Peterson, and S. E. Brodt. "Team Negotiation: An Examination of Integrative and Distributive Bargaining." *Journal of Personality and Social Psychology* 70 (1996): 66–78.

27. Mandel, D. R. "Economic Transactions Among Friends: Asymmetric Generosity But Not Agreement in Buyers' and Sellers' Offers." *The Journal of Conflict Resolution* 50(4) (2006): 584–606.

28. Kurtzberg, T., and V. H. Medvec. "Can We Negotiate and Still Be Friends?" *Negotiation Journal* 15(4) (2009): 355–361.

29. Mandel, D. R. "Economic Transactions Among Friends: Asymmetric Generosity But Not Agreement in Buyers' and Sellers' Offers." *The Journal of Conflict Resolution* 50(4) (2006): 584–606.

30. Kurtzberg, T., and V. H. Medvec. "Can We Negotiate and Still Be Friends?" *Negotiation Journal* 15(4) (2009): 355–361.

31. *Ibid.*

32. *Ibid.*

33. Fry, W. R., I. J. Firestone, and D. Williams. "Negotiation Process and Outcome of Stranger Dyads and Dating Couples: Do Lovers Lose?" *Basic and Applied Social Psychology* 4 (1983): 1–16.

34. Halpern, J. J. "The Effect of Friendship on Personal Business Transactions." *The Journal of Conflict Resolution* 38(4) (1994): 647–664.

35. Sondak, H., M. A. Neale, and R. L. Pinkley. "Relationship, Contribution, and Resource Constrains: Determinants of Distributive Justice in Individual Preferences and Negotiated Agreements." *Group Decision and Negotiation* 8(6) (1999): 489–510.

36. Olekalns, M., and P. L Smith. "Social Value Orientations and Strategy Choices in Competitive Negotiations." *Personality & Social Psychology Bulletin* 25(6) (1999): 657–668.

37. Sondak, H., M. A. Neale, and R. L. Pinkley. "Relationship, Contribution, and Resource Constrains: Determinants of Distributive Justice in Individual Preferences and Negotiated Agreements." *Group Decision and Negotiation* 8(6) (1999): 489–510.

38. Druckman, D., and B. J. Broome. "Value Differences and Conflict Resolution Familiarity Or Liking?" *The Journal Of Conflict Resolution* 35(4) (1991): 571–593.

39. Olk, P., and M. Elvira. "Friends and Strategic Agents: The Role of Friendship and Discretion in Negotiating Strategic Alliances." *Group & Organization Management* 26(2) (2001): 124–164.

40. http://www.unca.edu/FBF/statistics.html, accessed 8/4/10

41. Slowinski, G., G. F. Farris, and D. Jones. "Strategic Partnering: Process Instead of Event." *Research Technology Management* 36(3) (1993): 22–25.

42. *Ibid.*

43. *Ibid.*

44. Gersick, K. E., J. A. Davis, M. M. Hampton, and I. Lansberg. *Generation to Generation: Life Cycles of the Family Business.* Cambridge, MA: Harvard Business School Press, 1997.

45. La Porta, R., F. Lopez-de-Salanes, and A. Shleifer. "Corporate Ownership Around the World." *Journal of Finance* 54(2) (1999): 471–517.

46. Nicholson, N. "Evolutionary Psychology and Family Business: A New Synthesis for Theory, Research, and Practice." *Family Business Review* 21(1) (2008): 103–118.

47. *Ibid.*

48. Beehr, T. A., J. A. Drexler Jr., and S. Faulkner. "Working in Small Family Businesses: Empirical Comparisons to Non-Family Businesses." *Journal of Organizational Behavior (1986–1998)* 18(3) (1997): 297–312.

49. Stark, O. *Altruism and Beyond: An Economic Analysis of Transfers within Families and Groups.* Cambridge, U.K.: Cambridge University Press, 1995.

50. Lubatkin, M. H., W. S. Schulze, Y. Ling, and R. N. Dino. "The Effects of Parental Altruism on the Governance of Family-Managed Firms." *Journal of Organizational Behavior* 26 (2005): 313–330.

51. Beehr, T. A., J. A. Drexler Jr., and S. Faulkner. "Working in Small Family Businesses: Empirical Comparisons to Non-Family Businesses." *Journal of Organizational Behavior (1986–1998)* 18(3) (1997): 297–312.

52. Nicholson, N. "Evolutionary Psychology and Family Business: A New Synthesis for Theory, Research, and Practice." *Family Business Review* 21(1) (2008): 103–118.

53. Davis, P. S., and P. D. Harveston. "The Phenomenon of Substantive Conflict in the Family Firm: A Cross-Generational Study." *Journal of Small Business Management* 39(1) (2001): 14–30.

54. Jaffe, D. T. "The World of Family Business Consulting." *Consulting to Management* 17(1) (2006): 21–24.

55. Amarapurkar, S. S., and S. M. Danes. "Farm Business-Owning Couples: Interrelationships among Business Tensions, Relationship Conflict Quality, and Spousal Satisfaction." *Journal of Family and Economic Issues* 26(3) (2005): 419–441.

56. Beehr, T. A., J. A. Drexler Jr., and S. Faulkner. "Working in Small Family Businesses: Empirical Comparisons to Non-Family Businesses." *Journal of Organizational Behavior (1986–1998)* 18(3) (1997): 297–312.

57. Teachman, S. V. "Influences on the Duration of Wars, Strikes, Riots, and Family Arguments." *The Journal of Conflict Resolution (1986–1998)* 37(3) (1993): 544–568.

58. Giuseppe, L., D. J. Brass, and B. Gray. "Social Networks and Perceptions of Intergroup Conflict: The Role of Negative Relationships and Third Parties." *Academy of Management Journal* 41(1) (1998): 55–67.

59. Nicholson, N. "Evolutionary Psychology and Family Business: A New Synthesis for Theory, Research, and Practice." *Family Business Review* 21(1) (2008): 103–118.

60. Lubatkin, M. H., W. S. Schulze, Y. Ling, and R. N. Dino. "The Effects of Parental Altruism on the Governance of Family-Managed Firms." *Journal of Organizational Behavior* 26 (2005): 313–330.

61. http://www.unca.edu/FBF/statistics.html, accessed 8/4/10

62. Ward, J. L. *Keeping the Family Business Healthy: How to Plan For Continuing Growth, Profitability, and Family Leadership.* Marietta, GA: Business Owners Resources, 1997.

63. Astrachan, J. H., and C. E. Aronoff. "Succession Issues Can Signal Deeper Problems." *Nation's Business* 86(5) (1998): 72–74.

64. Gersick, K. E., J. A. Davis, M. M. Hampton, and I. Lansberg. *Generation to Generation: Life Cycles of the Family Business.* Cambridge, MA: Harvard Business School Press, 1997.

65. Davis, P. S., and P. D. Harveston. "The Phenomenon of Substantive Conflict in the Family Firm: A Cross-Generational Study." *Journal of Small Business Management* 39(1) (2001): 14–30.

66. Nicholson, N. "Evolutionary Psychology and Family Business: A New Synthesis for Theory, Research, and Practice." *Family Business Review* 21(1) (2008): 103–118.

67. *Ibid.*

68. Danes, S. M., R. D. Leichtentritt, M. E. Metz, and C. Huddleston-Casas. "Effects of Conflict Styles and Conflict Severity on Quality of Life of Men and women in family business." *Journal of Family and Economic Issues* 21(3) (200): 259–286

69. Creasey, G., K. Kershaw, and A. Boston. "Conflict Management with Friends and Romantic Partners: The Role of Attachment and Negative Mood Regulation Expectancies." *Journal of Youth and Adolescence* 28(5) (1999): 523–543.

70. *Ibid.*

71. Van der Heyden, L., C. Blondel, and R. S. Carlock. "Fair Process: Striving for Justice in Family Business." *Family Business Review* 18(1) (2005): 1–21.

72. Lubatkin, M. H., W. S. Schulze, Y. Ling, and R. N. Dino. "The Effects of Parental Altruism on the Governance of Family-Managed Firms." *Journal of Organizational Behavior* 26 (2005): 313–330.

73. Beehr, T. A., J. A. Drexler Jr., and S. Faulkner. "Working in Small Family Businesses: Empirical Comparisons to Non-Family Businesses." *Journal of Organizational Behavior (1986–1998)* 18(3) (1997): 297–312.

74. Nicholson, N. "Evolutionary Psychology and Family Business: A New Synthesis for Theory, Research, and Practice." *Family Business Review* 21(1) (2008): 103–118.

75. Mock, D. W. *More Than Kin and Less Than Kind: The Evolution of Family Conflict.* Cambridge, MA: Belknap Press of Harvard University Press, 2004.

76. *Ibid.*

77. Teachman, S. V. "Influences on the Duration of Wars, Strikes, Riots, and Family Arguments." *The Journal of Conflict Resolution (1986–1998)* 37(3) (1993): 544–568.

78. Sonfield, M. C., and R. N. Lussier. "The Influence of Family Business Size on Management Activities, Styles and Characteristics." *New England Journal of Entrepreneurship* 11(2) (2008): 47–56.

79. Siler, J. F. *The House of Mondavi: The Rise and Fall of an American Wine Dynasty.* New York: Gotham Books, 2007

80. Nicholson, N. "Evolutionary Psychology and Family Business: A New Synthesis for Theory, Research, and Practice." *Family Business Review* 21(1) (2008): 103–118.

81. *Ibid.*

82. Giuseppe, L., D. J. Brass, and B. Gray. "Social Networks and Perceptions of Intergroup Conflict: The Role of Negative Relationships and Third Parties." *Academy of Management Journal* 41(1) (1998): 55–67.

83. Stybel, L. J., and M. Peabody. "Friend, Foe, Ally, Adversary . . . Or Something Else?" *MIT Sloan Management Review* 46(4) (2005): 3–16.

84. Giuseppe, L., D. J. Brass, and B. Gray. "Social Networks and Perceptions of Intergroup Conflict: The Role of Negative Relationships and Third Parties." *Academy of Management Journal* 41(1) (1998): 55–67.

85. Kaye, K., and S. Hamilton. "Roles of Trust in Consulting to Financial Families." *Family Business Review* 17(2) (2004): 151–163.

86. Kurtzberg, T., and V. H. Medvec. "Can We Negotiate and Still Be Friends?" *Negotiation Journal* 15(4) (2009): 355–361.

87. LaChapelle, K., and L. Barnes. "The Trust Catalyst in Family-Owned Businesses." *Family Business Review* 11(1) (1998): 1–17.

88. Davis, P. S., and P. D. Harveston. "The Phenomenon of Substantive Conflict in the Family Firm: A Cross-Generational Study." *Journal of Small Business Management* 39(1) (2001): 14–30.

89. Amarapurkar, S. S., and S. M. Danes. "Farm Business-Owning Couples: Interrelationships among Business Tensions, Relationship Conflict Quality, and Spousal Satisfaction." *Journal of Family and Economic Issues* 26(3) (2005): 419–441.

90. Giuseppe, L., D. J. Brass, and B. Gray. "Social Networks and Perceptions of Intergroup Conflict: The Role of Negative Relationships and Third Parties." *Academy of Management Journal* 41(1) (1998): 55–67.

91. Van der Heyden, L., C. Blondel, and R. S. Carlock. "Fair Process: Striving for Justice in Family Business." *Family Business Review* 18(1) (2005): 1–21.

92. *Ibid.*

93. *Ibid.*

94. Nicholson, N. "Evolutionary Psychology and Family Business: A New Synthesis for Theory, Research, and Practice." *Family Business Review* 21(1) (2008): 103–118.

95. *Ibid.*

96. Krasnow, H. C. "What To Do When Talking Fails: Strategies for Minority Owners to Turn Stock Certificates into Money." *Family Business Review* 15(4) (2002): 259–268.

97. Makgosa, R. "Exploring the Impact of Ethnicity on Conflict Resolution in Joint Purchase Decisions." *Journal of American Academy of Business* 11(2) (2007): 205–212.

98. Hubbard, A. S. "Cultural and Status Differences in Intergroup Conflict Resolution: A Longitudinal Study of a Middle East dialog Group in the United States." *Human Relations* 52(3) (1999): 303–325.

99. Jun, Y., and R. L. Sorenson. "The Influence of Confucian Ideology on Conflict in Chinese Family Business." *International Journal of Cross Cultural Management: CCM* 4(1) (2004): 5–17.

100. *Ibid.*

Exercise 9.1   Obtaining the Assistance of Acquaintances in Your Job Search

Overview:

When you graduated from college a year ago, you took a job as an entry level manager in another state in order to spread your wings and gain work experience. The job has not turned out to be all that you had hoped. The economy declined and your employer had to make a number of cutbacks. As a result you are now working fifty hours every week and your morale is very low. You have had to terminate a number of employees and deal with others who are very disgruntled. It has been great experience, but you have had enough. You have decided to look for a different job that would be located closer to your family. You know you need to be proactive in finding another job, but you are not sure where to start. You have met a number of people in your field in the past year and you think they may be helpful in your job search. You need to contact them and get them to agree to let you use them as a reference.

Identify people you would contact and all of their contact information (i.e., title, business address, phone number, email address). Draft an email requesting their assistance.

Name	Title	Business Address	Phone Number(s)	Email Address

Exercise 9.2   Assessing a Conflict between Close Friends or Relatives

For this exercise you need to think of an actual conflict between close friends or relatives that you or someone you know has experienced. This could be something from your childhood, a current situation, or anything in between. Try to remember as much detail as possible—the who, what, where, and when of the situation. Using the following worksheet, evaluate the conflict and identify what each of the participants or a third party might have done to resolve or speed the resolution of the conflict.

Worksheet: Exercise 9.2 Assessing a Conflict between Close Friends or Relatives

Parties/personalities involved: _____

_____

_____

_____

_____

Reason for conflict: _____

_____

_____

_____

Duration of conflict: _____

_____

Others involved: _____

_____

_____

_____

_____

Turning point(s) in the resolution of the conflict: _____

_____

_____

_____

_____

Long-term effect on the relationship: _____

_____

_____

_____

_____

What might the participants have done to resolve the conflict sooner: _____

_____

_____

_____

_____

What might a third party have done to resolve the conflict sooner: _____

_____

_____

_____

_____

Exercise 9.3 Let's Start a Business Together!

In this exercise you will begin by identifying a business that you could start with a close friend or a relative. After selecting a business and a partner, identify the issues involved in forming and operating the business that you would need to address. Be sure to address both substantive (e.g., financing, decision making, salaries, time off) and relationship (e.g., personality differences, work ethics) issues. Use the following worksheet to organize your work.

Worksheet: Exercise 9.3 Let's Start a Business Together!

Business partner/your relationship:		
Type of business:		
Issues	Your views	Partner's views

Exercise 9.4   It's Not Always Easy Going Green

Instructions:

In this exercise you will be assigned the role of Randy Richman, Frieda Frugal, or an observer. Your instructor will provide you with confidential role sheets based on your assigned role. Read all information provided, complete the worksheet, and prepare for the negotiation based on your knowledge of the situation.

Overview:

Randy Richman and Frieda Frugal have been friends and business partners for a number of years. Thus far, they have always been able to agree on business decisions. But now, Randy has become quite environmentally conscious and told Frieda he would like the business to go green. When Randy raised the issue, Frieda was surprised and said she would need time to think about it. Frieda never said another word about it. Several weeks later Randy raised the issue again and they have decided to talk about it today.

Worksheet: Exercise 9.4 It's Not Always Easy Going Green

Randy Richman

Interests: _____

_____

_____

Issue	Opening Demand	Target	Resistance

Frieda Frugal

Interests: _____

_____

_____

Issue	Opening Demand	Target	Resistance

Exercise 9.5   All in the Family: The Company in the Hands of the Second Generation

You have recently started a business as a consultant to small businesses and are ready to begin work with your first client. It is a million dollar–a-year technical services company that was started by two friends, Sherman and Kelly, twenty years ago. Kelly is a little older than Sherman and has reduced his work schedule to part time. Sherman is still working full time, but would like to slow down and enjoy the fruits of his labor. Each has three children. Kelly has two sons and a daughter, all of whom have worked in the business at one time or another. Kelly has a very good relationship with all of his children. Sherman has two daughters who have never had any interest in the business and a son, J.R., who had worked in the business for a time until he and Sherman had a falling out when Sherman divorced J.R.'s mother fifteen years ago. It was a bitter divorce that had a very negative impact on Sherman's relationship with his children, especially his son. They had no contact for a number of years. While the ice has thawed a bit in recent years, the relationship is still very strained.

Sherman and Kelly want you to help them decide who should take over the business when they retire. You will be meeting with them for the first time tomorrow and are thinking about how you will approach the situation. You understand the importance of this job. It could chart the course for your consulting business for years to come. You want to be prepared and have decided that you should go in with a list of prepared questions to help you gain a better understanding of the business and all the people involved. Draft a list of questions that you would ask to help you assess the situation and identify any additional information that you would gather in preparation for your meeting with the partners.

Exercise 9.6   Not So Happily Ever After: The Family Business in Divorce Court

Instructions:

In this exercise you will be assigned the role of Cal Hanson, Kitty Hansen, mediator, or an observer. Your instructor will provide you with confidential role sheets based on your assigned role. Read all the information provided, complete the worksheet, and prepare for the negotiation based on your knowledge of the situation.

Overview:

Cal and Kitty Hansen have been married for thirty years. They both came from farm families and took over the operation of the Hansen family farm from Cal's parents soon after they were married. In their household, each had assumed traditional gender roles. Cal was the head of household, responsible for providing for the family. He worked very long hours and made all of the decisions having to do with the business. Kitty was a homemaker who was responsible for maintaining the household and making sure Cal and the children were well cared for. The house was always clean and the meals were always on the table at the appropriate time. Kitty was active in the children's school activities and always supported her husband. Now that their children are grown with families of their own, Kitty often takes care of the grandchildren.

Over the last five years Kitty and Cal have experienced marital difficulties. Kitty felt that her contributions were not being recognized and wanted to have a life of her own. Three years ago she moved out and they were separated for about six months. Cal has always been opposed to divorce and thinks Kitty should appreciate all that he has given her. Ultimately they decided to try to work things out and Kitty moved back in. Initially things were better, but in the end they reverted to their old patterns. Kitty again became very unhappy and moved out. A few months later she filed for divorce. Cal was still opposed to divorce, but there wasn't anything he could do to stop it from happening.

Neither Kitty nor Cal has a college education. The farm provided a good income for the family over the years, but Cal is ready to get out of the business. They have discussed this for a couple of years, but selling the business is not a quick or easy task. After moving out and filing for divorce, Kitty found a clerical job but the pay is quite low. She wants her share of the money out of the business to help support herself and to provide for her retirement.

An attorney suggested that Cal and Kitty take their case to mediation to try to come up with a way to handle the dissolution of the business and division of the marital property. They are meeting with the mediator for the first time today. Each has been asked to bring a list of what they would like to receive in the settlement.

Worksheet: Exercise 9.6 Not So Happily Ever After: The Family Business in Divorce Court

Cal Hansen

Interests: _____

_____

Issue	Opening Demand	Target	Resistance

Kitty Hansen

Interests: _____

_____

Issue	Opening Demand	Target	Resistance

CHAPTER 10

International Negotiations

> *"Culture is more often a source of conflict than of synergy.*
> *Cultural differences are a nuisance at best and often a disaster."*
> Prof. Geert Hofstede, Emeritus Professor,
> *Maastricht University*

Chapter Objectives

After studying this chapter and completing the exercises you should be able to:

- Assess the challenges that may arise when engaging in cross-cultural negotiations.

- Describe the five dimensions of Hofstede's cross-cultural differences and how each one impacts the process of negotiations.

- Identify what research needs to be done to effectively prepare for a cross-cultural negotiation, as well as options for obtaining the needed information.

- Hypothesize the nondomestic negotiating partner's expectations for your culturally influenced behavior in a cross-cultural negotiation.

- Assess the importance of the relationship in cross-cultural negotiation and how that varies among cultures.

- Evaluate the communication style, practices, and expectations for verbal and nonverbal behavior among different cultures and its impact on negotiation processes and outcomes.

- Examine customs (e.g., gift-giving), laws, and protocol (e.g., greetings), and the importance of understanding and demonstrating appreciation for these differences in cross-cultural negotiations.

Roberta from the opening scenario would certainly agree with Hofstede. That she was not only the secretary but likely the person most qualified to tell the man who just insulted her that his plant was the source of a critical manufacturing defect was indeed a disaster waiting to happen. As this example illustrates, the already complicated process of negotiation, when done in a global economy—wherein geographic boundaries are no longer impediments to doing business—creates even greater complexity and challenge. In this global marketplace, organizations large and small buy from, sell to, merge with, network among, and, in general, do business with other organizations around the world. Business transactions within and among international organizations occur regularly. In fact, international managers might find themselves spending half or more of their time in cross-cultural negotiations.[1]

With negotiations between domestic and foreign firms becoming more prevalent, it has become more important than ever that in addition to basic negotiation skills, individuals involved in global business have a solid understanding of how different cultures, practices, and customs affect negotiations.[2] While one chapter could never completely cover the complexities of effectively negotiating in each and every country, our goal is to provide a framework and other strategies that can be applied successfully in many international settings.

Chapter Scenario, Part I:

Roberta Matthews, the 33-year-old project manager for the pacemakers produced by her global biotech firm, had spent the last three weeks painstakingly checking every step in the manufacturing process in the South Florida plant after receiving the disturbing news that the pacemakers were estimated to fail 2% of the time. "This is completely unacceptable," she thought. "Pacemakers failing 2% of the time may not sound like much—especially when many of them function more as heartbeat monitors rather than regulators—but anything more than zero defect is unacceptable. Especially if the pacemaker is monitoring and ensuring the proper function of your loved one's heart!"

She presented her findings to upper management, and explained how there was no evidence suggesting that the defect was being caused in the South Florida plant. Instead, she explained that the problem must be coming from the partially assembled pacemakers they received from the Dutch firm with whom her firm contracted. (Assembly was completed and the product tested in the South Florida plant.) She requested and was given approval to visit the Dutch plant to help find and fix whatever was causing the pacemakers to fail.

When Roberta arrived, sharply dressed in a well-fitting suit and standing beside Carlos, the lead engineer who reported to her, Dennis van der Reis, VP of Operations in the Netherlands, looked her up and down and said, "OK, so you're the secretary. Is he (looking at Carlos) the project manager?" Roberta, with a master's degree in biomedical engineering, two patents to her credit, and a successful track record as both engineer and manager, was floored. She could barely speak. . . .

Points to Ponder

1. Imagine you are Roberta. What is your first reaction to the Dutch VP's comment?
2. What would be the likely result if you voiced your first reaction?
3. How might you handle this situation tactfully?
4. What if anything could have been done to prevent this awkward situation?

CROSS-CULTURAL DIMENSIONS

In his landmark research, using data collected from IBM employees in fifty countries between 1967 and 1973, Geert Hofstede observed several dimensions of culture among which countries vary.[3] These differences affect individual and group beliefs and behaviors, and show up as differences in, for example, communication, decision making, and negotiating practices. From the initial results, Hofstede developed a model that identifies four primary dimensions to assist in differentiating cultures: Individualism/Collectivism, Power Distance, Masculinity/Femininity, and Uncertainty Avoidance. Later, after conducting additional research on Chinese employees and managers, Hofstede added a fifth dimension, Long-Term Orientation.[4] We describe these dimensions (summarized in Table 10.1) and their impact on negotiation below.

Individualism/Collectivism

It is the degree to which individuals are integrated into groups. In societies that are individualistic (e.g., United States, United Kingdom, Australia, and Netherlands), the ties between individuals are loose—everyone is expected to look after himself and his immediate family.[5] Individual motivation and achievement is emphasized, decisions can be made by anyone, and it's okay to be interested in focusing on and improving oneself. After all, the squeaky wheel gets the grease. On the collectivist side, we find societies (e.g., Japan, many Latin American countries, South Korea) wherein people from birth onwards are integrated into strong, cohesive groups and extended families (with uncles, aunts, and grandparents), and these groups and families continue

TABLE 10.1	Summary of Hofstede Dimensions		
Dimension	**What It Means**	**Extremes**	**Impact on Negotiation**
Individualism/ collectivism	Degree to which members of a society act as individuals or members of a group.	Individualists: actors are motivated by individual achievement and ego gratification; "every man for himself"; Collectivists: actors set aside personal needs for the good of the group; group harmony, cohesion, and consensus.	Individualists may find themselves impatient with collectivists' need to check back with all organizational members to ensure consensus and group benefit.
Power distance	Degree to which members view and expect elders and those senior to them in the hierarchy as possessing significant amounts of power and authority compared with younger and junior members.	High: hierarchy and titles are important and respected; Low: egalitarian approach to decision making, along with informal adherence to processes and procedures.	The low-power-distance negotiator approaches the negotiation informally with the expectation that all present have the same power to decide and are willing to question the process and rules of the negotiation.
Masculinity/ femininity	Degree to which a culture's prevailing behaviors are dominated by masculine characteristics (e.g., aggressiveness, materialism) or feminine characteristics (e.g., collaboration, nurturing).	Masculine: strong focus on the task at hand and the status of those negotiating; Feminine: strong focus on building the relationship and arriving at collaborative solutions.	Masculine negotiators are more focused on the task (i.e., terms of the contract) than the process (i.e., building the relationship) and can be perceived as brutish and insensitive.
Uncertainty avoidance	Extent to which a culture programs its members to feel either uncomfortable in or threatened by unstructured situations.	High members prefer clear operating procedures and hierarchical processes; being told exactly what to do is preferred over what Low members prefer— being told "you're empowered . . . do what you think makes sense and get back to me."	Those high in uncertainty avoidance prefer clear agendas and procedures whereas those who are low in uncertainty avoidance "go with the flow" and can adapt fairly easily to new goals, terms, or negotiators.

Long-term orientation	Approach to the relationship and project, whether long term or short term.	Long-term orientation
		  –persistence
		  –ordering relationships by status and observing this order
		  –thrift
		  –having a sense of shame
		Short-term orientation
		  –personal steadiness and stability
		  –saving face
		  –respect or tradition reciprocation of greetings, favors, and gifts.
			Those who think long term look at the negotiating process as one of many within a long-term relationship, and, therefore, the issue of reciprocity is averaged over multiple negotiating events as opposed to those who think short term, who are likely more concerned about instant and equal reciprocity.

protecting them in exchange for unquestioning loyalty.[6] Decisions are made collaboratively, though typically articulated by the most senior member of the group, in an effort to maintain harmony and benefit the group as a whole. To be clear, collectivists can and do "squeak" if they feel something is amiss, but they do so not for personal gain but to benefit the collective. The word *collectivism* in this sense has no political meaning—it refers to the group, not to the state.

This dimension has an obvious impact on the way negotiations are conducted. Whereas individualistic negotiators are empowered representatives who can accept or reject an offer when it is presented, collectivistic negotiators will defer making a decision until all concerned parties—those at the table as well as back at the organization—are informed, provide their input, and reach agreement. Individualists may see this lack of or delay in decision making as uncooperative or uninterested behavior. However, collectivists may perceive individualists' need for the spotlight as confusing (e.g., "We weren't sure who was in charge or whom to speak with") or displaying a lack of unity (e.g., "Each one had his or her own ideas to share . . . I was surprised to see that they would willingly, almost with pride, display to us this lack of unity and cooperation.").[7] Furthermore, while individualists seek and expect individual recognition for their efforts, as it serves as motivation, singling out an individual for his or her achievements (e.g., "Yoshi, you did a great job in presenting the market analysis") can be unproductive if not destructive to collectivists.[8]

Power Distance

It is the extent to which lower-status members of organizations and institutions (like the family) accept and expect that power is distributed unequally.[9] Interestingly, this dimension represents less a top-down depiction of how power is shared and more the perspective of followers or subordinates.[10] In high-power-distance societies, such as Latin America, Arab countries, and France, there is great respect for age, titles, and seniority (e.g., an employee will never bypass the hierarchy), and the management philosophy tends to be paternalistic. All are expected to rigidly follow established procedures and protocol. In low-power-distance societies, such as the United States, Australia, Nordic countries, and Israel, the members value competence over seniority, are less impressed by (or deferent to) titles or status, and generally engage in a more democratic, participative style of management.

In negotiations among those representing low-power-distance societies, the tone and process of communication is informal and individuals openly question rules if they don't seem to make sense. To someone from a high-power-distance culture, such behavior appears disrespectful if not entirely insubordinate. In general, when negotiating internationally, it's best to adopt a formal posture when it comes to hierarchy and status and then move to informality only if the situation warrants it.

Masculinity/Femininity

It refers to the distribution of gender-based behavior among society members. Hofstede's IBM studies revealed that (a) there was more commonality among women's (versus men's) values in all societies and (b) men's values from one country to another range from very assertive, competitive, and materialistic (termed "masculine") to modest, collaborative, and caring (termed "feminine").[11] While the women in feminine countries (e.g., Sweden, Norway, Thailand) tend to share similar modest, caring values as the men, those in masculine countries (e.g., Japan, Italy) are somewhat assertive and competitive, though not as much as the men.

In countries that are more masculine, negotiators value status (e.g., titles are very important) and will remain focused on the task at hand (and seek to win), even if it means working late into the night. Negotiators in more feminine countries place a high value on family, relationships, and the overall quality of life, and are more likely to discontinue negotiations to return to their families in the evening. Another implication of this difference appears in merger or acquisition negotiations. Whereas more masculine negotiators tend to be concerned about the bottom line and financial impact of the merger, those from a more feminine culture will raise issues related to the well-being and satisfaction of the individuals impacted by such a change.

Uncertainty Avoidance

Deals with a society's tolerance for uncertainty and ambiguity; it indicates to what extent a culture programs its members to feel either uncomfortable in or threatened by unstructured situations. Unstructured situations are novel, unknown, surprising, and different from usual. Uncertainty avoiding cultures (e.g., Greece, Guatemala, Japan) try to minimize the possibility of such situations by enacting strict laws and rules, and safety and security measures. Countries with low needs for certainty, such as Jamaica, Hong Kong, and Singapore, are often characterized by high levels of entrepreneurial and intrapreneurial (i.e., within company innovation) behavior.[12]

Negotiators from low-uncertainty-avoidance societies are more able to adapt to situations that change quickly (e.g., new or different terms, negotiators) or when the rules of engagement are either unclear or shifting;[13] the negotiators also expect things to move quickly and aren't afraid to show their emotions.[14] By contrast, negotiators from high-uncertainty-avoidance cultures are uncomfortable with ambiguity and prefer having clear-cut rules and procedures articulated at the start of the negotiation.

Long-Term Orientation (LTO) vs. Short-Term Orientation

This fifth cross-cultural dimension was found in a study among students in twenty-three countries around the world using a questionnaire designed by Chinese scholars. Both the positively and the negatively rated values of this dimension are found in the teachings of Confucius, the most influential Chinese philosopher who lived around 500 B.C.; however, the dimension also applies to countries without a Confucian heritage.[15] At one end, we find thrift and perseverance among the values associated with Long-Term Orientation; at the other end are values associated with Short-Term Orientation, which include respect for tradition, fulfilling social obligations, and saving face.[16] Not surprisingly, people from LTO cultures are likely to remain with their employer for many years. Americans, who embrace a short-term orientation, "live for the day," change jobs frequently, and are on the whole unconcerned about saving for the future. Whereas the top management team of some American companies might push themselves to establish a strategic plan that looks five years into the future, their Chinese and Japanese counterparts will create and place high value in long-term strategic plans (as much as 150 years) and accept that business results take time to achieve.

PREPARING FOR INTERNATIONAL NEGOTIATIONS

When negotiating abroad, preparation—the first and most important stage of negotiation—is key. As in domestic negotiation, you need to clarify what you want and why, determine your BATNA, gather data to present and compare (i.e., objective criteria) your arguments/proposals, consider ways to learn the other parties' wants and needs, and collaborate to discover mutual benefits. However, your strategy and the way in which you implement it will likely vary based on what you know about the practices and customs of your global negotiating partner. Because the process of negotiation may look and feel very different from that to which you are accustomed, preparation is key. Start by doing background research on the organization's culture, practices, and business. Some information can be found on the Internet by searching government pages from the State Department website (go to www.state.gov/r/pa/ei/bgn/ and then click on the region of interest). Other information can be obtained by identifying other firms that have done business with this organization or individuals who were born or spent time in the country. In addition to basic information, it is a good idea to learn about the ways that a particular culture influences negotiation—from the way it is viewed, to the process, and the negotiation's ultimate goal or purpose. Table 10.2 provides a framework for viewing the range of responses countries have in how they approach and behave in negotiations.

In terms of the nature of agreements negotiated, whereas Americans expect to develop detailed, multipage contracts filled with legal terminology and clarifying all possible circumstances, the Chinese prefer a contract that establishes general principles versus detailed rules.[18] Americans negotiate a contract, while Japanese negotiate a personal relationship. A negotiator's style—which includes how she dresses, interacts with, and speaks to others—can be seen as formal or informal. Informal negotiators, such as Australians and Americans, try to set a personal, friendly tone by using first names, removing one's jacket, rolling up sleeves, and sharing personal anecdotes. To an Egyptian, Japanese, or French negotiator, these informal actions are seen as a sign of disrespect.[19]

TABLE 10.2 Ten Ways That Culture Can Influence Negotiation[17]

Negotiation Factors	Range of Cultural Responses From:	To:
Nature of agreements	Specific	General
Definition of negotiation	Contract	Relationship
Negotiating attitude	Distributive	Integrative
Selection of negotiators	Experts	Trusted associates
Personal style	Informal	Formal
Communication style	Direct	Indirect
Time sensitivity	High	Low
View of time	Monochronic	Polychronic
Risk propensity	High	Low
Emotionalism	High	Low

FIGURE 10.1 Some Examples of High-Context Communication

- In Japan, when an American asked a Japanese friend to translate some letters, the Japanese man said "ahhhh, that would be difficult"—which meant "no."
- In Italy, a man went to a wedding wearing a turtleneck shirt and a jacket. An Italian professor said: "If the man objected so much to the wedding, he should have stayed home!"
- In Saudi Arabia, men wear the same style of clothing—but you can tell who has higher status by the quality of the materials used.
- In Thailand, the height of two peoples' hands when they greet each other indicates who has higher status.
- In Mexico, if a man wants to let a woman he's dating know that he thinks of her more as a friend than a future wife, he can send her yellow flowers and she'll understand the message.

In terms of communication, realize that some cultures (e.g., Germans) value simple and direct communications while others (e.g., Japanese) rely on indirect and complex methods (e.g., facial expressions, gestures, greetings, even formality of dress) to communicate meaning. These contrasting examples illustrate low- and high-context cultures. When the words used are direct and to the point, the less we need to rely on nonverbal cues to interpret what is being said. The more we need to read into nonverbal and indirect clues to decipher what's going on, the higher the importance of context in that particular culture. Figure 10.1 provides examples of high-context communication in five different countries.

What about the content of or what is being said during negotiation? Verbal behaviors in negotiations differ among cultures as well. For example, one researcher studied how frequently certain verbal behaviors occurred per half hour bargaining session among Japanese, Brazilian, and American negotiators. He found that while the frequency of self-disclosing statements was quite similar across the three groups (between 34 and 39 per half hour), there were significant differences in other areas.[20] These differences are shown in Table 10.3.

It's also important to realize that even when negotiations that involve Americans are conducted in English, negotiations won't necessarily be without challenges. Just because your Canadian, Australian, or British counterparts speak the same language as you (though some would say this is debatable), don't pay short shrift to preparation, thinking that "since we speak the same language, we must share similar values." First

TABLE 10.3 Verbal Communication Differences among Japanese, American, and Brazilian Negotiators			
Frequency Per Half-Hour		**Bargaining Session**	
Behavior	Japanese	American	Brazilian
Self-disclosure (the speaker's statements that reveal information about himself)	34	36	39
Promise (the speaker's statements indicating his intention to provide a reinforcing consequence that the target would evaluate positively)	7	8	3
Commitment (the speaker's statements indicating his promise that future bids will not go above or below a certain level)	15	13	8
Command (statements in which the speaker asks the target to reveal information about himself)	8	6	14
Use of the word *no*	<2	<5	>40

of all, even when the language is shared, there are differences in meanings ascribed to words or phrases. For example, Americans use the phrase "Let's table this" to indicate that the subject should be deferred until a future meeting. However, in Australia, this means to put the topic on the table to be discussed, literally, to put the topic "on the table." There is also a tendency to assume that language adjustments need not be made. This is simply untrue and unwise, as can be seen from Figure 10.2. Following that, Figure 10.3 offers some guidelines to consider.

Some additional important communication differences concern nonverbal communication in the form of eye contact and the use of the smile and silence.

FIGURE 10.2 That's Not What I Meant![21]

In Persian, the word "compromise" does not have the English meaning of a midway point that gives both sides some of what they want and can accept; instead, the connotation to Persian speakers is "surrendering one's principles." Also, a "mediator" is a meddler—someone who is barging in uninvited. In 1980, U.S. Secretary General Kurt Waldheim flew to Iran to deal with the hostage situation. Persian radio and television broadcasted a comment Waldheim made upon his arrival in Tehran: "I have come as a mediator to work out a compromise." Less than an hour after the broadcast, his car was stoned by angry Iranians.

FIGURE 10.3 Guidelines to Follow When International Negotiations Are Performed in English[22]

1. *Keep your English simple.* Use common words and phrases and refrain from using slang (e.g., "my bad"), idioms (e.g., "here's a ballpark figure"), colloquialisms (e.g., "run that by me again") and words that have multiple meanings (e.g., right, hard).
2. *Speak slowly.* Take your time and enunciate the words. There's no need to shout or dumb down the language, but a slower speed will give the listener adequate time to translate as you speak.
3. *Avoid repeating yourself.* If you speak slowly, you'll not need to repeat—which just provides additional opportunities for being misunderstood.
4. *Avoid humor.* It doesn't translate well, and it might be cause for embarrassment for either or both of you.
5. *Begin on a formal note.* Use Dr./Mr./Mrs. and last names and titles, even if you refer to yourself by your first name. Err on the side of conservative and courteous; use first names only if you are given permission to do so.
6. *Confirm understanding.* Even when all parties speak the same language, there's room for misunderstanding. Errors in understanding expand exponentially in the presence of language and cultural differences. Use listening skills to paraphrase or repeat back what you understand after a decision is made or important information is exchanged.

Americans place great importance on eye contact, as eyes are "the window to the soul," and the means by which Americans judge the trustworthiness and veracity of a negotiator and her claims. The Japanese, who avoid direct eye contact to show respect, report discomfort at the "aggressive staring" of Americans, who in turn report frustration in not knowing where they stand in a negotiation with Japanese counterparts.[23]

While in many cultures, a smile indicates friendliness and perhaps agreement, Japanese use smiles to show happiness as well as to mask shame, disappointment, and discontent.[24] Because of their concern to save face, Japanese often use smiles in concert with phrases like "That would be difficult to do," when what is meant is, "We will not be agreeing to your terms."

You've heard the phrase *pregnant pause*, right? The idea behind this phrase speaks to the discomfort many Americans feel during periods of silence. According to Professor Nancy Adler, Japanese are the biggest users of silence in negotiation.[25] Because Japanese tend to respond and not react, and strive to reach consensus among decision makers, their silence represents the time needed to achieve these ideals. However, Americans have been known to interpret Japanese silence as rejection and respond impatiently by making typically unnecessary concessions.

In terms of the view of time in negotiations, we've already mentioned that Americans like to get down to business quickly because "time is money." Similarly, Germans are known—and expect others—to be punctual; however, negotiators from Spanish-speaking cultures tend to view start times as approximate. The Japanese take as much time as needed—away from the negotiating table—to arrive at a consensus among multiple representatives of the organization.[26] The silence and waiting causes many Americans to offer an even better deal before waiting to hear if the original proposal is accepted. Or, Americans might offer to compromise and "split the difference," which while expedient, may be viewed by French negotiators as "an insult to their carefully crafted logic."[27]

Another dimension of time relates to what's known as monochronic versus polychronic time. Negotiators from such countries as America and Germany tend to view negotiations as linear and give great weight to deadlines. In this monochronic mode, issues are negotiated one at a time, in order; once decisions are made, they are rarely resurfaced.[28] However, in countries like France, Mexico, and Central and South Asian countries, negotiations are seen as more fluid or circular. As the name implies, polychronic negotiations are those in which multiple issues are discussed simultaneously, and completed issues are readdressed from time to time. Moreover, long conversations are common in polychronic cultures; people would not cut a good conversation short in order to make an appointment. To a monochronic negotiator, this approach may amount to inefficiency at best and chaos at worst. From a polychronic perspective, it's a much more relaxed way of life. As a woman from India once told me, "In India, we are run by our hearts but in America you are run by your watches." You can learn whether you tend to be more monochronic or polychronic by completing Exercise 10.6.

Finally, while the public expression of deep emotion is considered ill-mannered in most countries of the Pacific Rim (because of the separation of one's public and personal persona), to withhold emotion while negotiating in Latin America would signal mistrust.[29] It is important not only to learn as much as possible about the differences between countries involved in a negotiation prior to the negotiation, but also to monitor and check subtle (and not so subtle) signals during the negotiation. With all there is to remember, it might be helpful to prepare for your negotiation by practicing role reversal.[30]

CUSTOMS, LAWS, AND OTHER PROTOCOL

Aside from these differences, it is important to know about customs and laws specific to each country. For example, while a firm handshake is common in American business, in other countries, a handshake might be quick (e.g., Europe) or limp (e.g., Asia).[31]

In still other countries, negotiators greet one another with an exchange of kisses (yes, men kiss other men) or bows. Americans who put their feet on their desk are said to be taking it easy; however, to do so in an Arabic country, where the soles of the feet are regarded as dirty and represent the bottom of the body, would be considered sinful. We could go on with examples, however, our point here is that what may seem a typical or common courtesy in one country (e.g., burping, slurping, or directing all remarks to the eldest male) may be considered offensive in another. Again, do your research.

Offering gifts to a negotiating partner is expected in some countries (and considered bribery in others). The Chinese often engage in gift giving, but you would be wise not to present your Chinese counterpart with a clock—it symbolizes death in China.[32] Even how you present and where you open a gift is no small detail.[33] You would also do well to know whether certain foods (e.g., pork, artificial sweetener) and drinks (e.g., alcohol) are forbidden in a particular country. In fact, an American firm sent a business proposal bound in fancy pigskin portfolio to a country in which pigs were considered unclean. The proposal was never opened.[34] Gift-giving presents other problems as well. For example, while the Japanese are known to exchange gifts—often expensive ones—during the course of conducting business, many Western businesspeople see this custom as not only different but wrong. To accept gifts, from the perspective of Western businesspeople, is tantamount to accepting bribes, and is unacceptable.[35]

Understanding the laws and regulations of your negotiating partners' country is even more complicated. The degree to which the government regulates industries and organizations varies widely.[36] Except for highly regulated industries (e.g., defense, airlines), American businesses enjoy a fairly laissez-faire approach; the opposite is the case in some developing and communist countries.[37] Depending on the nature and goal of a particular negotiation, it might be wise to hire a local intermediary to facilitate negotiations in heavily regulated countries.[38]

Clearly there is much preparation to be done before traveling abroad. While preparation is key, there is still more you need to do once you've arrived at your destination to be effective, as shown in Figure 10.4.

Points to Ponder

1. Think of people from other cultures with whom you have interacted. What about their mannerisms or behaviors were different than your own?
2. Which mannerisms or behaviors, if any, made you uncomfortable?
3. How might you handle such situations?

FIGURE 10.4   Adapting Abroad

Observe: Do you notice patterns of behavior? Do people act differently around older people or people of authority? Do people put money on the counter or in the cashier's hand? Do people on the street look almost mean as they avoid direct eye contact and keep a serious expression on their face? How close do people stand to each other? What is considered appropriate dress?

Listen: Do people speak in softer voices than where you are from? Or, maybe men speak loudly while women are quieter. Do people roar with laughter or cover their mouths and bow their head slightly when they laugh? Do they interrupt each other in a lively conversation or listen quietly while one person talks at length?

Ask questions: People appreciate it when you try to understand their culture. Note that if you ask a question and people start laughing, it may not mean they thought it was funny. Laughter can mean the person is nervous or embarrassed. You may have asked a question about a subject that is not discussed in their culture.

WHAT IT MEANS TO BE AN AMERICAN

It seems almost paradoxical to discuss the domestic perspective in a chapter on being successful in international negotiations. However, according to negotiation expert Kathleen Reardon, it is impossible to understand another's culture without understanding one's own.[39] Knowing how we think and act gives us a reference point for understanding how and why diverse others think and act the way they do.[40] Notice we say *reference point* as opposed to *measuring stick*. It is important to evaluate others' differences as just that—unique (to us) ways of thinking and behaving in a negotiation situation. If you can understand, respect, and adapt to these differences, you will be effective in building cross-cultural relationships and negotiating internationally. Those who judge, or adopt an ethnocentric stance toward diverse others, will be seen as condescending, insensitive, and untrustworthy. Such ethnocentrism from Americans explains the origin and use of the unkind term "Ugly American".

Understanding the impact of your culture on you also helps you understand how others view you and how they expect you to act in a negotiation situation. For example, Americans are known to be impatient and individualistic; representatives tend to work alone (granted the authority to do so on behalf of the organization) and strive to "get down to business" and make decisions quickly. We've discussed other American "traits" as they relate to the Hofstede cross-cultural dimensions. While not all Americans are alike—and there are significant differences among dimensions when comparing mid-Westerners to East Coasters and the like—don't be surprised when your European counterpart says something like, "Well, I know you want to get down to business, but there's this wonderful little café a block away. . . ." It's not meant as an insult.

Points to Ponder

1. Think of interactions you have had with people from other cultures. What about your mannerisms or behaviors may have made them uncomfortable?
2. How might you prepare for and handle such situations to reduce others' discomfort?

WHEN IN ROME . . . DO AS THE ROMANS DO?

So far, we've discussed the ways in which countries differ in their values, culture, and customs, and how these differences impact negotiation. When preparing to negotiate with Italians (taking our cue from this North American idiom), one would expect that to be successful, an American businessperson would research Italy's culture and behave in a way that conforms to the Italian approach to doing business. Simple enough? Well, it's not that simple. Italian employees preparing to negotiate with the Americans are doing the same thing. So, will it be effective for the Italians to act like Americans and the Americans to act like Italians? Or maybe, as some have suggested, there's a "home court advantage." In other words, if the negotiations take place in Italy, that culture and those practices would prevail. Do you agree? Still others have suggested that the primary culture would be of the one who has the upper hand or the most to gain from the negotiation. While all of these ideas are arguably logical, none are completely right.

The rule of thumb for international negotiations is this: When in Rome, non-Italians should be respectful of differences among their Italian counterparts and be at least somewhat true to the characteristics of their own culture. They should not attempt to act like Romans. To do so might come across as insincere at best and mocking at worst. Besides, in the same way you are advised to thoroughly prepare so you can understand and display sensitivity toward cross-cultural differences, you should expect negotiators from other nations to do the same: thoroughly prepare to successfully negotiate with you. Others expect Americans to *be* American. Non-Japanese should not try to act like Japanese (but should gladly participate in customs and events to which they're

Chapter Scenario, Part II:

While Roberta was collecting her thoughts and managing her anger at Dennis for his degrading comment, Carlos calmly mentioned to Dennis that he was the engineer and Roberta was the project manager. Dennis apologized, but Roberta didn't believe his apology was totally sincere. In their initial conversation, Dennis made far more eye contact with Carlos than he did with Roberta. It took a while, but things changed. Roberta clearly impressed Dennis with her extensive knowledge of the pacemaker, the manufacturing process, and the implications on patient health. She cited several studies—including her own in-house investigation of the defect—and shared detailed findings of each. Before long, Dennis acted as though his opinion of Roberta was that of an equal. They engaged in long conversations, where he asked her input on several key concerns, and then he took her and Carlos on a tour of the plant. It took a few hours, but Roberta was able to identify the issue in the process that resulted in the 2% failure rate. By the end of the day, it was clear from Dennis's behavior that he was embarrassed on two counts: first for the error that occurred in his plant and second for the way he treated Roberta.

invited) and non-Muslims should refrain from praying with their Muslim negotiating counterparts.

A word of caution, however. While we have provided general guidelines for understanding how members of different societies think and behave, it is important not to generalize. Not all Americans or Japanese behave the same as all other Americans or Japanese and in all circumstances. Realize that humans are always full of surprises, and that there may be a tendency to select out or incorrectly interpret unfamiliar behavior based on such generalizations. Furthermore, it is important not to lump together seemingly similar groups. For example, Asians share some similarities, but there are key differences between Japanese, South Koreans, Malaysians, and Singaporeans. Similarly, while Arabic countries tend to exclude women (in conversation and in business), some countries (e.g., Oman, Lebanon) are increasingly less conservative about the role of women in business.[41]

Points to Ponder

1. Evaluate Roberta's response to Dennis's comment. What would you have done?
2. Evaluate Carlos's response to Dennis's comment. Is there anything you might have done differently and why?
3. What lessons do you think Dennis might have learned in this situation?
4. What lessons do you think Roberta might have learned in this situation? What will she do differently the next time she is sent overseas to represent her company?

THE RELATIONSHIP AND THE NEGOTIATION

While we've said it before, it bears repeating. Undoubtedly, your understanding of and sensitivity to cross-cultural differences and their impact on negotiations will pay dividends when negotiating abroad. However, despite these similarities and differences among our global negotiating partners, one constant is the importance of the relationship. Research demonstrates that better negotiators focus on establishing a collaborative climate where relationships are nurtured and needs are met, and both sides emerge as winners.[42] This is true for negotiations, in general, and even more so in the international arena. In most other cultures, doing business begins first and foremost with establishing a relationship. To many Americans, however, the "business" of negotiations is all about persuasively presenting your case, sealing the deal, and signing the contract, and doing so expeditiously, so that you can move on to the next negotiation or business challenge. The notion of participating in a casual conversation, learning about one another's likes/dislikes and customs, touring the city and its monuments, and even exchanging gifts is often seen by aggressive, time-is-money Americans as not only "not business" but a waste of time that should be saved for after the contract is signed, if at all. However, to successfully negotiate with international partners, Americans (in particular) need to learn that negotiation is first and foremost about developing trust and mutual respect—the relationship—among individuals at the table. This could take hours, days, or even weeks (and continues to develop over time) and requires extreme patience on the part of "let's get down to business" Americans. American negotiators need to think of relationship building as an investment in the future (or alternatively as "an ounce of prevention worth a pound of cure"). The time required to repair a relationship damaged by a negotiator's impatience (assuming repair is even possible) exceeds the time likely spent by negotiating partners who focus on building the relationship before discussing the mechanics of a deal. Put simply, focusing on building relationships—at whatever cost in time—will pay dividends over the course of multiple negotiations and years to come.

Summary

Global negotiations are admittedly complex and uncertain. Planning is crucial to the process. Gathering information about a country and its practices and customs is a necessary step to understanding how to approach your negotiating partner. Understanding differences and similarities between your and your foreign counterpart's communication style, behaviors, and practices can help you manage the negotiations and increase the likelihood that both parties leave the global negotiating table with satisfactory outcomes and a desire to continue the business relationship.

Summary: The Big Picture

Hofstede's dimensions of culture	Individualism/Collectivism: the degree to which individuals are integrated into groups. Power Distance: acceptance and expectation that power is distributed unequally. Masculinity/Femininity: distribution of gender-based behavior among people. Uncertainty Avoidance: tolerance for uncertainty and ambiguity. Long-Term Orientation: long term versus short term.
Preparing for international negotiations	Research country, culture, and organization. Beware of all differences in communication, use of silence and time, laws, and protocol.
What it means to be e.g., an American	Anticipate what others expect from you. Be at least somewhat true to the characteristics of your own culture.
When in Rome . . .	Be respectful of differences but don't attempt to take on (or imitate) the characteristics or practices of diverse others.
The relationship and the negotiation	Take the time to establish a collaborative, trusting relationship before rushing into details of a deal or contract.

Key Terms and Concepts

Individualism/collectivism   The degree to which individuals are integrated into groups.

Long-term orientation   The degree to which individuals focus on the long term versus short term.

Masculinity/femininity   The distribution of gender-based behavior among people.

Power distance   The extent to which lower-status members of organizations and institutions accept and expect that power is distributed unequally.

Uncertainty avoidance   The tolerance for uncertainty and ambiguity.

Discussion Questions

1. Discuss the challenges that are likely to arise in cross-cultural negotiations.
2. Describe the impact of Hofstede's five dimensions of cross-cultural differences.
3. Imagine your employer has asked you to handle contract negotiations with a supplier in Honduras. Describe the steps you would take to prepare for the negotiation and what your negotiating partner is likely to expect from you.
4. Describe the role of the relationship in cross-cultural negotiation and its variation among different cultures.

Ethical Dilemma[43]—Take It or Leave It: This Is the Way We Do It Here

Michael Woodson, the CEO of a major college publishing company headquartered in the United States with three offices in major U.S. cities as well as a recent expansion in the United Kingdom, had been considering expanding his company's operations to India. According to his research, with one of the highest literacy rates in the world, a highly educated and moderately priced workforce, and burgeoning distribution channels for noncollege publications, India was the ideal location for the newest office. Following multiple conversations with Ranjit Singh, handpicked to be the operations manager of the proposed New Delhi office, Michael and his wife Anita (Vice President of Human Resources) made the twenty-one-hour trip to New Delhi.

At the start of their meeting, Ranjit corroborated Michael's research, and demonstrated a real eagerness to head operations in New Delhi. The three of them discussed the market, the labor needs, and even various real estate options. All the boxes—so to speak—were seemingly checked . . . except two. First, as Ranjit informed the Woodsons, it would not be possible for the Woodsons to own more than 49% of the New Delhi Office. By Indian law, no foreign national could own a majority stake in a local business. That, thought Michael, was an issue, but not an insurmountable one. However, the next "box" presented a real problem. As Ranjit described it, in order to get the process started and secure governmental approval, a handful of local, regional, and governmental officials would have to be paid off. These "payments," as described by Ranjit, were nonnegotiable. "This is how one does business in India."

Shocked and appalled, Anita and Michael couldn't believe what they were hearing. "You mean we have to bribe officials in order to bring new jobs, taxes, and revenue to your country? Surely, there must be another way. That's not how our company does business! Besides, once bribes are requested and received, when would it ever stop?"

Ranjit matter-of-factly explained the Indian ways of doing business, and even shared a few stories that demonstrated how failing to do so resulted in a failed (or stopped before it started) enterprise.

The Woodsons excused themselves from the meeting. "What are we going to do?" they asked each other.

Questions

1. Michael Woodson did his research before entering the negotiation; however, he missed a key issue. What steps could he have taken to avoid missing the ownership and bribery requirements prior to initiating the negotiation?
2. What choices do the Woodsons have at this point?
3. If they ended the negotiation at this point, what will likely happen? Why?
4. If you were Michael or Anita and chose to continue the negotiation, what would you say or do at this point? Why?
5. When ethical norms differ among the countries represented in a negotiation, which country's norms prevail? Explain.

Endnotes

1. Perlmutter, H. 1983, 1984. "More than 50% of international managers' time is spent in negotiating – in interpersonal transaction time influencing other managers." Statement made at the Academy of Management Meeting, August 1983, and at The Wharton School, 1984, as cited in Adler, N. J. International Dimensions of Organizational Behavior, 3rd ed. Cincinnati, OH: Southwestern College Publishing, 1997, p. 214.
2. Wanis-St. John, A. "Thinking Globally and Acting Locally" *Negotiation Journal* 19(4) (October 2003): 389.
3. Hofstede, G. *Cultures and Organizations: Software of the Mind.* Burr Ridge, IL: McGraw–Hill–Irwin, 1991.
4. It is also worth noting that a more recent and large scale research project, GLOBE (under the direction of Robert J. House of Wharton) has identified nine cultural dimensions. They include: performance orientation, uncertainty avoidance, humane orientation, institutional collectivism, in-group collectivism, assertiveness, gender egalitarianism, future orientation, and power distance. For more information on the GLOBE framework and study, see R. J. House et al., Culture, Leadership, and Organizations: The GLOBE Study of 62 Societies, Thousand Oaks, CA: Sage Publications, 2004.
5. Hofstede, G. http://www.geert-hofstede.com/hofstede_dimensions.php, accessed September 14, 2009.
6. Foster, D. A. *Bargaining across Borders: How to Negotiate Business Successfully Anywhere in the World.* Burr Ridge, IL: McGraw-Hill, 1992.

7. *Ibid.*

8. *Ibid.*

9. Lewicki, R. J., D. M. Saunders, and B. Barry. *Negotiation* (4th ed.). Burr Ridge, IL: McGraw-Hill Irwin, 2003.

10. Hofstede, G., http://www.geert-hofstede.com/hofstede_dimensions.php, accessed September 14, 2009.

11. Hofstede, 1991.

12. Foster, 1992.

13. Lewicki, R. J., D. M. Saunders, and B. Barry. *Negotiation* (4th ed.). Burr Ridge, IL: McGraw-Hill Irwin, 2003.

14. Foster, D. A. *Bargaining across Borders: How to Negotiate Business Successfully Anywhere in the World.* Burr Ridge, IL: McGraw-Hill, 1992, p. 269.

15. Hofstede, G., http://www.geert-hofstede.com/hofstede_dimensions.php, accessed September 14, 2009.

16. *Ibid.*

17. Adapted from Lewicki et al., *Negotiation*, p. 420.

18. Salacuse, J. W. *Making Global Deals: What Every Executive Should Know about Negotiating Abroad.* New York: Times Books, 1991, p. 66.

19. *Ibid*, p. 63.

20. Graham, J. "The influence of culture on the process of business negotiations in an exploratory study," *Journal of International Business Studies* (Spring 1985): 88.

21. Fisher, R., W. Ury, and B. Patton. *Getting to Yes*, 2nd ed. (New York: Penguin Books, 1991).

22. Adapted from Foster, 1992, pp. 61–64.

23. Graham, J. L., and Y. Sano. *Smart Bargaining: Doing business with the Japanese.* Los Angeles: Sano Management Corporation, 1989.

24. *Ibid.*

25. Adler, N. J. *International Dimensions of Organizational Behavior* (3rd. ed.). Cincinnati, OH: Southwestern College Publishing, 1997, p. 214.

26. Graham, J. L., and Y. Sano. *Smart Bargaining: Doing business with the Japanese.* Los Angeles: Sano Management Corporation, 1989.

27. Reardon, K. *Becoming a Skilled Negotiator.* Hoboken, NJ: Wiley, 2005.

28. Foster, D. A. *Bargaining across Borders: How to Negotiate Business Successfully Anywhere in the World.* Burr Ridge, IL: McGraw-Hill, 1992.

29. *Ibid*, p. 281.

30. Adler, 1997.

31. Foster, D. A. *Bargaining across Borders: How to Negotiate Business Successfully Anywhere in the World.* Burr Ridge, IL: McGraw-Hill, 1992, p. 281.

32. *Ibid.*

33. See Reardon, *Skilled Negotiator*, p. 170 and K.K. Reardon, *Gift Giving Around the World.* Stanford, CA: Passepartout, 1986, for more details.

34. R. Robert, Patricia, D., Marshall, S., and Carl, P. *Global Literacies: Lessons on Business Leadership and National Cultures: A Landmark Study of CEOs from 28 Countries.* New York: Simon and Schuster, 2000.

35. Thomas Donaldson (1996, September/October) Values in tension: Ethics away from home. *Harvard Business Review*, reprint #96502.

36. Lewicki, R. J., D. M. Saunders, and B. Barry. *Negotiation* (4th ed.). Burr Ridge, IL: McGraw-Hill Irwin, 2003.

37. *Ibid*, pp. 408–409.

38. Salacuse, J. W. *Making Global Deals: What Every Executive Should Know about Negotiating Abroad.* New York: Times Books, 1991.

39. Reardon, K. *Becoming a Skilled Negotiator.* Hoboken, NJ: Wiley, 2005.

40. Foster, D. A. *Bargaining across Borders: How to Negotiate Business Successfully Anywhere in the World.* Burr Ridge, IL: McGraw-Hill, 1992.

41. *Ibid.*

42. *Ibid*, p. 239.

43. Case is adapted from Whiting, Victoria & Reardon, Kathleen. (1993). "Sage Publications India: A Strategic Alliance." In Braaton, David (ed.) *Cross Cultural Alliances.* Gulf Publication.

44. Bird, A., M. Mendenhall, M. J. Stevens, and G. Oddou. "Defining the content domain of intercultural competence for global leaders." *Journal of Managerial Psychology* 25(8) (2010): 810–828.

Exercise 10.1   How Cross-Culturally Competent Are You?

According to recent research, there are three dimensions of cross-cultural competence: perception management, relationship management, and self-management.[44] Increasing your competence in these areas will improve your ability to effectively interact and negotiate with members of another culture.

The questions below are intended to help you assess your current level of competence. Reflect on situations when you've been involved in interactions (e.g., conversations, business transactions, team projects) with members of a culture different from your own, whether in your country or in another country. Honestly assess your level of competence on the dimensions below as either low, moderate, or high (L, M, or H). Next, provide a brief example that illustrates your belief.

Perception management	Assessment of my competence	A positive or negative recollection that illustrates my competence (or lack thereof) with this dimension
To what degree am I able to withhold or suspend negative judgments about people upon meeting them?	L M H	
To what degree am I curious about other cultures, such that I take steps to learn about others' ideas, values, norms, and ways of behaving?	L M H	
How comfortable am I when I don't know exactly what is going on in a cross-cultural interaction?	L M H	
When in cross-cultural interactions, how likely am I to focus on our similarities instead of differences?	L M H	
Relationship management		
In general, how curious am I about people and how best to relate to them?	L M H	
How interested am I in initiating and maintaining relationships with people from other cultures?	L M H	
To what degree do I recognize and respond to others' feelings?	L M H	
How well do I know my strengths, weaknesses, and biases (and the impacts of these behaviors) when it comes to interacting with diverse others?	L M H	
How well can I adjust my behaviors to fit the situation and connect with people I do not know?	L M H	

The third dimension, self-management, encompasses your outlook on life, your ability to cope with difficult or stressful situations, and your willingness to learn from these situations. In the table below, identify your competence in these dimensions and then provide a brief example that illustrates your belief.

Self-management	Assessment of my competence	A positive or negative recollection that illustrates my competence (or lack thereof) with this dimension
To what degree do I maintain a generally positive outlook toward people, situations, and events?	L M H	
To what degree do I feel that if I work hard enough, I can learn what I need to in order to accomplish a goal?	L M H	
How likely am I to remain calm and resilient in the face of opposition and adversity?	L M H	
How well do I handle stress, failure, and frustration?	L M H	

Finally, choose one dimension from each of the three competencies and set a near-term (three to six months) and a slightly longer-term (six to twelve months) goal that, if accomplished, would significantly improve not only your competence but also your comfort interacting with people from cultures different from your own.

Perception Management

Near-term goal:	Potential challenges to achieving this?	Plans to overcome these challenges?
Long-term goal:	Potential challenges to achieving this?	Plans to overcome these challenges?

Relationship Management

Near-term goal:	Potential challenges to achieving this?	Plans to overcome these challenges?
Long-term goal:	Potential challenges to achieving this?	Plans to overcome these challenges?

Self-Management

Near-term goal:	Potential challenges to achieving this?	Plans to overcome these challenges?
Long-term goal:	Potential challenges to achieving this?	Plans to overcome these challenges?

Exercise 10.2 Researching Cross-Cultural Differences and Values

Imagine you've been asked to negotiate in one of the following countries (pick the one your employer is most likely to send you to):

Brazil
China
Germany
Indonesia
Japan
Mexico
Netherlands
New Zealand
Philippines
Spain

Part 1: Using the website www.geert-hofstede.com/hofstede_dimensions.php (or other resource), research the dimensions of the two countries—your country and the country you are being sent to. Note your findings in the chart below.

Dimension	Your Country: _____	Other Country: _____
Power distance		
Individualism/collectivism		
Masculinity/femininity		
Uncertainty avoidance		
Long-term orientation		

Part 2: Select two of the dimensions that are most relevant or interesting to you, and:

a. Describe how these differences will likely affect negotiations: before (preparation), during, and at (or shortly after) the closing of the negotiation.

b. Develop a plan/strategy for how you will manage conflicts or challenges related to the impact these differences will have on your negotiations.

Exercise 10.3   Sharing with and Learning from Diverse Others[*]

Part 1: Imagine you were asked to give a talk on how best to negotiate with people from your country. It could be the country where you grew up or the country where you are currently. Using the dimensions listed and described below, write down tips (one from each dimension) for preparing and negotiating effectively with someone from your country in the second column.

Dimensions	Advice about negotiating with someone from my country	Advice about negotiating with someone from another country
Space (social distance, queuing, seating arrangements in meetings, office layout, etc.)		
Time (norms of punctuality, interruptions, meeting culture, etc.)		
Status (how respect is shown, how power is expressed, how important is hierarchy, communication styles, dress code, etc.)		
Relationships (greetings, friendships, formality and informality, gifts, sharing personal information, dining out, drinking, karaoke, gender-specific rules, etc.)		
Agreement (explicit vs. implicit, contract vs. network, contract negotiations, handshake, my word is my bond, etc.)		

Part 2: Pair up, preferably with someone from another country. Take turns sharing advice and asking questions for clarification or examples. Use the third column to write down the advice you receive.

---

[*]Exercise created and adapted from (1) a suggestion from one of our reviewers, from Wayne State University and, (2) an in-class exercise developed and used by John Weeks, IMD professor, 2010.

Exercise 10.4   Case Study: Give Up or Keep Going?[**]

It was four o'clock on the afternoon of Friday, December 19th. Charlotte looked out of a tenth-floor window with a view of Paris. Her thoughts drifted away for a second, thinking about the traffic congestion ahead on the famous grand departs of the city, and what excuse she would find this time to give to her husband for being late again. However, she quickly refocused her mind on the small group of people in the meeting room.

She looked at the VP of purchasing of Renault Nissan Alliance, together with his Japanese counterpart at the other end of the conference table, and laughed to herself about the complicated relationship she had developed with them over the years. Everyone knew that the stakes were high. Depending on how the negotiations proceeded, it was possible that a U.S.-based company would take over the business from a deeply infringed French supplier and for an amount of money too big to imagine. This was the moment Charlotte was waiting for . . . for two years.

It wasn't easy, especially for a woman, to get where she was. Charlotte realized that her status as an outlier—someone who didn't fit the mold—helped her immeasurably. While she was fluent in French and familiar with Japanese traditions, her appearance bewildered most in the male-dominated automotive industry; they were not sure how to handle her combination of nearly 5'11" with a sporty engineering style, friendly demeanor, and nonthreatening smile. Over the years, she survived all kinds of tough negotiations with a kaleidoscope of raw male emotions from men of all nationalities by always staying focused on the content and delivery of customer service. Her ability to think three steps ahead and respond more quickly than the competition, combined with her tenacity and professionalism, was rare—regardless of gender. This positioned her favorably at the negotiating table.

In fact, because of her track record of winning big business for her company over the last fifteen years, Charlotte's management willingly provided her the support and resources that were necessary throughout the typically complicated and lengthy negotiation processes around the globe. By now, her team had delivered twelve months' work of three-dimensional drawings, new plant layouts, and a complete new concept, with intellectual knowledge that was difficult to protect. She also knew she could not go back and ask for another bucket of money without a clear contract in her hands. But strangely enough, the closeness of the mega deal did not deliver the adrenaline rush she would normally encounter in this stage. She actually felt like not wanting to win the game . . . and suddenly she realized that months and months of sleeping only five hours a night had brought her to this stage of indifference. On top of that, her French boss an old-school manager with responsibility for the whole division—had decided to join the negotiations. Charlotte knew he wanted to dominate the meeting. He was new in his role and he wanted to rack up risk-free success stories to support his global career within a rather American culture while keeping his French ego intact in front of the customer. What this customer was unaware of, however, was that only an hour ago, he called Charlotte in a panic after having seen last-minute changes in a business case worth several million dollars. He would not sign off and considered walking away from the deal.

At that moment, Takahashi-san started to speak. Instantly, Charlotte knew something was wrong. It would be the first time in the two years since the negotiations began that he would open the meeting. . . .

Two hours later, while stuck in traffic on the Boulevard Périphérique, Charlotte revisited her options. Christmas holiday was supposed to start at this moment. Her customer had left already, for either Marseille or Tokyo. Her boss was clear in his message: "zero support." Her team desperately needed a break. Her husband would ban her computer from the kitchen table. The U.S. headquarters would certainly not be in favor of releasing another budget.

[**]We wish to thank Josephine Schoolkate, Executive Director at IMD, for contributing this case study in January 2011.

Her rational mind told her that nothing was lost; she knew the financials and business risks by heart and she needed to spend time with the team to develop a roadmap to profitability. Her customer wanted to get the maximum out of the deal and did not realize that his key supplier was ready to walk away from this major strategic business due to exhaustion and potential intellectual property risks. The customer's explanation was simple and took only ten minutes. Although Charlotte's company was certainly the preferred supplier, it was still not decided at the board level that Renault Nissan Alliance was ready for such a major strategic shift. More time was needed to reflect. As price and product design were almost equal between the two suppliers (the new one and the incumbent one), it was difficult.

Questions

1. What should Charlotte do in the next two (holiday) weeks in order to save the business for the company? She had already invested two years of work and saw a real potential to win. Yet, she was testing the limits of her marriage, her own hardiness, and her role as leader and caretaker of an exhausted team.
2. What information would you need to make this decision? Where would you get it?
3. What are the potential implications of Charlotte moving forward versus stopping at this point? Realize that the decision was not in her hands; rather, it rested with the board.
4. How do you keep acquisition teams and sponsors motivated, energized and focused in such long negotiation processes?
5. How do you build the necessary trust between all stakeholders knowing that your customer is in a position to provide your complete competitive edge to your key competitor.

Exercise 10.5   Johannes van den Bosch Sends an Email***

Read the case (provided by your professor), which is based on an email exchange between a Mexican manager and a Dutch manager, both partners in a global accounting firm. Then, answer the following questions:

1. What is van den Bosch's intention in sending this email?
2. What will the response likely be?
3. Do the respective cultures of the characters affect your responses to the previous two questions, and if so, how?

***Professor Joseph DiStefano, 2000. With permission from IMD-International Institute for Management Development, Lausanne, Switzerland.

Exercise 10.6 The Case of the Floundering Expatriate[†] (Harvard Business Review Case Study)

Your instructor will be distributing this exercise and specific roles each person will play. Upon completion of the negotiation, each team must submit their answers to the following questions:

1. Discuss the team's overall opinion about the negotiation outcome (what you "got") relative to what your team strategized for. What explains the discrepancy (if any) or similarity between planned and actual outcome? (This discussion might include reference to what might have been done differently to achieve the desired outcome . . . or more, if you got what your team wanted too easily.)

2. Discuss two successful and two unsuccessful persuasion attempts, linking specifics to course concepts in your explanation. These attempts may have occurred on your team, the opposing team, or both.

3. To what degree were both sides' key interests satisfied? Describe elements of the negotiation process that helped you get there (or not), as well as evidence to support your opinion that key interests were satisfied (or not).

4. Share specific examples from the negotiation which demonstrate your team's use of its knowledge of Hofstede's (power distance, individualism versus collectivism, masculine versus feminine, uncertainty avoidance, long-term versus short-term orientation) and other cross-cultural dimensions (e.g., view on time—polychronic versus monochronic, high-context versus low-context culture) discussed in class. You need not comment on each of these dimensions, just those that were germane to the negotiation (e.g., they demonstrated your team's credibility in the negotiation), or those that if addressed adequately may have positively impacted the negotiation.

[†]Adler, G. (1995, July/August) *Harvard Business Review*, reprint #95401X. Used with permission.

Exercise 10.7   Campbell Soup-Arnott's Ltd.

You will be assigned to one of two negotiating teams in this negotiation concerning the possible merger of two well-established companies (your instructor will distribute additional materials). Campbell's (since 1869) CEO, David Johnson, seeks to acquire Australia's Arnott's Ltd. Arnott's (since 1865) is one of the largest food companies in the Asia Pacific region (world's seventh largest cookie manufacturer; has 67% market share in Australia). Specializing in cookies and crackers, its Tim Tam is the highest selling chocolate biscuit in the world (per capita)—an equivalent of 17 Tim Tam for every man, woman, and child.

As of December 1992, Campbell owns 33% of Arnott's. The Arnott family, which holds about 25% of the company, has already rejected the offer ($6.34 U.S. per share = $890 million) as too low. Board Chairman, Bill Purdy, is not feeling pressure to sell, particularly to Ugly Americans.

A meeting is scheduled between the Campbell team of Johnson, his director of marketing, and director of operations and the Arnott team of Purdy, a member of the Arnott family, and the director of marketing to discuss the merger. . . .

Exercise 10.8   The Polychronicity Attitude Index[††]

Please consider how you feel about the following statements. Circle your choice on the scale provided.

I do not like to juggle several activities at the same time.	Strongly disagree 5	Disagree 4	Neutral 3	Agree 2	Strongly agree 1
People should not try to do many things at once.	Strongly disagree 5	Disagree 4	Neutral 3	Agree 2	Strongly agree 1
When I sit down at my desk, I work on one project at a time.	Strongly disagree 5	Disagree 4	Neutral 3	Agree 2	Strongly agree 1
I am comfortable doing several things at the same time.	Strongly disagree 1	Disagree 2	Neutral 3	Agree 4	Strongly agree 5

Add up your points and divide the total by 4. Then plot your score on the scale below.

1.0	1.5	2.0	2.5	3.0	3.5	4.0	4.5	5.0

Monochronic   **Polychronic**

The lower the score (below 3.0), the more monochronic your orientation; the higher your score (above 3.0), the more polychronic your orientation.

1. What are the potential benefits of your tendencies toward time? Explain.

2. What are the potential downsides of your tendencies toward time? Explain.

[††]Kaufman, C., P. Lane, and J. Lindquist. "Exploring more than 24 hours a day: A preliminary investigation of polychronic time use." *Journal of Consumer Research* 18 (1991): 392–401.

Team and Multiparty Negotiations

When most people think about negotiation, they imagine two people engaged in an interaction that involves an attempt to resolve differences, agree on contract terms, or conduct a business transaction (e.g., barter or exchange, purchase, sale, lease). While this may be the more traditional form, many negotiations involve multiple parties where "more than two parties are working together to achieve a collective objective."[1] One type of **multiparty negotiation** involves three or more "sides," each represented by one or more individuals. This is the situation represented in the Chapter Scenario, where each party attempts to maximize his or her goals and interests while working toward a solution that all can accept. Another type of multiparty negotiation is the **team-based negotiation**, where each side is represented by at least two individuals who work together as a team to achieve the goals and interests within a negotiation. For example, you might have multiple homeowners working together to negotiate with a construction company to reduce the noise, mess, and traffic that have increased as a result of a building project in the neighborhood (see Exercise 11.2). Or university employees from various groups or organizations (e.g., faculty, administrators, custodians) may work collectively within their groups and across groups as they bargain with the university's leadership team in an effort to increase salaries and benefits for all. This chapter clarifies the benefits and challenges of team and multiparty negotiations, and provides strategies and tactics to improve your chances of minimizing the challenges and maximizing the benefits.

Chapter Scenario, Part I

MaryAnn and Julio are planning a ten-day vacation to be taken over the winter holidays. They asked their children, nineteen-year-old Marco and seventeen-year-old Lydia, about their destination preferences. Compared to all the previous family vacations, planning this one will be the most difficult. Marco is going to be coming home from college for the break, and could easily choose to hang out with his friends rather than be stuck with his not-so-cool family. The same is true for Lydia; however, at only seventeen, she realizes that her options are more limited. In an effort to make the family vacation idea appear more enticing, MaryAnn mentioned to Lydia the possibility of her bringing a friend along if the family decides to drive to the small cottage they own one block from the beach three hours away. The cottage is okay, though, in addition to it not being beach weather, the accommodations will be a bit cramped since one of the bedrooms has had to be renovated due to a mold problem in that part of the house. Julio cares less about where they go. His company just completed a major reorganization and he is desperate for some peace and quiet. Perusing deals on the Internet, MaryAnn found an all-inclusive vacation in the Caribbean that caught her eye. She loves all outdoor activities and water sports, and sees the all-inclusive vacation as a great value for the family. Will all members of the family be able to find a solution that satisfies everyone?

BENEFITS OF TEAMS IN NEGOTIATIONS

Honing your skills in one-on-one as well as multiparty and team-based negotiations is a very good idea, given organizational trends and recent research that suggest that negotiation teams achieve better, more satisfying outcomes than individual parties.[2] For the last thirty years, work teams have become common in businesses, non-profit organizations, and schools. This is not surprising given the abundant empirical and anecdotal evidence that work accomplished by a team of diverse individuals is of greater quality, creativity, and effectiveness than the sum of the efforts of individuals working alone.[3] In fact, it is estimated that between 70% and 82% of U.S. companies use teams and teamwork as a means of getting work done.[4] This trend toward teamwork is reflected in negotiations that take place within and between groups and organizations. Moreover, recent research suggests that negotiation effectiveness can be increased when more parties are involved. One study showed that during team negotiations (team/team and team/solo), much more time was spent exchanging information (e.g., asking questions and providing preferences) than during solo negotiations (solo/solo).[5] In another study comparing three types of negotiation situations—teams versus teams, teams versus solo negotiators, and solo versus solo negotiators—findings demonstrated that having at least one team at the bargaining table resulted in higher joint gains.[6]

Another benefit of team-based negotiations concerns the implementation of the negotiated outcome. When multiple individuals from a single organization collaborate in representing the organization in negotiation, not only are there significantly more ideas generated from the combined set of skills and abilities but also the likelihood that the resolution will be accepted by the departments represented on the negotiating team is greater. For example, let's say that a manufacturing organization was evaluating the proposals of two vendors offering enterprise software, such as SAP. A negotiating team is assembled and it represents the various departments that will be using the software, including materiel, accounting, operations, quality assurance, and human resources. Each team member will recognize and voice department-specific concerns that the software needs to address during the proposal evaluation and negotiation processes. Because these issues are raised and addressed in the negotiation, each team member will feel a greater commitment to the final agreement and its implementation (i.e., installation of and training for the new software). Imagine MaryAnn and Julio forcing their vacation wishes on their teenagers. Marco could choose not to come, but Lydia, if unhappy about the choice, could isolate herself (and her friend) from the family and complain incessantly. Such reactions to having a choice forced upon her would likely detract from everyone's vacation experience.

However, for anyone who has ever worked on a team project, it should come as no surprise that gains in the process and outcome of multiparty or team-based negotiation are not automatic. More is not necessarily merrier, so to speak. When more people and perspectives are involved, to a point, there is a greater amount of information shared (e.g., issues, interests, ideas) and potential for creative, synergistic (i.e., mutually beneficial) solutions. There is also greater complexity and potential for conflict or even failed negotiations.[7] We discuss these challenges next.

CHALLENGES IN TEAM OR MULTIPARTY NEGOTIATIONS

While multiparty negotiations share many similarities with traditional, two-party negotiations, there are several key differences that make such negotiations more complex and therefore more difficult to manage.

Increased Competition for and Usage of Airtime

First, the more people that are involved in a negotiation, the greater the quantity and variety of perspectives put forth, information shared, objectives sought, and approaches discussed for achieving the diverse objectives. Whereas it might take a couple of hours for two individuals to arrive at a negotiated resolution, expect it to take significantly more time to reach a resolution for each additional person involved in the negotiation. The amount of time would depend on the importance of the issue and decision rule selected (i.e., more time is needed to arrive at consensus while less time is needed to implement a majority rule decision). Ideally, throughout a negotiation, the varied interests, issues, and positions would all be voiced and taken into consideration in an effort to identify a resolution that all parties support. However, if the resolution sought is choosing between two mid-range restaurants on the same block in which to hold the follow-up meeting, a simple majority vote would suffice and be expedient.

Few negotiation decisions are this uncomplicated. The expression of a multitude of viewpoints makes the conversation difficult to navigate and manage, particularly when negotiators—insistent on being heard—speak simultaneously. You might think that at a minimum, the members who collectively represent a single firm or organization in a multiparty negotiation would all be on the same page. But that's not always the case. Even within the same team, it's not unusual to find members disagreeing—subtly or not so subtly—about their negotiation goals or tactics. These differences can be magnified when such individuals represent different functional areas (e.g., accounting, operations, marketing) or management levels.[8] For this reason, time invested in preparation is time well spent.

Chapter Scenario, Part II:

MaryAnn decides to convene a family meeting. She starts by clarifying the dates of the proposed family vacation, and then proceeds to pitch the all-inclusive vacation. "Look at all the things we can do there!" she notes. Julio responds, "Well, I just want to relax and read a few books. Lydia, shares her concern: "If we go to the all-inclusive resort, will I still be able to bring Maggie?" Before MaryAnn could respond, Marco rolls his eyes and fumes, "Maggie? What a witch! If she goes, I'm not coming!"

Points to Ponder

1. Can you think of any solution that will satisfy each member of the family? What might that be?
2. If you were the family's next door neighbor, and happen to serve as a volunteer mediator in the family court from time to time, what advice would you give the family: a) right now? b) (turning back the clock . . .) before the meeting?
3. Has something like this ever happened in your family? How did the discussion proceed and end? What might have been done differently to improve both the outcome and the parties' acceptance of the outcome?

Preparation Challenges

As we've said many times in this book, preparation is key to effective negotiation. However, as the number of "sides" grows, so too does the task of gathering information needed to better understand the goals and interests of each party and then integrating that information into potential mutually beneficial solutions. When you negotiate one on one, you spend time identifying and prioritizing your interests—and taking educated guesses about the interests of the other party—to facilitate the integrative bargaining process. When three or more sides are involved, however, the process of give and take, that is, considering potential tradeoffs among primary and secondary interests, becomes less straightforward. Planning for these contingencies is complicated yet important.

Another issue that may complicate the process is the assigning of responsibility for preparation. In a multiparty negotiation where each side is represented by a single individual, responsibility for preparation is clear. However, when the number of individuals per side grows, so too does the possibility for social loafing, or hiding in the crowd.[9] The adage, "when everyone's responsible, no one's responsible," applies here. One member might defer to others who are more senior, while another might see his role as more tangential, and "allow" the key players to prepare. It is critical to take time to clarify roles and responsibilities before (preparation), during, and after the negotiation.

Procedural Chaos

Another challenge involves the need for formal or informal rules of engagement. Whereas a one-on-one negotiation involves each side taking turns, the procedural rules in a multiparty negotiation become less clear.[10] Does the selling team begin by presenting their goods or services, followed by a question and answer period from the buying team? Or, does the group of negotiators take turns speaking, starting with the highest ranking individual and then moving in a clockwise pattern to ensure an orderly flow of communication? Such might be the case with the Chapter Scenario where those with power (the parents) have priority over those without (the children). How should decisions be made—majority rule or consensus? Once agreement on an issue is reached, can it be reconsidered? Anything is possible; however, it would be best to expect more chaos than order, making it more important for the parties to establish an agenda, allow sufficient time to get through it, and establish ground rules for interaction.

Development of Trust

Another issue in multiparty and team-based negotiations deals with the development of trust necessary for integrative resolutions. Developing trust in one-on-one negotiations is neither automatic nor easy, as it requires negotiators to be vulnerable—showing weaknesses and admitting mistakes.[11] As the number of people involved in the negotiation increases, one would expect the ability to determine the trustworthiness of each party involved to decrease. This is especially true when there are relatively unknown players within a negotiating team as well as unknown players across the negotiating table. Not surprisingly, a study by Polzer found that team members—both from within and between negotiating teams—perceive their counterparts to be less trustworthy and cooperative than do individual negotiators.[12] This lack of trust negatively affects negotiators' ability and willingness to openly discuss goals and interests and search for commonality among others' goals and interests, leading to a greater emphasis on claiming value than on creating value.

Formation of Alliances and Coalitions

In multiparty negotiations, there is a natural tendency for coalitions—when two or more parties work together in an effort to exert greater influence on the outcome—to emerge.[13] Sometimes, coalitions can be helpful in moving the group toward agreement, and can be useful—if managed properly—when negotiators need to rely on others to implement an agreement.[14] However, by their very nature, coalitions can form in an effort to stall or even destroy negotiations that threaten to undermine their goals. If a strong coalition disrupts the negotiation process, it may be difficult to make progress. When this happens, it might be best to conclude the negotiation.

Impact of Cultural Differences

As difficult as all of these challenges may be, we haven't even considered what happens when companies or individuals representing them hail from different countries. At this most basic level, consider the impact of Hofstede's individualism/collectivism dimension of cross-cultural differences. For negotiators from a collectivistic culture (e.g., Mexico, Japan), working collectively toward a superordinate goal comes naturally and fairly easily. However, the nature of team-based negotiations may cause negotiators from individualistic cultures (e.g., United States, United Kingdom) to struggle more than negotiators from collectivistic cultures in finding an integrative, collaborative solution. In fact, two studies found that negotiators from collectivistic cultures reached more integrative solutions,[15] and higher joint outcomes[16] than negotiators from individualistic cultures.

Potential for Dysfunctional Group Dynamics

As the number involved increases, so does the likelihood that **group dynamics** will affect the negotiation.[17] Group dynamics describes the different behavioral patterns that occur when individuals are working collectively to complete a task or achieve a goal. Some of these behaviors can facilitate the process, for example, by bouncing-off of and building on one another's ideas, the creative potential for a collection of diverse individuals can be tapped. However, some of these behaviors can hinder the process. We describe some of these below:

Simultaneous conversations/overtalking.   Even in a one-on-one negotiation, individuals—even those who are good listeners—can become impatient and "need" to interject their points during a negotiation conversation. Of course, speaking and listening simultaneously is neither possible nor desirable. As the number of negotiators present increases, so does the likelihood of multiple people speaking at once. This dynamic makes it difficult to listen, to problem solve collaboratively, and ultimately, move the negotiation toward agreement.

Silence/withdrawal.   The larger the group, the more likely that those who are naturally shy or feel less confident about themselves or their rank/inherent power in a situation will be silent. This could happen in a family negotiation (such as that chronicled in the Chapter Scenario) where the less powerful feel like their voices wouldn't be heard. On the face of it, fewer people talking means an easier route to a negotiated agreement. However, it would be risky to ignore the silent person. Effective negotiators realize the value gained from each person contributing to and thereby increasing buy-in from the negotiation conversation and outcome.

Side conversations.   Another dynamic that appears in groups is side conversations. The natural tendency to whisper comments—related or not—to one's neighbor increases as the number of those involved in a negotiation increases. These side conversations can be seen as distracting, or worse, as strategizing by the opposing team; this perception may reduce any trust that remains. Sometimes, these side conversations take center stage, causing the negotiation to go in unintended or unrelated directions, diminishing the focus and lengthening the time needed to achieve resolution.

Groupthink.   Groupthink[18]—or individuals agreeing reluctantly with a group's decision because they are more concerned about maintaining harmony and cohesiveness than critically thinking about problems or alternative approaches—is a potential problem in negotiation. It occurs when negotiators "avoid promoting viewpoints outside the comfort zone of consensus thinking . . . to avoid being seen as foolish or . . . to avoid embarrassing or angering other members of the group."[20] In an effort to make the process finish quickly or efficiently, a group of negotiators affected by groupthink may agree to suboptimal or even harmful decisions for the companies they represent. Efficiency is not the same as effectiveness!

Dominating or blocking.   As the competition for airtime increases, some negotiators will compete harder, monopolizing the conversation by talking longer and louder, effectively blocking others from participating. This behavior can frustrate not only the other side but also other members of the dominator's team.

As you can see, there are many challenges that arise when negotiations consist of more than two parties. However, there are negotiation situations in which teams are actually preferred over traditional, one-on-one negotiations. When is it best to use a team in negotiation? Cornell University professor and negotiation expert, Elizabeth Mannix, offers the following advice.

FIGURE 11.1   When to Use a Team in Negotiation[19]

Working as a team can be particularly beneficial in the following situations:

1. The negotiation is complex, requiring a diverse set of knowledge, abilities, or expertise.
2. The negotiation has great potential for creative, integrative solutions.
3. Diverse constituencies and interests must be represented at the table, as in union negotiations.
4. You want to display your strength to the other side, for example, in international contexts where teams are expected.
5. You want to signal to the other side that you take the negotiation very seriously, as in a merger or acquisition.
6. You trust and respect available team members.
7. You have sufficient time to organize and coordinate a team effort.

PREPARING FOR TEAM OR MULTIPARTY NEGOTIATIONS

As we have advised throughout this book, preparation for any negotiation is critical. Start by clarifying your goals (including your BATNA) and interests, right? That's true; however, it's not a good idea to assume that all members on the same team are on the same page. Your team will need to meet to discuss its goals, BATNAs, a proposed agenda, and roles that each member will play during the negotiation. Clarifying goals should be the first step. Imagine your team is planning to meet with a group of employees who represent a firm that supplies machinery needed by your company; your current supplier will be closing his doors in six months when the owners retire and move to Mexico. Your team is led by the VP of Operations and includes three other members—from quality control, manufacturing, and finance. It may seem that everyone on the same team has the same goals, but that's probably not the case, or at least not in the same priority order. The VP of Operations is a busy man who has been placed on the team by the CEO to ensure top management is represented. The VP of Operations would like the deal to be completed quickly and at the best price for the company. However, the quality control supervisor is more concerned about the variability in the machining processes. She is a "zero defects" guru who has trained the employees to do daily reviews of the process control charts. To her, acquiring a lower priced machine with greater variability will result in a short-term savings that costs the company significantly more in the long term in terms of rework and possibly customer returns. The manufacturing supervisor is primarily concerned about reliability: a machine that does what it is supposed to do, when it is supposed to do it. A machine

FIGURE 11.2   Negotiation in the News[21]

NFL owners and the NFLPA (National Football League Players Association) are at opposite extremes in their collective bargaining agreement. As it stands, the NFL players get 60% of revenues brought in by teams. This six-year contract is in its last year. The NFLPA wants to extend this contract for another six years. On the other hand, the teams' owners believe that the contract is not fair. They assume 100% of the costs and gain only 40% of the revenues. Players believe that the owners are getting a fair share of the pie. They back this up by saying that all the lucrative television deals, prices of teams going up, and small-market teams having success in the postseason should offer the owners plenty of money. The owners oppose these ideas by saying that the amount of money they put back into the teams, new facilities, new stadiums, and increasing player costs during a down-time in the economy makes it hard for them to operate their businesses. Through eleven sessions between these two parties, nothing can be established or agreed upon. There is plenty of time for these negotiations to play out, but it will more than likely be later than sooner. What would you do if you were called in to mediate this multiparty negotiation?

that needs to be reset frequently will cause downtime among the employees and make it more difficult for him to schedule downstream processes. Last, there's the finance manager. She was recently promoted after completing her MBA part-time, and wants to prove that she belongs in her position. Her plan is to try to negotiate a deal with the best terms possible—a net present value that matches or improves the company's current asset-related bottom line.

This scenario is not exaggerated, and illustrates why preplanning and open communication among a negotiating team is especially critical. The negotiation team needs to clarify roles and responsibilities—for the preparation as well as the negotiation processes. Who will be the lead negotiator? How much should others contribute (and how) during the negotiation? What if there is dissent at the negotiating table—will the group caucus or defer to the lead negotiator? One example of a multiparty negotiation that has gained media attention is illustrated in Figure 11.2.

With regard to negotiation preparation, accountability regarding who will do what, by when and with what resources must be clearly understood by each team member. Before dividing and conquering the preparation task, however, the team should discuss and agree upon its goals, interests, and BATNAs. Finally, while an agenda should be agreed upon by all parties prior to the start of the multiparty negotiation, it would be helpful for each team to draft an agenda to ensure that key goals and interests are represented. This should be done in advance of the negotiation. Another possibility is that one team—possibly the host team—will take responsibility to draft an agenda and send it to the lead negotiator of the other team, with the stated goal of agreeing upon a basic goal, key issues to be discussed (and not), and a time frame in which to complete the negotiation.

Points to Ponder

1. Nearly all of today's employees have access to the Internet.
   a. In what ways can technology facilitate the planning of a team or multiparty negotiation?
   b. In what ways can technology get in the way?
2. As discussed in the chapter, the greater the number of people involved in a negotiation, the greater the likelihood that dysfunctional team dynamics impact the process. Should those involved in such a complex negotiation decide that the services of a facilitator or mediator would be helpful,
   a. what options are available for engaging such a professional?
   b. what are the advantages and disadvantages of engaging such a professional?
3. Looking back on multiparty (or team-based) negotiations in which you've been involved, would you say that the advantages outweighed the challenges or vice-versa? Explain.

GUIDELINES TO FOLLOW DURING A TEAM OR MULTIPARTY NEGOTIATIONS

Agree Upon and Use an Agenda

All parties should work together to agree upon a plan that specifies the time allotted, issues to be discussed, and order of topics. When allotting times to different topics, remember to allot more time for decisions to be made than for information to be reported.

Introduce Players and Clarify Roles

In addition to naming lead negotiators, consider selecting a time keeper, scribe, and facilitator. When the negotiation begins, allow each member to introduce herself, including their position in the organization (e.g., representing engineering, contracts, human resources) and role to be played during the negotiation (e.g., team leader, time keeper).

Decide on Procedural Rules

These rules include how to run the meeting, who talks first, and how the group makes decisions and resolves conflict. Once negotiations move past two individuals, the process becomes less clear and procedural rules become more important.[22] Lawrence Susskind, Harvard professor and negotiation expert, notes that it is critical for those involved in the negotiation to discuss and agree upon the overriding decision rule *before* the negotiation proceeds.[23]

Utilize Public Note-Taking

In addition to any private notes individuals will take, having someone record key decisions or actions publicly ensures that decisions are not rehashed, and facilitates the clarification and questioning of important decisions made. This helps keep all members on the same page and assured that their views count as the team moves forward with their goals and tasks.[24] The recorder or scribe can make good use of technology during and after the negotiation session by recording everyone's ideas on a laptop, with the entries appearing before the group either on a large monitor or projected onto the wall.[25] Following this, a summary of the agreements made can be easily emailed to all participants.

Utilize Active Listening and Summarize Regularly

Paraphrasing and restating key points made—even those with whom you don't agree—is an important way to show others you are listening. It also builds trust and facilitates the recognition of common interests. Regular summarizing will help ensure all parties are on the same page, clarify what has and has not been agreed upon, and generally keep the negotiation on track.

Consider Using a Facilitator or Mediator

Facilitators, or group process consultants,[26] are invaluable in team processes. They monitor group dynamics—intervening when necessary—and help teams utilize effective interpersonal skills to ensure that outcomes are achieved effectively and efficiently. Facilitators, who tend not to be vested in the outcome and are therefore seen as objective process consultants, may come from within the participating organizations or are contract employees from external organizations. A mediator is a special type of process consultant who is trained in the art of negotiation and demonstrates his or her neutrality toward the outcome of the negotiation.[27] This objectivity can be valuable when teams are locked in disagreement and need help finding common ground. The use of process consultants varies with the type of organizations involved and the value and potential impact of what is being negotiated.

Find Early Agreement on Some Issues

The more issues and people involved in a negotiation, the more frustrating it can become to all involved when resolution doesn't appear to be forthcoming. Look for and secure early agreement on what might seem to be smaller issues. This common ground can be used to help resolve more difficult and complicated issues that follow.[28]

Use Subgroups to Secure Tentative Agreement

One way to move a larger group toward consensus is to appoint one or more subgroups to temporarily leave the group to arrive at a tentative agreement. Typically, when the range of perspectives is reduced, the ability to find commonality is increased. When the subgroup returns, a spokesperson should explain the subgroup's decision and how it arrived at that agreement. This can then be discussed and tweaked further by the large group.

As Appropriate, Use Caucuses

The **caucus**, or time-out, allows groups to make midcourse corrections, discuss different strategies or tactics, or consider offers made. Even if the offer on the table is as hoped for, taking time to discuss among the team builds consensus toward and support for the outcome, and gives an opportunity for more silent members to voice any concerns previously unvoiced. In addition to face to face, teams could use their laptops or pass notes to signal a need for a caucus. Note that the seating arrangement matters. Some negotiation teams purposely sit across from each other and rely on eye contact with their teammates.

Confirm Agreements, Next Steps

You should always schedule a specific ending time for the negotiation. Toward the end of the negotiation, use the notes that were taken publicly to guide a recap of key decisions made and any follow up actions or meetings required or planned. Allow sufficient time for this step; don't start as everyone is packing up and running for the door.

Summary

Team and multiparty negotiations are complicated and challenging. Planning is crucial to the process, as is clarifying the agenda, roles, and rules of engagement at the start of the negotiation. The process is prone to many challenges—as the more people that are involved, the greater the difficulty in reaching agreement and likelihood that dysfunctional group dynamics emerge. However, there are many strategies and tactics that can be used to facilitate an effective negotiation process and resolution.

Summary: The Big Picture

Multiparty negotiation	Negotiation which involves three or more "sides" represented by one or more individuals, where each party attempts to maximize his or her goals and interests while working toward a solution that all can accept.
Team-based negotiation	Negotiation wherein each side is represented by at least two individuals who work together as a team to achieve the goals and interests within a negotiation.
Benefits of multiple parties and teams in negotiations	Include diverse perspectives as well as increased creativity, opportunities for integrative solutions, and increased buy-in to the agreement.
Challenges of multiple parties and teams in negotiations	Include increased competition for airtime, preparation challenges, trust development, formation of alliances and coalitions, impact of cultural differences, procedural chaos, greater likelihood of dysfunctional group dynamics.
Strategies and tactics for preparing and conducting multiparty and team negotiations	Include managing preparation and negotiation role responsibilities, utilizing public note taking, using a facilitator, finding early agreement on some issues, using subgroups for agreement, etc.

Key Terms and Concepts

Caucus A break that allows the parties to speak privately to make midcourse corrections, discuss different strategies or tactics, or consider offers made.

Dominating or blocking Monopolizing the conversation by talking longer and louder, effectively blocking others from participating.

Group dynamics The range of behavioral patterns that occur when individuals are working collectively to complete a task or achieve a goal.

Groupthink Individuals agreeing reluctantly with a group's decision because they are more concerned about maintaining harmony and cohesiveness than critically thinking about problems or alternative approaches.

Multiparty negotiation A negotiation that involves three or more "sides" represented by one or more individuals.

Side conversations Parties whispering comments—related or not—to each other during a negotiation.

Silence/withdrawal When one or more parties cease to participate in a negotiation.

Simultaneous conversations/overtalking Parties speaking simultaneously.

Team-based negotiation A type of multiparty negotiation where each side is represented by at least two individuals who work together as a team to achieve the goals and interests within a negotiation.

Discussion Questions

1. Describe the differences between team and multiparty negotiations and highlight the advantages and disadvantages of each.
2. Discuss the challenges (e.g., procedural, process, reaching resolution) involved in team and multiparty negotiations.
3. Discuss how team dynamics impact team and multiparty negotiations.
4. Describe the process of preparing for team and multiparty negotiations, in particular, how that differs from one-on-one negotiations.
5. Discuss strategies and approaches for preventing or managing dysfunctional team dynamics in team and multiparty negotiations.

Ethical Dilemma—Are We on the Same Team?

Maria, Peter, and Eduardo have spent the last two weeks working diligently on their presentation. After several failed attempts, they have a chance to provide advertising services to a major consumer products organization. After dotting all their I's and crossing all their T's, they hop on the metro together to go the downtown offices where they'll be making their pitch.

They are greeted warmly by Johan, the VP of Operations, and three product line managers. After a brief chat in the reception area, they are escorted into a large conference room. The presentation goes smoothly and Maria, Peter, and Eduardo secretly exchange "we nailed it" winks.

Johan asks a few questions about past and current client campaigns for which they are responsible. Just then, Peter takes over and proceeds to drop names. At first, Maria and Eduardo watched and smiled in support of their teammate. But as the tale grew longer (and more exaggerated), their smiles began to neutralize. Maria thought to herself, "What is he doing? We don't have that client." Eduardo could feel his temperature rise as he contemplated, "Sure, landing this account would be a major coup for the company and possibly even a promotion for me, but if they find out about Peter's lies, we'll lose the account—and maybe even our jobs!"

Questions

1. What ethical and other issues are at play in this scenario?
2. If you were a member of Peter's team, how would you react to this situation? What, if anything, would you say or do and why?
3. What options for resolving this situation exist—during and/or after the negotiation? Describe two or three, and discuss the advantages and disadvantages of each option.
4. What, if anything, could have been done to have prevented this situation?

Endnotes

1. Lewicki, R. J., D. M. Saunders, and B. Barry. *Negotiation* (5th ed.). Burr Ridge, IL: McGraw-Hill Irwin, 2006.
2. For a review, see Bazerman, M. H., J. R. Curhan, D. A. Moore, and K. L. Valley. "Negotiation," *Annual Review of Psychology* 51 (2000): 279–314.
3. For a review, see Cohen, S. G., and D. E. Bailey. "What Makes Teams Work: Group Effectiveness Research from the Shop Floor to the Executive Suite." *Journal of Management* 23 (1997): 239–290.
4. Chaney, L., and J. Lyden. "Making U.S. Teams Work." *Supervision* (January 2000): 6.
5. Thompson, L., E. Peterson, and L. Kray. "Social context in negotiation: An information processing perspective." In R. Kramer & D. Messick (eds.), *Negotiation as a Social Process*. New York: Russell Sage, 1995, pp. 5–36.
6. Thompson, L., E. Peterson, and S. E. Brodt. "Team Negotiation: An Examination of Integrative and Distributive Bargaining." *Journal of Personality and Social Psychology* 70 (1996): 66–78.
7. Bazerman, M. H., J. R. Curhan, D. A. Moore, and K. L. Valley. "Negotiation," *Annual Review of Psychology* 51 (2000): 279–314.
8. See for example Dougherty, D. "Interpretive Barriers to Successful Product Innovation in Large Firms." *Organization Science* 3 (1992): 179–202 and S. E. Jackson. Team Composition in Organizational Settings: Issues in Managing an Increasingly Diverse Workforce. In S. Worchel, W. Wood & J. Simpson (Eds.), *Group Process and Productivity*. Newbury Park, CA: Sage, 1991.
9. DuBrin, A. *Essentials of Management*. Mason, OH: South-Western, 2009.
10. Lewicki, R. J., D. M. Saunders, and B. Barry. *Negotiation* (5th ed.). Burr Ridge, IL: McGraw-Hill Irwin, 2006, p. 352.
11. Lencioni, P. *The Five Dysfunctions of a Team*. San Francisco: Jossey Bass, 2002.
12. Polzer J.T. "Intergroup negotiations: The effects of negotiating teams." *Journal of Conflict Resolution* 40 (1996): 678–698.
13. Carrell, M. R., and C. Heavrin. *Negotiating Essentials: Theory, Skills, and Practices*. Upper Saddle River, NJ: Pearson Prentice Hall, 2008, p. 22.
14. Lewicki, R. J., D. M. Saunders, and B. Barry. *Negotiation* (5th ed.). Burr Ridge, IL: McGraw-Hill Irwin, 2006, p. 524.
15. Lituchy T. R. "Negotiations between Japanese and Americans: The Effects of Collectivism on Integrative Outcomes." *Canadian Journal of Administrative Sciences* 14 (1997): 386–398.
16. Arunachalam, V., J. A. Wall, Jr., and C. Chan. "Hong Kong versus U.S. Negotiations: Effects of Culture, Alternatives, Outcome Scales, and Mediation." *Journal of Applied Social Psychology* 28 (1998): 1219–1244.
17. Lewicki, R. J., D. M. Saunders, and B. Barry. *Negotiation* (5th ed.). Burr Ridge, IL: McGraw-Hill Irwin, 2006, p. 352.
18. Janis, I. I. *Groupthink* (2nd ed.). Boston. MA: Houghton-Mifflin, 1982.
19. Reproduced with permission from Elizabeth Mannix, "Strength in Numbers: Negotiating as a Team," *Negotiation*, 8(5), Harvard Business School Publishing, May 2005.
20. Editorial, "EGF Should Think about 'Groupthink'," *Knight Ridder Tribune Business News*, June 27, 2007, p. 1.
21. Adapted from http://www.nfl.com/news/story?id=09000d5d815dc70b&template=with-video-with-comments&confirm=true
22. Susskind, L. "Winning and Blocking Coalitions: Bring Both to a Crowded Table." *Negotiation*, Harvard Business School Publishing, January 2004, Volume 7.
23. *Ibid*, p. 352.
24. de Janasz, S.C., K.O. Dowd, & B.Z. Schneider (2009) *Interpersonal Skills in Organizations. (3/e)*. Burr Ridge, IL: Irwin McGraw-Hill.
25. The Future of Business Meetings, available at http://www.allbusiness.com/technology/telecommunications-conferencing/12305-1.html, accessed 31 July, 2010.
26. de Janasz et al. *Interpersonal Skills in Organizations*, 2009.
27. Technically speaking, mediators are trained in mediation, not negotiation, although there is some overlap. Training in negotiation is opening demands, target, resistance points, and strategies to get what you want. Training in mediation is getting the parties to talk (air their differences and share their needs) and work toward resolution, not necessarily an optimal solution.
28. Carrell, M. R., and C. Heavrin. *Negotiating Essentials: Theory, Skills, and Practices*. Upper Saddle River, NJ: Pearson Prentice Hall, 2008, p. 24.

Exercise 11.1   Moving Up . . . and Moving Out?

Anil, Beth, and Carlos have been friends since the sixth grade when all three were in the school band. Throughout middle and high school, some subset of the threesome would be taking classes together, attending school functions, and participating in extracurricular activities. They stood by each others' sides through failed romances, school-related disappointments, and other challenges. One such challenge was when Anil and Beth were accepted to State College while Carlos, who had a weaker application, was forced to complete two years at the local community college in order to have a chance at being accepted as a transfer student at State College. Despite this setback, the three friends remained close, visiting one or two weekends a month and on extended breaks.

Things changed two months ago. Carlos got his acceptance letter from State College and the three spent time over the summer finding the perfect apartment to share. The first week living together was bliss—conversations until the wee hours of the morning, taking turns shopping and cooking dinner, and the appearance of an occasional guest or two. By week two, tensions began to mount. Though each had a private bedroom, it appeared as though Beth moved into the living room. All of her books, electronics, and various clothing items were strewn about the sofa and coffee table. Carlos kept his room fairly neat, but his large and growing array of hair products and colognes began to clutter up the bathroom he shared with Anil. Anil's course load—twenty-one units—plus a part-time job (ten hours a week in one of the college's computer labs) kept him busy; he rarely spent time in the apartment or doing any of the chores he agreed to do back when they signed the lease.

Then the bills came: cable, phone, electricity, trash. Beth's parents sent her a monthly allowance, but the last check she sent to the cable company was returned. "Insufficient funds," Beth explained to her roommates, while simultaneously realizing that the 500+ text messages she sent last month created a $150 overage on her cell phone bill. "I'll have to get unlimited text messaging," Beth thought to herself. The bills were divided equitably initially, but Carlos added several sports channels (adding $20 per month to the cable bill), and the hotter than normal fall made for higher than normal electric bills.

Even the cost of groceries had gone up; however, since Anil was spending less time at the apartment—eating many of his meals on campus, he felt that the even three-way split on groceries was no longer equitable. Plus, he fumed to himself, Beth's boyfriend stays over every weekend and has yet to replace any of the food—or beer—he consumes.

Lately, the three of them are rarely talking to one another. It's almost as if they're avoiding the issues. Their friendship of eight years is on the verge of destruction if they don't talk and renegotiate shared costs, chores, and even guest arrangements. Deborah, their next door neighbor and a psychology major, has offered to mediate their negotiation if need be.

> Step 1: After roles are assigned, each person should spend time planning his or her goals, BATNAs, and other components of his or her negotiation strategy. Consider using the Negotiation Strategy Outline at the end of this exercise.
>
> Step 2: Have the negotiation. Each person present should introduce himself or herself (and the role he or she is playing) and share any relevant information. Consider jointly developing an agenda. Your instructor may allow up to one hour for this negotiation.
>
> Step 3: Debrief/self-assessment

1. Discuss the actual implementation of the negotiation concepts, for example, as shown here.
   - What role did your strategy preparation play in the negotiation?

- Was the negotiation integrative or distributive? Please provide evidence. Why was this approach best, given the situation?

- How well did you articulate your goals and interests? How well did you understand the other parties' goals and interests? Please provide evidence?

- How persuasive were you and your opponents? Please provide evidence to support your opinion.

- How well did you focus on interests (as opposed to positions) and problems (as opposed to the people)?

2. Comment on the results of your negotiation. Objective criteria are preferred for the evaluation of your attempt. Were they better or worse than expected? How creative were the solutions you and your partner developed?

3. Overall, were you satisfied with the negotiation? Why or why not? If you had the option to redo this negotiation, what would you do the same and what would you do differently? Explain.

Negotiation Strategy Outline
Negotiation Strategy

1. What do I/we ideally want?

2. Why do I/we want this? What are my/our interests?

3. What is my/our BATNA?

4. What does our opposition likely want? Why?

Negotiation Frame

1. What is my/our frame (be creative)? How does this further our goal for the negotiation? How might my/our frame be twisted/turned around?

2. What do we anticipate our opposition's frame to be?

3. Are there ways to frame this opportunity differently, to facilitate the negotiation?

Assumptions

1. What assumptions are being made regarding my/our opposition that may not be accurate?

2. What assumptions might our opposition be making that I/we may wish to change, or to use in my/our favor?

Questions

What questions should I/we be asking?

Enhancing Credibility

Which of the criteria (e.g., expertise, energy, composure, trustworthiness) will we incorporate and how?
Two things I/we want to be sure to say in our favor to establish credibility:

1.

2.

Persuasion

1. What persuasion methods (emotion, logic) or theories (e.g., inoculation, ACE model, etc.) might prove useful? How should we use them in this case?

Mutual Gain

1. What options for mutual gain might we propose?

Objective Criteria

1. By what standards should we evaluate arguments/data/options presented?

Agenda

1. What will we suggest as the topics and order in which we will discuss them?

Exercise 11.2   Goodbye Greeks?

Midwestern U has had a long-standing Greek system. Ten fraternities and seven sororities account for 18% of the student body. However, the last three years have seen a significant increase in the number of incidents on Greek Row, as well as rising complaints from area residents. Aside from overall rowdiness, public drinking, and property defacement, there have been parent complaints of hazing. Doug Amrhein, VP of Student Affairs, decides to take action. He invites two groups—MU's Student Council leadership (president and three vice presidents) and MU's Greek Leadership Council (the elected fraternity and sorority presidents and their alternatives)—to review the incidents and develop a solution that will appease the multiple stakeholders, such as neighbors, parents, Greek organizations, current students, and possibly, future students.

You will be assigned to one of these two teams. In your groups, decide on the roles, and then devote 20–30 minutes to planning and addressing the following points (at a minimum):

- Clarifying your party's assumptions, goals, and interests
- Identifying the other party's assumptions, goals, and interests
- Thinking of potential solutions that would create value/be mutually beneficial
- Deciding on ways of arriving at solutions in the negotiation
- Discussing how you will manage the negotiation within the time limit; the negotiation will last approximately 30–40 minutes.

Debrief/Team Assessment

1. Discuss the team's overall opinion about the negotiation outcome (what you "got") relative to what your team strategized for. What explains the discrepancy (if any) or similarity between planned and actual outcome? (This discussion might include reference to what might have been done differently to achieve the desired outcome, or more, if you got what your team wanted too easily.)

2. Discuss the dynamics of the negotiation: Specifically explain two dynamics or issues that threatened to undermine the effectiveness of the negotiation. What actions were taken to overcome or manage these issues? In what ways were the actions successful? What other actions might have been taken, and toward what likely effect?

3. To what degree were both sides' key interests satisfied? Describe elements of the negotiation process that helped you get there (or not!), as well as evidence to support your opinion that key interests were satisfied (or not).

Exercise 11.3   Going Across the Pond?

John Monroe is a senior vice president for one of the North America's largest hotel chains. Given his well-earned reputation as an industry leader in improving customer focus and satisfaction, it's not surprising to learn that a competitor based in the United Kingdom is attempting to lure John away from his company. In fact, the initial contact with Rupert Kingston, the CEO, progressed to two additional phone conversations, and most recently, a face-to-face visit where Rupert and members of the senior management team wined and dined John and ended with "an offer he can't refuse." While John has had some concerns about his present employer, he hadn't been actively looking for another position. In addition, he is concerned about how his wife and fourteen-year-old daughter would react to a move. They moved 800 miles away from their home when he took his current position five years ago, and both ladies had a tough time making new friends and adjusting to a town that was substantially larger (in size and population) than what they were used to. Should John accept the offer, his wife and daughter would have to adapt to a new country.

Your instructor will distribute additional information for the roles to be played in this multiparty negotiation that will last no more than one hour.

Step 1: After roles are assigned, each person should read his or her additional information and plan his or her goals, BATNAs and other components of his or her negotiation strategy. Consider using the template on page 266.

Step 2: Have the negotiation. Each person present should introduce himself or herself (and the role he or she is playing) and share any relevant information. Consider collaboratively developing an agenda.

Step 3: Debrief/self-assessment

1. Discuss your opinion about the negotiation outcome (what you got) relative to what you strategized for. What explains the discrepancy (if any) or similarity between planned and actual outcome? (This discussion might include reference to what might have been done differently to achieve the desired outcome, or more, if you got what you wanted too easily.)

2. Discuss the dynamics of the negotiation: Specifically explain two dynamics or issues that threatened to undermine the effectiveness of the negotiation. What actions were taken to overcome or manage these issues? In what ways were the actions successful? What other actions might have been taken, and toward what likely effect?

3. To what degree were all sides' key interests satisfied? Describe elements of the negotiation process that helped all parties get there (or not), as well as evidence to support your opinion that key interests were satisfied (or not).

Exercise 11.4 When a Manager Stumbles (Harvard Business School Case)[*]

Your instructor will be distributing this exercise and specific roles each person will play within the two teams: one which consists of Bulwark's management of Jim Slake, Paul MacKinley, and Gloria Ludlow, and the other which consists of three consultants representing Anders Arthurson, Inc. These two teams will be meeting to address the following questions put forth by Bulwark CEO, Chris Woodbone:

> Who's at fault? Should Goldstone be demoted or fired? How can his team be improved? How do we avoid this kind of problem in the future? Your job is to use your opinions, knowledge, and the perspective of Goldstone (advanced in the case) to formulate a plan to improve the current situation for Bulwark and to avoid future ones like it.

Upon completion of the negotiation, each team must submit their answers to the following questions:

1. Discuss the team's overall opinion about the negotiation outcome (what you got) relative to what your team strategized for. What explains the discrepancy (if any) or similarity between planned and actual outcome? (This discussion might include reference to what might have been done differently to achieve the desired outcome, or more, if you got what your team wanted too easily.)

2. Discuss the dynamics of the negotiation: Specifically explain two dynamics or issues that threatened to undermine the effectiveness of the negotiation. What actions were taken to overcome or manage these issues? In what ways were the actions successful? What other actions might have been taken, and toward what likely effect?

3. To what degree were both sides' key interests satisfied? Describe elements of the negotiation process that helped you get there (or not), as well as evidence to support your opinion that key interests were satisfied (or not).

Exercise 11.5 Rolling Hill Turkey Company

Overview

Rolling Hill Turkey Company has been in business for well over fifty years and is located in Tinytown, USA. Rolling Hill is well known in its community, as it is one of the biggest employers in the area, employing fifty full-time workers. The relationship between management and the workers of Local 731 has traditionally been good. This fact was illustrated in contract negotiations three years ago.

In the last five years, competition in the turkey slaughter and packaging market has become brutal. In response to this situation, at the last contract negotiation, the workers of Local 731 agreed to a salary freeze for the length of the contract. Since that time, Rolling Hill has made the company profitable again, and the workers of Local 731 believe they were an integral part of this recovery.

At one time, the union workers at Rolling Hill were among the best paid in their industry. Now they lag substantially behind the industry average. The contract negotiated three years ago is due to expire in a few days. Union workers believe that it is time for the company to pay them back for their loyalty. Management is still concerned about containing costs because many competitors are automating their plants, leaving Rolling Hill with higher costs, primarily due to labor.

Rolling Hill is an S-corporation with fewer than fifty shareholders. Most shares are tightly held by the family that started the company and other relatives.

In this contract renegotiation, management is represented by the director of human resources, and two employee relations representatives. Local 731 is represented by three union officials—elected by the fifty employees who are members of the union. Your instructor will distribute additional instructions and materials related to this exercise.

Team-Based Assessment Questions

1. How did your team go about preparing for your negotiation (how did it come up with its goal, BATNA, and approach)?

2. Upon what criteria did your team base its goals? Explain.

3. Was an agenda used in the negotiation? Were there any caucuses? Explain the effect, if any, these tools had on the outcome and process of the negotiation.

4. Did any conflicts arise in the negotiation process? Explain, and discuss key approaches used to resolve the conflict.

5. Overall, was the negotiation primarily distributive or integrative? Give examples to illustrate your opinion.

6. What tactics or strategies did your team use to achieve its goals? Discuss one successful and one unsuccessful tactic or strategy.

7. What tactics or strategies did the other team use to achieve its goals? Discuss one successful and one unsuccessful tactic or strategy.

8. In what ways was the negotiation successful? Factors to consider: persuasive arguments made, tactics used, goals achieved, relationship strengthened, creative solutions jointly developed.

9. In what ways could the negotiation have been more effective? If you could redo the negotiation, what do you wish you or your team would have done differently, and what effect would likely have resulted?

Exercise adapted from one developed by Christine Roeder, MBA, Management Program, College of Business, James Madison University, Harrisonburg, Virginia, 2004. Reprinted with permission.

PART IV

Negotiation and Dispute Resolution Applications

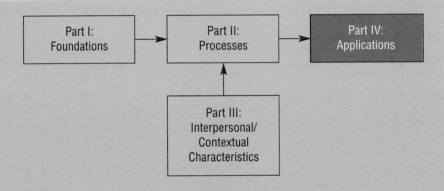

CHAPTER 12

Negotiating in the Workplace

Chapter Objectives

After studying this chapter and completing the exercises you should be able to:

- Assess your human, social, and relational capital and identify ways to increase it to enhance your value to, and leverage with, an employer.

- Identify and evaluate the challenges of negotiating in the workplace.

- Prepare for and execute a variety of workplace negotiations.

- Evaluate the challenges of negotiating with outside organizations on behalf of your employer.

- Apply integrative negotiation principles to situations where you are representing your employer.

- Develop a plan for dealing with excessive demands in the workplace.

T hus far, we have considered the processes of, components of, and influences on negotiation and dispute resolution in general terms. In the remaining chapters we shift the focus to the application of what you have learned to specific situations you are almost certain to encounter as you go forward in your professional and personal lives. We begin with a closer look at negotiations in the workplace.

The workplace is rife with negotiations, whether you are an actual employee of the organization or a self-employed independent contractor.* In some cases the negotiations involve the terms and conditions of an individual's employment (e.g., work schedule, pay, job duties, relationships with co-workers), while in others, an individual is representing his or her employer in negotiations with others (e.g., customers, suppliers). In this chapter, we explore these and other situations that involve negotiating and resolving conflict in the workplace. Appendix A contains additional information and exercises for those interested in the unique aspects of negotiating with labor unions.

---

*For more on the difference between employees and independent contractors see http://www.irs.gov/businesses/small/article/0,,id=99921,00.html

Chapter Scenario, Part I

Jacinta joined CMC, a large auto manufacturer, a month ago when she graduated from college with a degree in engineering. She is a quality assurance specialist whose job involves working with supplier companies to review and implement improvements to their quality processes and resolve quality problems. She is still learning the ropes and has noticed that some of her co-workers have more success in negotiations with her manager than others. One of her co-workers, James, seems to get what he wants when he negotiates—and he negotiates regularly. He consistently has the best work schedule, and recently, got the manager to send him to an expensive training seminar in Orlando. James seems to be on very friendly terms with the manager and is often seen having lunch with him. At the other end of the spectrum there is Ramon, who is rarely seen talking to the manager and is consistently given the worst tasks. Last month Ramon's adult daughter, who lives in another state, came for a visit. Jacinta noticed that Ramon didn't take any time off while his daughter was in town. When she asked him about it, Ramon said that he didn't ask for any time off because it was very short notice and he was sure the manager would just say no. Jacinta feels sorry for Ramon, but she wants to emulate James.

Hypothetically, managers should behave similarly with all of their employees. In the United States, differential treatment of employees—if based on race, color, national origin, sex, religion, age, or disability—is illegal. However, as we saw in the opening scenario, there are often differences in the supervisor-subordinate relationship,[1] which can influence negotiations. We know from Chapter 4 that having an open and trusting relationship with the other party—in this case your supervisor—is the basis for integrative negotiations where both parties achieve their objectives. As it applies to your supervisor, two factors have been shown to lead to a better relationship—competence and having personality characteristics that are similar to that of your superior.[2] While your education and prior experience prepare you for the former, the latter is more ambiguous. In some cases, you may happen to have much in common with your boss. But what if you don't share a common history or the same values, attitudes, and beliefs? How do you remain true to yourself while building a good working relationship?

The answer is that you need to learn to negotiate your position within the norms for the organization. Since there are vast differences in supervisors and organizations, the first step is to learn the expectations and norms of the organization, and recognize that they may differ from official company policy. What is acceptable behavior in one organization may be unacceptable in another. Consider the case of KD Corporation where the stated work hours for white collar employees were from 8 a.m. to 5 p.m. Monday through Friday. The reality was that the organization's culture dictated that everyone arrive closer to 7:30 a.m. and not leave before 5:30 p.m. In some departments, there was an expectation that everyone would work on Saturday mornings as well. It was even common for an employee who left at 5:00 p.m. to be chided by co-workers for leaving work early or "working part-time." Most employees accepted the situation and put in the extra time, even though there was no additional compensation for doing so. Employees who didn't follow the norm often lost their jobs during one of the company's regular reductions in workforce. Even though they were meeting the stated requirements of the job, they were not meeting the expectations on which they were actually evaluated.

We are not suggesting that you should become a chameleon and give up your own identity. To the contrary, the goal should be to fit in while preserving your own values, attitudes, and beliefs, and where there are differences, negotiate a mutually beneficial solution. As you work your way through this process, gather as much information as possible to ensure you are prepared for subsequent negotiations. Talk to

Points to Ponder

1. Think about organizational norms that might be in conflict with your values, attitudes, and beliefs. Which ones might be the easiest to negotiate and why?
2. To what extent might you have a difficult time adapting to the norms of your organization and work group? What would be your resistance point?

others—especially those who are productive, engaged, and approachable—and ask questions to help you understand the environment as well as the interests and priorities of those with whom you will be negotiating.

IDENTIFYING AND INCREASING YOUR LEVERAGE

We know from the discussion of power in Chapter 3 that the more you have to offer the other party, the greater your leverage in a negotiation. In the workplace this means the more valuable you are to your employer, the more likely you are to be successful when negotiating employment-related matters. Labor economists have long studied **human capital**—the knowledge, skills, and abilities a worker possesses as a result of native ability and "raw labor power," plus specific skills acquired through education and training.[3] In general, the more human capital one possesses, the greater his worth and leverage in negotiations with an employer. This is why employees who have an MBA command higher salaries—and also why more people today are pursuing MBAs.

Social capital is the sum of the resources a person possesses as a result of investments in social networks and provides an advantage based on a person's location in a structure of relationships. It explains how some people are more successful negotiating in a particular setting as a result of their superior connections to other people. Social capital is clearly a critical resource for those in any type of position where you develop a customer base and rely on repeat business, such as sales and small businesses ranging from consultants and lawyers to event planners and hairdressers. It is also valuable in negotiations where a creative, integrative solution involves bringing in others. For example, an interior designer who is negotiating a contract to redecorate a company's headquarters may gain an edge because he has strong connections to contractors who are known for doing superior work.

Negotiation researchers have also recently identified **relational capital**, a negotiation-specific form of social capital, which focuses on the relational assets that accumulate within a specific dyadic negotiation relationship.[4] Components of relational capital include mutual liking, knowledge, trust, and commitment to continuing the relationship.[5] When the parties know, like, and trust each other, and want to continue the relationship, it follows that negotiations will be more integrative, with a focus on producing the best outcomes for both parties. For example, an electrical contractor who has built a good relationship with a facilities manager is likely to be the first one called when there is any electrical work to be done.

Once you have identified the capital you already possess, the next step is to pinpoint what your employer needs, paying particular attention to needs within the organization that are currently unsatisfied. The possibilities could range from a need for a particular skill, such as knowing how to use a new computer program, to a need for someone to take on a special project. You should focus on needs that are both important to the organization and a good fit with your knowledge, skills, abilities, and interests. If you don't currently have all of the skills or knowledge needed, think of how you might acquire it. Increasing your value to your employer increases your power in the relationship, which carries into all of your employment negotiations. Exercise 12.1 at the end of this chapter provides a useful framework for this assessment.

Chapter Scenario, Part II

Jacinta had been at CMC for only six months when there was a problem at one of its suppliers that required someone from CMC to be on site to resolve the problem. Normally this would have been handled by the senior QA specialist Doug, but he had just left for a two-week safari in Africa. Jacinta had to handle this by herself, which had her more than a little intimidated. Not only was this her first time representing CMC, but the supplier was known to be difficult. Jacinta knew that she had to win the supplier over to get them to resolve the problem as soon as possible.

The problem was that she was quite shy, especially around people she didn't know well. She was away from familiar surroundings and completely out of her comfort zone. She could talk technical details at great length, but had a hard time with small talk and getting to know people. In college she excelled at the technical aspects of the work, but never learned how to approach this type of situation. She was concerned that she wouldn't be able to get them to correct the problem in a timely manner and that they might try to push her around.

Jacinta's situation was not unique. Many jobs today involve working with someone from outside your department, if not outside the organization. Obviously, suppliers must work with customers and vice versa, but employment-related relationships go beyond just salespeople and buyers. Depending on the nature of the product, a variety of people from engineering, manufacturing, production control, and even accounting may be involved. Depending on your position, you may also have to work with outside auditors, representatives of accreditation bodies, consultants, the media, or even the government. You may also be involved in interviewing job applicants and hiring new employees. All of these examples can involve negotiating and resolving disputes.

In Chapter 6 we explored a number of personality traits that influence negotiations. In general, people who are extroverts will have an edge because they are more comfortable dealing with new people. Similarly, high self-monitors are able to read their negotiating partners and adjust their behavior accordingly. Together, these traits help in establishing a relationship with a new negotiating partner inside or outside of the organization. Being upbeat and optimistic sets the tone for integrative negotiations, and displaying positive emotion increases the likelihood of a future business relationship, coming to agreement, and gaining concessions from the other party.[6]

Points to Ponder

1. How comfortable are you with dealing with new people in a business setting?
2. What might you do to increase your confidence?
3. What is the potential downside of being extremely extroverted and high in self-monitoring?

THE ART OF NEGOTIATION IN SALES

It has been said that the art of negotiating may be the most difficult skill for any salesperson to develop[7] and that many salespeople aren't effective negotiators because they're often too willing to do whatever it takes to make the sale.[8] This is likely due to the incentives built into their compensation plans. In most cases, part, if not all, of a salesperson's income comes from commissions—typically a percentage of the dollar value of the sale. While some employers structure their commission system to pay a higher rate for products that are more profitable, the bottom line in sales is that if you get a sale—any sale—you get paid. We learned in Chapter 1 that people are motivated by incentives. Thus, it follows that salespeople will do whatever it takes to make a sale. Taken to the extreme, it can involve making unrealistic promises or engaging in hardball tactics just to get the sale.

Good negotiation skills are about much more than simply using distributive tactics to close the deal. Negotiation requires a different way of thinking: The aim is to satisfy the client, without giving up too much in the process.[9] Using the integrative approach discussed in Chapter 4, a salesperson must consider both her employer's and

FIGURE 12.1 The Sales Perspective Redefined

Approaching negotiations from a sales perspective, Conlin posits that salespeople can be turned into strong negotiators by following five steps.[10] The first is to avoid discussing price and focus more on value. People are often willing to pay more for an item if they believe they are getting value. It is why some people buy a Rolex instead of a Timex or a BMW instead of a VW. The second step is to build credibility with the customer. When a salesperson is viewed as an expert who is trying to help the customer find solutions that meet his needs, the customer is likely to disclose more about his needs, increasing the likelihood of an integrative solution. Conlin's third step is to "plan effectively and early" so as to anticipate the customer's needs. At the same time, a good sales negotiator understands the needs of her employer. Does your company have excess capacity that it needs to use? Is your company trying to expand into new markets or get a foot in the door with a potentially large customer? The fourth step is to manage information so you are not disclosing information that could put you at a disadvantage if the customer decides to play hardball. The fifth step, managing concessions, is ensuring that the concessions you make are indeed worth it. If they aren't, ending the negotiation may be appropriate.

customer's interests and seek to create additional value for mutual gain. While receiving/ paying a fair price is obviously an interest, you need to think about other things that are valuable. For both parties, there is likely value in building a long-term relationship. Other common interests include quality level of the products and services offered, ongoing product service and support, delivery schedules and terms, and even transfer of ownership. Of course, if you are negotiating these types of issues, people from other areas (e.g., quality assurance, service, operations, production control, and shipping) will also likely be involved.

To help identify the customer's interests, respond to a demand with questions seeking to reveal the reason for the demand.[11] For example, if the customer asks for modifications to your standard product, ask what she needs to accomplish. The additional information may help you find a way to meet the customer's objectives in a more efficient or less costly manner. If a customer requests a shipper that you do not normally use, ask why. The customer may simply not be familiar with your preferred method of shipping. Taking this approach from the first meeting with the customer is apt to lead to better outcomes in the end. While many salespeople view negotiations as occurring only at the end of the sales process, the reality is that selling and negotiating take place concurrently.[12] Figure 12.1 provides an example of how the sales perspective can be reframed.

THE NEGOTIATION PERSPECTIVE

We know from Chapter 9 that the relationship you have with the other party has a significant impact on subsequent negotiations. When you approach sales from a negotiation perspective, the focus shifts from a list of dos and don'ts to developing a good relationship with customers. In most cases salespeople want repeat business. Satisfaction with the relationship encourages expansion of the relationship.[13] The best way to ensure that is to work to develop an ongoing relationship with the customer from the beginning. This means getting to know the customer, her situation, and her needs. In Chapter 2, we learned that reciprocity is a powerful force and helping others achieve their objectives often results in them helping us to achieve ours. Thus, you should try to understand the customer's challenges and look for ways that your company can assist her in meeting them. Be responsive to your customer's requests for information and provide technical assistance as appropriate. In all your dealings with the customer and her representatives, be honest and forthcoming. If you know that you won't be able to deliver on a promise, don't make it. It is better for the long-term relationship to risk losing a sale than to risk losing the entire relationship.

Seek to create value beyond the customer's basic criteria for the product or service. Think about this as the sales equivalent of preferred qualifications for job applicants. A basic assumption about job applicants is that they meet the required qualifications or they wouldn't have applied for the job. What sets them apart is the extent to which they possess the preferred qualifications. In a sales context, the basic requirements are just that—*required*. The supplier must provide them. If you go beyond the basic requirements, you create value to the customer that sets you apart from the competition. Think about the trend in light bulbs. The basic requirement for someone buying a light bulb is that she needs a product that will produce light. Historically, most people viewed light bulbs as basically all the same and would buy whatever brand happened to be on sale. Today, however, people are spending three or four times as much to get the new CFL bulbs because they use far less energy and last much longer. Not only do customers save on their energy costs, they save time because they don't have to change the bulbs as often and they help the environment by using less energy.

As a salesperson you may need to educate the customer so he appreciates the added value. In some cases, you may need to educate more than just the people who work in purchasing. If you are selling a raw material or component part that will result in a higher-quality product for the customer, you may need to educate the customer's quality assurance engineers. If you are selling a product that reduces the customer's manufacturing time, you may need to educate the customer's operations or manufacturing engineering staff. To do this you will need to gain access to people outside of purchasing. Remember our discussion of the value of professional networks in Chapter 9? In this situation, if you have a good relationship with the buyer, she will be more likely to help you make the right connections. Of course, educating the customer requires additional effort on your part, but if the customer appreciates the added value, she will be less likely to focus solely on the price of your product.

Although the success of cooperative relationships depends in large part on how the parties develop the relationship over time, negotiation of the initial agreement is critical in setting the stage for subsequent development of the exchange relationship.[14] This is not a time to engage in distributive bargaining or play hardball. Research has shown that the use of coercive techniques during negotiation has a negative effect on satisfaction with the negotiation.[15] Gaining a small amount on profit margin is generally a hollow victory if the customer leaves the negotiation vowing to never do business with you again. Thus, you should come to the table with a cooperative mindset and avoid the use of coercive tactics. In addition to its effect on the relationship, a cooperative orientation has a positive effect on the formalization of the design of the contract between the parties.[16]

When large, complex products are involved, it is common for a negotiating team to be involved. The team may include representatives from finance, operations, and engineering in addition to sales. Who takes the lead can affect the general direction of the negotiation, as each functional area has an inherent interest in different aspects of the negotiation. For example, engineering is more likely to focus on product specifications, while finance is more likely to focus on profit margins. Thus, while everyone on the negotiating team has an interest in the negotiation, each individual's priorities may be different and perhaps even in conflict. You must ensure that all parties on the negotiating team understand the overall objectives and work together to make sure they are attained, recognizing that individual goals may or may not be fully achieved as the overall goal is pursued.[17] As Figure 12.2 illustrates, achieving the overall goal may even require that you negotiate with your own employer on behalf of your customer.

BEYOND OUTSIDE SALES

Thus far, we have focused on negotiating with customers on behalf of your employer from the perspective of an outside salesperson; however, there are many more subtle, informal negotiations that happen daily with customers in a wide variety of settings. The principles are the same whether one is in retail sales, food service, customer service, or any of a myriad of other jobs that involve working with a customer. While we typically don't think of this as negotiation, it is essentially what we are doing.

FIGURE 12.2   The Flip Side: Representing Your Customer to Your Employer

> When we think of salespeople negotiating, we typically think about their negotiations with customers, but they also negotiate with other employees in their own company on behalf of their customers. They may be called upon to negotiate the inclusion of special features/options, production/delivery schedules, credit terms, and even the return of merchandise. In these situations, the salesperson assumes a dual role in the negotiation, representing both the employer and the customer simultaneously. When this happens, the salesperson must balance loyalty to the customer with loyalty to her employer, both of whom want the best deal possible. This requires the salesperson to walk a fine line in the negotiations. If she puts more emphasis on the employer's interests, she risks losing the customer, but if she favors the customer, there may be negative repercussions for her employment.

Employees in retail and food service persuade customers to purchase additional products and continue to frequent the business. Employees involved in all kinds of customer service build relationships with and offer service to customers in exchange for their continued patronage. Negotiators in all arenas can learn lessons from people in these professions.

In most of the customer service positions, employees are taught that service is paramount and to treat all customers with extreme courtesy, even if the customer is rude or obnoxious. It's the old adage that "the customer is always right." There are stores whose return policy is to accept virtually anything a customer returns in an effort to make the customer happy so he will continue to frequent the business. These retailers see the value of repeat business and are willing to accommodate even difficult customers to ensure that happens. When you find yourself negotiating with a difficult person, before walking away, consider whether the long-term relationship is worth dealing with difficult behavior in the short term.

Consider too the work of a server in a restaurant. In most restaurants, servers are taught to "up-sell" the customer, going far beyond the cliché "would you like fries with that order sir?" Depending on the type of restaurant, servers may entice customers to try an appetizer or a dessert, to add sautéed mushrooms or onions to their steak, or to opt for bottled instead of tap water. With desserts, customers are often tempted with a tray of samples the server brings by at the end of the meal. So why is this not common practice for appetizers? Because at the beginning of the meal, customers are hungry and order food without much added encouragement. However, by the end of the meal, customers are usually satiated and the added incentive of seeing the luscious choices can lead to increased sales of what are often high-profit items.

But the use of incentives to encourage the other party to comply with your requests isn't limited to food service. A good salesperson will try to sell you a shirt when you buy a suit or a tie when you buy a shirt. Similarly, stores offer incentives to encourage customers to purchase more. This might be a buy one get one half off offer or discounts based on the amount of your purchase, where larger purchases result in larger discounts. This has also become common in telecommunications where you get a better price on your cable, Internet, and phone service by bundling them into a multiproduct package. A common incentive for online retailers is to offer "free" shipping so the customer perceives there is no additional cost to making purchases online. Of course the retailers have to cover the cost of shipping, whether they call it a shipping charge or allow for it in the price of the product. Still in the minds of consumers they are getting a better value if the shipping is "free."

Similarly, you may need to offer incentives when negotiating to close the deal. You should identify the range of possible incentives when you are preparing for the negotiation. Think about what it might take to entice the other party to agree to your proposal. Consider how important it is to your employer that you complete the negotiation. Of course this will depend on your BATNA. The more and better your alternatives, the less you will have to rely on incentives.

Points to Ponder

1. Think about times that you have sold goods or services either as an employee or in a fundraising capacity. To what extent were you comfortable selling the goods or services? What made you comfortable or uncomfortable?
2. How likely are you to purchase more when there is an incentive involved? What types of incentives influence you the most?

PURCHASING ON BEHALF OF YOUR EMPLOYER

Purchasing is the mirror image of sales; thus, the interests and issues involved are fundamentally the same. The difference is your perspective. Generally speaking, as a customer you want the price to be lower and the quality higher than you would if you were the supplier. You want the delivery exactly when you want it—sometimes sooner and sometimes later—as in the case of just-in-time inventory control. As a customer, you may need special service or the expertise of the supplier or you may need to provide a supplier with your expertise if you are asking the supplier to develop a new or highly specific product.

As a customer, you must be careful not to give suppliers the impression that you are trying to manipulate them. Know what you want and when you want it, be complete and precise about your expectations, and be honorable in all of your dealings. Cutting corners or using hardball negotiating tactics may lead to gains in the short term, but will likely damage the long-term relationship. From a customer standpoint, there are tangible benefits to developing a good relationship with your suppliers. Preferred customers often obtain better outcomes in negotiations with suppliers. It goes back to the basic principle of reciprocity. If you work with the supplier when he has problems, he will be more likely to respond in kind when you need special consideration. If you do a significant amount of business with a supplier, in return, you are likely to receive special benefits. This is true whether you are a customer on an industrial or a personal level.

Essentially these are incentives to maintaining the relationship and there are many common examples. Regulars at restaurants typically get better tables and service. Preferred customers of department and other retail stores often receive coupons for special savings or access to special "preferred customer" sale hours. Airlines offer preferred customers first access to free upgrades to first class and exit row seating, and access to special lounges in airports. Members of museums, zoos, and other organizations receive invitations to special members-only events. Supporters of various arts groups (e.g., symphony, theatre) often have an opportunity to purchase advance tickets to special performances. People who belong to professional organizations receive access to information that is not available to the general public.

The same practices apply in industry. Preferred customers often have better access to product support, and obtain more favorable delivery schedules and payment terms. That is not to say they automatically get everything they want. Indeed, large customers sometimes engage in hardball tactics to dictate terms and conditions to suppliers. Over the last 20–30 years, customers such as the U.S. government and auto manufactures have used such tactics to require suppliers to implement major changes, including the use of bar-coded labels for product identification, Electronic Data Interchange (EDI), and Total Quality Management (TQM), and as shown in Figure 12.3, even the way products are manufactured.

That is not to say that customers should give suppliers a "do it or else" ultimatum. The trend in business today is quite the opposite. Customers need to focus on total value because buying by price, rather than total value, can destroy trust.[18] Beyond the negative impact on the relationship, focusing on price alone may result in substantive problems as well. The cheapest product may be of inferior quality or the supplier may not provide the level of service you need. Suppliers who are experiencing internal problems may offer low prices to attract customers, but may not be able to deliver on their promises. A low price on a needed item provides no value if the supplier declares bankruptcy before the goods are delivered.

In some cases, negotiations in which you are involved may adversely affect your co-workers, creating additional challenges. On the surface these may seem to be

FIGURE 12.3   Customer Hardball Tactics in Action: The Evolution of Manufacturing

Historically in manufacturing, customers maintained a receiving/inspection department, quite literally, to receive the shipment and subsequently inspect raw materials and component parts that they had purchased to ensure they met quality specifications. If the quality did not meet certain standards, the customer would send the product(s) back to the supplier to have them reworked or exchanged. During the 1980s and 1990s, when negotiating with their suppliers, large customers used hardball tactics telling them that they were no longer going to inspect every product they purchased. Instead, the suppliers had to provide statistical evidence that their products met all specifications. To say this revolutionized manufacturing is an understatement. Suppliers were forced to transform themselves from a "if it comes off the machine in one piece, it gets shipped" mentality to the current model of checking quality at every step of the manufacturing process and halting production to correct any problems. Not only has this virtually eliminated inspection of incoming products, it has had a dramatic impact on the work of machine operators who now have the added responsibility of tracking statistics and making production decisions.

unintended consequences, but in most cases, they are to be expected. Looking beyond the immediate negotiation and anticipating potential problems can better position you for resolving conflicts that surface and conducting additional negotiations that may arise from your initial negotiation. Negotiations involving the procurement of outside services and idiosyncratic deals in the workplace are particularly susceptible to this.

Negotiating the Procurement of Outside Services on Behalf of Your Employer

In an effort to reduce costs, many organizations today are **outsourcing** (i.e., transferring work to outside suppliers rather than completing it internally). With so many organizations today opting to outsource, there is a good chance that you will be involved in this at some point in your career. When this happens, you must be prepared to deal with the fallout.

Once a decision to outsource is made you must find a suitable vendor and negotiate a contract to govern the relationship. As a customer, you need to understand your needs and be able to fully articulate them in a **Request for Proposal (RFP)**. Because this is an ongoing arrangement, the relationship between the parties is particularly important. You must get to know your negotiation partner and be sure to check his references. Because the contract is the primary mechanism to ensure that both yours and the vendor's expectations are realized,[19] you must ensure that it details your expectations in terms of the scope of desired services, work arrangements, the level of service required, and objective performance measures. You may also include protection clauses for arbitration, confidentiality, and penalties for noncompliance. As you would expect, building incentives into the contract encourages desired behaviors from the vendor.[20]

These negotiations are more complex because there are typically deep-seated emotional issues for the current workforce who fear losing their livelihood and having their lives turned upside down. If you are involved in negotiating the outsourcing, you may encounter hard feelings and bear the brunt of their frustration and anger. The key to managing personnel issues in these situations is open communication.[21] Being forthright with workers about outsourcing plans from the time outsourcing is first considered will help prevent speculation, squelch the rumor mill, and maintain the relationship with the employees. Essentially, you are conducting two negotiations simultaneously, one with the vendor and one with the current employees. The latter is as important as the first because you still need the employees' services until the contract has been negotiated and the outsourcing begun.

Points to Ponder

1. To what extent would you be comfortable in negotiating outsourcing of work?
2. What might you do to alleviate the fears of, and ease the impact on, the employees?

Negotiating Individual Employment Agreements on Behalf of Your Employer

A second type of negotiation that may create additional challenges is the negotiation of individual employment agreements to entice an applicant to accept your offer of employment or convince an employee to remain with the organization. These are **idiosyncratic deals**—often referred to as **"i-deals"**—and may involve anything from granting additional paid vacation to allowing non-standard schedules or compensation. I-deals can be effective in recruiting and retention, but you must be prepared to live with the consequences. In general, problems that arise are related to the impact such deals have on other employees. It's been said that other employees are the i-deal's "most interested third party."[22] Even when organizations try to keep special arrangements private, you must always assume that any deals you make will become public knowledge as people talk and share information with others. Even when the exact terms of the arrangement are private, others are likely to learn about these in an incomplete and inaccurate manner.[23] When other employees find out about a special deal that someone negotiated, they may want similar treatment. If they don't get it, you must be prepared to deal with a variety of problems. The more nonstandard work arrangements there are in an organization, the less favorable attitudes toward supervisors and peers, the higher the level of turnover intentions, and the fewer work-related helping behaviors.[24] Thus, before you agree to anyone's requests, consider the likely repercussions down the road and make sure they are something you can handle.

For example, consider a situation where a new employee negotiates to be able to work from her home one day each week. If the other employees are not interested in that type of work arrangement, there should be no problem. If they would be interested and it would not be a problem for the employer, it is simply a matter of working out the logistics. In either case, the other employees are happy and it isn't costly for the employer. In contrast, suppose a new employee negotiates a starting salary that is substantially higher than what current employees earn. A reasonable assumption would be that the existing employees would seek a substantial raise to bring their pay in line with that of the new hire. Needless to say, this could become very costly for the employer.

Clearly, employers in these situations find themselves in a predicament. If they don't offer more lucrative compensation packages or agree to i-deals, they won't be able to hire the applicants they wish to hire. But if they make the deals, they may risk alienating, and potentially losing, current employees. If you are negotiating these types of deals for your employer, in addition to issues about legality and fundamental fairness, you must also consider the potential domino effect and ensure you are able—and have the resources—to deal effectively with the consequences. If you are not in a position to extend the terms and conditions negotiated in an i-deal to other employees who seek the same privileges, you should think twice about making the deal.

Points to Ponder

1. How would you react if a new employee had negotiated special privileges?
2. Should applicants refrain from attempting to negotiate i-deals? Why or why not?

Chapter Scenario, Part III

Jacinta has been on the job for two years. She has done extremely well and is generally viewed as the top performer in her department. She has taken on many responsibilities and is regularly asked to work on special projects. She always agrees regardless of what is involved. Management is very good to her, but lately she has been feeling like all she does is work so she is questioning her priorities in life. What started out as an effort to establish herself as a valuable employee has become detrimental to her well-being.

WHEN YOU ARE OVERCOMMITTED

We all know someone like Jacinta, who never seems to be able to say no when asked to help out or take on a new project. Helping others succeed is often a goal in itself, even if doing so is at the expense of your own needs.[25,26] Women in particular seem to get caught in this trap. Getting in the habit of negotiating when you are facing excessive demands on your time and resources can help preserve your health and well-being, and help you find a balance between your professional and personal lives. The question is where do you begin?

If the task you are being asked to do isn't something that will help your career or something that you really want to do, you must learn to say no. This can be tricky to do without impacting the relationship with the person making the request. Thus, it is often beneficial to take some time before responding. You might say that you want time to think about it to be sure you would be able to do the best possible job. While you often can't make people wait a long time for a response, you can almost always have a night "to sleep on it." If, after thinking about it, you decide that you really don't want to do it, decline gracefully. Instead of saying "I'm too busy with more important things" try something like "I would really like to help you out, but I have so many other things on my plate right now, that I don't think I would be able to give it my full attention." The end result is the same, but the impact on the relationship is generally quite different.

If you are being asked to do something that you want to do, but you are already stretched thin, it is still a good idea to ask for time to think about it. This gives you time to plan how you will negotiate away some of your other less desirable tasks. Think of creative options for getting the less desirable tasks done. Could they be handled by a lower-level employee who might see it as an opportunity to increase his value to the organization? Could the time required to complete the task somehow be reduced? Might some of the steps in the process be combined or eliminated?

Consider the example of weekly department meetings. A one hour meeting with twenty people is the equivalent of twenty hours per week—one-half of a full-time employee. The problem is exacerbated when the meetings don't start on time, leaving those who are punctual sitting around. Time is also wasted when not all of what transpires in the meetings is particularly important. Instead of complaining about the lost time, negotiate a different arrangement. For example, if part of the meeting is dedicated to some type of announcements, negotiate to have that part done electronically. Similarly, you might negotiate to have weekly meetings become biweekly meetings. Given a little time to think about it, people often come up with creative integrative solutions that benefit all involved. Once you have identified alternatives for improving the situation, the solution is only a negotiation away. As suggested in Figure 12.4, you should not assume that the boss' solution is automatically the best one.

FIGURE 12.4 Have You Met Peter?

You may be familiar with the "Peter Principle"—the notion that people rise to their highest level of incompetence in an organization. On the surface it is humorous, that is until you have to work with, or worse yet for, Peter. Just because a person is good in his current job, doesn't guarantee he will be good in a higher-level position. A classic example is the topnotch salesman who is subsequently promoted to sales manager even though the skills required for each job are very different. Salespeople need to know their products and be able to work effectively with customers to satisfy their needs. A manager on the other hand, needs to be skilled in planning, organizing, leading, and controlling human and material/financial resources. Unfortunately, organizations sometimes promote people who are good in the technical aspects of their jobs to management positions where their skills may be lacking. When negotiating with these people, it is important to remember that they may have needs that they are reluctant or even unwilling to articulate. For example, if you are negotiating something that has complex financial or budgetary implications, you may need to offer more detailed explanations than you would for those who are more knowledgeable, and do so without being asked or coming across as condescending.

Summary

Supervisors have varying relationships with different employees. Employees who enjoy better relationships with their supervisors are likely to have greater success when negotiating. Similarly, employees who have higher levels of human, social, and relational capital are generally more valuable and have greater leverage when negotiating with their employers. To increase their leverage, employees should understand what their employer values and seek opportunities to increase their value to their employer.

In addition to negotiations involving one's employment, people in a wide variety of occupations negotiate and resolve disputes with people outside of their organization. Extroverts and high self-monitors are particularly successful in such negotiations. Salespeople often focus on simply getting the sale instead of building a relationship, creating value, and negotiating the best deal possible with the customer. When you negotiate the outsourcing of work or an i-deal, you must be aware of and prepared to deal with the reactions of other employees. You may also need to negotiate your own workload.

Summary: The Big Picture

Identifying and increasing your leverage	It is important to understand your human, social, and relational capital that is valuable to your employer and seek ways to increase it.
The art of negotiations in sales	The sales perspective seeks to make a sale.
	The negotiation perspective seeks to build a relationship, create value, and negotiate the best deal possible.
	Beyond outside sales, many employees interact and negotiate with customers to sell additional goods and increase business.
Purchasing on behalf of your employer	You may be involved in purchasing goods or services for your employer, negotiating contracts to outsource work, or negotiating individual employment agreements.
Other negotiations on behalf of your employer	Negotiations involving outsourcing or i-deals with employees may lead to difficulties with current employees and additional negotiations.
When you are overcommitted	Negotiate a more manageable workload by learning to say no and negotiating away some of your responsibilities.

Key Terms and Concepts

Human capital The knowledge, skills, and abilities a worker possesses as a result of native ability and "raw labor power," plus specific skills acquired through education and training.

Idiosyncratic deals/I-deals A nonstandard agreement between an employer and an individual employee.

Outsourcing The organizational practice of transferring work to outside suppliers rather than completing it internally.

Relational capital A negotiation-specific form of social capital, which focuses on the relational assets that accumulate within a specific dyadic negotiation relationship.

Request for Proposal (RFP) A formal request from a customer for a potential supplier to submit a proposal to supply goods or services.

Social capital The sum of the resources a person possesses as a result of investments in social networks and provides an advantage based on a person's location in a structure of relationships.

Discussion Questions

1. Describe the challenges of negotiating in the workplace.
2. Discuss the importance of human, social, and relational capital in the workplace and provide examples of when each may be used.
3. Evaluate personal characteristics that may or may not be helpful when negotiating with those outside your organization.
4. Compare and contrast the sales and negotiation perspectives.
5. Discuss the importance of establishing and maintaining a good relationship with suppliers.
6. Discuss the challenges of negotiating outsourcing contracts for your employer.
7. Discuss the potential problems of negotiating i-deals with employees.
8. Develop a plan for dealing with excessive demands in the workplace.

Ethical Dilemma: Cash Sales

You and four others are the "bar team" in an upscale restaurant. Everyone works very well together—so well that you pool your tips and divide them equally at the end of each shift. Recently, management has voiced concerns about liquor costs being too high. You know that part of that is because the bartenders "pour heavy" when mixing drinks, but that doesn't account for all of the costs. A couple of weeks ago you were working with Nathan and noticed that he didn't seem to be ringing all of his cash sales into the cash register. It appeared that he was just putting the cash into the bar team tip box. The next day you talked with another team member Jamie about it and the two of you started paying more attention to what Nathan was doing. You have come to the conclusion that Nathan isn't recording all of his cash sales, but you have no real proof.

Questions

1. What is the potential conflict?
2. What could be negotiated to resolve the situation and prevent future conflict?
3. Do you have any obligation to Nathan as a fellow member of the bar team?
4. Do you have an obligation to voice your suspicions to management?
5. What risks do you face if you do/do not speak up?
6. Based on your value system, what would you do?

Ethical Dilemma: Declining Sales

You are a salesperson for Visions Medical Equipment, a distributor of high-end CAT scan, MRI, ultrasound, x-ray, and mammography equipment. Lately, business has not been good and you have lost a number of customers to your largest competitor. Your boss has been on you about it and the declining sales have dramatically affected your commission checks. You have curtailed your spending, but your finances are starting to get really tight. You are barely able to make the minimum payments on your credit card bills and you are afraid that if your commission checks don't start to rebound, you won't be able to make your car and house payments. You don't understand the loss of business; you are very good at your job and are selling the top-rated products in the industry. Lately, you have begun to suspect that your competitor's salesperson is giving kickbacks to the hospital buyers. Recently, a buyer for your largest customer hinted that

he could help you secure a large order if there were "something in it" for him. If you land the order you will earn a very large commission. You have never done anything like this before, but you do have an expense account where you could bury the payoff and there would be little risk of getting caught. You are afraid that if you don't do it, your company will lose the sale and you will lose the commission.

Questions

1. What are your options? What are the advantages and disadvantages of each option for you and your employer?
2. What risks do you face if you give the kickback?
3. What risks do you face if you speak up?
4. What is the risk of doing nothing?
5. What would you do in this situation?

Endnotes

1. Graen, G. B., and M. Uhl-Bien. "Relationship-Based Approach to Leadership: Development of Leader-Member Exchange (LMX) Theory of Leadership Over 25 Years: Applying a Multi-Domain Perspective." *Leadership Quarterly* (1995): 219–247.
2. Wayne, S. J., L. M. Shore, and R. C. Liden. "Perceived Organizational Support and Leader-Member Exchange: A Longitudinal Test." *Academy of Management Journal* (1997): 82–111.
3. Reynolds, L. G., S. H. Masters, and C. H. Moser. *Labor Economics and Labor Relations* (10th ed.). Englewood Cliffs, New Jersey: Prentice Hall, 1991.
4. Gelfand, M. J., V. S. Major, J. L. Raver, L. H. Nishii, and K. O'Brien. "Negotiating Relationally: The Dynamics of the Relational Self in Negotiations." *Academy of Management Review* 32(2) (2006): 427–451.
5. *Ibid.*
6. Kopleman, S., A. S. Rosette, and L. Thompson. "The Three Faces of Eve: Strategic Displays of Positive, Negative, and Neutral Emotions in Negotiations." *Organizational and Human Decision Processes* 99(1) (2006): 81.
7. Conlin, J. "Negotiating Their Way to the Top." *Sales and Marketing Management* 148(4) (1996): 56–59.
8. Lorge, S. "The Best Way to Negotiate." *Sales and Marketing Management* 150(3) (1998): 92.
9. *Ibid.*
10. Conlin, J. "Negotiating Their Way to the Top." *Sales and Marketing Management* 148(4) (1996): 56–59.
11. *Ibid.*
12. Lorge, S. "The Best Way to Negotiate." *Sales and Marketing Management* 150(3) (1998): 92.
13. Dwyer, R. R., P. H. Schurr, and S. Oh. "Developing Buyer-Seller Relations." *Journal of Marketing* 51 (1987): 11–28.
14. Rognes, J. "Negotiating Cooperative Supplier Relationships: A Planning Framework." *International Journal of Purchasing and Materials Management* (Fall, 1995): 12–18.
15. Atkin, T. S., and L. M. Rinehart. "The Effect of Negotiation Practices on the Relationship between Suppliers and Customers." *Negotiation Journal*, 22(1) (2006): 47–65.
16. *Ibid.*
17. *Ibid.*

18. Moody, P. E. "Supplier-Customer Integration: Why Being an Excellent Customer Counts." *Business Horizons* (1992): 52–57.

19. Sunoo, B. P., and J. J. Laabs. "Winning Strategies for Outsourcing Contracts." *Personnel Journal* 73(3) (1994): 69–76.

20. Barthelemy, J. "The Seven Deadly Sins of Outsourcing." *The Academy of Management Executive* 17(2) (2003): 87–98.

21. *Ibid.*

22. Rousseau, D. M. *I-deals: Idiosyncratic Deals Employees Bargain for Themselves*. Armonk, NY: M. E. Sharpe, 2005.

23. Rousseau, D. M., V. T. Ho, and J. Greenberg. "I-deals: Idiosyncratic terms in employment relationships." *Academy of Management Review* 31(4) (2006): 977–994.

24. Broschak, J. P., and A. Davis-Blake. "Mixing Standard Work and Nonstandard Deals: The Consequences of Heterogeneity in Employment Arrangements." *Academy of Management Journal* 49(2) (2006): 371–393.

25. Fletcher, J. K. "Relational Theory in the Workplace." *Work in Progress Series*, paper No. 77. Stone Center, The Wellesley Centers for Women, Wellesley College, Wellesley, MA, 1996.

26. Kolb, D. M., and G. Coolidge. 1991. "Her Place at the Table." In J. W. Breslin & J. Z. Rubin (Eds.), *Negotiation Theory and Practice* pp. 261–277, Cambridge, MA: Program on Negotiation, Harvard Law School, 1991.

Exercise 12.1   Assessing and Using Your Human and Social Capital

In this exercise you will begin with an inventory of your human and social capital, identifying when and how you use it, and identifying alternatives for increasing it. Start by identifying the knowledge, skills, and abilities you acquired and developed in school and other formal training venues such as seminars, workshops, and internships. In addition to the program-specific skills (e.g., accounting, engineering, human resources), be sure to include general skills such as written and oral communication, and the ability to work with others. Next, identify your natural talents and abilities. In addition to ingenuity, creativity, or artistic ability, this includes personality characteristics such as a strong work ethic, determination, conscientiousness, etc. Finally, identify your social capital—your work-related contacts, both inside and outside of the organization.

When you have identified the human and social capital that you already possess, identify human and social capital that you wish to acquire and the steps you need to take to obtain it.

Current: Human/Social Capital	When Used	How It Is Used	Strategy to Increase

Desired: Human/Social Capital	When Used	How It Is Used	Strategy to Obtain

Exercise 12.2   The Overdue Review

Instructions

In this exercise you will be assigned the role of the employee, supervisor, or an observer. Your instructor will provide you with confidential role sheets based on your assigned role. Read all the information provided and complete the worksheet for both the employer and employee based on the role sheets you have been given and your knowledge of the situation.

Overview

BHA Inc. is a small company that supplies component parts to the office furniture industry. It has few written policies for addressing human resource issues, and things are often handled in a haphazard manner. For the last several years, the company has been struggling with reducing costs to remain competitive. Bess has been the manager of the accounting department at BHA for several years and has been working on a special project for the president to identify areas in which the company could save money. About nine months ago she hired Kathy, a recent college graduate, as a staff accountant at a starting salary of $35,000. When Bess offered Kathy the job, she acknowledged that the salary was 5–10% less than what other larger employers in the area were offering, but promised Kathy she would receive a review and a raise after six months on the job. Kathy has now been on the job for nine months and the review still hasn't been done.

Worksheet

Employee: Kathy

Interests: _____

_____

Issue	Opening Demand	Target	Resistance

Supervisor: Bess

Interests: _____

_____

Issue	Opening Demand	Target	Resistance

Exercise 12.3 Negotiating a Salary Increase

Instructions

In this exercise you will be assigned the role of the customer service representative, customer service manager, or an observer. Your instructor will provide you with confidential role sheets based on your assigned role. Read all the information provided and complete the worksheet based on your knowledge of the situation.

Overview

Organic Foods Unlimited (OFU) is a supplier of fresh organic produce to the food service industry on the east coast. It specializes in supplying high-quality and unusual organic products to upscale dining establishments. Pat Pinchnikl is the customer service manager. He has been with the company since it was founded twenty years ago and remembers very clearly the early days when the company was stretched so thin financially that it almost went bankrupt. Even though the company is profitable today, Pat is still very careful to hold costs down.

Gwen Gougetr is a customer service representative and reports to Pat. She has been with the company since graduating from college two years ago. She has worked very hard to prove herself. Since coming to OFU, Gwen has taken on additional responsibilities that are not included in her job description and even took it upon herself to develop a system of tracking customer satisfaction. Her performance appraisals have all been very positive and she has received slightly above average raises. She is currently earning $35,000 a year.

Worksheet

Employee: Gwen Gougetr

Interests: _____

_____

Issue	Opening Demand	Target	Resistance

Manager: Pat Pinchnikl

Interests: _____

_____

Issue	Opening Demand	Target	Resistance

Exercise 12.4   The Competent Shall Be Punished

Instructions

In this exercise you will be assigned the role of assistant manager, operations manager, or observer. Your instructor will provide you with confidential role sheets based on your assigned role. Read all the information provided and complete the worksheet based on your knowledge of the situation.

Overview

Chris Costner is the operations manager at Island Treasure, a 500-room luxury resort located on the island of Maui. Ira Workman is the assistant manager and reports to Chris. Ira is a very dedicated, conscientious employee who has taken on additional tasks over time. He has the reputation for never saying no when asked to take on increased responsibility. Chris relies heavily on him, especially for important projects. Ira always gets the job done and done well.

Since its establishment in 1977, Island Treasure has provided world-class accommodations to upscale clients from around the world. It was the first luxury resort on the island, but in the last decade or so other resorts have opened and top management is concerned that the new resorts have diminished Island Treasure's leadership in the market. Management is looking at alternatives to reestablish the resort as the clear market leader. One option they are considering is applying for a Malcolm Baldrige national quality award. The two-phase application process is lengthy and requires extensive documentation of an organization's policies and procedures. The application materials are subject to multiple reviews by Baldrige examiners and judges.[**] The project will easily take a year or more to complete. Obviously, it would be a big undertaking, but if management is successful it will lend external support to Island Treasure's claim that it is the best of the best.

Worksheet

Employee: Ira Workman

Interests: _____

_____

Issue	Opening Demand	Target	Resistance

Manager: Chris Costner

Interests: _____

_____

Issue	Opening Demand	Target	Resistance

[**]For more information on the Baldrige National Quality Program see http://www.quality.nist.gov/

Exercise 12.5   The New Boss

Instructions

In this exercise you will be assigned the role of the employee, manager, or an observer. Your instructor will provide you with confidential role sheets based on your assigned role. Read all the information provided and complete the worksheet based on your knowledge of the situation.

Overview

Liquid Refreshments Limited (LRL) is a regional distributor of adult beverages. The owner, Anna Absolute, has recently decided to ease into retirement and turn the day-to-day operations over to her son Alex. Anna is known for being a very capable and caring employer, and is well-liked and respected by everyone. Alex is new to the company, having recently graduated with an MBA from a very expensive private university. He has yet to earn the respect of the employees. The general consensus is that he got the job only because he is Anna's son. He doesn't have the experience or personality compared to Anna, but then she is a tough act to follow.

Jess Miller was hired by the owner Anna twelve years ago and is currently the operations manager. He is very knowledgeable and well-liked by both customers and employees. Jess seemed to have a very good relationship with Anna and everyone thought he would be the one to take over when Anna retired.

Worksheet

Employee: Jess Miller

Interests: _____

_____

Issue	Opening Demand	Target	Resistance

Vice President: Alex Absolute

Interests: _____

_____

Issue	Opening Demand	Target	Resistance

Exercise 12.6   Dispute with Another Department

Instructions

In this exercise you will be assigned the role of Terri Tankman, Jean Greenleaf, or an observer. Your instructor will provide you with confidential role sheets based on your assigned role. Read all the information provided and complete the worksheet based on your knowledge of the situation.

Overview

Air Industries is a Fortune 500 company that produces air conditioning units for a wide variety of vehicle applications. The company is structured around four types of customers. The defense division designs and produces AC units for the military for use in tanks and armored personnel carriers. The agriculture division produces AC units for use in large farm machinery (e.g., tractors, combines, etc.). There are also divisions serving the transportation (planes, trains, and buses) and commercial building applications (hospitals, high rises). The divisions function independently and there is virtually no interaction between them.

A team from the defense division, led by Terri Tankman, is currently designing a new AC unit to be used in armored personnel carriers for the Army. The units must withstand high temperatures and dusty conditions for extended periods. It has recently been discovered that the agriculture division is working on a very similar project. The manager in charge of the project for the agriculture division is Jean Greenleaf. Throughout the corporation there is a very competitive environment with tight budgets and little sharing of information. In an effort to bolster sagging stock prices, corporate has decided to reduce costs by eliminating one of the projects. Everyone is aware that whichever division retains the project will avoid layoffs, while the other division will experience a reduction in workforce.

Worksheet

Manager #1: Terri Tankman

Interests: _____

_____

Issue	Opening Demand	Target	Resistance

Manager #2: Jean Greenleaf

Interests: _____

_____

Issue	Opening Demand	Target	Resistance

Exercise 12.7   You as a Sales Rep: Presenting Products/Services

Instructions

In this exercise you will present a product or service to the representative of a prospective customer using the persuasion process outlined in Chapter 8. Note: You will subsequently negotiate the sale of this product/service in Exercise 12.9. Your professor will explain how the products/services will be assigned. You will then research the product/service and prepare a sales presentation for your class. Use all sources available—the Internet, annual reports, and sales literature on the product—to prepare for your presentation. Audience members will use the following evaluation form to provide feedback on your presentation.

Sales Presentation Evaluation Form

_____
Your Name

Presenter: _____

Scoring key: 5 = Outstanding
             4 = Above average
             3 = Average
             2 = Needs some work
             1 = Needs a lot of work

Dimension	Score	Comments
Preparation/knowledge of product		
Enthusiasm		
Presence/confidence		
Use of time		

Exercise 12.8   You as a Buyer: Purchasing Products/Services for Your Employer

Instructions

This exercise consists of two rounds. In one round you will be a buyer representing your company in the purchase of a product or service. In the other round you will be playing the role of the sales representative negotiating the sale of your company's product/service to a buyer of a prospective customer.

First you must select a product/service presented in Exercise 12.7 that you would like to negotiate to purchase. Simultaneously, another student in your class will choose to negotiate for the product you presented. Your instructor will provide instructions for making these selections. For your role as a buyer, you need to research the product or service in preparation for the role play. Your professor will also provide instructions for completing the negotiation either in class or as an outside assignment.

Exercise 12.9   Hiring a New Employee

Instructions

In this exercise, you will be assigned the role of the applicant, director of sales, or an observer. Your instructor will provide you with confidential role sheets based on your assigned role. Read all the information provided and complete the worksheet based on your knowledge of the situation.

Overview

The *Northwoods Gazette* is a regional newspaper located in Smallville. The *Gazette* has been in business for nearly a century. The paper is run by Edward Longfellow, the editor-in-chief. It is known as a paternalistic organization that takes good care of its "family" of employees. Over the years, people who came to work at the paper stayed. Today, the average length of service of the employees is twenty-five years and the last person hired was the sports editor fifteen years ago. Over the years, employees have gotten raises that were at or slightly above the rate of inflation. The going market rate for employees in the industry has increased faster than the rate of inflation, primarily due to the increased use of technology and competition in the industry. *Gazette* employees, however, have not sought to increase their incomes by seeking jobs with newspapers in other areas. This is in part because they are comfortable in Smallville and in part because they are not skilled in state-of-the-art technology, making them less desirable applicants to other employers.

Ed understands that if the *Gazette* is going to compete in the current business environment, it needs to change with the times. He recently made the decision to implement a new printing process that will transform the operation of the newspaper. About six months ago, the editor of the business section of newspaper retired. Ed knows he needs to bring in new blood, a person who understands the technology and values the impact it can have on the organization, to fill this position. The problem is most people with these skills don't see the appeal of living in Smallville and are hesitant to work for less than they could earn elsewhere, even though Smallville's cost of living is low. Recently, Ed interviewed Angela for the position. Angela has an impressive background and credentials, and her family lives in the area. Ed is meeting with Angela today and is planning to offer her the job.

Applicant: Angela

Interests: _____

_____

Issue	Opening Demand	Target	Resistance

Editor-in-Chief: Edward Longfellow

Interests: _____

_____

Issue	Opening Demand	Target	Resistance

Exercise 12.10   Co-workers in Conflict

Carolyn is the customer service manager at Shoreline Industrial Supply, a position she has held for the last five years. She has recently hired five new account representatives and now has twenty-five direct reports. The people in the department generally work well together and often eat lunch as a group in the company cafeteria.

James is one of the recent hires in the department, having been lured away from a major competitor in another state. He has an impressive professional background and the general consensus is that Shoreline was lucky to hire him. James has been in a committed relationship with Bruce for eighteen years. He is open about his sexual orientation with his family and friends, but wants to get to know his new co-workers better before he shares it with any of them.

Stanley has been with Shoreline for fifteen years and is one of the senior employees in the department. He is hardworking and has always received favorable performance appraisals. Stanley is a devout Christian who readily shares his religious beliefs with others, often quoting the Bible to support his position. Historically, others in the department remained silent when Stanley proselytized, even if they disagreed with what he was saying, opting instead to maintain harmony in the department.

One day in the cafeteria, the lunchtime conversation turned to a recent story in the news of an effort to legalize gay marriage in the state. While some of the people at the table expressed support for the change, Stanley was very vocal in his opposition. He said that marriage should be only between a man and a woman, and that according to the Bible, anything else would result in eternal damnation. When Neo, another co-worker at the table, remarked that the Bible could be interpreted differently by different people, Stanley became angry. He stated that the Bible must be taken literally and that there is no room for interpretation.

James was very upset by Stanley's words, but didn't want to argue with him in front of his new co-workers. After all he didn't know them well enough to know whether or not they agreed with Stanley. Instead, he excused himself and went directly to Carolyn's office. He explained to Carolyn that he was very upset at what had happened and that he has been in a committed relationship for many years. Carolyn told him she would address the situation and James went back to his office.

The next morning Stanley came to Carolyn's office. He said he was very upset that Neo said the Bible is open to interpretation and felt that she was challenging his religious beliefs. He said he had discussed it with his minister, who agreed with him and encouraged Stanley to make sure "something was done." Stanley said if Carolyn wouldn't do something about it that he would "go over her head."

Questions

1. What aspects of this conflict make it difficult to resolve?
2. What options does Carolyn have for handling this situation?
3. What are the advantages and disadvantages of bringing in a third party to help resolve the conflict?
4. How would you attempt to resolve this conflict?

CHAPTER 13

Negotiating the Purchase or Sale of an Automobile

Chapter Objectives

After studying this chapter and completing the exercises you should be able to:

- Identify the unique aspects of and challenges involved in vehicle negotiations.

- Identify and prioritize the various interests inherent in acquiring a new or used vehicle.

- Evaluate the differences in purchasing a new or used vehicle.

- Develop a plan for negotiating the purchase of a new or used vehicle.

- Develop a plan for negotiating the trade-in or private-party sale of your vehicle.

- Assess the costs and benefits of purchasing an extended warranty.

INTRODUCTION

In 2008, in the United States alone, there were nearly 256 million registered vehicles in operation.[1] There are also 196 million drivers,[2] meaning there are approximately 1.3 vehicles per every person of driving age. As you can see, John is not alone in his desire or need for a car. Used or new, a car is needed to get students to school, employees to work, and people to their many activities. For many, a car purchase is the first major purchase. Even those who have cars—perhaps passed down by other family members who got new cars—will eventually tire of their old cars and want (or need) to buy a new—or new to them—car. Research suggests that the average length of time an owner keeps his car is approximately seven years.[3] Since you'll be involved in four or more automobile negotiations in your lifetime, it would be a good idea to master this skill. The good news is that no matter whether you buy or sell (or even lease), privately or through a dealership, a new or used car, you won't have to look far to gather relevant information to prepare for such a negotiation. In this chapter, we'll discuss what information is needed, how to get it, and what to do with that information, along with nuances and details specific to effective negotiation involving automobiles.

Chapter Scenario, Part I

Last year, as a freshman at the University of Miami, John Bento neither had nor needed a car. The Metrorail provided ample opportunity to get around Miami. Now a sophomore living off campus, John would like to buy a used car. The car should be dependable, be economical, must have air conditioning, and shouldn't cost more than $4,000. He noticed in the Sunday newspaper that an area auto dealer has numerous used cars for sale. He walks onto the lot with a classmate and zeroes in on a late model Toyota Corolla. It is in very good condition and has all the features he is looking for, including a killer stereo system. The car is priced at $4,995—about $1,000 more than he wants to spend. A salesman approaches, asking John if he'd like a test drive.

Points to Ponder

1. Imagine you are John. How would you react to the salesman?
2. What preparation might you have done before zeroing in on the Corolla?
3. If you really like the car after test driving it, how would you go about negotiating the price?
4. If you've ever purchased a car before, what about the experience was difficult and how could it have been easier?

As is generally the case, to be an effective negotiator, you must be able to put yourself in the shoes of the other party. Knowing the car dealer's perspective increases your ability to effectively bargain and persuade to achieve the best deal for you, as well as the dealer. In his book *Bare-Knuckle Negotiation*,[4] Raoul Felder shares words of wisdom from his friend and Volkswagen franchise owner, Howard Koeppel (p. 78). In terms of the price (of a car or service contract), "start high because then you can always lower the price down. But if you start low, you can never go up." Koeppel clearly takes a long-term view of client relationships, as evidenced by his view of the profit/relationship tradeoff:

> "If I let a customer walk out with a car where I've made too large a profit, I can replace the car but not the customer. Conversely, in some inventory situations, I may have one car too many and can let it go for a lower amount. My comfort level is lower but I've probably made a customer for life."

Koeppel's words certainly make sense from an ethical and business standpoint, even if the average person's perception of the auto industry may not match this viewpoint. However, you may not realize that dealers make more money, as a percentage, on service (over the life of the car) than on the sale of the car. Profit margins, in fact, are decreasing due to competitive pressures from both domestic and nondomestic manufacturers, as well as the current state of the economy. The continuing recession has been characterized by increased layoffs and home foreclosures as well decreased home sales and sales of other durable goods—including cars, which, in 2009, saw sales hit their lowest mark in 27 years.[5]

PURCHASING A NEW VEHICLE

According to the **National Automotive Dealers Association (NADA)**, there are currently 21,495 new vehicle dealerships in the United States, generating almost $700 billion in sales.[6] Your choices are many, and along with manufacturer's incentives and local dealers' competitiveness, you should be able to get what you want at a fair price. But the first question is . . . What do you want?

As with your preparation for any negotiation, the first step is to figure out what you want and why you want it. These two are inextricably twined when it comes to cars. For example, who wouldn't want to drive a sporty little convertible, particularly if you live someplace where there are 300 days of sunshine per year? However, if you need a car to transport your toddlers to daily daycare, a convertible is clearly the wrong choice. (Just rent a Miata or a Mustang convertible for a weekend and get it out of your system.) Think about your interests (e.g., proven safety record, good gas mileage, comfortable for long commutes) before constructing a list of possible car choices that would address those interests. (We've included a prioritization matrix in Exercise 13.4, number 2, to help you prioritize your interests in such a situation.)

When a customer walks on a car lot, the average car salesperson is looking to sell that customer a car—any car. Better yet, the customer walks in with an obvious emotional connection to a particular car. Such a situation simplifies the salesperson's job and gives him the upper hand in the eventual negotiation. While many a salesperson and dealership would be all too happy to close a sale, without regard to the more integrative goal of helping facilitate a customer's purchase decision now and in the future, your knowledge and preparation can level the playing field. The more time you spend thinking about your vehicle wants and needs, the greater the likelihood that you will get what you want for the price you want (and are able) to pay. Let's start by considering why you need a car, or more specifically, what will you be using it for? For example, will you be transporting people (e.g., how many seats?) or equipment (e.g., will the pick-up truck need a drop-down gate or bedliner)? How important is safety (e.g., multiple airbags, steel frame)? Will you be driving in snow or rough terrain (e.g., four-wheel drive)? Do you plan to keep the new car long term, or would you like to get a new car every few years, and therefore, consider leasing? While there are more questions, the primary interests include:

- Type of vehicle: car or truck.
- Size: economy/sub-compact up to twelve-passenger van.
- Number of passengers: from two to twelve or fifteen.
- Buy or lease?[7]
- Safety features and record: airbags, side curtains, steel frame.
- Transmission: automatic versus manual
- Fuel: gasoline versus diesel versus hybrid or possibly electric
- Traction needs: two- versus four- versus all-wheel drive
- Number of doors: two or four (or maybe an extra hatchback or back door)

Secondary interests, or wants (as opposed to needs), might include:

- Color choices
- Interior choices: available leather seats, heated seats, built-in child safety seat
- Infotainment: GPS, Blue-tooth voice activation, CD or MP3 player, automatic garage door opener or vehicle locator
- Roof-top luggage or bike rack
- Prestige factor

Knowing what you want and why you want it will help you make choices and tradeoffs between those choices. One tool for prioritizing these interests, particularly if more than a few of them seem equally critical, is the prioritization matrix (included in Exercise 13.4). Completing this matrix will facilitate the information gathering process and negotiation strategizing; it will also help you estimate the projected cost of the vehicle.

Now let's take a closer look at vehicle cost and how much you can afford. Being able to afford a certain car means different things to different people. Some people "just

FIGURE 13.1 **Steps for Buying an Automobile**

1. Figure out what you want and why you want it. Identify your primary interests (e.g., safety, size, transporting people or equipment).
2. Identify your secondary interests. What should the car look like (exterior and interior features) and what goodies should it have (e.g., entertainment, luggage racks)?
3. Prioritize these interests, using a prioritization matrix.
4. Determine how much you can afford to spend. Consider monthly payments as well as the cost of ownership (e.g., gas, maintenance, repairs, insurance).
5. Identify the expected price (target and resistance points) of the car you want using any and all national and local information available about the car's value (if used) and sales incentives (if new).
6. Determine the value of your trade-in, and decide if it's best to trade it in at the time of purchase or sell it to a private party.
7. As appropriate, visit your bank or credit union to get preapproved for the approximate amount of the loan you'll be seeking. This strengthens your negotiating position at the dealership.
8. Visit the dealership, armed with your data, as well as other options you are considering (e.g., other sellers, waiting until your income tax refund comes). Consider the time of month, day of the week, and time of day of your visit.

gotta have" that sports car and are willing to consume 30% of their monthly income on payments for their dream car. However, the price tag alone tells only part of the story. Every car has an approximate "cost of ownership." The biggest part of this cost is the price of the car, and how one pays for it. If John's Aunt Rita recently left him $5,000, he could buy the Corolla outright and not have to make monthly payments, which over the life of the loan, will amount to much more than the purchase price. However, spending his inheritance now leaves John without a small nest egg for another purchase down the line—such as a house. Fuel is another obvious cost of ownership, and some cars are more fuel efficient than others. John's Corolla will probably get between 25 and 32 miles per gallon, depending on whether he takes long highway trips versus short stop-and-start drives through Miami in rush hour. The other costs of ownership include auto insurance premiums, maintenance, and repairs. Insurance premiums are based on the value of the car and vary relative to the driver's age, location (city and specific location of the car when parked, for example, in a garage or on the street), driving experience, driving record, marital status, expected annual mileage, and the maximum value of the covered services required/desired as well as deductibles should an incident occur.[8] Manufacturers suggest that oil changes be done every 7,500 miles (about $30-40), and every 15,000 miles might entail more extensive servicing—some of which could amount to $300–400 or more if special services (e.g., timing belt replacement; usually every 100,000 miles), replacements (e.g., new tires; usually every 30,000 miles), or repairs are needed. These preventive services add to the cost of ownership, but ignoring getting them done can prove more costly in the long run. Imagine having to replace the brake rotors because you ignored the scraping sound and put off replacing brake pads (at nearly one-third of the cost) until it was too late and the rotors became warped. Even worse, imagine having to rebuild or replace an engine because yours ceased due to an insufficient amount of oil or water. So, while a bank will decide how large a monthly payment you can afford based on the price of the car, you now know that the cost of ownership can add as much as 50% or more to that figure. Clearly, there is a lot to think about when thinking about getting a new—or new to you—vehicle. But if you want to avoid making a bad purchase—one that might be with you for about seven years—it would be worth at least an hour of your time to consider and plan your decision. Moreover, if this decision involves others' input or approval, preparation becomes that much more important. Being prepared means making the best decision before, and being effective during, the ensuing negotiation.

How Much?

Prices of new cars vary from just over $10,000 to over $100,000. Of the nearly 17 million new cars sold each year,[9] the average sticker price on a vehicle sold in the United States is $29,746.[10] However, customers rarely ever pay the "sticker" or **manufacturer's suggested retail price (MSRP)**.[11] They instead pay a discounted price, which amounts to, on average, 16.8% off of MSRP, according to a 2004 report.[12] However, the rate of average discounts varies—the discounts tend to be the highest for domestic vehicles due to perceived declining quality and resale value. In 2007, the average selling price was discounted, on average, 20.6% below MSRP for a domestically produced car.[13] For Japanese and Korean cars, the average discount was 10% and 12.8% respectively. For European manufacturers, that average discount was 7.7% below MSRP.[14]

Another factor affecting the price of new cars is the incentives available to car dealerships and/or customers. Certain times of the year, and depending on a manufacturer's inventory and impending introduction of new models (typically in September for the coming year), are characterized by aggressive pricing, financing, or rebate campaigns. If you can wait until a more advantageous time to make your purchase, you will be able to negotiate a better deal.

How do you determine your target point and resistance point in preparing for your new vehicle negotiation? It depends. As we said, there are a number of factors involved in the actual selling price of a car. You need to know:

- the advertised price of the car—from your target dealership as well as its competitors. If you can demonstrate that other dealerships sell the same car for less, your target dealership may be willing to match its competitors' prices.
- how much the dealership paid for the car (www.cars.com is one website that contains dealer invoice information).
- any special incentives and rebates currently available—to the public and to dealerships.

Additionally, it is helpful to know how big a discount is typical for the car in which you're interested and how long the car has been in the dealer's inventory. In some states, you could just look at the state inspection sticker; if the month shown has passed, the car has probably been there at least one month. You could also ask the salesperson: she or he can find out from the computerized inventory listing. This information—while not offered readily—can also provide ammunition for your persuasive arguments. Dealers pay interest on every car during the time it sits on the lot. The best case scenario is for dealers to turn their inventory—sell their vehicles—before the first interest payment is due, typically thirty days. If you know that the car you want has been on the lot for some time, and in particular, if the sticker price is quite high, the dealer has an incentive to sell the car quickly, and perhaps for a bit less, just to move the car. Aside from the interest payment, dealers receive specific allocations from automobile manufacturers. They can't receive new cars until they sell the ones they have. Then there's also the issue of limited space on the lot.

Trade-Ins

Ideally, when you purchase a new car, you could trade in your current car and its value would provide a substantial down payment. Realistically, however, your car is worth less—to the dealership—than you might think. When the salesman tells you what the dealership will give you for your car, your first reaction might be to refuse to trade it in, opting instead to sell it to a private party. While you might get more for your car this way, realize that the path is neither as easy nor as profitable as it may seem. Dealers know that:

- they must buy low (especially if they have to put work into the vehicle before selling it) to make a profit upon resale
- you may not have the time or the finances to wait for the sale, particularly, if your subsequent car purchase is contingent upon the sale of your current vehicle
- there are costs (e.g., advertising and possibly time off from work) and even safety issues (e.g., unknown others taking you and your car for a test drive) involved in the process of private party sales

Therefore, research is essential in preparing you for what should be the second negotiation process of your car purchase. Why do we say this? If the salesperson knows that you have a vehicle that you plan to trade in upon purchasing your new vehicle, she knows that the completed transaction will have two opportunities for pricing that ensure ample profit for the dealership (and her commission). This is another reason why dealers offer so little for the trade. Any potential profit lost in the negotiation for the car purchase price can be made up in the price the dealership offers for your trade. If asked whether you will be trading in your current vehicle, you should indicate that you haven't decided yet. Negotiate the price of the new vehicle first—including any rebates, special financing rates, and other offers—and after that, ask the salesperson what the dealership would give you for your car in trade.

PURCHASING A USED VEHICLE

There are several options for purchasing a used vehicle, the two primary ones being through a dealership (new car/factory authorized or used car) and via a private party.* In either case, you need to carefully research your interests as they relate to particular car choices. In addition, in the case of car dealerships, it would be worthwhile to investigate each dealership's policies (e.g., some have limited return options and warranty service) and reputation.

In general, the used car business has acquired a reputation for being less than ethical in its dealings with customers. Part of this reputation is deserved—as many of us know people who've been taken advantage of or misled into thinking a car has never had major problems or been in an accident. The growing used car market and the growing disdain for dealing with unethical organizations has led to several innovative business models for selling used or pre-owned vehicles. One such firm, CarMax, based in Richmond, Virginia, with eighty locations and almost $7.5 billion in sales,[15] has been quite successful since its start-up in the early 1990s. It sells late model used cars, all of which have been carefully inspected, serviced, and certified with a warranty, for a fair price which is typically not negotiable. CarMax (www.carmax.com) has recently expanded its business model and now operates seven new car dealerships. Another dealership with a similar business model is AutoNation U.S.A. Headquartered in Florida, it has 257 dealership locations representing 331 new-vehicle franchises—selling across sixteen states. About 70% of its over $19 billion annual revenue comes from the sale of used cars.[16] Its website is www.autonation.com.

---

*Car auctions are another option. Some of these require a dealer's license, and some may use closed bidding. More information about these options and strategies for buying in these contexts (including virtual auctions such as Ebay and Craigslist) is included in the web-based material for the text.

Chapter Scenario, Part II

John's excitement about the Corolla is obvious. The salesman needs to ask only once, and after obtaining John's license to photocopy it, the salesman leaves John by the car while he retrieves the keys from inside the dealership. About a minute later, the salesman returns John's license and they both get in the car. John adjusts the mirrors and the seat, and then fastens his seat belt. The salesman periodically calls out directions, which John follows and for just a few seconds, he tests the car's acceleration on the open road, momentarily exceeding the speed limit. After all, the salesman said it should be okay. "Car handles well," John thought. "And the sound system is pretty chill. Yup, I want it!" After the test drive, the salesman escorts John into the dealership. John is a bit nervous about negotiating, but he takes a deep breath and sits down across from the salesman. He likes the car, but it is priced $1,000 more than he wants to spend. John wonders what the final outcome would be.

Similarly, a growing number of mid- (e.g., Honda) to high-end (e.g., Mercedes) dealerships are creating separate profit/loss centers—or in some cases, freestanding dealerships—for the purpose of selling pre-owned Hondas and Mercedes that have come off leases or were trade-ins for new cars. Many offer extended warranties or maintenance services, either included in the price or for an additional fee.

An important piece of information to remember, from the dealer's perspective, is that the profit margin is substantially larger for used cars than for new cars. That margin is determined by several factors, including supply and demand for cars both used and new (a popular new car tends to be popular used), where and how the dealer acquires used cars for sale (not all are trade-ins),[**] and how competitive the used car is in the particular local market (e.g., convertibles are hot in warm climates while four-wheel drives are popular in cold/high-snowfall regions). Another factor determining the price is geography. For example, cars in the Northeast—which are affected by the chemicals used to remove snow and ice—are more susceptible to rust than those sold in the South. Prices are adjusted accordingly. Still another factor is the current reputation of the manufacturer. In 2000, there were increasing reports of exploding tires and crashes involving Ford Explorers; Ford blamed Firestone, Firestone blamed Ford and Explorer drivers,[17] and sales of Explorers declined. A few years ago, the spiraling gas prices and burgeoning interests in ecofriendliness caused a downturn in sales of Chevy Suburbans, Hummers,[18] and SUVs. In 2007, Toyota's once stellar reputation for quality and reliability had declined so much that *Consumer Reports* reversed its trend of automatically recommending all new Toyota cars and trucks.[19] Suddenly, Toyota buyers had more power than ever before in negotiating the price of their new Toyota.

Points to Ponder

1. Why would you buy a pre-owned car over a new one? What are the advantages?
2. Why would you buy a new car over a pre-owned one? What are the advantages?
3. You can buy your next car—new to you—from the dealership or a private party. Which would you choose and why?

SELLING YOUR USED VEHICLE

There are several sources for determining the value of your car. National sources include NADA, **Kelly Blue Book** (www.kbb.com), and **Edmonds** (www.Edmonds.com); all of these allow the user to select the characteristics of her car (or desired car) and determine several values: retail (the dealer's asking price), private party (the price

---

[**]Cars returned at the expiration of a lease are usually returned to whomever financed the lease. Then these cars are auctioned off to car dealers, who buy them and put them up for sale.

you would expect to receive if selling your car to a private party in your area), and trade-in (what the dealer will give you for your car). Once you determine the base value (the year, make, and model of the car), you then add or subtract for mileage (charts show you how to add value if your car's mileage is below the expected annual 10–12,000 miles or reduce the value if your mileage is above); the general condition of the car (excellent/mint, good, average, fair); and any extra features (e.g., leather or heated seats, upgraded wheels or stereo system).

Next, you should look at the local sources to see what is popular and at what price in your geographic region. Two local sources include the classifieds of your local (or regional) newspaper and focused periodicals such as the **Autotrader** (www.autotrader.com). Beyond the value established by these trusted sources, you must realize that your car is worth what others will pay for it. Simply put, if no one is interested in your car— at the price you think it is worth—you may have trouble finding a buyer, no matter how wonderful a car you think it is. You might learn this the hard way after paying for multiple weeks of advertising with little or no response to your ad. This is one reason why dealers are able to offer less for your trade.

There are also sources for specialty (e.g., limited edition, exotic, antique) and high-end (over $70,000) vehicles. One such source is the Dupont Registry (www.dupontregistry.com). Another less specialized but potentially useful source for specialty vehicles is Ebay (www.ebay.com). You might also visit specialized dealerships and private brokers to learn more about what such vehicles are worth.

VEHICLE FINANCING

In the same way buyers are advised to arrange a loan preapproval before purchasing a home, doing the same for a vehicle purchase is a good idea for at least three reasons:

1. Working with a bank representative, you will learn just how much of a monthly loan payment you can afford.[20]
2. If you get a car loan at the bank where you do most of your personal banking, you might have a slight advantage on rates.
3. By researching financing options before you visit the dealership, you are able to minimize the effect "falling in love" with a particular car may have on your accepting whatever the dealership offers you. For the dealership, selling you a car *and* arranging the financing gives them two sources of profits from the sale.

By having already arranged financing elsewhere, you are in a stronger negotiating position for the car price and any financing arrangement the dealership might offer. The dealership would prefer to sell a car than not. Any lot visitor is a potential customer, but someone with arranged financing or cash in hand is serious about and ready for purchasing.

You might decide to finance the vehicle with the dealership, especially if special incentives are offered. However, by investigating your options in advance of your visit, you make this decision instead of having it made for you.

THE EXTENDED WARRANTY

For a new car, the **extended warranty**, which comes in many shapes and sizes and can be added to your monthly car payment for "just a few dollars," provides the owner with warranty services (at no cost), beyond the manufacturer's warranty. So if the car comes with a three-year, 36,000-mile warranty (replacing or repairing anything that needs it beyond traditional "wear and tear" items like tires, brake pads, wiper blades, and batteries), any factory authorized dealer of your new car will replace or repair the broken or damaged part free of charge until the three-year or 36,000-mile mark is reached (whichever comes first). An extended warranty will expand this time/mileage up to a prescribed level, for example, five years or 100,000 miles.

Keep in mind that the extended warranty works the same as insurance. From a cost/benefit perspective, the dealership (or manufacturer) is betting that the car won't

Chapter Scenario, Part III

Now that John and the salesman have arrived at the price of the car, John thought he was done. Not so fast. The salesman tells John about the availability of an extended warranty for his car. At first, John thinks to himself, "Sure, what else does he want to sell me?" but the more he listens to the salesman's explanation of what the warranty will cover, the more carefully he considers this option. Knowing he's neither handy nor able to afford several hundred dollars if a costly (and out of warranty) repair were needed, John begins to think the warranty is a good idea. But the price tag is higher than he expected. Sure, financed along with the purchase of the car, the warranty adds "only" $24 more a month. What should he do? And, is the price of the warranty negotiable?

need repair, while you're betting that in the event that it does, your small payments now will protect you from unexpected and expensive payments later (the ounce of prevention idea). If all goes well, your car won't require any major work beyond the standard interval services. Your extended warranty will have covered peace of mind and nothing else. Should something complicated go wrong, for example, the transmission fails, the few dollars per month paid would have been a great investment. You might also be able to negotiate the purchase of an extended warranty on certain used cars as a growing number of manufacturers are offering this option with the purchase of their certified pre-owned vehicles.

Points to Ponder

1. You've noticed that the monthly payments on a lease are lower than those of a sale. What factors would you consider in deciding whether to buy or lease your next vehicle?
2. Some would say that extended warranties are pure profit for car dealerships. What do you think and why?
3. How would you decide whether to purchase an extended warranty?

Summary

More than a few times in your life, you will find yourself negotiating the sale or lease of a new or used car. Being comfortable in this situation is important for your confidence as well as your finances. Effective preparation is key, and the good news is that more than ever, much of the information you'll need is readily available.

Summary: The Big Picture

Purchasing a new vehicle	Identify and prioritize primary and secondary interests and determine what you can afford (including cost of ownership).
Cost	Conduct research to establish target and resistance points.
Trade-ins	Essentially a second negotiation. Negotiate purchase price of new vehicle first.
Purchasing a used vehicle	Decide whether you will buy from a dealership or a private party. Then proceed to prepare for the negotiation as if you were buying a new vehicle.
Selling your used vehicle	Perform research to determine its value. This information is critical in your preparation for negotiating the sale of your used vehicle.
Financing	Prior to negotiating the purchase of a new or used vehicle, arrange a loan preapproval from your current or preferred bank or credit union to strengthen your bargaining position.
Extended warranty	Essentially an insurance policy against future, costly repairs.

Key Terms and Concepts

Autotrader   A periodical for advertising vehicles available for sale.

Edmonds   An online resource for determining the value of a vehicle.

Extended warranty   An insurance policy that covers the costs of certain repairs for a specified period of time after the manufacturer's warranty expires.

Kelly Blue Book   An online resource for determining the value of a vehicle.

Manufacturer's Suggested Retail Price (MSRP)   The list price for an automobile which may or may not be the dealer's opening offer.

National Automotive Dealers Association (NADA)   An industry group that represents the interests of new car and truck dealers to the public, media, Congress, and vehicle manufacturers.

Discussion Questions

1. Discuss the interests and issues that might be included in vehicle negotiation. How would you prioritize and address them?
2. Describe how you would prepare for negotiating the purchase of a new or used vehicle. How does the extended warranty fit into this preparation?
3. Describe how you would prepare for trading in or selling your current vehicle.
4. Discuss how you would evaluate the choice of purchasing or leasing your next vehicle.

Ethical Dilemma: Buyer Beware[21]

Bill sold his three-year-old motor home to Gus, a colleague. Gus received a great price of $10,000 in the as-is sale. When asked about the condition, Bill said, "It uses a lot of oil, but all of these motor homes do. I've not had any problems with it." A few days later, the motor home quit on the freeway, and Gus had it towed to a repair shop. The repairman said, "This vehicle has a badly cracked block and needs a new engine. It'll cost about $5,000." Gus returned to Bill, asking him, "What are you going to do for me here? You sold me a defective vehicle." Bill responded, "I didn't know anything about the cracked block. I sold the vehicle as is, and I don't intend to do anything about it."

Questions

1. How would you feel if you were in Gus's shoes? How does your belief about Bill's honesty about his knowledge of the motor home's condition affect your feelings about the situation?
2. When asked about the condition of the motor home, Bill explained that it used a lot of oil. At this point, what should Gus have done?
3. What else should Gus have done before considering this purchase?
4. Is Bill obligated to pay for the repairs on the motor home? Why or why not? What do you think is fair?

Endnotes

1. http://www.bts.gov/publications/national_transportation_statistics/html/table_01_11.html, accessed July 16, 2011.
2. U.S. Bureau of Transit, 2003, p. 18.
3. For light trucks it is 6.6 years and for cars, it is 9 years.
4. Raoul, F. *Bare Knuckle Negotiation*. Hoboken, NJ: John Wiley & Sons, 2004, p. 78.
5. Bertel Schmidt, "U.S. Car Sales in 2009: Worst in 27 years," http://www.thetruthaboutcars.com/2010/01/u-s-car-sales-in-2009-worst-in-27-years/, accessed September 22, 2011.
6. www.nada.org "Driving the United States' Economy," accessed April 11, 2007.
7. Leasing means lower monthly payments (you are paying only for the value of the car during the period you drive it: current value minus salvage [end-of-lease] value), but at the end of the lease period, you do not own the car.
8. There are several online sites which enable a driver to estimate the cost of insuring a particular vehicle, e.g., www.geico.com, www.progressive.com, www.statefarm.com.
9. *AutoExec magazine*, May 2006, p. 19
10. This figure is from July, 2004, according to Edmunds.com.
11. http://www.edmunds.com/help/about/press/102825/article.html, accessed on April 13, 2007
12. This figure is from July, 2004, according to Edmunds.com.
13. http://www.edmunds.com/help/about/press/102825/article.html, accessed on April 13, 2007
14. http://www.theautochannel.com/news/2003/07/29/165850.html, accessed on April 13, 2007

15. Fiscal year ending February 28, 2007. March 29, 2007 press release "CarMax Reports Record Fourth Quarter and Fiscal Year 2007 Results," available from www. CarMax.com, accessed April 16, 2007.

16. http://corp.autonation.com/about/profile.asp, accessed April 16, 2007.

17. Dan, A. "Ford, Firestone Face Off," *Forbes*, June 19, 2001.

18. In fact, General Motors ceased production on Hummer in 2009.

19. MSN Money. (October 2007). http://articles.moneycentral .msn.com/Savingsand Debt/Advice/ToyotaIsSlipping ConsumerReportsSats.aspx, accessed August 5, 2010.

20. You can also access an online budgeting tool that can help you with this. One example can be found at http://www. edmunds.com/car-loan/how-much-car-can-you-afford. html, accessed July 16, 2011.

21. Spangle, M. L., and M. W. Isenhart, *Negotiation: Communication for Diverse Settings.* Thousand Oaks, CA: Sage, 2003, p. 175.

Exercise 13.1 Researching Market Values

Imagine you were going to sell your (or a family member's) car to a private party. You will have to know the year, make, and specific model of the car, as well as the current odometer reading and an inventory of the car's features.

Go to at least one national site (e.g., Edmonds, Kelly Blue Book), and one local site (the classifieds for your local or near-local newspaper). Starting with the national site, research the value of your car, and then adjust that estimate based on values for similar cars advertised in the local market, and how quickly you need to sell your car. Keep a record of the total estimate, as well as how you arrived at that estimate (e.g., additions/subtractions for extra, missing, or poor elements of your car).

Base value: _____

Additions: + _____

Subtractions: – _____

Other adjustments: +/– _____

Realistic asking price: _____

Exercise 13.2   Selling Your Car

Step 1: Using the information you gathered in Exercise 13.1, create an advertisement that could be included in the classifieds section of your local newspaper. The ad must be factual (not falsely embellished) and should indicate the year, make, model, and price of the car. In addition, you may include any/all pertinent features and benefits and contact information (e.g., phone number, email address). Note that there is a forty-word limit for your ad.

Step 2: Prepare a strategy outline for selling your car by completing the following:

1. How much do you want for your car?

   _____

2. Why do you want this price? What elements of your research suggest this price?

   _____

   _____

   _____

3. What are you willing to accept? What is this based on?

   _____

   _____

   _____

4. What is your BATNA? If you don't receive a satisfactory offer for your car, what is your best alternative?

   _____

   _____

   _____

   _____

5. How is this price a good value? Be prepared to explain key elements of your research.

   _____

   _____

   _____

   _____

6. What persuasive arguments will you make to convince the buyer that your price is fair and the deal is a good one? Consider using the ACE and inoculation theories (discussed in Chapter 8), as well as arguments that are logical and/or appeal to the buyer's basic instincts.

   _____

   _____

   _____

   _____

   _____

Exercise 13.3   The Car Swap

This activity may be completed using an in-class bulletin board or an electronic discussion board (e.g., WebCT, Blackboard).

Step 1 (Selling your car):

1. You will need to have completed initial research (Exercise 13.1) and have composed an ad (Exercise 13.2) to "sell" your car.
2. In the designated area, you will post your ad (additional information is available from your instructor) by a given deadline. In an electronic environment, you will post a new thread with the title that includes the year, make, and model of your car.

Step 2 (Buying a car):

1. By another deadline, you must indicate the used car (of one of your classmates) that you want to "buy." This may be done by sticking a Post-it note (e.g., "I want this") with your name on it, or in an electronic environment, by clicking on the thread/car of your choice and clicking Reply and typing "I want this." If your desired car has already been selected, you must choose another car. All participants must choose a car (*not* their own), and all cars must be chosen—that is, no multiple buyers on a single car. Clearly, the earlier you respond after the ads are placed, the better selection you'll have.
2. Now that you know the car in which you're interested, it's time to do some research. Before the class session that features the car swap negotiation, gather whatever pertinent data you'll need to successfully negotiate the purchase of your new used car. The following outline will help:

   1. How much do you want to spend on this car?

   _____

   2. Why? What elements of your research suggest this price?

   _____

   _____

   3. How much are you willing to pay? Why (what is this figure based on)?

   _____

   _____

   4. What is your BATNA? If the seller doesn't agree to your preferred price, what is your best alternative?

   _____

   _____

   5. What questions will you ask to understand relevant information about the car, the buyer, and the situation?

   _____

   _____

   6. What persuasive arguments will you make to convince the seller that your price is fair and the deal is a good one? Consider using the ACE and inoculation theories, as well as logical arguments, to construct these persuasive arguments.

   _____

   _____

   _____

Exercise 13.4   Negotiating a New Car

The goal of this exercise is to apply the skills you have been honing in an actual dealership. The purchase of a vehicle is *optional*; however, engaging in preparation and negotiation is not.

1. Thinking about your near-term vehicle needs and interests, determine what for you would be up to five ideal or nearly ideal choices. The "Purchasing a New Vehicle" section of this chapter lists many of these for your consideration.
2. Use the prioritization matrix below to narrow down your selection to the top choice for you. To do this:
   a. List the five vehicles (make and model) in first column.
   b. Next, write in at least six criteria that are most relevant to your interests in the top row.
   c. Using a scale of 1 (low/worst) to 5 (high/best), devise a ranking system for each criterion, such as cost, quality reputation, fuel economy, trunk/cargo space, "cool" factor. Ensure that the direction of each criterion's scale is consistent, for example, while quality should be from 1 (low) to 5 (high), cost should be from 1 (high) to 5 (low).
   d. As appropriate, weight these criteria using the bottom, shaded row. If price is twice as important as available leather seats, indicate "2" in the weighting for price and "1" for available leather seats.
   e. Using the various respected vehicle information sources (e.g., cars.com, *Consumer Reports*, NHTSA, NADA), research these five cars in order to help you arrive at ratings for each of the criteria for each car. Some websites will actually do comparisons for you.
   f. Sum across each row (car choice), weighting the scores as appropriate. If you think cost is twice as important as the other criteria, multiply the score you gave in that column by two, and add that figure to the rest of the scores in the row to arrive at a total.
   g. Determine your top choice, which is likely the car with the highest score in the "Total" column.

Car choices / Criteria Scale (1–5) →								Total
Weighting								

3. Armed with your research, visit a neighborhood dealership that carries your desired car. When asked, be honest about your intentions, for example, "I'm not ready to buy today, but I'd like to have a sense of what to expect when I'm ready to buy in the near future." Have the salesperson show you the car in which you are interested, and engage him or her in any questions that are relevant to—and demonstrate your knowledge regarding—a future purchase.
4. If the salesperson begins to talk price, you may remind him or her that you are probably not ready to make a purchase today. However, should you feel comfortable doing so, commence a price negotiation discussion.
5. Once your business is complete, thank the salesperson for his or her time.

Exercise 13.5   Self Assessment—Car Negotiation

1. What went well in the car negotiation you participated in (Exercise 13.4)? Describe at least two things you said or did before, during, or after the negotiation that you would like to do again in a future opportunity.

   _____

   _____

   _____

   _____

   _____

2. What didn't go so well? Describe at least two things you said or did before, during, or after the negotiation that you felt were opportunities for improvement. Discuss why these things were less than satisfactory to you; in particular, how they would have resulted in a less than satisfactory outcome should the deal have been consummated.

   _____

   _____

   _____

   _____

   _____

3. Based on this experience, what are some lessons learned? In particular,
   a. What are your strengths, or in what dimensions of car negotiations do you feel most comfortable and why?

   _____

   _____

   _____

   _____

   _____

   b. What are your weaknesses, or in what dimensions of car negotiations do you feel least comfortable and why?

   _____

   _____

   _____

   _____

   _____

   c. What one thing would you do differently in the future, and how would this change likely impact the process or outcome of a future car negotiation?

   _____

   _____

   _____

   _____

   _____

Exercise 13.6   Going for a Ride[*]

This assignment will help you integrate what you have learned throughout the text. The context is a used car negotiation. Dive deeply into this negotiation by analyzing the negotiation and persuasion skills, strategy, and tactics used by both Judy and Ed. Refer to paragraph numbers in your analysis, and provide support for your opinion. You need not discuss every paragraph in your analysis; your instructor will advise you of his/her expectations.

1. It was a beautiful summer day, typical of early June in Cleveland, when Judy Berne pulled into Lee Road Chevrolet. She came directly from her service station, where the mechanic gave her twelve-year-old Chevy Cavalier two to three months left to live. Without much thought, she got out of her rusting heap and began to peruse the new cars. Within seconds, a nicely dressed, middle-aged man approached her, introduced himself as Ed Wargo, and asked, "What can I do for you today?"

2. "Well, I just started looking because my car is about to fall apart. I'm not really sure what I want," Judy replied honestly.

3. Seizing the opening, Ed whisked Judy away from the practical into the sporty. He showed her the red Crystal GT, a little sports coupe with a not-so-little price. "This baby's loaded: sunroof, AC, power steering, power brakes, AM/FM quad stereo with CD, magnesium hubs, full options package. They've been very popular with you "young professional" customers," he added, knowing full well that there would be a $400 bonus waiting for him if he unloaded this overloaded model that had been stuck on the lot for weeks.

4. Judy could hardly contain her excitement. "I've always wanted a car like this!" she exclaimed, her eyes reflecting genuine enthusiasm.

5. "Hey, take it for a test drive and tell me what you think." Ed tossed her the keys and sat back to prepare his strategy.

6. Judy returned, her hair tousled (she had obviously tried out the sunroof) and looking as if she had genuinely enjoyed the drive. "How did you like it?" Ed asked, knowing full well how the Crystal would outclass a 1987 Cavalier. "Nice . . . really nice," she responded, "but it's a little more than I need." It was obviously wise to guard her true feelings. "How much is it?"

7. There, the question had finally been asked. "The sticker price, including all options and dealer preparation, is $19,750." Ed noticed the immediate slumping of her shoulders. "Of course, there is a $1,000 factory rebate or 2.9% manufacturer's financing available." She was still looking at the ground. "And you do have a trade-in. Let's have a look!" With that, the wind was returning to her sails, and something of her previous smile returned to her face.

8. "Not too bad. I think that we could give you $1,000 for it. Of course, I'll have to have my "trade-in specialist" look at it. Can I give him your keys so he can check it out more closely?" Ed asked. Judy handed them over and they walked back over to the Crystal GT. This time Judy looked more closely at the sticker. "I know what Suggested Retail Price, options, and rustproofing are, but what are the charges: $300 for A.D.M. and $200 for N.D.A.?"

9. "Well. A.D.M. is a dealer prep charge; for instance, cleaning and checking the car out," he admitted, acting a bit annoyed at such an obvious question. "And the N.D.A.?" Judy persisted. "That's the National Dealer Advertising charge, for those ads on TV. Advertising is very expensive for us, you know.

10. Judy paused a minute. $19,750 was a lot of money for her budget. Finally she began to speak, "even with the trade-in, the price is. . . . " Sensing that the intoxicating new-car aroma was beginning to wear off, Ed interrupted, "I'll give you the rustproofing, fabric finish, and floor mats at cost. That's $300 off, only $17,450 for the car after trade-in."

[*]This exercise was prepared and presented at the 2010 Organizational Behavior Teaching Conference by Professor E. Wertheim, College of Business Administration, Northeastern University. It is used here with his permission.

11. "I don't know," Judy said, with Ed's arithmetic going by pretty quickly.
12. "Come back into my office and we'll work this out." With that, Ed led her into a small office near the rear of the dealership. He spent the next fifteen minutes convincing her that she could not find a better deal on such a popular car.
13. Suddenly, Judy interrupted with conviction. "I really don't need the magnesium wheels, quad stereo, or most of the options." Ed was surprised by her sudden assertiveness. He explained that the car was a package and that they just couldn't take the options out of it for her. Judy was beginning to feel claustrophobic. With no windows and the door shut, she wondered if she would ever get out of this small office. With a mental start, she realized that even if she escaped, she no longer had her keys.
14. Seeing that he wasn't getting anywhere. Ed decided to go for broke. "Since you're such a nice person, and I would like to help you out, I'll give you the wheels and the stereo at cost if you take the car today. That's another $400 off, $2,700 off the sticker price, or $17,050 with your trade-in."
15. I'm not sure that I can afford that much," Judy responded.
16. What if I told you I can sell you this car for less than what you are paying monthly now?
17. "That sounds pretty good," responded Judy.
18. "How much can you spend per month on your car?" Ed asked.
19. "Under $450."
20. "Well, Ms. Berne, I will keep my word. All we have to do is stretch the payments out to four years and that makes it only, let's see . . . $437 a month. We did it. What do you say?" As Ed leaned over his desk awaiting her response, Judy began to reconsider buying a new car, especially without shopping around first. She got up to make her escape and to thank Ed for his time when he blurted out, "Are you a first-time new car buyer?"
21. "Why . . . yes," Judy answered.
22. "I almost forgot," Ed announced, "I can offer you $300 off invoice just to get your business and begin what I'm sure will be a long-term relationship with this dealership. Even if we don't make anything on this car, we're in it for the long haul. This will bring the payments down to $429. You can't beat that; the car you want at your price. But we have to make the deal today. There has been a lot of interest in that particular car and I'm not sure how long it will be around." That was just enough to halt her exit; besides, at this point, Ed was really trying to help her out. Judy took the deal.
23. "Just let me clear this with my sales manager," Ed explained as he left the room. When he returned, he was solemn. "He didn't go for it. He got after me for getting carried away, especially with the new buyer discount. Bottom line, he says you can't have the new car buyer discount and the options at cost." Judy was angry with the sales manager, but empathized with Ed's predicament and agreed to his suggested solution of giving up the magnesium wheels. After a quick check, Ed indicated with evident relief that the sales manager had accepted.
24. Now it was time for the paperwork. Ed began by filling in the sales discount. Judy noticed an $80 processing fee, but she did not mention it because it was printed on the form and therefore must have been a standard charge. She also noticed the $120 "etching" fee. Ed filled in the proper price, $19,870, and the $1,000 factory rebate, but then wrote in a mysterious $105 charge. "What's that?" Judy inquired.
25. "Oh, I forgot about that. That's the paint sealant we put on all our cars to protect our customer's investment," Ed answered.
26. "And what is the etching fee?"
27. "That's for theft protection; it gets you a major discount on your insurance."
28. Judy responded, "I think I remember my employer having a program last year where the police come to the parking lot and do the etching for $15."
29. Ed countered, "It's preprinted on the sales sheet here; we provide the service and it's standard; all our customers get it. Your insurance company needs this."

30. The next line was the trade-in value, which Ed had to check with his trade-in specialist. Ed left the room and returned with the specialist who stated that the 1987 Cavalier was in worse shape than Ed had thought and the dealer could only offer $500 for it and would probably lose money even at that price. Judy thought back to the morning. Five hundred dollars was close to what her mechanic said it was worth, so she had to agree.

31. Ed said that he felt terrible. "I thought that we could get more for it, but he's the expert." Ed added, "You know, with a new car like that, you really should have an extended warranty. I have a six-year/60,000-mile warranty available on the Crystal. We usually sell it for $750, but since I was wrong on the trade-in, you can have it for $500." Knowing that she would have the car for a long time (the payments alone would last four years), she took him up on the offer.

32. "Now just take this over to the finance department and I'll meet you out front with your new car. It's been a pleasure." With that, Ed smiled and led Judy to the finance window.

33. The finance manager looked over her papers and asked Judy to sign on the dotted line. A last check of the forms revealed a $230 life insurance fee, which would pay off her auto loan if she died before she could. Angered by this late addition, Judy thought back over her three hour ordeal and, not feeling too well, reasoned that life insurance might not be such a bad investment after all. So with a sigh of relief, she signed the papers not knowing how much she really paid for the car or whether or not she got a good deal.

Exercise 13.7   You Want *How Much* for That Repair?

Karen was having trouble with the window on her minivan. Seems one of the power windows would get stuck, usually in an awkward position. The brake pads also needed replacing. She brought it to the dealership and they said it would be ready by the end of the day. When she got the bill for over $1,600, she nearly fell over. She paid the bill, but then immediately called a friend of hers who knew a lot about cars and the industry. He also thought the price was exceedingly high and agreed to accompany her on a return trip to the dealership. When the service manager showed Karen's friend the bill, the first thing that stood out was the fact that over seventeen hours of labor were charged when the car had only been at the dealership for less than eight hours. When asked, the service manager replied that the dealership's practice—consistent with industry standards—was to charge "book" on any procedure or repair, even if multiple procedures may be done more quickly when done together (e.g., once the hood is open and parts removed for one procedure, this time is saved for completing another procedure). "Book" is the average amount of time that an average mechanic would take to complete a particular task. Even though only one mechanic worked on the car, the fact that he worked faster than "book" just meant a bonus for the dealership. In other words, they did nothing wrong. Karen was infuriated and was thinking about stopping payment on her check.

Two roles to be played in the negotiation: Karen, service manager.

(Your instructor will distribute the information necessary to perform this negotiation.)

Real Estate Negotiations: Commercial and Residential

CHAPTER **14**

Chapter Objectives

After studying this chapter and completing the exercises you should be able to:

- Identify the unique aspects of real estate negotiations.
- Develop a plan for negotiating the purchase of a home.
- Assess the options for financing a home.
- Evaluate the importance of third parties (e.g., realtors, attorneys) in real estate negotiations.
- Identify the unique issues involved in leasing retail and industrial space.
- Evaluate the differences in negotiating commercial versus residential real estate transactions.

wning a home is a goal for many people. In addition to purchasing a home, more people today are leaving giant corporations and opting to open a small business; doing so will require them to negotiate rental, lease, and purchase agreements to house their businesses. At the most basic level, negotiations involving real estate are like other negotiations—you identify your interests and the issues to be negotiated and establish opening offers, target, and resistance points for each issue. There are, however, a number of unique aspects that make real estate negotiations significantly different than other types of negotiations. The process used for negotiating real estate is fairly well defined and often involves the use of a third party, a realtor. Often there are many issues involved including purchase price, financing, date of possession, and a multitude of other details. Whether the real estate involves a home or a business, it is an investment and involves much more money—and risk—than other purchases. With more at stake, preparation is even more important. You need to have a good understanding of the subject matter and the long-term implications. Sadly, in the last few years, a number of people buying homes in the United States didn't have this knowledge and got in over their heads. Indeed, the U.S. housing crisis that began in 2007 has been attributed in part to people who bought houses they ultimately couldn't afford, with the mortgaged houses ending up in foreclosure. More than ever, it is critical to understand and build your skills in real estate negotiations—which is the goal of this chapter.

317

Chapter Scenario, Part I

Jake and Stephanie have been married for almost a year. Jake manages a local deli and Stephanie is a representative for a wine distributor. Their dream is to one day open their own deli, wine, and catering business; for now, they are focusing on learning as much as they can in their current jobs and networking so they are better prepared to start their own business in a few years. They currently live in an apartment complex and their lease is about to expire. They have been debating whether they should renew their lease for another year or take the plunge and buy their first house. After much discussion they decided to buy a house so they can build equity to help finance their business down the road. They have looked at a few houses and have come to the realization that there is a lot they need to learn about buying a house.

Jake and Stephanie's situation is fairly typical. Home ownership is the dream of many. The decision to buy a home is particularly intense since it is the place you will be living complete with all the emotional issues involved.[1] A home is usually the largest purchase a person makes, yet most people are not well versed in the process. In this chapter we take you through the basics of negotiating real estate transactions, that is, buying, selling, leasing, renovating, and resolving disputes involving real estate, both residential and commercial. We begin with residential because it is typically the first type of real estate transaction a person will encounter.

REAL ESTATE BASICS: RESIDENTIAL

As with any negotiation, the first step in finding and purchasing a home is to identify your interests. At the most basic level a home provides shelter from the elements. Beyond that your home can be a symbol of your status (e.g., living in an upscale neighborhood), of your dedication to the environment (e.g., an eco-friendly or green home), or of your commitment to the community (e.g., a refurbished home in a blighted area), among other things. Your home can help meet your need to be near to your extended family or friends. A home can even help meet your need for recreation if it comes with access to a beach, golf course, or health club. A home can also help meet a need to increase wealth. In fact, many people who are purchasing their first home do so with the intent of making improvements to the home and then selling it for a profit. The television show *Flip This House* was created to give viewers examples of what can be done. Taking time up front to identify and evaluate your interests will help ensure you are happy with your purchase in the long term.

After you have identified your interests the next step is to determine how much home you can afford. This will be based on the size of your down payment and your mortgage. The size of the mortgage for which you can qualify depends on your income, your other debts, and your credit rating. In general, the larger your down payment and income, the lower your other debts, and the better your credit history, the more expensive house you can afford. There are some standard heuristics used in the mortgage industry. Typically, the total of your principal, interest, taxes, and insurance (**PITI**) can be no more than 28%—and total debt can be no more than 36%—of your gross monthly income. In some situations lenders may go higher, such as when a buyer has significant assets (e.g., investments, other property). But these are just general guidelines. To get a more accurate number that reflects your specific situation, you can prequalify for a loan to see what you can afford. There are several mortgage websites that allow you to do this online. If you are serious about purchasing a home, it is helpful to be preapproved, which means that the lender guarantees what she will loan you for a house that meets her requirements. We'll discuss more about financing later in the chapter.

Once you have an idea of what you can afford, the next question is whether you want a house or a condominium (i.e., condo). There are major differences, as described in Figure 14.1, and you need to make sure you understand the implications of each type.

Identifying how much you can afford and deciding on the type of home you want is only the beginning. As with all purchases, you need to identify what you must have

FIGURE 14.1 Houses vs. Condos

You've decided you want to own your own home, but will it be a house, condo, or manufactured home? With a house you are responsible for all maintenance indoors and out. For the most part you can do what you want to do with the house, provided you don't violate any local zoning ordinances or other restrictions. For example, if you are in an historical area there will likely be restrictions on what you can do (e.g., construction style, paint color choice) to the exterior of your home. In general these restrictions exist to maintain the character of the neighborhood as a historical area. Similarly, if your house is in a subdivision that has restrictive covenants, you will be limited as to what you can do with the exterior of the home and property. Often these include using only approved building materials, meeting requirements for fencing if it is allowed at all, prohibitions on keeping a car, boat, trailer, and so on, outside of a garage, and even whether you are permitted to have a garage sale. How problematic such restrictions are depends on you. Some people appreciate living in a neighborhood where they can be assured their neighbors won't be storing old cars or doing other things with their property that might diminish property values in the neighborhood. Conversely, others see such restrictions as infringing on their rights as property owners. In their eyes, their house is their property and they believe they should be able to do as they wish with it.

Condos can be attached or detached. Attached condos can range from two to many units per building, while detached condos, which are sometimes referred to as townhouses, can be two on a lot, carriage homes, or look like single family homes. When you own a condo, everything on the exterior is maintained by the condo association (e.g., lawn, landscaping, roofs, siding). The cost of this is covered by an association fee, which can be as much as several hundred dollars per month. The fees paid to the association are held in reserve and used as needed for maintenance. Before you purchase a condo, you need to consider the reserves of the association. The higher the reserves, the less chance that the association fees will increase unexpectedly. If the reserves are low and a number of roofs start leaking or siding needs replacing, the fees could increase dramatically to cover those costs. In a condo, you are also usually limited as to what you can do with the exterior of your home. You may not be able to plant additional trees or other plants or even display exterior holiday or other decorations.

and what you would like to have. The most basic questions include the number of bedrooms and bathrooms, the size of the house in square feet, the number of floors (e.g., ranch versus two story), an eat-in kitchen or a formal dining room, a garage or carport, and so on. You also need to think about how long you plan to live in the home. If this is a starter home and you plan to live there for only a few years before moving up, you will likely place more emphasis on the resale value than if you plan to live there for many years.

There is an old saying in real estate: "it's all about location, location, location." You could have identical homes, one in a desirable location and one in a not so desirable location, and the difference in value of the two homes can be enormous. The neighborhood and schools are important; even if you don't have (or plan to have) children, the quality of the local schools affects the value of your home. Good neighborhoods and schools generally mean the demand for housing is higher, which increases the value of homes in the area. Generally speaking, people want to live in "nice" neighborhoods, which they perceive are safe from a variety of intrusions and hazards. For example, most people don't want to live next to a railroad track or in the path of planes arriving and departing from a local airport where they may be disturbed by noise. Similarly, homes located near a nuclear power plant or a large factory that dumped toxic waste on nearby property, or even those near a strip club or a blighted retail center are less desirable. People also usually prefer to avoid homes on busy streets where they would hear a lot of noise and be near heavy traffic.

If you think there are a lot of details to consider when you are preparing to buy a home, you are right. After looking at several homes it is easy to confuse the details. Thus, it is helpful if you have a checklist, like the one offered by Mortgage101 shown in Figure 14.2, to keep track of the properties under consideration.

For the best resale value, you should avoid buying the most expensive home in the neighborhood and be careful not to "over improve" your house. Homes in a neighborhood tend to sell in a common price range. If you buy a house for $200,000 in a

FIGURE 14.2 Checklist for Buying a Home

Home Buyer Checklist	Property #1	Property #2	Property #3
Property address			
Asking price			
Real estate taxes			
Near work			
Near schools			
Near shopping			
Near expressways			
Near public transportation			
Near doctors/dentists			
Near churches			
Garbage collection			
Street lights			
Sidewalks			
Streets/alleys well maintained			
Traffic volume			
Parks			
Neighbor's property well maintained			
All utilities installed			
Neighborhood covenants/restrictions			
Near trains/airport			
Area zoned as residential			
Near industry			
Proposed special assessments			
Environment concerns/influences			
Age of house			
Number of stories			
Wood frame			
Brick frame			
Wood and brick frame			
Aluminum siding			
Roof condition			
Foundation condition			
Overall exterior condition			
Garage size			
Number of bathrooms			
Number of closets			
Number of bedrooms			
Oil heat			
Gas heat			

FIGURE 14.2 (Continued)

Home Buyer Checklist	Property #1	Property #2	Property #3
Electric heat			
Hot water heat			
Insulation			
Central AC			
Energy conservation features			
Age of heating system			
Age of water heater			
Capacity of water heater			
Age of electrical wiring			
Plumbing condition			
Estimated water bill			
Estimated heating bill			
Estimated electric bill			
Living room			
Fireplace			
Separate dining room			
Family room			
Drapes: Number of rooms			
Carpeting: Number of rooms			
Kitchen eating area			
Refrigerator			
Stove/oven (gas/electric)			
Garbage disposal			
Dishwasher			
Broken windows			
Storm windows/screens			
Washer/dryer outlets			
Laundry space			
Finished basement			
Attic			
Sump pump/drainage			
Connected to sewer system			
Patio			
Backyard fence			
Landscaping			
Property boundaries			
Security (dead bolts, detectors)			
Building code compliance			
Ability to expand/enlarge house			

Source: Mortgage101, http://www.mortgage101.com/article/home-buyer-checklist. Used with permission.

neighborhood of homes valued from $175,000–$275,000, you would be ill-advised to undertake a $200,000 remodeling project. Doing so would mean that you have $400,000 invested in your home in a neighborhood where other homes sell for only $175,000–$275,000 and it would be unlikely that you would be able to recoup your investment if you were to sell your house.

Property Value: What Is It Really Worth?

The first indicator of what a home may be worth is the list or "asking" price. This is essentially the seller's opening demand[2] and there is almost always room to negotiate. The list price may or may not be close to the true market value of the property. Some homeowners have an inflated view of what their home is really worth because they own the home and attach a higher subjective value to it,[3] particularly if they have spent a lot of money on home improvements. Realtors typically look at recent sales of comparable homes when helping a client establish the list price. Essentially, the asking price set by the seller attracts buyers who are looking for a home in a particular price range, but who then inspect the home to determine its value to them.[4]

A second indicator of what a home may be worth is the **state equalized value (SEV)**. SEV is the taxable value of the home and property; however, it can vary considerably from the true market price. If the home was purchased a number of years ago and real estate values have increased faster than the rate of inflation, the SEV is probably low. Conversely, if you bought the house recently and the housing market has been flat or declining, the SEV could be higher than what you might reasonably be able to sell the property for. This is likely the case with homes that are advertised as being priced "below SEV."

What a home is worth in the eyes of a lender is based on an appraisal. Appraisals can be done by an independent appraiser, a lender, or a realtor and the result is not always the same. Historically, some lenders had a tendency to appraise homes higher so they could lend you more money. The risk is that if the housing market declines or something happens that requires you to sell your home (e.g., being transferred or losing your job) before building any equity, you may end up owing more than the home is worth. During the housing crisis that began in 2006–2007, many people walked away from their homes when they went "upside down" and owed more on the home than it was worth.

Finally, a home is worth what a buyer is willing to pay for it. You have likely seen homes that have been on the market for months, sometimes even years. In many cases they are priced high relative to comparable homes in the neighborhood. Or perhaps the price set months or years ago remained unchanged despite the economic and housing market declining markedly. If you are interested in a home that you think is priced too high, you can always make an offer based on what you think it is worth. The worst the seller can say is no. Sometimes, however, the seller might be willing to accept your offer or negotiate something close to it, especially if he is anxious to sell the property. You have probably even seen real estate ads that state the sellers are "motivated." This almost always means that the seller is at a disadvantage in terms of bargaining power. Not surprisingly, research has found that bargaining power has a significant effect on sale prices.[5] There are a number of reasons a seller may have reduced bargaining power.

On a community level, local supply and demand conditions can either reinforce or weaken the seller's bargaining position for particular houses in specific markets.[6] Communities suddenly hit by a natural disaster, as was the case with hurricane Katrina in 2005 or the floods in Tennessee in 2010, almost always experience a sudden sharp decline in property values as people seek to relocate to areas they perceive to be more safe. Similarly, the closure of a major business, especially in smaller communities, can devastate the local real estate market as the former employees/homeowners relocate in search of other employment. At the same time there may be some who need to sell their homes in order to reduce their expenses as their income declines.

On an individual level, a seller may be relocating to another city and not want to be responsible for maintaining a home in the old location. Even if the seller is remaining in the same area, she may have purchased another home and needs to be free of the cost of owning two homes—despite the perceived attractiveness of being a landlord and receiving rental income on your property. Similarly, the sellers may need to sell their home to cover other financial obligations, as might happen in a divorce.

In the absence of any direct statements, whether a home is currently occupied or vacant can be an indicator of a sellers' motivation to sell. If a home is vacant, the owner is paying to maintain the home without the benefit of living there. It is generally understood that sellers of vacant homes are at a disadvantage relative to other sellers.[7] As a buyer, this can be to your advantage in the negotiation. Accordingly, you need to be sure to take this into consideration when you are establishing your opening offer and target point. The lower the purchase price you negotiate, the less you will have to finance.

Financing

The difference between the purchase price and the amount of your down payment is the amount you will need to finance. There are a number of options when it comes to financing, the most common of which are conventional and **adjustable rate mortgages** (**ARM**). Depending on your situation, you might also qualify for Veterans Administration (**VA**) or Federal Housing Administration (**FHA**) financing. In some cases, the seller may even be willing to provide complete or partial financing by agreeing to sell on a land contract.

Conventional financing is for a predetermined number of years, often thirty, at a fixed interest rate. Conventional financing provides the least risk to the borrower because the borrower's house payments, excluding property taxes and insurance, will not increase over the life of the loan. Because the lenders are locking themselves in for a long period of time, the interest rates are typically slightly higher for a conventional fixed rate mortgage than for an ARM. ARMs typically offer a lower rate of interest for the first few years of the loan, but then the interest rate is adjusted periodically, sometimes annually, based on predetermined economic indicators, such as the prime lending rate. During periods of inflation, the ARM's monthly payments increase, sometimes dramatically. From the borrower's perspective, the advantage is lower payments in the early years, which allows him to buy a more expensive house than he could otherwise afford when his career—and thus earning potential—has not reached its full potential. If you plan to stay in the home only for a short time, an ARM may be the most cost effective way to go. However, if you are considering such a loan, be sure to read the fine print so you understand how much your payment can increase and how frequently. Indeed, many of the home foreclosures during the housing crisis were the result of homeowners finding themselves with larger mortgage payments than they could afford due to higher interest rates.

FHA and VA are government sponsored programs to promote home ownership. FHA, established in 1934, accomplishes this by providing mortgage insurance to lenders to cover their losses should borrowers default on their loans, which encourages lenders to make loans to people who may not otherwise qualify. As the name implies, VA loans help veterans qualify for mortgages, again by insuring the lender will be paid if the borrower defaults. While the FHA and VA programs help people qualify for mortgages with little or no down payment, they require extra paperwork, adding another step to the process of purchasing a home.

Seller-financed means the seller is loaning you the money (and assuming the risk) for the home. Many sellers simply cannot afford to do this; they need to get the equity out of their current house to put into their next house. Even if the sellers can afford to provide financing, they are often reluctant to assume the risk of a buyer defaulting on the loan. An exception is when supply exceeds demand in the housing market, perhaps due to a poor economy and/or high interest rates. An excess supply of housing can be isolated to certain geographic areas or can be nationwide as was the case in the 1980s when mortgage interest rates were 15–20% and there was both double digit inflation and unemployment. During that time, land contracts became popular in many areas because the land contract interest rates were limited by law in many states to 11%. Today, such land contracts seem unbelievable, but back then it was the only way many people could afford to buy a home. There is often a "balloon" clause that specifies that the loan must be repaid (or refinanced) after a certain period of time (e.g., three to five years). This means that the seller is obligated to hold the mortgage for only that period of time and allows the buyer time to obtain other financing. Of course all of this is negotiable.

Regardless of who is lending you the money, the lender will want to protect her investment and make sure the loan gets repaid. At the same time, you want to negotiate the best deal possible on a mortgage. Anything you can do to show that you are a good credit risk strengthens your bargaining position. The most commonly used measure of your credit record is your **FICO score**—named for Fair, Isaac & Co., the firm that developed the calculation. Your FICO score determines whether you are able to obtain a loan. If your FICO score is relatively high you may even qualify for a slightly more favorable interest rate. While there is not a lot of room to negotiate interest rates, you might be able to reduce your rates by 0.25–0.5% if you agree to automatic payments deducted from your checking account.

Typically, lenders will loan only 80% of the appraised value of the home on a primary or first mortgage. Historically, lenders required the remaining 20% to be in the form of a down payment. This meant the borrower had his own money invested in the house, which made it less likely that he would default on the mortgage. In an effort to get a bigger share of the market, lenders began backing off the requirement for a 20% down payment in the early 1990s. Initially some lenders protected their investment by requiring buyers to obtain **private mortgage insurance (PMI)** that would pay off the mortgage in the event the buyers weren't able to do so. A more recent alternative is a **piggyback mortgage**, essentially a second mortgage, which closes simultaneously with the first, for the difference between the purchase price and the first mortgage plus the down payment. The primary mortgage holder is the first secured party on the house, which means that if anything happens to the house or your ability to repay the loan, the primary mortgage holder gets paid first. When lenders give second mortgages, they are not first in line for repayment, so rates for second mortgages are typically 1–2% higher than for first mortgages. Whatever financing you use, be sure to investigate multiple alternatives and read the fine print, watching out for early-termination fees and prepayment penalties.

In addition to requirements for a down payment or PMI, lenders establish other requirements that must be met, including title and homeowner's insurances. Title insurance involves a one-time payment based on the value of the home and property. This insurance protects both you and the lender from someone claiming that he or she is the rightful owner of your home. Similarly, homeowner's insurance provides protection to both you and the lender in case of theft, fire, and so on; however, damage from a natural disaster, such as a flood or earthquake, is usually not covered under a basic policy. If you are buying a home in an area that is prone to such disasters, you may need to obtain a separate policy which may be government subsidized. It is important to note that when you are talking about the value of a home for insurance purposes, you are talking about the value of the buildings (called capital improvements) on the property, not the value of the property itself. This is because even if your home is destroyed, you still own the property. While most of this is pretty standard and there is not much room to negotiate, there are a number of other issues that are commonly negotiated.

As was the case when comparing homes, there are a multitude of details to consider when you are evaluating financing options and it is helpful if you have a checklist. Figure 14.3 is an example of one available from the Federal Reserve Board.

FIGURE 14.3 Mortgage Comparison Worksheet

	Lender 1	Lender 2
Name of Lender:		
Name of Contact:		
Date of Contact:		
Mortgage Amount:		

	Mortgage 1	Mortgage 2	Mortgage 1	Mortgage 2
Basic Information on the Loans				
Type of mortgage: fixed rate, adjustable rate, conventional, FHA, other? If adjustable, see below.				
Minimum down payment required				
Loan term (length of loan)				
Contract interest rate				
Annual percentage rate (APR)				
Points (may be called *loan discount points*)				
Monthly private mortgage insurance (PMI) premiums				
How long must you keep PMI?				
Estimated monthly escrow for taxes and hazard insurance				
Estimated monthly payment (principal, interest, taxes, insurance, PMI)				
Fees **Different institutions may have different names for some fees and may charge different fees. We have listed some typical fees you may see on loan documents.**				
Application fee or Loan processing fee				
Origination fee or underwriting fee				
Lender fee or funding fee				
Appraisal fee				
Attorney fees				
Document preparation and recording fees				
Broker fees (may be quoted as points, origination fees, or interest rate add-on)				
Credit report fee				
Other fees				
Other Costs at Closing/Settlement				
Title search/Title insurance				
For lender				
For you				
Estimated prepaid amounts for interest, taxes, hazard insurance, payments to escrow				
State and local taxes, stamp taxes, transfer taxes				
Flood determination				
Prepaid private mortgage insurance (PMI)				
Surveys and home inspections				
Total Fees and Other Closing/Settlement Cost Estimates				

FIGURE 14.3 (Continued)

	Lender 1	Lender 2				
Name of Lender:						
			Mortgage 1	Mortgage 2	Mortgage 1	Mortgage 2
Other Questions and Considerations about the Loan						
Are any of the fees or costs waivable?						
Prepayment Penalties						
Is There a Prepayment Penalty?						
If so, how much is it?						
How long does the penalty period last? (e.g., three years? five years?)						
Are extra principal payments allowed?						
Lock-Ins						
Is the lock-in agreement in writing?						
Is there a fee to lock-in?						
When does the lock-in occur—at application, approval, or another time?						
How long will the lock-in last?						
If the rate drops before closing, can you lock in at a lower rate?						
If the Loan Is an Adjustable Rate Mortgage:						
What is the initial rate?						
What is the maximum the rate could be next year?						
What are the rate and payment caps each year and over the life of the loan?						
What is the frequency of rate change and of any changes to the monthly payment?						
What is the index that the lender will use?						
What margin will the lender add to the index?						
Credit Life Insurance						
Does the monthly amount quoted to you include a charge for credit life insurance?						
If so, does the lender require credit life insurance as a condition of the loan?						
How much does the credit life insurance cost?						
How much lower would your monthly payment be without the credit life insurance?						
If the lender does not require credit life insurance, and you still want to buy it, what rates can you get from other insurance providers?						

Source: Federal Reserve Board, http://www.federalreserve.gov/pubs/mortgage/mortb_1.htm#head7. Used with permission.

Beyond Price: What Else You Can Negotiate

Along with negotiating a favorable purchase price, wise homebuyers negotiate a multitude of other issues including who pays the closing costs, home inspections and warranties, and what remains with the home (i.e., what is conveyed with the home). As with purchase price, the worse the real estate market, the more power the buyer has when negotiating these items. A 2006 survey of homebuilders revealed that 55% were offering more amenities, 42% were paying closing costs, 26% were absorbing points on mortgages, and nearly 45% were trimming prices.[8] While there are a plethora of individual issues that can be negotiated, we address them here in general terms.

Closing costs include a variety of loan fees (e.g., application, commitment, document preparation, underwriting), title and settlement fees (e.g., appraisal, credit report, pest inspection, survey, title insurance), and taxes and other prepaid items (e.g., homeowners insurance, association fees, and prorated interest). Many of the closing costs are required; however, one cost that is optional is "points," which can be paid to buy down the interest rate. A point equals 1% of the loan and typically reduces the mortgage rate by 0.25–0.5%. Closing costs vary considerably from state to state. A 2006 survey of loan, title, and settlement fees (excluding taxes and other prepaid items) by Bankrate.com found that the average in the United States for a $200,000 loan was $3,024, with the highest at $3,887 in New York and the lowest at $2,713 in Missouri.[9] Closing costs are often paid by the seller or split between the buyer and seller, but again, this is negotiable.

Generally speaking, when you purchase a home, you are assumed to be buying whatever is nailed, screwed, or bolted down. You may, however, also negotiate to have some of the sellers' possessions included in the sale, even if they have been specifically excluded in the listing. Most often this involves window coverings and kitchen appliances, but you can negotiate that other items, such as furniture, also be included. During the housing meltdown that began in 2007, many real estate developers holding new homes that weren't selling began offering large rebates, free swimming pools, and even luxury cars that they referred to as "driveway jewelry" to buyers of high-end homes. While this might seem extreme, remember, such extras may provide the extra incentive for a buyer to purchase one home instead of another.

It is important to note that both buyers and sellers may make contingent offers, which means they may back out of the sale depending on the specified contingency. This effectively gives the parties an out if they decide not to complete the sale. A buyer's offer may be contingent on obtaining financing, a favorable home inspection, or selling his current house. Similarly, a seller can make her offer to sell contingent. For example, a seller might make the sale contingent on her finding suitable housing, which means she may decide not to sell if she doesn't find other appropriate living arrangements.

Buyers of existing homes commonly make their offers contingent on a favorable home inspection. A professional home inspector is hired to check for problems (e.g., heating/air conditioning, plumbing, electrical, roof, water heater, termite, or structural damage) that could be costly to repair. If the home inspector finds problems, you can negotiate who pays for the repairs or you could back out of the negotiation completely. Of course who pays for the home inspection is also negotiable. As a buyer you might also negotiate for the seller to warrant the home against problems for a specified period of time after the purchase.

Realtors: Do You Need One?

The answer to this question depends on whether or not you are willing to put the time and effort into doing the work yourself. The main function of a real estate agent is to match buyers and sellers, a process complicated by the fixed location and heterogeneity of homes, infrequent transactions among buyers and sellers, and complexity arising from the financial and legal dimensions of the transaction.[10] For a commission, a realtor

TABLE 14.1	Impact of a Higher Sale Price		Difference
Sale price of home	$250,000	$260,000	$10,000
Total commission (6%)	$15,000	$15,600	$600
Amount to seller	$235,000	$244,400	$9,400
Listing realtor's share of commission (1.5%)	$3,750	$3,900	$150

will place a value on and market your property, offer advice and assistance on making your home more appealing to buyers, host open houses, show the property to prospective buyers, handle all of the paperwork, and facilitate the negotiation. Research suggests, however, that the benefit of using an agent may be predominantly in the matching of buyers and sellers rather than in facilitating negotiation.[11]

If you decide to list your property with a realtor, you will sign a listing contract which usually continues for three to six months. There are three types of real estate listing contracts, the most common of which is an **exclusive-right-to-sell listing**.[12] Under this type of contract, the real estate agent is entitled to a commission if the property is sold during the life of the contract, even if you find your own buyer. Courts in some states allow the inclusion of extension clauses in these contracts, which state that if the property is sold during a specified period of time after the listing expires (e.g., six months) to a buyer who was procured by the broker during the original contract, the broker is still entitled to collect a commission.[13] As you might guess, this is the listing arrangement that is preferred by most realtors.

The two other types of contracts—exclusive agency and open listings—are much less common. With an **exclusive agency contract**, the seller agrees that a particular broker is the only one who can sell the property; however, if the seller finds her own buyer, the realtor is not entitled to a commission. Interestingly, one study found that sellers are better off with this type of contract because it results in greater effort by the agent and a faster sale without a sacrifice in price.[14] Unfortunately for sellers, many brokers are reluctant to take such listings. The third, and the least common, type of listing agreement is an **open listing** which allows the seller to contract with multiple realtors and pay a commission only to the one who actually sells the home. For obvious reasons, realtors are not fond of this arrangement.

The traditional commission on a residential real estate transaction is 6%. There is a popular belief that because of the commission, realtors are motivated to obtain the highest possible sale price on their listings.[15] But closer evaluation of this suggests otherwise. The listing realtor splits the commission with the buyer's agent so that each receives 3%. Each agent then typically splits her 3% with her company, which means each agent earns 1.5% of the sale price of each home sold. Consider the example in Table 14.1, which compares the commission on a home that is sold for $250,000 and the same home if it were to sell for $260,000.

The difference in purchase price of $10,000 to the home buyer is substantial. The same is true for the seller, who after paying a 6% commission receives $9,400 more. The difference to the individual realtor however is only $150. From a purely economic standpoint, there is little incentive for a realtor to invest the extra effort and waiting time in getting a higher sale price, and risk not receiving any commission if the home doesn't sell, for an additional $150. A reasonable assumption is that he would be more anxious to close the sale, guaranteeing the receipt of a $3,750 commission, and put his effort into selling another property.

Historically, people contracted with a realtor primarily because realtors had access to information on comparable home sales and could advertise homes for sale via the Multiple Listing Service (MLS), which was accessible only to realtors. Today however, in large part due to the Internet, home sellers have access to information once controlled by realtors[16] and can advertise their homes with a variety of listing services. As a result, there is a trend toward an unbundling of real estate services so that individuals—for a fee—can purchase desired services without formally listing their home with a realtor. Companies such as Assist2sell.com offer a menu of services ranging from a flat fee for handling paperwork to a full service MLS listing arrangement. From the seller's perspective, he can save by selecting the services he desires without having to pay for services he doesn't want or need. From the realtor's perspective, it is better to keep some aspects of the business than to lose it all. There is yet more good news for people who don't want to put the time and effort into selling their home themselves. Because of the competitive pressures, realtors are more willing to negotiate lower commission rates when listing properties[17] with the average real estate commission today at about 5%.[18] Using the example of a $250,000 home, a 1% difference in commission equals a difference of $2,500, which most people would find worth negotiating.

Attorneys: Do You Need One?

If you opt not to use a realtor at all, you should have an attorney draw up, or at least review, the paperwork whether you are purchasing or selling any property. These are major legal transactions and you need to make sure that the paperwork is done properly to avoid any problems in the future. This is also true if you are leasing property. Since a lease agreement is a legal contract, you need to make sure you understand the terms of the lease and are protected if there are problems with the property. Without proper protection, often referred to as "an escape clause," you could be liable for the remainder of the lease if you break it before the expiration date.

Points to Ponder

1. What kinds of things would be most important to you if you were planning to buy a home?
2. What is your level of comfort with assuming a large amount of debt to purchase a home?
3. How comfortable would you be in purchasing a home without a realtor?

Chapter Scenario, Part II

After five years of learning the business, making contacts, and saving money, Jake and Stephanie have decided it is time to start their business, J & S Café and Catering. Since they are just starting their business, they are not in a position financially to purchase a building, and even if they were, they don't want to commit to buying a building since they aren't sure how well their business will do. They know how important it is to have a good location and have been looking for commercial space to lease.

NEGOTIATING COMMERCIAL LEASES

As with residential real estate, location has a substantial influence on the parties' power in a negotiation, especially for office and retail space where the physical location can have a significant impact on the success of the business. For example, a retail business located in a high traffic area will generate a higher sales volume than an identical business located off the beaten path, simply because more customers are likely to come in. Similarly, the supply of and demand for space will have an effect on power and, subsequently, price. If there is a lot of vacant space available, building owners are in a weaker position to negotiate high rents. Rental property is a perishable commodity in that every month that it remains vacant represents rental income that is lost forever. Thus, property owners may be willing to accept a lower rent just to have the property occupied and generating some income.

There are several considerations when leasing commercial space. Commercial space is usually priced per square foot, but it is important to understand whether the square footage leased is based on total space or usable space. The rent may or may not include utilities, and there may be a charge for building maintenance or management. Depending on the situation, there may be a need for **build-outs**, which involve customizing space for a particular business. In this case, all the details of the construction, as well as who pays for it, are negotiable. Whoever is paying will likely want an escape clause in the lease agreement in case the renovations become too costly. Similarly, there may be a need for permits or approvals for the tenant's use of the premises. The lease should make it completely clear which party (usually the tenant) has the obligation to obtain the permits and approvals.

The lease should specify the initial length of the agreement and any options to renew or extend it. Tenants may also want to include an option to increase the amount of space they lease so they are prepared if their business does well and they need to expand their operations. Similarly, the lease should specify the date that rental charges begin. This is especially important if build-outs, permits, or approvals are required before the business can open and start generating income. In some cases tenants are able to negotiate a rent abatement period, much like apartment complexes that offer tenants free rent for the first month.

Most leases address subletting to a third party and often place restrictions on the practice. This can have a negative impact on tenants who find they don't need the full amount of space they have leased and would like to recoup some of their costs by subletting a portion of the leased space. Restrictions on subletting can also be major drawback for businesses that fail, leaving the owners with lease payments they can't afford. If subletting is permitted, the lease should specify if there is to be any release of the original tenant's obligation to the landlord upon assignment, although this is generally not the case in commercial leasing.[19]

Landlords almost always require a security deposit to cover the cost of any damage done to the property while the tenant is occupying it. At the end of the lease, assuming there is no damage, the security deposit should be refunded, and depending on the contract, with interest. From a landlord's perspective, security deposits can help sort out lower-quality tenants[20] in that businesses that are not well financed, and thus more likely to fail, will find it more difficult to put up a large security deposit.

Retail Leases

Thus far, we have addressed commercial leasing in general, but there are unique considerations when leasing retail space. A retail lease may be for space in a shopping center, mall, or stand-alone store. In some cases the rent will consist of a base rent and a **percentage rent**, which is based on a percentage of sales. Of course how sales are calculated should also be negotiated and specified in the lease. While security deposits might sort out lower-quality tenants, percentage rent may sort out lower-quality landlords,[21] in that landlords who don't plan to reinvest in the property may be less likely to put part of the rent proceeds at risk. Percentage rent can also help build the relationship between the landlord and the tenant because the landlord has a financial interest in the success of the tenant. Thus, the landlord may be more responsive to the tenant's requests for improvements or repairs.

In addition to rent, retail leases for tenants in a shopping center or mall will likely address **common area maintenance (CAM)**, tax and insurance expenses, and possibly, management or administrative fees. Of course this is all negotiable, and savvy tenants will negotiate limits on annual increases in these fees. In addition tenants may negotiate a cotenancy clause, which addresses the required occupancy by "anchor" tenants. In a mall, the anchor stores are generally located at opposite corners of the property and are usually well-known chain stores (e.g., J.C. Penney, Macy's, Nordstrom, Sears) that draw customers to the mall, helping generate traffic for the smaller stores. A cotenancy clause may also stipulate that a tenant is not required to open and/or operate unless a certain percentage of all shopping center tenants are also operating.

A detailed and accurate description of permissible uses is particularly important in a retail lease,[22] and there may be limitations on changing how the property is used. For example, the landlord may prohibit uses that she finds objectionable or inconsistent with the nature of the facility, or uses for which other tenants have negotiated exclusive rights (e.g., no more than one high-end beauty salon in a mall). There may also be so-called radius restrictions that specify the distance outside the door of the leased space that the tenant may use for things such as displaying merchandise or conducting sidewalk sales. Also particularly important in retail leasing is the subject of signage—where, how large, lighting, and so on—as it can have a substantial impact on the success of the business.

Industrial Leases

Different considerations come into play when you are leasing industrial space. Industrial real estate leases fall on a continuum from gross leases to triple net leases. In a gross lease, the landlord has the responsibility for all building costs and maintenance of the property. Conversely, in a triple net lease the tenant is responsible for all costs, including building upkeep. Most industrial leases fall somewhere between these two extremes.[23] When you negotiate the lease, it is important to clearly specify the responsibilities of each party, including who is responsible for any environmental damage that might occur. If the use of any hazardous materials is anticipated, this should be addressed in the early stages of the negotiation.[24]

If build-outs are required, the parties may negotiate to have the landlord pay the cost of improvements, particularly if they add value to the building. If the landlord isn't willing to incur the cost, he might agree to pay for the build-outs up front and have the tenant repay the cost over the life of the lease. When the supply of industrial space exceeds the demand, landlords may provide such incentives to rent the space.[25] It's important to note that there is a legal difference in the ownership of improvements depending on whether they are classified as chattels or fixtures. **Fixtures** are things that are attached to the building (e.g., truck docks) and automatically become the property of the landlord at the end of the lease unless specifically exempted. Conversely, **chattels**, which are not attached to the building (e.g., freestanding shelving), are the property of the tenant and can be relocated by the tenant at any time. Obviously tenants will likely have more success in negotiating to have the landlord pay for fixtures than chattels.

Chapter Scenario, Part III

J & S Café and Catering has been in business for three years and is very successful. Its catering services are very popular with local businesses, and customers often have to wait to get a table. It now needs more space in the kitchen to accommodate the catering business and in the dining area to provide space for customers dining at the café. The building it is leasing has no room for it to expand. They know it is a big step, but Jake and Stephanie are ready to purchase a building of their own.

PURCHASING COMMERCIAL PROPERTY

Commercial real estate negotiations involve most of the issues addressed in residential real estate transactions and more. There are still listings, commissions, title insurance, prorated taxes, and so on, the details of which are all negotiable. Purchase prices for commercial property are usually higher, which means the buyer is usually financing a larger amount. Of course this means that obtaining financing is more complex. You will still need to obtain title insurance; however, it too can be more complex if there are shared parking lots or driveways involved. If part of the property is leased to others, prorated rent proceeds should be addressed in the negotiation. Just as you can negotiate to have personal possessions remain with a home, you can negotiate to have office furniture or other equipment, such as phones and computer equipment, remain with a commercial property.

Offers may be contingent on a variety of things ranging from obtaining financing or zoning variances to favorable building inspections or environmental hazard reports. If you are buying an existing business or rental property, you should obtain financial records, including tax returns, to verify the seller's claims as to profitability. You will also have to obtain public liability insurance to provide protection in case someone is hurt on your property and sues you.

Because all of the details take time to address, you might offer to pay the seller an "option fee" that would grant you the right to buy the building within a certain time period at an agreed upon price. This prevents the seller from selling to someone else while you are finalizing arrangements. If you offer an option fee, you might negotiate to have part or all of fee applied toward the purchase price when the deal closes.

Real estate negotiations for the purchase of commercial property are also more complex because there are often others involved beyond the buyer and seller. Frequently you end up negotiating with these parties as well. For example, buyers typically need to make at least a 20% cash down payment. Some small business owners take out a second mortgage on their home or borrow from family members. For larger transactions, buyers often obtain outside investors. Whether you are dealing with your rich Aunt Jenny or Warren Buffet, you will need to negotiate the details of the financing. Similarly, if there are shared driveways or parking lots, you may need to negotiate the maintenance of, and access to, the space. If there are tenants, you will ultimately need to negotiate or renegotiate their lease agreements, and if build-outs or other renovations are needed, you will be negotiating with contractors.

You may also need to negotiate with representatives of the local government or regulatory agencies. For example, if you need to have the property rezoned for a different use or want to erect signage that exceeds local restrictions, you will need a zoning variance. If this is the case, you will need to gain the approval of the local government and possibly neighbors to gain their support for your request. Similarly, if you are seeking tax abatements, you may negotiate the amount and duration with the local government officials. If you are negotiating the purchase of a business that involves a liquor license, you may need to negotiate with the state liquor control commission.

Because of the complexity of commercial real estate negotiations, you may begin with an exchange of **letters of intent**. These are typically nonbinding, but allow you to make a preliminary determination as to whether you will be able to reach agreement on the major terms of the transaction. If you can resolve the more significant issues up front, the letter of intent is generally viewed as saving time in documenting the transaction.[26] Similarly, if you can't reach agreement on the key items, you can walk away from the negotiation before investing a great deal of time and effort.

Summary

Real estate negotiations have unique characteristics that make them more complex than other purchases. They run the gamut from buying a home to multi-million dollar commercial real estate deals. In negotiating to purchase a home, you begin by identifying your wants and needs and what you can afford. Next, you identify potential properties and research the value of the property to aid in determining your opening offers and target and resistance points for each negotiable issue. While you may or may not use a realtor, you should always have an attorney review the paperwork.

Commercial real estate may be leased or purchased. If you are negotiating to lease property, the issues will likely include the cost per square foot, maintenance fees, security deposit, subletting, and possibly build-outs. Negotiating the purchase of commercial property involves most of the same issues involved in purchasing residential property and more. Commercial transactions are likely to result in subsequent negotiations with neighboring businesses and government and regulatory officials.

Summary: The Big Picture

Basics of residential real estate	Types: house, condo Identify interests and what you can afford. Determine value, list price, SEV, appraisal.
Financing	Fixed versus variable, FHA, VA, seller-financed. Closing costs.
Realtors	May or may not use. If you use a realtor, issues are type of listing and commission rate. May negotiate for specific services.
Attorneys	Necessary if you don't use a realtor.
Commercial property: Leasing	Types: office, retail, industrial. Priced per square foot. Issues: utilities, maintenance, build-outs, permits/approvals, subletting, security deposits, permissible uses.
Commercial property: Purchasing	Additional issues, more complex financing, zoning variances, building inspections, outside investors. May use letter of intent.

Key Terms and Concepts

Adjustable rate mortgages (ARM)   A type of financing available through banks and other financial institutions for residential property at a variable interest rate.

Build-outs   Additional construction to a commercial property to customize space for a particular business.

Chattels   Items that are not attached to the building that are the property of the tenant and can be relocated by the tenant at any time.

Common area maintenance (CAM)   An additional charge in a commercial lease to help cover the costs of maintaining an area used by multiple tenants.

Conventional financing   A type of financing available through banks and other financial institutions for residential property at a fixed interest rate.

Exclusive agency contract   A contract where the seller agrees that a particular broker is the only one who can sell the property, however if the seller finds her own buyer, the realtor is not entitled to a commission.

Exclusive-right-to-sell listing   A contract where the real estate agent is entitled to a commission if the property is sold during the life of the contract, even if the seller finds her own buyer.

FHA mortgages   A type of financing for residential property available through the Federal Housing Administration.

FICO score   The most commonly used measure of one's credit.

Fixtures   Things that are attached to the building which automatically become the property of the landlord at the end of the lease unless specifically exempted.

Letters of intent   Typically nonbinding documents that allow you to make a preliminary determination as to whether you will be able to reach agreement on the major terms of the transaction.

Open listing   A contract which allows the seller to contract with multiple realtors and pay a commission only to the one who actually sells the home.

Percentage rent   An arrangement for leasing retail space where the rent consists of a base rent and an additional amount that is based on a percentage of sales.

Piggyback mortgage   A second mortgage, which closes simultaneously with the first, for the difference between the purchase price and the first mortgage plus the down payment.

PITI   The total amount of the principal, interest, taxes, and insurance for a residential property.

Private mortgage insurance (PMI)   Insurance that pays off the mortgage in the event the buyers aren't able to do so.

Seller-financed   When the seller loans the buyer the money to purchase her property.

State equalized value (SEV)   The taxable value of the home and property.

VA mortgages   A type of financing available through the Veterans Administration.

Discussion Questions

1. Discuss the issues that might be included in a residential real estate negotiation.
2. Describe how you would prepare to negotiate the purchase of a home.
3. Evaluate the options for financing a home.
4. Assess the role of third parties (e.g., realtors, attorneys) in real estate negotiations.

5. Describe the issues involved in leasing retail and industrial space.
6. Compare and contrast the differences in negotiating commercial and residential real estate transactions.

Ethical Dilemma: Subprime Mortgages

In early 2007 we started hearing about the meltdown in the subprime mortgage market. Essentially, subprime lending involved loaning money to people to purchase a house who couldn't qualify for a regular mortgage, usually because of poor credit. From the consumers' standpoint, subprime lending allowed them to purchase homes when they would not have otherwise qualified. From the lenders' standpoint, they were able to charge higher interest rates and other costs on these loans because they were taking on additional risk. The problem arose when the borrowers were unable to make the payments and the homes went into foreclosure.

Questions

1. How much responsibility should the lender bear for insuring the consumer can afford his mortgage?
2. How much responsibility should the consumer bear for ensuring he can afford his mortgage?
3. Should lenders be allowed to loan more than the value of the borrowers' home?
4. Does the government have an interest in regulating the size of home mortgages?

Ethical Dilemma: Cape Wind: Not in My Backyard!

Cape Wind is a project to create the United States' first offshore wind farm on Horseshoe Shoal in Nantucket Sound. The towers for the 130 wind turbines will stand 258 feet above the water with the tip of the highest blade reaching 440 feet into the air. They will be spaced six to nine football fields apart to allow the shallow draft boats that pass through or fish Horseshoe Shoal to navigate. Once operational, Cape Wind will produce up to 420 megawatts of clean, renewable energy, helping to reduce air pollution, dependence on petroleum, and energy costs for the local residents. It will also create up to a thousand jobs in manufacturing, assembly, and ocean construction, boosting the local economy and creating 150 permanent jobs, including 50 highly paid maintenance and operations jobs based on Cape Cod.[27]

While Cape Wind enjoys support from many individuals and organizations, there are also those who have vigorously opposed the project. The project faced staunch opposition from, among others, two well-known environmental advocates, the late Senator Edward Kennedy and his nephew, Robert F. Kennedy Jr., whose family compound has a view of Nantucket Sound that would be forever changed by the giant windmills,[28] as well as former Massachusetts Governor Mitt Romney.[29]

Questions

1. How much influence should property owners have in controlling their view?
2. How much influence should property owners have in controlling projects on neighboring property?
3. Should projects that are considered to be "good" for society or the environment be treated any differently than any other project?

Endnotes

1. Halpern, J. J. "The Effect of Friendship on Decisions: Field Studies of Real Estate Transactions." *Human Relations* 49(12) (1996): 1519–1547.
2. Arnold, M. A. "Search, Bargaining and Optimal Asking Prices." *Real Estate Economics* 27(3) (1999): 453–481.
3. This effect is discussed by Kahneman and his colleagues (1990, 1991) in reporting results of an experiment regarding subjects who owned (versus didn't own) their coffee mugs. See Kahneman, D., J. Knetsch, and R. Thaler.

"Experimental Tests of the Endowment Effect." *Journal of Political Economy* 98 (1990): 1325–1348; and Kahneman, D., J. Knetsch, and R. Thaler. "The Endowment Effect, Loss Aversion, and Status Quo Bias." *Journal of Economic Perspectives* 5 (1991): 193–206.
4. Arnold, M. A. "Search, Bargaining and Optimal Asking Prices." *Real Estate Economics* 27(3) (1999): 453–481.
5. Harding, J. P., J. R. Knight, and C. F. Sirmans. "Estimating Bargaining Effects in Hedonic Models: Evidence from the

Housing Market." *Real Estate Economics* 31(4) (2003): 601-622.

6. *Ibid.*

7. *Ibid.*

8. Chatzky, J. "Builders to Buyers: Take This House, Please!" *Money* 35(11) (2006): 44.

9. Bankrate.com http://www.bankrate.com/brm/news/mortgages/ccmap2006a1.asp?caret=6, accessed August 24, 2007.

10. Mantrala, S., and E. Zabel. "The housing market and real estate brokers." *Real Estate Economics* 23(2) (1995): 161.

11. Yavas, A., T. J. Miceli, and C. F. Sirmans. "An Experimental Analysis of the Impact of Intermediaries on the Outcome of Bargaining Games." *Real Estate Economics* 29(2) (2001): 251–276.

12. Ruterford, R. C., T. M. Springer, and A. Yavas. "The Impacts of Contract Type on Broker Performance." *Real Estate Economics* 29(3) (2001): 389–409.

13. Miceli, T. J. "Renegotiation of Listing Contracts, Seller Opportunism and Efficiency: An Economic Analysis." *Real Estate Economics* 23(3) (1995): 369–383.

14. Ruterford, R. C., T. M. Springer, and A. Yavas. "The Impacts of Contract Type on Broker Performance." *Real Estate Economics* 29(3) (2001): 389–409.

15. Bajtelsmit, V. L., and E. Worzala. "Adversarial brokerage in residential real estate transactions: The impact of separate buyer representation." *The Journal of Real Estate Research* 14(1/2) (1997): 65–75.

16. Levitt, S. D., and S. J. Dubner. *Freakonomics.* New York: William Morrow (Harper Collins), 2005.

17. Mantrala, S., and E. Zabel. "The housing market and real estate brokers." *Real Estate Economics* 23(2) (1995): 161.

18. Money.cnn.com http://money.cnn.com/2006/03/31/pf/saving/willis_tips/index.htm, accessed August 30, 2007.

19. Brooks, S. D., and R. J. Sykes. "A Practical Guide To Using Letters Of Intent." *Journal of Property Management* 65(2) (2000): 80–86.

20. Benjamin, J. D., and P. Chinloy. "The Structure of a Retail Lease." *The Journal of Real Estate Research* 26(2) (2004): 223.

21. *Ibid.*

22. Brooks, S. D., and R. J. Sykes. "A Practical Guide To Using Letters Of Intent." *Journal of Property Management* 65(2) (2000): 80–86.

23. Luton, D. "Understanding industrial leasing." *Modern Materials Handling* 54(9) (1999): 43.

24. Brooks, S. D., and R. J. Sykes. "A Practical Guide To Using Letters Of Intent." *Journal of Property Management* 65(2) (2000): 80–86.

25. Luton, D. "Understanding industrial leasing." *Modern Materials Handling* 54(9) (1999): 43.

26. Brooks, S. D., and R. J. Sykes. "A Practical Guide To Using Letters Of Intent." *Journal of Property Management* 65(2) (March/April 2000): 80–86.

27. Cape Wind (2007). http://www.capewind.org/article24.htm, accessed November 3, 2010.

28. Kahn, H. May 16, 2007. On Cape, gales of hypocrisy, Boston Globe http://www.b#ton.com/news/globe/editorial_opinion/oped/articles/2007/05/16/on_cape_gales_of_hypocrisy, accessed November 3, 2011.

29. Daly, Beth January 15, 2008. Cape Wind proposal clears big obstacle. Boston Globe, http://www.boston.com/news/local/articles/2008/01/15/cape_wind_proposal_clears_big_obstacle, accessed November 3, 2010.

Exercise 14.1 Researching Property Values

Instructions:

This exercise provides you with experience researching property values. Identify the type (e.g., residential or commercial) and location of the property you wish to research. If you are researching residential property, imagine you are ready to buy your first (or next) home. If you are researching commercial property, identify a business you would like to start (e.g., retail, office-based, restaurant, industrial).

Using the worksheet, identify and prioritize your interests. Determine whether each item is something you must have, something you would like to have, or something you absolutely cannot live without. Identify five properties that are currently available in your area that meet or come close to meeting your criteria. For each property identify the list price, SEV, current taxes, and so on. Rate each property against your criteria and identify the property that best meets your needs.

Exercise 14.1 Researching Property Values Worksheet

Criteria	Weight*	Criteria
A		
B		
C		
D		
E		
F		
G		

Note: *+2 = must have, +1 = nice to have, 0 = neutral, –1 = rather not have, –2 = must not have

Property #1:

      Address: _____

      Price: _____ SEV: _____ Taxes: _____

      Improvements needed: _____

      Comments: _____

Property #2:

      Address: _____

      Price: _____ SEV: _____ Taxes: _____

      Improvements needed: _____

      Comments: _____

Property #3:

      Address: _____

      Price: _____ SEV: _____ Taxes: _____

      Improvements needed: _____

      Comments: _____

Property #4:

        Address: _____

        Price: _____ SEV: _____ Taxes: _____

        Improvements needed: _____

        Comments: _____

Property #5:

        Address: _____

        Price: _____ SEV: _____ Taxes: _____

        Improvements needed: _____

        Comments: _____

Rate each property against your criteria and multiply by the weight you assigned to that criterion to obtain the score.

Rating scale:

5 = substantially exceeds requirements
4 = slightly exceeds requirements
3 = meets requirements—no more, no less
2 = slightly less than desired
1 = does not meet requirements at all

Criteria	Weight	Property 1 Rating/Score	Property 2 Rating/Score	Property 3 Rating/Score	Property 4 Rating/Score	Property 5 Rating/Score
A						
B						
C						
D						
E						
F						
G						
Total Score						

Property that best meets your needs: _____

Pleasant surprises: _____

_____

Disappointments: _____

_____

Exercise 14.2   Buying/Selling Property without a Realtor

This exercise consists of two rounds. In one round you will be negotiating as a buyer for the property that you identified as best meeting your needs from Exercise 14.1. In the other round, you will be playing the role of the seller for another student.

Your instructor will provide instructions for posting your property description for the other students in the class to review. Each student then selects a property description for which she or he would like to portray the seller. While you will have already researched the property you will be negotiating to buy, you will also need to research the property you will be negotiating to sell. Once student dyads for each round are determined, you should prepare for your negotiations including drafting a written offer for the property you wish to purchase.

Exercise 14.3   Sandy's by the Shore: Leasing Retail Space

Instructions:

In this exercise you will be assigned the role of Sandy, Robin, or an observer. Your instructor will provide you with confidential role sheets based on your assigned role. Read all information provided, complete the worksheet, and prepare for the negotiation based on your knowledge of the situation.

Overview:

Sandy is planning to open her own gift shop, Sandy's by the Shore, featuring unique and handmade items in Clear View, a chic resort community. She has been looking for approximately 1,500 square feet of retail space to lease in a high-traffic area. After much searching, she thinks she has found the right location at the Bayside Shops, an upscale shopping center. The 1,600 square foot property is advertised as leasing for $9/square foot, which equates to $14,400 per year or $1,200 per month, plus utilities and a monthly CAM fee of $300. Robin is the property manager for Bayside Shops and negotiates all leases. Sandy is meeting with Robin to discuss leasing the property.

Worksheet: Exercise 14.3 Sandy's by the Shore: Leasing Retail Space

Prospective Tenant, Sandy

Interests: _____

_____

Issue	Opening Demand	Target	Resistance

Property Manager, Robin

Interests: _____

_____

Issue	Opening Demand	Target	Resistance

Exercise 14.4   The Agency Needs Additional Space

Instructions:

In this exercise you will be assigned the role of the executive director, landlord, or observer. Your instructor will provide you with confidential role sheets based on your assigned role. Read all the information provided, complete the worksheet, and prepare for the negotiation based on your knowledge of the situation.

Overview:

Westshore Community Resource Center (Westshore) is a nonprofit agency that provides a variety of services to people in the local community. As a community nonprofit agency, it operates on a very tight budget. For the last five years, Westshore has leased office space from Turner, Williams & Associates (TWA). There is now one year left on the lease which specifies that Westshore could lease additional space in the building and that TWA would remodel the space to meet Westshore's needs. One year ago Westshore determined that additional space was needed to accommodate its growing outreach programs and notified TWA's managing partner, Lynn, of Westshore's need to exercise its option for additional space. To help cover the cost of remodeling, Westshore has been paying a monthly fee of $800 for the past year while the remodeling has been in process. Progress has been very slow until the last month when TWA brought in a construction manager to expedite the progress. The remodeling is now complete but TWA just rented the space to another business.

Worksheet: Exercise 14.4 The Agency Needs Additional Space

Executive Director, Dave

Interests: _____

Issue	Opening Demand	Target	Resistance

Managing Partner, Lynn

Interests: _____

Issue	Opening Demand	Target	Resistance

Popular Real Estate Websites

www.assist2sell.com offers sellers a "menu" of services ranging from a flat fee for handling paperwork to a full-blown Multiple Listing Service (MLS) marketing program.

www.bankrate.com provides information on mortgage rates and home equity loans.

www.forsalebyowner.com is a listing service for home sellers, search feature for buyers, and includes neighborhood information.

www.fsboprimer.com provides information for buyers and sellers on saving money on real estate commissions, includes a list of for sale by owner websites by state.

www.helpusell.com is a full service set fee realtor.

www.mtgprofessor.com is a website developed by Jack M. Guttentag, Professor of Finance Emeritus at the Wharton School of the University of Pennsylvania, and founder of GHR Systems, Inc., a mortgage technology company. The website has a number of spreadsheets available to calculate a variety of things, including amortization of simple interest loans, extra payments on different types of mortgages, loan repayment versus investment, and the benefit of making a larger down payment versus investing the money elsewhere.

www.owners.com is an online marketplace for people selling their own homes.www. propertypig.com is a listing service for home sellers and a search feature for buyers.

www.realestate.com is a listing service for home sellers, search feature for buyers, and includes information on home values and financing.

www.realestatejournal.com is the Wall Street Journal guide to property and includes information on residential and commercial real estate.

www.realtor.com is a website owned by the National Association of Realtors; it excludes homes for sale by owners.

www.zillow.com is a website for real estate listings, comparables, and other information.

CHAPTER 15

Negotiating Your Future

Chapter Objectives

After studying this chapter and completing the exercises you should be able to:

- Describe the importance of identifying your ideal work situation and taking steps to find or create it.

- Identify ways of marketing yourself on the internal and external job markets.

- Assess how managing expectations can be used to prevent conflicts among work and nonwork relationships.

- Identify options for resolving conflicts, particularly those which arise out of changes in your personal or professional responsibilities.

- Evaluate the challenges particular to negotiating with loved ones when pursuing professional goals.

- Determine the degree of alignment between your values and behaviors (choices) and identify ways for facilitating improved alignment and creating a contract with yourself.

By now it is abundantly clear how critical negotiation skills are for your success in both your professional and personal lives. Many of the negotiations discussed in this book focus on a planned situation, be it buying a house, negotiating a contract for repairs, or collaborating with members of a team to resolve a crisis in the workplace. In this chapter, however, we address how you can negotiate your future—in both the personal and professional realms of your life. This involves identifying preferred outcomes and negotiating with the appropriate parties to ensure you accomplish these outcomes.

Chapter Scenario

Gabe and Natalie have been married six years. They met while attending college in Los Angeles; he majored in engineering while she majored in economics. Shortly after graduation, both obtained positions in Fortune 500 firms near one another, got married, and rented an apartment near downtown L.A. With both salaries, Gabe and Natalie could afford a comfortable though not extravagant lifestyle. They were happy in their relationship, and were contemplating a change. Natalie wanted to start a family, but Gabe didn't feel quite ready to become a father. Instead, based on informal conversations with colleagues at work and at a recent conference he attended, Gabe thought it was a good time for him to pursue an MBA. His engineering studies prepared him well for the projects he worked on, but to successfully manage others in the organization seemed to require a general management degree. Gabe's company would pay for his education, but only if he remained a full-time employee and attended school part-time. This education benefit was great, but at two to three classes per year, it would take Gabe three to four years to obtain his MBA. Alternatively, Gabe could go back to school full time, though that would halve their total income and create additional student loan debt to pay for graduate school. Gabe and Natalie were at a crossroads. What would they do? How should they decide?

While both work and nonwork issues are at play for Gabe and Natalie, we focus on work issues first. In negotiating your professional future, you will need to address the following questions:

- How do I identify my ideal work situation?
- What do I need to know about marketing myself to future (and current) employers?
- How do I prepare for my interviews?
- How do I evaluate and negotiate job offers?
- If additional skills or knowledge are needed, how do I negotiate this support from my employer, while also managing expectations of others who rely on me?

THE IDEAL WORK SITUATION

Unless you inherit a vast sum of money or happen to win the lottery, you can expect to be involved in regular activity that produces income that helps pay for the necessities of life, while you are working and after you retire. There are many ways to generate income, and not all involve a nine-to-five lifestyle. This is why we use the term *ideal work situation* as opposed to *job*. There are entrepreneurs, artists, musicians, and even day traders who work and generate sufficient income in what most would not refer to as "jobs." So, whether you are working now or looking for work, you would be wise to think critically about how you want to spend what for most is a substantial portion of your waking hours. The fit (or lack thereof) between you and your work situation will affect you and those around you in significant ways.[1] Moreover, because your needs and wants evolve over time, you must realize that this process of evaluating and realizing your ideal work situation is one that must be carried out regularly. In some cases, you may be able to obtain the ideal fit without changing jobs, by engaging in what is termed "job crafting"— a process of redefining your job to better meet your wants, needs, and strengths.[2]

If you are unsure of what type of work would best meet your needs, the O*NET Resource Center (www.onetcenter.org), sponsored by the U.S. Department of Labor, offers a number of Career Exploration Tools that can help you identify your interests and career options. Once you have an idea of what you would like to do, the worksheet in Figure 15.1 will help you begin the process of identifying the characteristics of your ideal work situation.

To begin, identify what you have to offer and what job and organization characteristics are important to you, and compare these with what the employer is seeking and offering. Is the type of work a good fit with your knowledge, skills, and abilities? Will the job allow you to grow and develop additional skills? Are your values compatible with those of the organization? To what extent will the job satisfy your needs—and will

FIGURE 15.1 Ideal Work Situation Worksheet

Type of Organization
Industry ——————————————————————————
For profit/nonprofit ———————————————————————
Organization's values ——————————————————————
Social/environmental consciousness ——————————————

Nature of the Work
Work tasks ——————————————————————————
Individual versus team ——————————————————————
Reporting relationships —————————————————————
Internal versus external customers ——————————————
Long-versus short-term projects ————————————————
Routine versus creative ————————————————————
Single versus multiple projects ————————————————
Opportunities for growth —————————————————————

Work Environment
Preferred work hours ——————————————————————
Standard versus flexible schedule ——————————————
Travel opportunities/requirements ——————————————
Relationship with supervisor ——————————————————
Relationship with co-workers ——————————————————

Compensation
Salary/hourly wage ——————————————————————
Health insurance ——————————————————————
Vacation ——————————————————————————
Retirement ——————————————————————————
Tuition reimbursement —————————————————————
Other perks ——————————————————————————

you satisfy the organization's? Once you are confident that the job would be a good fit, the focus shifts to negotiating the best employment arrangement. As with all negotiations, research and preparation is the key.

MARKETING YOURSELF EXTERNALLY

In the current economy, it is common for employers to receive 100–200 resumes for a single job. In fact, with the ease of attaching one's resume to an email or uploading it to a company portal, you can expect there will be plenty of similar-minded individuals in pursuit of the job you want. Now the question becomes, how do you stand out among your competition? Simply put, you must market yourself. It is no longer sufficient to send out a resume and cover letter to a prospective employer and then wait for a response. In today's competitive environment, that is akin to asking the employer to ignore you.

To be successful in the job search, you must actively market yourself. This involves networking with others who might work for—or know others who work for—your target employers and following up with the individual recruiters (e.g., "Hi, Mr. Matthews. I sent you my resume a week ago and wanted to be sure you received it. I'm very interested in your company and would welcome an opportunity to learn more about the position."). Once these connections are made, you need to clearly and confidently communicate your interests as well as the specific knowledge, skills, and abilities that you possess that make you suitable for the position. Despite the criticality of these job search skills, most students neither possess nor have been taught these skills. Almost all graduate students in a psychology program reported that no one formally discussed job search strategies with them and that all discussions regarding employment occurred informally among peers or sympathetic faculty members or practicum supervisors.[3] Not surprisingly, most students who majored in areas other than business have never taken a basic marketing course or been taught to apply marketing principles to market themselves. Even with one or more courses in marketing, business students rarely view the job search as an opportunity to apply what they have learned about marketing to their own job situation.[4] Surprisingly, even those who major in marketing do not have an edge. A study by McCorkle and colleagues found that marketing majors are no more prepared for the job search than other business students.[5]

MARKETING YOURSELF INTERNALLY

Not everyone in the job market is looking to join a different company. Some employees would like to remain with their current employer, but feel it is time to move on to a different (lateral) or higher (more senior) level position. Even though they know their supervisor and others in the company, few employees reveal their internal job searches. Changing this mindset is a good idea as there are several advantages to pursuing an internal job:

- You are more likely to know the inside track and have a better idea of what the employer wants in an applicant.
- You are a known commodity to the employer. The axiom "better the devil I know than the one I don't know" suggests that it is better to deal with someone whose weaknesses are known than someone whose weaknesses are unknown because the stranger's weaknesses could be much worse.
- The company is assured of a good fit between you and the organization, its culture, and its values; why else would you have been successful and in pursuit of another position within the firm?
- The company—by hiring from within—sends the message that employees are valued.

However, there are some downsides as well.

- If a supervisor feels threatened or put off by his subordinate's desire to move elsewhere in the company, the supervisor might be less than helpful, or could possibly sabotage the search.
- Unlike their internal counterparts, external employees have no vested interest in keeping things the way they have always been and therefore are less risk averse and more willing to challenge the status quo and bring in new ideas and ways of looking at the business.
- Hiring from within means that one job search ends while another begins. An external candidate fills a hiring gap while an internal hire simultaneously fills and creates an open position.
- In some organizations, not all job postings may be "real." The employer may be following the stated policy of posting even when she already knows who she wants for the job or may plan to go outside the organization to bring in "fresh blood." Of course, employees who learn of this bait and switch will become disenfranchised with and soured on the company.

There are several ways to market yourself to your current employer. First, during the initial interview process, or when you accept the job, make sure you are ready to discuss your career goals. Doing so sets the stage for what you want and are willing to do. Your supervisor might expand these into a more formalized development plan and integrate these goals into those of the work group. Second, when your supervisor offers you formal or informal feedback on your performance and progress toward individual and group goals, demonstrate willingness to learn and improve. Ask questions for clarification, ask for suggestions and offer your own, and request an opportunity for further feedback once you overcome a particular issue. Similarly, ask for feedback when you complete a major task or project. Don't get into the "no news is good news" mode. Realize that feedback may not be forthcoming unless you seek it as many managers are uncomfortable giving feedback.[6] Third, volunteer for assignments—especially those that will stretch your capabilities. Doing so demonstrates your willingness to grow and take risks, and also shows that you are a good organizational citizen—someone who is willing to go the extra mile for the good of the work group or organization. Fourth, pay attention to the internal postings that fit your knowledge, skills, abilities, and career goals. Ask your colleagues if they know anyone in that part of the company, and then ask for an introduction. This can occur via phone, email, or face to face. Once you have been introduced, ask the person to tell you about the position and work group, and be prepared to discuss your interests and fit with the job. Fifth, participate in company-sponsored activities and training. All things considered, those who are known (and seen in a positive light) are more desirable than those who do good work but seldom leave their offices. Of course, there is a fine line between confidence and arrogance. Colleagues are looking for competent team players, not arrogant loners or prima donnas.

RESEARCHING THE JOB

Once you've lined up an interview, learn as much as you possibly can about the position, organization, and the people with whom you will be interviewing. Most organizations have a website that contains information on the history of the organization, its products or services, its organizational structure, its people, and its policies. Even if you are an internal candidate, it is a good idea to review the most current information available, especially if the position you are seeking is in a different department or division. By demonstrating your knowledge of the position and company, you show that you are interested in the job and the organization. The time you spend preparing enables you to formulate intelligent questions to ask in the interview and prepare to negotiate a job offer. For example, if the company's website provides a full description of its tuition reimbursement program and it meets your needs, there is no need to ask if the company has one or be prepared to negotiate it. What are the company's policies on flexible schedules, time off, tuition reimbursement, and so on? Look for information on its compensation policies. Does the company website say that it offers competitive salaries or excellent benefits? The terminology used on the website can help you anticipate what the employer might offer and help you establish your target and resistance points.

PREPARING FOR THE INTERVIEW

Whether you are an internal or external candidate, a successful interview or series of interviews increases your chances of being offered the job and strengthens your position to negotiate a job offer. While we consider the interview to be a part of preparation for the negotiation, you must also prepare for the interview. Prepare to give a brief description of your skills and job experience, and why you are interested in the position. In preparing your responses to likely questions, think about specific examples of both your accomplishments and the challenges you have overcome. Instead of saying, "People see me as a real leader," it would be better to give an example that demonstrates this quality. For example, "Two weeks after I started my current job, my supervisor took a leave of absence to deal with a family emergency. I took on several of her responsibilities, including a, b, and c. Within a few weeks, we were able to achieve increased sales, on time deliveries, and satisfaction." Realize that providing specifics is about marketing yourself as well as providing the recruiter information needed to more accurately determine if you are a good fit for the job. This is especially important for women, who, according to research, are less likely to talk up their achievements.[7]

Even if you feel that you interview well, it is a good idea to rehearse your delivery, practicing in front of a mirror or a trusted friend or colleague. You might even determine the availability—and take advantage of—mock interview services provided by the career services office in many colleges. Instead of anticipating the worst, the mock interview provides an opportunity to practice in a "safe" environment. The feedback you receive, combined with positive imagery (i.e., imagining yourself successfully completing the interview and accepting a fabulous job offer), can really boost your confidence. A recent study demonstrates that an applicant's self-confidence about interviewing is more relevant to interview success than her personality attributes.[8]

In addition to increasing your self-confidence about interviewing, the time you spend preparing will also help reduce apprehension. Unfortunately this doesn't mean you won't experience any nervousness. In reality, a certain level of stress and anxiety will always remain with the job search process, regardless of the amount of preparation.[9]

Researchers and practitioners alike encourage applicants to engage in assertive social behaviors during the job search.[10] Whether they realize they are doing it, applicants typically engage in a variety of influence tactics during an interview to persuade the employer to extend an offer of employment. Remember our discussion on self-monitoring in Chapter 6? Applicants who are high in self-monitoring—who are aware of and adjust their behavior to fit their surroundings—typically use more influence tactics during an employment interview than those who are low in self-monitoring.[11] At the most basic level is your physical appearance and body language. Projecting a professional appearance to the interviewers helps establish credibility, which is an important component of the persuasion process covered in Chapter 8.[12]

The use of influence tactics goes beyond your physical presentation to your behavior in an interview. Two of the most commonly used behavioral tactics are ingratiation and self-promotion.[13] Applicants seeking to ingratiate themselves to an interviewer typically agree with the interviewer's opinions (or perceived opinions) and are complimentary. Applicants may also offer small favors, such as holding a door or picking up something that was dropped. Self-promoting applicants talk themselves up, emphasizing their positive characteristics to convince the interviewer of their competence. But do these tactics make a difference? Yes, although there is some disagreement on how. One study found that these tactics often lead to second interviews and job offers,[14] while another study found that the influence of these tactics is indirect through their effect on the interviewer's perception of fit, which is developed throughout the course of the interview.[15]

While ingratiation and self-promotion can clearly be effective tactics, they can also be used to excess and have a negative impact, especially if you come across as obsequious or a braggart. Ideally, you use tactics with which you are comfortable, are honest but diplomatic in your responses, and are positive about your past and future employment. Prospective employers who hear an applicant bad mouth former supervisors might project that the same could happen were the applicant to leave their organization and might believe that the problem was not with the supervisor or organization but with the applicant. Negativity will not help your cause. Finally, ask for the job. If that is not something you are comfortable with, you should at least express your interest and desire to work there, assuming of course that you really do.

Toward the end of the interview, most employers will ask if you have any questions. Even if the employer doesn't, be ready to ask a few questions, as it shows your interest in the interviewer and organization, and as Figure 15.2 suggests, questions may help you decide if the job would be a good fit for you. One of your follow-up questions might be to ask where they are in the hiring process. This will give you an idea of what to expect and the time frame involved. Applicants often assume that the employer will get back to them within a few days when that is not always the case, especially if there was a large response to the posting or last-minute changes to the job requirements. Other good questions to ask include "What would a typical week look like for a person in this job?" and "Why the position is vacant?" That the incumbent was promoted may mean something different than if the person quit.

FIGURE 15.2 Another View of Interviews

Obviously interviews provide an opportunity for an employer to assess the extent to which an applicant would be a good fit for an open position. For savvy applicants, interviews also provide an opportunity to evaluate the extent to which the job would meet his or her needs. Does the job offer appropriate challenges and opportunities for growth? Are the values of organization congruent with those of the applicant? Would the applicant, supervisor, and co-workers be compatible? Accepting a job that doesn't provide a good fit with the applicant's needs is more likely to result in the employee leaving.

After the interview you should send a thank you note to the interviewer(s)* While this might be viewed as another ingratiation tactic, a thank you note shows good manners and demonstrates that you are genuinely interested in the job. Such gestures are appreciated and effective in keeping your name in the forefront of the interviewer's mind. If your note mentions your plan to follow-up with them, make sure you do—showing the prospective employer that you follow through on your commitments. Remember, everything you do during the application and interview process helps set the stage for negotiating an offer of employment.

Points to Ponder

1. What is your experience with interviewing?
2. To what extent are you comfortable with the job search process?
3. What do you need to do to increase your comfort level and skill?

EVALUATING AND NEGOTIATING THE JOB OFFER

From a purely economic standpoint, everyone should negotiate when presented with any job offer. This is especially true for recent graduates whose first job after college has been shown to be a major predictor of future career status and earnings.[16] Your first job sets the stage for the rest of your working life. With the exception of long-term employees whose raises have not kept pace with market increases, almost all pay inequity within organizations can be traced back to the hiring process and the initial salary.[17] Indeed, negotiating your initial job offer can have a substantial effect on your lifetime wealth.[18]

While there is a dearth of research on actual salary negotiations, one study found that 56% of graduating MBA students who negotiated for larger salaries obtained increases ranging from $1,000 to $7,000.[19] We use these numbers to illustrate the difference in lifetime income resulting from negotiating a higher starting salary in Table 15.1. The example assumes forty-five years in the workplace,** a starting salary of $40,000,*** and annual raises of 3%.

The example shows that negotiating a starting salary of only $1,000 more than the initial offer results in a lifetime difference of $92,720, while negotiating $7,000 more results in a difference of $649,039. While this is a large amount of money, it is also a conservative estimate, since it assumes that a person will remain in the same job for his or her entire working life. Realistically, people will change jobs, employers, and even careers several times during their working life,[20] providing additional opportunities to negotiate their salary. Of course, the final outcome of a salary negotiation will vary from person to person depending on the individual's—and the employer's—negotiation skills, the industry, the economy, the organization's policy on starting salary, and a multitude of other factors. How can you ensure that you negotiate a salary that is in line with what you are worth? Table 15.2 identifies five active/assertive and five reactive/defensive negotiation tactics to justify higher salary demands that have been used in several studies of salary negotiations.[21]

Active/Assertive Tactics

First in this list is maintaining a confident, professional attitude. Identify your particular skills and abilities that the employer needs. If you have experience with a software product that the employer has or is just about to acquire, you might remind the employer that because of your experience you would be able to assist with the training of other

---

*Today, hand-written, typed, and emailed thank you notes are all considered acceptable. Email may actually be preferred when the process is short and the position makes use of technology skills.
**From age 22 to age 67, which is currently the age at which one can receive full social security retirement benefits in the United States.
***Our example uses a starting salary of $40,000, however the differences in lifetime earnings would be the same regardless of starting salary.

TABLE 15.1	Income Difference Resulting from Negotiating a Higher Starting Salary		
Year	Salary	Additional $1,000	Additional $7,000
1	40,000	41,000	47,000
2	41,200	42,230	48,410
3	42,436	43,497	49,862
4	43,709	44,802	51,358
5	45,020	46,146	52,899
6	46,371	47,530	54,486
7	47,762	48,956	56,120
8	49,195	50,425	57,804
9	50,671	51,938	59,538
10	52,191	53,496	61,324
11	53,757	55,101	63,164
12	55,369	56,754	65,059
13	57,030	58,456	67,011
14	58,741	60,210	69,021
15	60,504	62,016	71,092
16	62,319	63,877	73,224
17	64,188	65,793	75,421
18	66,114	67,767	77,684
19	68,097	69,800	80,014
20	70,140	71,894	82,415
21	72,244	74,051	84,887
22	74,412	76,272	87,434
23	76,644	78,560	90,057
24	78,943	80,917	92,759
25	81,312	83,345	95,541
26	83,751	85,845	98,408
27	86,264	88,420	101,360
28	88,852	91,073	104,401
29	91,517	93,805	107,533
30	94,263	96,619	110,759
31	97,090	99,518	114,081
32	100,003	102,503	117,504
33	103,003	105,578	121,029
34	106,093	108,746	124,660
35	109,276	112,008	128,400
36	112,554	115,368	132,252
37	115,931	118,829	136,219
38	119,409	122,394	140,306

(Continued)

TABLE 15.1 (*continued*)

Year	Salary	Additional $1,000	Additional $7,000
39	122,991	126,066	144,515
40	126,681	129,848	148,850
41	130,482	133,744	153,316
42	134,396	137,756	157,915
43	138,428	141,889	162,653
44	142,581	146,145	167,532
45	146,858	150,530	172,558
Total income	$3,708,794	$3,801,514	$4,357,833
Difference due to negotiation		$92,720	$649,039

TABLE 15.2 Negotiation Tactics

Active/Assertive	Reactive/Defensive
Maintaining a confident, professional attitude.	Using prolonged silence to indicate the other party's unreasonableness.
Phrasing demands to appeal to employers' interests.	Avoid reaching premature resolution by focusing on the parties' interests.
Framing demands favorably through the use of contrasts.	Persistently reiterating key points.
Proposing options for contingent mutual gain.	Verbally recognizing intimidating behavior.
Proposing options for non-contingent mutual gain.	Reframing weaknesses as potential strengths.

employees and serve as an in-house resource when questions or problems arise. Keep the negotiation professional by focusing on what you will contribute to the organization as opposed to what you want from it. It is much more effective to support your request for a higher salary by citing the contributions you will make instead of your need to pay off your student loans. Provided you are realistic about what you will bring to the organization, you will appear capable but not arrogant.

The second tactic is phrasing your demands to appeal to the employer's interests. This is consistent with persuasion tactics and processes discussed in Chapter 8. For example, if you are asking the employer to pay for you to obtain a professional certification, cite the benefits to the employer. Third is framing your demands favorably through the use of contrasts. This includes explaining why your demands are in the employer's best interests and what the organization doesn't gain, or even loses, by not granting your request. For example, if you would like to begin work later in the day so you can take your child to school, you might point out that working later in the day would allow you to provide coverage for your department after your co-workers have completed their shifts.

Fourth is proposing options for contingent mutual gain. A common example of this is to propose a review of your performance after some period of time, typically three to six months. If your performance meets an agreed-upon standard, then you receive a raise. This tactic lets the employer know that you are willing to prove yourself and can be especially effective for those who are just entering a profession. The fifth active-assertive tactic is proposing options for non-contingent mutual gain. This involves highlighting benefits that you bring to the organization, but which aren't directly linked to your compensation. This might include contacts you have outside of the organization. For example, if you are active in a professional or community organization, you can demonstrate your employer's commitment to the community through your continued involvement.

Reactive/Defensive Tactics

These tactics are commonly used to counteract various intimidation attempts. The first is using prolonged silence to indicate that the other party is being unreasonable. Americans, in particular, tend to be uncomfortable with silence, as discussed in Chapter 10. You can often send a powerful message that the other party's proposal is extreme or unfair by simply not immediately responding. The second is avoiding reaching premature resolution by focusing on the interests and issues involved. Sometimes the parties in a negotiation are so anxious to reach an agreement that they lose sight of what they are really trying to accomplish. The result is usually a suboptimal agreement. It may not be a terrible agreement; just not as good as they might have reached had they not rushed.

Third is persistently reiterating key points when the other party is unyielding. For years, Barbara represented employees in negotiating labor contracts. Unlike some of the others at the bargaining table, she never raised her voice or displayed any negative emotion even when the negotiators for the employer presented extreme demands or counterproposals. She would simply smile and nod, and then explain yet one more time why the union's requests should be met. In most cases, the other side would ultimately agree. She simply wore them down. The fourth tactic is calling out an opponent's intimidating behavior. If the other party is talking nonstop and not letting you present your arguments, you might say something like "Excuse me, may I explain my position?" The final reactive/defensive tactic is reframing weaknesses as potential strengths. You can reframe the weakness of not having years of experience in a particular industry as the strength of bringing in a fresh perspective.

Hopefully you will receive offers from more than one employer. When that happens it is important that you compare all aspects of the offers so as to make an informed decision. You can use the worksheet in Figure 15.3 to help you organize and compare multiple offers.

If after negotiating, the employer's final offer is still below your resistance point, you basically have two choices: either reconsider your resistance point or break off negotiations. Rethinking your minimum may be prudent, especially if you have been on the job market for some time and haven't received other offers. Be sure you consider the entire package, not just the salary. Things like retirement or 401k contributions, dental or vision insurance, tuition reimbursement, even subsidized childcare or memberships to health clubs represent tangible, valuable benefits. Especially when evaluating multiple offers, you need to take the whole package—and its worth to you now and in the near future—into account. If you opt to decline an organization's offer because you have a better one, it is still important to end the negotiation on good terms. Thank the employer for his or her time and the offer. Be genuine and honest in everything you say. You never know when you might deal with this person or this employer again.

Here we must interject a word of caution. If, despite your best efforts, you are not selected for the job, be very careful about your attitude and your actions. It is human nature to be offended and even angry if you aren't offered the job, but you need to remain professional. If you are an internal candidate and decide to seek employment elsewhere, you will still want a good reference. If you decide to stay with your present employer, you need to continue to perform well in your present position. Resist the temptation to complain to co-workers as this can get back to your superiors. Similarly, be aware of your performance and make sure you are not slacking off, coming in late, leaving early, or using more sick days. Remember the importance of maintaining the relationship with your employer.

NEGOTIATING SUPPORT FOR MOVING FORWARD IN YOUR CAREER

Perhaps like Gabe, you recognize one or more areas for improving your skills and knowledge and would like to make these improvements. As we have said before, you don't get what you don't ask for. When it is clear that additional education, whether

FIGURE 15.3   Job Offer Comparison Worksheet

	Offer #1	Offer #2
Employer		
Position/job title		
Job duties		
Hours		
Base salary		
Commission (if applicable)		
Potential bonus (range)		
Medical insurance cost and coverage		
Dental insurance cost and coverage		
Vision insurance cost and coverage		
Disability insurance cost and coverage		
Life insurance cost and coverage		
Paid vacation (number of days)		
Paid holidays (number of days)		
Tuition reimbursement		
Commute time		
Length of time before first review/salary increase		
Opportunities for advancement		
Impression of supervisor		
Impression of co-workers		
Impression of organization		
Additional benefits/advantages		
Additional costs/disadvantages		

it is an in-house development program, a certificate program, or a part- or full-time degree program, would be beneficial, your preparation begins. After you've clarified your goals, as Gabe did in determining that he wanted to manage other engineers, you need to research the experience and education gap between where you are currently and where you need to be. Look for this information in your network—both colleagues at work and those within your profession (e.g., at a professional conference). Ask people in positions that would interest you about their education and experience, and as appropriate, probe for details to get a sense of what you should do. If you are considering further education, remember that not all graduate degrees/programs are created equally, in terms of reputation, clearly, but also in terms of your own needs. For example, an increasing number of graduate programs are available online. While that sounds convenient (as well as easy on one's car and busy schedule), it takes a certain type of person to be successful in the virtual classroom. Even identical degree programs have different foci—some are more theoretical versus hands-on, some rely more heavily on online delivery, some take a more quantitative as opposed to qualitative approach, and some have a clear philosophy (e.g., social responsibility and ethics, globalism).

Once you've done your research, consider the cost to the company of your top two or three options, and more importantly, the benefits. How would your having a graduate degree help your work group, supervisor, and company? For example, will your skills enable your manager to focus on more strategic tasks, while you manage the day-to-day operations? If so, that benefit should be emphasized. Realize that even when a company has a stated education benefit, it is up to you to ask and negotiate. Gabe's company may not only believe that a graduate degree in engineering is more relevant for Gabe, but it may also be the only advanced degree they would ordinarily subsidize. Knowing this up front would allow Gabe to build a better case for the employer financing a management degree. Needless to say, thorough preparation enables you to communicate and negotiate more effectively.

NEGOTIATING EXPECTATIONS TO FACILITATE ACHIEVEMENT IN THE WORK SITUATION

So far, we have focused primarily on your professional future. As you would expect, many of the professional goals we set for ourselves cannot be achieved or maintained without the frequent negotiation of expectations with others. Think about your first job. Whether it was babysitting, lawn mowing, or working at a fast food restaurant, you had to negotiate with others. Parents often want to ensure that time spent earning money doesn't interfere with the time needed to complete required schoolwork or chores. After all, time is a finite resource. You may have negotiated with your parents and agreed to complete certain tasks or maintain a certain GPA, if they allowed you to work a certain number of hours per week. Or perhaps you negotiated for the use of a family car. You had your interests, but fulfilling them typically required negotiating with others. Even now as an adult, to be successful in your professional life, you need to be able to address the following in your personal life:

- How do I clarify roles and responsibilities with my significant other/family/friends/roommates?
- How do I manage expectations and negotiate additional support—whether within the family, the workplace, or with subcontractors (e.g., housekeepers)—especially when the demands for my time and attention shift?
- How do I establish a contract with myself to ensure that I make choices among my work and nonwork domains that are consistent with my values?

CLARIFYING ROLES AND RESPONSIBILITIES

Let's catch up with Gabe and Natalie. At the conclusion of the scenario, you might have thought of several questions for Gabe and Natalie to consider:

- Should they start their family? If so, will Natalie go back to work after her maternity leave expires?
- Should Gabe go back to school? Full time or part time?
- Can they do both (start a family and have Gabe go back to school)?
- Can they afford to live on one income? What about no income?
- Can they take a loan? Should they take a loan?

As with any negotiation, the parties should begin by clarifying their goals and interests. In this case, the stakes are quite high. Having a child, quitting a job, and starting a graduate program are all significant decisions with significant financial, emotional, and logistical implications. Making these decisions is difficult enough; however, in this case, at least Gabe and Natalie have the luxury of choice. That is not always the case.

Imagine for a moment that despite efforts to hold off having children, Natalie becomes pregnant. Imagine further that news of her pregnancy comes after Gabe quits his job and goes to school full time. We are not suggesting that all issues or concerns can be thought of, discussed, and resolved in advance. However, it is likely that you know people whose decisions may have been made for them because of poor planning or communication.

As you learned in Chapter 9, there are several challenges that are unique to negotiations with loved ones. First is the history with this person. Over time, patterns of communication and decisions form and consciously or subconsciously provide the foundation for current and future interactions. For example, if the husband tends to be domineering and the wife tends to be meek, the parties will approach a negotiation—what to buy, where to eat, whom to hire to babysit—in a manner similar to prior negotiations, that is, the husband emphatically expresses his wishes and the wife acquiesces. These patterns create inertia and, combined with uncommunicated expectations, will dictate an outcome that might not optimize or even recognize the interests of both parties. Such an interaction might sound like:

WIFE: I really like this dinette set. It reminds me of the one we had when I was growing up.

HUSBAND: Are you kidding? Look at the price tag!

WIFE: Our old set is falling apart and we need to replace it. This one is really nice.

HUSBAND: No way! I'm not paying for that!

WIFE: I suppose we can wait a bit. . . .

In fact, sometimes these patterns can run so deep that a conversation such as the one above doesn't even take place. The wife "knows" that her husband will refuse her request so she chooses not to ask and face another rejection.

In addition to the history between loved ones, there is the projected future. While the nature of the relationship suggests the importance of approaching negotiations among loved ones integratively, Thompson notes that loved ones may make suboptimized decisions—sometimes referred to as "satisficing"—because it is more important to get along (i.e., reduce or resolve the conflict and negative emotions therein) than to find an optimal solution that achieves the interests of both parties.[22] Unfortunately, this pattern of compromising or accepting a "good enough" outcome can result in post-decision rationalization ("I guess it made sense to pass on that opportunity") or even resentment. It is possible that the thought of living for many years with the decision reached can cause one to dig his or her heels more deeply into a particular position.

Negotiation expert Leigh Thompson explains that when there is conflict between loved ones, it is possible that their perceptions of what is happening are not in sync, as illustrated in Table 15.3.[23] A conflict seen by one party may not be perceived by the other party. If one partner does something that creates a conflict, for example, refuses to pay her share of a monthly expense, unless and until the other partner becomes aware of this, the conflict is hidden. When all is well and conflicts are neither perceived nor real, there is harmony. However, if you determine that a conflict is real, you have to decide how you will respond to it. Psychologist Carol Rusbult suggests four possible reactions: exit (leave the relationship), loyalty (stay with and tolerate the partner), neglect (avoid conflict), and voice (actively engage in discussion regarding the conflict and preferences for resolving it).[24] Needless to say, you are not reading this textbook to obtain relationship advice. Our point is that everyone has choices when dealing with conflict with a significant other and it is best if you evaluate your alternatives and decide how you will approach the conflict in advance.

TABLE 15.3	Perceptions of Conflict	
	Actual conflict	**No actual conflict**
Perceived conflict	Real conflict	False conflict
No perceived conflict	Latent conflict	Harmony

MANAGING EXPECTATIONS AND NEGOTIATING ADDITIONAL SUPPORT AMIDST CHANGES

You often hear phrases like, "I don't have time to exercise (or meditate or attend religious services, etc.)." The truth is we all have 168 hours a week. How we choose to spend those hours is just that—our choice. Some choices are made for us, as in the time we are expected to be at work or in class, while other time slots are left for us to choose. Having a spouse or children certainly constrains those choices further, although it still comes down to choice. How we choose is or should be a function of our values and priorities, which change over time. For the person who says that he doesn't have the time, the reality is that he has already chosen to allocate his discretionary time to other pursuits or activities, whether it is watching TV, playing tennis, reading, or participating in social activities. The important thing to remember is that your choices with your time should reflect your values. This alignment (or lack thereof) will have significant consequences for your satisfaction at work, home, and even with yourself. Exercise 15.8 gives you an opportunity to consider your alignment and possible adjustments where necessary.

What if you are aligned and then circumstances change? Suppose Gabe decides to work on his MBA part-time while maintaining his full-time employment? Clearly, the time required in the classroom and outside (for assignments and group work) has to come from somewhere. Does he sacrifice his weekend vacations with Natalie? Does he reduce the time he spends in the gym? Does he abandon his buddies and their occasional happy hour after work engagements? Does he function on less sleep? Does he reduce the time he spends helping to keep their home clean and things in good working order?

As you can see, all of the options represent a change from Gabe's current way of operating and a trade-off among competing choices. Many of the options require trade-offs and, more specifically, communication and negotiation between Gabe and one or more parties. To avoid or delay having these interactions would be to invite conflict and strain in the relationship. Let us illustrate.

Until now, Gabe and Natalie have an enjoyable and somewhat predictable lifestyle. They can expect to have evenings and weekends together, dinners out, occasional short trips, and an annual vacation. Once Gabe starts taking two classes per week, the interactions between Gabe and Natalie will necessarily change. Typically, and especially in a relationship of some length, the tendency would be to assume that the other partner understands and supports the changes. After all, it was common goals and values that brought the partners together. However, change is uncomfortable for most, and this situation is no different.

How should Gabe handle this situation? First, it would be best not to wait until classes begin to have a discussion with Natalie about the potential impact of working toward his MBA part time. In an effort to manage expectations, Gabe should start the conversation early, perhaps once he receives word from the school that his application has been accepted. Better yet, the conversations should begin when he starts thinking about pursuing a graduate degree. Knowing how the change might affect the parties individually and collectively will prepare them for what will change and how. Communicating and negotiating expectations early and often can help prevent conflict and strife in the relationship. The conversation might sound something like this:

GABE: Natalie, I know that we talked about the benefits of getting my MBA. But I am concerned about how much time I will have to devote to the program to be successful . . . and how that time will affect some of the things that we like to do together.

NATALIE: Like what?

GABE: Well, obviously, during the evenings I have class, we won't be able to go out to dinner together, nor will I be able to eat with you at home.

NATALIE: I expected that.

GABE: There may also be evenings and weekends where I am studying alone or with my work group.

NATALIE: Hmmm . . . weekends too? All weekends? I have a feeling I am going to be alone a lot, and I don't like it.

GABE: I don't like it either. I love you and want to be with you. But I also know that this program will not last forever. We'll have some tough periods, but we'll also make sure to continue our annual week-long all-inclusive vacation. That's really important to me.

NATALIE: So are you not going to be able to do the grocery shopping or vacuum the house?

GABE: I hadn't thought about that. Let's look at this more carefully. It's not fair that you do more housework and I do less. Would you mind asking your friends for a recommendation for a house cleaner? Maybe we can afford to do this twice a month.

NATALIE: Thanks for understanding, sweetie. I don't think we can afford NOT to do this. I don't want to be angry at you for not doing your share, but I don't want to do it either.

Maybe this conversation sounds too civil to be realistic. Think about it this way. When you know what to expect—even if it is bad news—it is easier to handle than when things happen without warning. Using a simple example, imagine that you order a meal at a restaurant. It is at least thirty minutes since you've ordered, your drink has been empty for fifteen minutes, and you are feeling ignored and uncared for. When the server finally brings your food, you think to yourself, ". . . hmmmm, I guess he won't be getting a big tip." Now imagine that you order your meal, and after ten minutes, the server tops off your drink and informs you that things are backed up a bit in the kitchen because two employees called in sick. Five minutes later, he stops by again, apologizes for the delay, and brings more bread. He comes back ten minutes later and tells you that the chef is working on your meal right now, and it should be ready in a few more minutes. Four and half minutes later, he delivers your meal and thanks you for your patience. Now how do you feel about his service and potential tip? It is the same thirty minutes, but an entirely different experience. Therein lies the benefit of managing expectations.

Let's assume that Gabe has entered the MBA program at a nearby university. Classes start at 6:00 p.m., and after the first few weeks of attending two classes per week, Gabe's boss seems less accommodating. Most days, Gabe leaves when his work is done . . . 5 p.m., 6 p.m., even 8:00 p.m. on occasion. But on Tuesdays and Thursdays, Gabe must leave by 4:45 p.m. in order to get to class on time amidst rush-hour traffic, and leaving late means driving on more congested roads and getting to class twenty or more minutes late. Last week, he was over an hour late and was lost during most of his finance class.

Points to Ponder

1. How should Gabe handle this situation?
2. Was there anything Gabe could have done to prevent this?
3. Using the previous dialog between Gabe and Natalie as a template, what conversation Gabe should have had with his boss?

CONTRACTING WITH YOURSELF

We have discussed the key dimensions of negotiating your future, focusing on finding the ideal work situation, and managing expectations and relationships that support excelling in your ideal work situation. As discussed, it is important to manage and negotiate expectations with those in your work and nonwork realms to ensure a smoother journey into your future. However, there remains the issue of you. How do you ensure that you stay focused, balanced, and true to your values while you pursue the path into your future? Wouldn't we all like to know?

A visit to your local bookstore will reveal a plethora of self-help books. However, there are a few thoughts we want to leave you with:

- Realize that you can decide what you want to do. As we said earlier in the chapter, too many people follow the path of least resistance—a path that may have been inconsistent with who you are or want to be from the outset.
- Realize that you are responsible for setting and navigating your path. Of course, there are others who can help you, such as parents, teachers, career counselors, bosses, and significant others. Remember, however, you don't get what you don't ask for, and you get more of what you want when you research and prepare fully for conversations or negotiations with these potential goal facilitators.
- Frequently engage in self-reflection. What am I good at? How does this add value to my organizations and relationships? What should I improve, and in what ways will these improvements pay off professionally and personally?
- Once you understand what you want, set appropriate goals and contract with yourself (and loved ones) for achieving those goals. You might need to manage expectations in the process, remembering that change can bring about conflicts, which put stress on your relationships.
- When you fall off your path, and most will, don't get discouraged. Most successful people have failed, and failed more than once on their roads to success. Remember the axiom, "If you don't fail, you're not trying hard enough"? Promise yourself that you will accept failure as a means for growth and necessary adjustments on your path. Success is sweeter and more appreciated when you had to overcome challenges along the way.

Summary

The days of your organization being responsible for your career—from hiring after graduation until retirement—are long gone. You are responsible for negotiating your career—and all the work situations that entails, as well as the relationships within the work and nonwork domains that facilitate a successful and fulfilling career. Furthermore, you need to continually and proactively identify and pursue your ideal work situation via negotiations with your employer, colleagues, and loved ones.

Summary: The Big Picture

The ideal work situation	Because work occupies a significant amount of time for most people, it is important that you take time to find or create employment that is congruent with your wants, needs, and strengths.
Marketing yourself	Whether you are seeking a job with a new employer or a different position with your current employer you need to make efforts to make your skills, capabilities, and desires known, as opposed to assuming your work and wishes will speak for themselves.
Preparing for the interview	In addition to researching the company and developing and rehearsing answers to likely questions, you need prepare to negotiate a job offer. The better your interview, the stronger your position in the subsequent negotiation.
Evaluating and negotiating the job offer	Based on your preparation and goals, you may choose a combination of active/assertive or reactive/defensive tactics.
Negotiating support for career moves	Research and preparation can help you identify benefits to communicate to your employer in order to gain necessary support when you are considering changing jobs or responsibilities.
Negotiating expectations	It is important to clarify roles and responsibilities, manage others' expectations, and negotiate additional support when unexpected or planned changes arise. This should be done early and often.
Contracting with yourself	Taking steps to stay true to yourself and your values in pursuing a balanced, fulfilling life.

Key Terms and Concepts

Active/assertive tactics. Approaches used in a negotiation that are direct, tactful, and fair while taking into account the rights and feelings of others.

Reactive/defensive tactics. Approaches commonly used in a negotiation used to counteract various intimidation attempts.

Discussion Questions

1. Discuss the importance of identifying your ideal work situation and taking steps to find or create it.
2. Develop a plan for marketing yourself on the external job market.
3. Develop a plan for marketing yourself for a different/higher-level job with your current employer.
4. Discuss three examples of how managing expectations can be used to prevent conflicts among work and nonwork relationships.
5. Compare and contrast the options for resolving conflicts that arise out of changes in your personal or professional responsibilities.
6. Discuss the challenges particular to negotiating with loved ones when pursuing professional goals.

Ethical Dilemma: Should You Apply?

You are in your last semester of college and have been looking for a job. You have registered with the placement office and posted your resume online, but the jobs that are available leave a bit to be desired. In one of your classes you overhear a classmate, Bernardo, talking about an interview he had last week. Bernardo said that he really wanted the job but didn't think his interview went particularly well. He is currently waiting to hear back from the employer. As Bernardo was describing the position, you thought it sounded very interesting, but you wondered if it would be right for you to pursue the position since Bernardo had found it first.

Questions

1. Should you apply for the job? Should you wait until Bernardo hears from the employer?
2. Do you have any obligation to tell Bernardo if you apply for the job?
3. If you interview for the job, how would you respond if asked how you heard about the opening?

Endnotes

1. Saks, A. M., and B. E. Ashforth. "Is Job Search Related to Employment Quality? It All Depends on the Fit." *Journal of Applied Psychology* 87(4) (2002): 646–654.
2. Wrzesniewski, A., J. M. Berg, and J. E. Dutton. "Turn the Job You Have Into the Job You Want." *Harvard Business Review* (June 2010): 114–117.
3. Plante, T. G. "How to Find a First Job in Professional Psychology: Ten Principles for Finding Employment for Psychology Interns and Postdoctoral Fellows." *Professional Psychology: Research and Practice* 29(5) ((1998): 508–511.
4. McCorkle, D. E., J. F. Alexander, J. Reardon, and N. D. Kling. "Developing Self-Marketing Skills: Are Marketing Students Prepared for the Job Search?" *Journal of Marketing Education* 25(3) (2003): 196–207.
5. *Ibid*.
6. Jackman, J. M. "Fear of Feedback." *Harvard Business Review* (November 2003): 54–63.
7. Barron, L. A. "Ask and You Shall Receive? Gender Differences in Negotiators' Beliefs about Requests for a Higher Salary." *Human Relations* 56(6) (2003): 635–662.
8. Tay, C., S. Ang, and L. Van Dyne. "Personality, Biographical Characteristics, and Job Interview Success: A Longitudinal Study of the Mediating Effects of Interviewing Self-Efficacy and the Moderating Effects of Internal Locus of Causality." *Journal of Applied Psychology* 91(2) (2006): 446–454.
9. McCorkle, D. E., J. F. Alexander, J. Reardon, and N. D. Kling. "Developing Self-Marketing Skills: Are Marketing Students Prepared for the Job Search?" *Journal of Marketing Education* 25(3) (2003): 196–207.
10. Kanfer, R., C. R. Wanberg, and T. M. Kantrowitz. "Job Search and Employment: A Personality-Motivational Analysis and Meta-Analytic Review." *Journal of Applied Psychology* 86(5) (2001): 837–855.
11. Higgins, C. A., and T. A. Judge. "The Effect of Applicant Influence Tactics on Recruiter Perceptions of Fit and Hiring Recommendations: A Field Study." *Journal of Applied Psychology* 89(4) (2004): 622–632.
12. For more information on how to present yourself in an interview, check with a career services office or the following detailed and helpful website from Washington State University (http://amdt.wsu.edu/research/dti/index.htm); it contains clothing examples and comments from people in industry.

13. Stevens, C. K., and A. L. Kristof. "Making the right impression: A field study of applicant impression management during job interviews." *Journal of Applied Psychology* 80 (1995): 587–606.

14. *Ibid*.

15. Higgins, C. A., and T. A. Judge. "The Effect of Applicant Influence Tactics on Recruiter Perceptions of Fit and Hiring Recommendations: A Field Study." *Journal of Applied Psychology* 89(4) (2004): 622–632.

16. Steffy, B. D., K. N. Shaw, and A. W. Noe. "Antecedents and Consequences of Job Search Behaviors." *Journal of Vocational Behavior* 35 (1989): 254–269.

17. Turnasella, T. *The Salary Trap, Compensation and Benefits Review*, Nov/Dec. 1999, pp 27–30.

18. Babcock, L., and S. Laschever. *Women Don't Ask: Negotiation and the Gender Divide*. Princeton, NJ: Princeton University Press, 2003.

19. Gerhart, B., and S. Rynes. "Determinants and Consequences of Salary Negotiations by Graduating Male and Female MBAs." *Journal of Applied Psychology* 76 (1991): 256–262.

20. Sullivan, S. E. "The Changing Nature of Careers: A Review and Research Agenda." *Journal of Management* 25(3) (1999): 457–484.

21. See for example: Gist, M. E., A. B. Bavetta, and C. K. Stevens. "Transfer Training Method: Its Influence on Skill Generalization, Skill Repetition, and Performance Level." *Personnel Psychology* 43 (1990): 501–523; Gist, M. E., C. K. Stevens, and A. G. Bavetta. "Effects of Self-efficacy and Post-Training Intervention on the Acquisition and Maintenance of Complex Interpersonal Skills." *Personnel Psychology* 44 (1991): 837–861; and Stevens, C. K., A. G. Bavetta, and M. E. Gist. "Gender Differences in the Acquisition of Salary Negotiation Skills: The Role of Goals, Self-Efficacy, and Perceived Control." *Journal of Applied Psychology* 78(5) (1993): 723–735.

22. Thompson, L. *The Truth about Negotiations*. Upper Saddle River, NJ: Pearson Education Inc, 2008.

23. *Ibid*.

24. Drigotas, S. M., Whiteney G. A., and Rusbult, C. E. "On the peculiarities of loyalty: A diary study of responses to dissatisfaction in everyday life." *Personality and Social Psychology Bulletin* 21 (1995): 596–609.

Exercise 15.1 Blue-Sky/Ideal Job

If you could craft your ideal job, what would it look like? How would you describe the job to others such as colleagues, family, or friends? Be specific about the tasks in which you would be involved, the people with whom you would interact, the nature of the work (long- versus. short-term projects, individual versus team work, internal versus external customers, single versus multiple projects), your work schedule, travel requirements, reporting relationships, and the values of the organization. Use the space below to describe the job of your dreams.

Exercise 15.2   Preparing Your Resume and Cover Letter

For this exercise, you will be creating a resume and cover letter targeted toward a job for which you would like to apply. You may have one that you can edit, or you may be starting from scratch. Use a style (chronological or functional) that is most appropriate for you (see Appendix B for more information).

Next you will draft a targeted cover letter (see Appendix B for more information about what to include).

When you have drafted your resume and cover letter, identify at least three people to critique it. At least one of these people should be working in the field you are targeting. Provide each person with a copy of your resume and cover letter and ask for his or her input. Be prepared to discuss your resume and cover letter and the input you received in class.

Exercise 15.3 Researching Prospective Employers

This exercise provides an opportunity to practice researching a prospective employer. Your professor will explain how the employers will be assigned. You will then find out as much as you can about the organization you are assigned. Use all sources available (the Internet, annual reports, people you know who are associated with the organization) to complete the Prospective Employer Worksheet. Be sure to list your sources of information.

Prospective Employer Worksheet

Organization name: _____

Products/services: _____

_____

Location(s): _____

_____

Number of employees: _____

Public/private (if public, include stock performance): _____

_____

Company history: _____

_____

_____

_____

Organizational structure: _____

_____

_____

Compensation policy: _____

_____

News items (big contracts, scandals, etc.): _____

_____

_____

Contacts:

Name	Title/Department	Phone	Email	Notes

Sources for information:

_____

_____

_____

_____

Exercise 15.4   Employment Negotiations: Interests, Issues, Opening Demands, Target and Resistance Points

In this exercise you will identify interests and issues and develop opening demands and target and resistance points for an employment negotiation.

Using the Employment Negotiation Worksheet, identify your interests, that is, what you hope to accomplish in the negotiation, and what is most important to you in a job. Is it an opportunity for advancement or to gain a particular type of experience? Is it flexibility, job security, the compensation package, geographic location, or something else? Looking at the list of interests, prioritize them by assigning values (1 is the most important while 7 is the least important).

Next identify the issues (the specific items that you would like to negotiate) and your opening demands and target and resistance points for each. Remember the resistance point is the point at which you would break off negotiations.

Employment Negotiation Worksheet

Priority	Interests

Issue	Opening Demand	Target	Resistance

Exercise 15.5   Determining Your Worth

For this exercise you will research your worth in the job market for a position you would like to have. In selecting a job, chose one for which you are currently qualified or will be qualified for upon graduation. Pay special attention to the job description to ensure it is a realistic job for you.

Pick two diverse geographic locations for comparison. If you are from a relatively small town one could be your hometown and the other a major metropolitan area. Conversely, if you are from a large city you could use that and another smaller city from a different part of the country.

Use multiple sources and be sure to cite them.

Job Title/ Description	Location 1	Location 2
Salary		
Benefits		
Cost of living		
Source		
Salary		
Benefits		
Cost of living		
Source		
Salary		
Benefits		
Cost of living		
Source		
Salary		
Benefits		
Cost of living		
Source		

Exercise 15.6   Practicing Your Interview Skills

This exercise consists of two rounds. In one round, you will be interviewing for a job that you would like to have. In the other round, you will be playing the role of the employer and interviewing another student.

First, you must obtain a job description for a job that you would like to have. If you completed Exercise 15.3, the job should be for that employer. Your instructor will provide instructions for posting your job description for the other students in the class to review. Each student then selects a job description for which she or he would like to portray the employer. For each of the two roles you will be playing, you need to research the position, the industry, and the organization in preparation for the role plays. You should also prepare a list of questions about the position/organization to ask at the end of the interview. Once student dyads for each round are determined, you will then supply your interviewer with a copy of your resume, cover letter, and job description. Your professor will also provide instructions for completing the interview.

Exercise 15.7 Negotiating a Job Offer

This exercise consists of two rounds. In one round, you will be negotiating an offer for a job that you would like to have. In the other round, you will be playing the role of the employer for another student.

If you completed Exercise 15.6, continue with the information you already have. If not, you must find a job description for a job that you would like to have. Your instructor will provide instructions for posting your job description for the other students in the class to review. Each student then selects a job description for which she or he would like to portray the employer. For each of the two roles you will be playing you need to research the position, the industry, and the organization in preparation for the role plays. Once student dyads for each round are determined, you should prepare questions for both your role as a prospective employee and your role as an employer.

Exercise 15.8   Check Your Alignment

When you are aligned, you know what you value and behave in accordance with those values. One way to do this is to compare your values with how you spend your time.

First, imagine you have $100 to allocate among domain buckets. Obviously, there are no right answers; however, the total across the six columns must not exceed $100.

Family (immediate—spouse, children, parents and extended—cousins, uncles, aunts, grandchildren, grandparents)	Friends	Work (current and future)	Community (neighborhood, nonprofit organization)	Religious/ Spiritual	Self (exercise, diet, education, self- development)	
$	$	$	$	$	$	Total: $100

Next, take a look at a recent but typical (i.e., non-vacation) week in your calendar. Looking at your work schedule and other appointments/activities, estimate the number of hours (out of 168) that you spent in each of the following activities:

Activity	Approximate Hours/Week	Activity	Approximate Hours/Week
Sleeping		Running errands (include travel time)	
Working		Watching TV	
Commuting		Spending time with family	
Eating (include cooking/prep time if applicable)		Spending time with friends	
Exercising or other physical activity		Partaking in individual or group religious activities	
Hygiene-related activities		Engaging in community activities	
Reading (news, magazines, books, Internet)		Other	
School-related activities		Other	

Now compare the percentage of time you spend doing the following activities activities (divide total hours spent on an activity per week by 168) with the value you place on the various buckets or domains of your life.

1. Where are the percentages aligned?

_____

_____

2. Where could they be adjusted?

_____

_____

3. What impact would making these adjustments have on you and others in your life?

_____

_____

4. What two or three steps could you take to begin making these adjustments?

_____

_____

Exercise 15.9   Aren't I Management Material?

Maurice was a hospitality major who worked as a server in an upscale hotel restaurant for several years while in college. During that time, he was a dedicated employee who could always be counted on to fill in when others called in sick. Everyone in the management team liked him and respected his work ethic and dedication except for Doug, the food and beverage director. When Maurice graduated from college he applied for an opening for assistant manager with his current employer. He passed all the required employment tests for that position, but Doug insisted that he spend time as a trainer. Maurice was not pleased with this since he had been responsible for training new servers for some time, even though he didn't officially have the title of trainer. He was angry and believed this was just Doug's way of keeping him from getting the job as assistant manager.

1. While we don't know what happened in Maurice's initial interview (where he landed the job as server), what are some things Maurice could have done to effectively signal his intentions and market himself within the company?

   _____

   _____

   _____

   _____

   _____

   _____

   _____

   _____

2. What should Maurice have done or said when Doug insisted he spend time as a trainer? Why? How would this have impacted the outcome?

   _____

   _____

   _____

   _____

   _____

   _____

   _____

   _____

3. What would you advise Maurice to do? Explain.

   _____

   _____

   _____

   _____

   _____

   _____

   _____

Exercise 15.10 Negotiating Your Mid-Career: The Case of João Oliveira[†]

João Oliveira was torn. A senior manager at Consumer Products Firm (CPF), a global manufacturer, Oliveira had been running CPF's largest factory in Portugal for the last five years. Now he had been offered a post as manufacturing director at CPF in Argentina, an upward promotion and in a far bigger market. It was a rare opportunity, one that would allow Oliveira to develop both his global skills and his general management potential.

For the bulk of his career, the forty-six-year-old Oliveira had worked for CPF in Portugal. A native of Lisbon, he had trained as an engineer at the top national university. After spending three years as a junior engineer with a local industrial firm, he had been recruited to join CPF at the age of twenty-five.

Oliveira worked very hard running the factory. For the bulk of the last five years, he had been putting in sixty-five-hour weeks. His wife, who had given up a career in law to bear and care for their two children, now nine and five, had complained more and more bitterly about Oliveira being "married" to his job. Finally, two years before, the couple had divorced. Now single, Oliveira lived alone in a small apartment not far from his ex-wife and children. The divorce had been a painful wake-up call; Oliveira described his son and daughter as the two most important things in his life, and made a point of seeing them frequently.

Oliveira knew that for the time being he had gone as far as he could in the CPF hierarchy in Portugal. To become director of manufacturing or country general manager it was clear he would have to work outside the country first. To date, other than spending a semester of university in England and serving on a couple of global manufacturing project teams, he had never done so. It was obvious that the offer to go to Argentina was, in part, an invitation to remedy this deficiency. And Oliveira knew that, at forty-six, he was unlikely to receive another such offer from CPF, most of whose international executives had taken their first expatriate assignments when they were ten to fifteen years younger.

Oliveira had heard of the offer just before coming on a two-week executive development course at a global business school. He would have to decide immediately upon his return whether or not to take the job. On the fourth day of the course, the topic was "developing talent globally." The professor had emphasized something he called the "mobility principle": "You cannot learn as much staying in one place as you can by moving around."

Oliveira was committed to developing himself, and had ambitions to rise further within CPF. He also felt keenly the pain of the divorce and a strong attachment to his children. As he pondered his options, he wished that somehow the decision could be made for him.

Questions

1. What are Oliveira's options?
2. What are the pros and cons of each option?
3. How should he decide?
4. With whom should he discuss his options?
5. Are there ways to prioritize his needs and wants when evaluating the options? Explain.
6. If you were Oliveira, what would you do and why?

[†]This case (©2006) was prepared by Professor Maury Peiperl and is used with permission from IMD International.

APPENDIX A

Negotiating with Organized Labor

Some employees may find themselves involved in negotiations on behalf of their employer when other employees are represented by a labor union. We limit our coverage of this topic to an overview for several reasons. First, relatively few people are involved in this type of negotiation due to the overall decline in unionization in the United States. The employers who do negotiate with unions tend to be clustered by industry and to some extent geographically. For example, employers in the automotive industry are still typically unionized, but the office furniture industry is predominately nonunion. Many of the employees in the hospitality industry are unionized in big cities such as Las Vegas, New York, and Atlantic City, but in smaller markets employees are usually nonunion. Similarly, there are more unions in the north and east than in the south and west. Even if your employer is unionized, almost all labor contract negotiations involve the use of bargaining teams, and employers often hire a labor attorney to serve as the chief negotiator. Thus, even if you were asked to serve on your employer's bargaining team, you would almost certainly be working under the direction of the chief negotiator.

Whenever there is a union involved, negotiations are more complex in part because both parties must abide by the requirements of the **National Labor Relations Act*** **(NLRA)** as amended if you are in the private sector, or other state and federal laws if you are in the public sector. The NLRA identifies three categories or subjects of bargaining: mandatory, prohibited, and permissive. The mandatory subjects of bargaining are just that, *mandatory*, and include wages, hours, and terms and conditions of employment. You must negotiate these subjects in good faith with the union (and they with you) or risk being charged with an **unfair labor practice (ULP)**. The courts have generally interpreted "wages, hours, and conditions of employment" very broadly. Thus, employers have no choice but to negotiate things such as insurance, vacation, tuition reimbursement, employer-required uniforms or safety equipment, breaks, training, overtime requirements, and layoff and recall policies. The courts have even gone so far as to rule that the price of food in a company-subsidized vending machine is a mandatory subject of bargaining because it provides an economic benefit to the employees.

The prohibited subjects are any topics that would be illegal under the NLRA or any other statute. For example, an employer and a union could not legally agree that women performing the same job as men should be paid less simply because they are female, as this would be illegal under the Equal Pay Act of 1963** and Title VII of the Civil Rights Act of 1964.*** The permissive subjects are those that are neither mandatory nor illegal, such as union representation on the board of directors. Employers may agree to negotiate such issues, but are not required to do so. There are two different general situations when an employer has to negotiate with a union: when they are negotiating a complete labor contract and when they are attempting to resolve grievances that arise under that contract. We discuss them in that sequence.

NEGOTIATING A LABOR CONTRACT: THE PROCESS

Negotiating a labor contract is generally very involved, and unfortunately, too often adversarial. Each side selects a group of people to serve as the bargaining team. It is generally best if the team members possess a variety of skills and backgrounds. There is almost always an accountant or finance person on the team to cost out the various contract proposals. Conversely, CEOs virtually never participate. This allows the management team an escape hatch if the union demands an immediate answer to a proposal.

---

*For more on the National Labor Relations Act see http://www.nlrb.gov/nlrb/legal/manuals/rules/act.pdf
**For more on the Equal Pay Act see http://www.eeoc.gov/policy/epa.html
***For more on Title VII see http://www.eeoc.gov/policy/vii.html

The management team simply replies they need to check with top management before they can respond. From the union perspective, this occurs automatically since union members have to vote to ratify the final contract. Once the bargaining team is formed, they begin preparing for the negotiation. This is a critical step in the negotiation process, and when done well, often takes months.

The bargaining team begins by seeking input from functional departments and reviewing the existing contract and previous grievances to identify areas where there have been problems or questions in the past to aid in the development of contract language the team thinks will address the issues. The team also gathers information on pay and benefits, along with workforce demographics so they can calculate the costs of various proposals. This prepares them to quickly project the cost of various union proposals and give a reasoned and prompt response. For example, the cost of expanding a tuition reimbursement program to cover books will be affected by how many employees participate in the current program. If a relatively small number of employees participate, the issue may be considered fairly inexpensive to agree on. On the other hand, agreeing to a union demand to fully fund top-of-the-line health care insurance for all employees could be cost prohibitive. Of course what is affordable or not depends on the organization's financial health and how many employees are involved. It is much easier for an employer to be generous when it is very profitable than when it is barely breaking even. When profits are held constant, it is easier for a company to be generous when it has fewer employees. It is the organizational equivalent of buying holiday gifts for your children. If the parents are wealthy and only have one child, they will typically spend more on that child than parents of more modest means would spend on each of their six children.

To fully assess the organization's financial condition, the bargaining team must also gather information on sales projections to help provide assurance that the organization's financial situation will not deteriorate over the life of the contract. Similarly, they need to assess the impact of any pending legislation that might affect the organization negatively. In some industries (e.g., hospitality and food service) changes in the minimum wage can have dramatic effects on a company's bottom line, which could have a large impact on contract negotiations. Bargaining teams typically use computer software to aid in calculating and projecting costs. Even a relatively simple spreadsheet can make the process of evaluating proposals quite straightforward.

As with any negotiation, the bargaining team must identify the interests and issues, opening demands, and target and resistance points for each issue. Asking questions aids in this process. For example, how important is it to control costs? Do we need more flexibility in terms of work rules? Is it important to encourage employees to gain new skills? The bargaining team should also research industry and community data to identify trends in settlements. What is the average pay increase? Are other employers providing more or less in terms of benefits? The bargaining team should also assess the union's position. What are the union's likely interests, issues, and probable demands? How strong is worker support for the union? Does the union have the ability to stage a strike if the negotiations break down? While the union typically presents their opening demands first, management needs to give careful consideration before providing their response to the union's demands because this often sets the tone for the rest of the negotiations. If the initial offers of both parties are extreme, there is an increased likelihood that the negotiations will be both protracted and contentious.

While both labor and management generally want to successfully negotiate a new agreement, there is always the chance that negotiations will break down and the workers will strike. Management must prepare for that possibility by identifying their BATNA. Depending on the nature of the business there are several common alternatives. If it is a manufacturing facility that produces nonperishable goods, they might produce additional products before the current contract expires to build inventory. If it is a multi-plant operation and there is another plant that is not covered by the same labor contract, they may be able to shift some of the production to the other plant. In some cases, the employer may be able to continue operations with management and nonunion employees or even replacement workers. As always, the better your alternatives, the stronger your position at the bargaining table.

Once negotiations begin, both sides have a legal obligation to bargain in good faith. This does not mean that either side must agree to any demand from the other party or make any concessions. It simply means that the parties must meet and confer at reasonable times in reasonable locations with an open mind and the intent of reaching an agreement. This is a very vague requirement and one that has led to the filing of many ULP charges alleging that the other party is not bargaining in good faith. Sometimes one of the parties will even file a ULP complaint as a scare tactic in the negotiation. Such moves are common in distributive bargaining in an attempt to win the negotiation. Research has shown that negotiators who are representing others assume that their constituents want them to behave competitively,[1,2,3] which helps explain the historically adversarial relationship between labor and management. From an integrative bargaining perspective, these hardball tactics more often than not harm the negotiation process by putting the other party on the defensive and creating a climate of distrust, which reduces the sharing of information. Thus, they should be avoided.

Typically the parties begin with small issues and work their way up to the larger ones. By getting early agreement on small issues they set a tone of cooperation for the rest of the negotiation. These issues often involve changes to the existing contract language to clarify or correct one thing or another without making any substantive changes in the contract. As they gain agreement on the easy issues, the parties proceed to increasingly larger and more difficult ones. The last issues to be negotiated are usually wages and benefits. Because there can be large amounts of money involved in issues related to wages and benefits, negotiating these issues is usually the most difficult. Often there are trade-offs involved. For example, the employer may agree to contribute more to the employees' health insurance if the union agrees to a smaller wage increase. While these issues are more difficult, as time goes on there is also more pressure to reach an agreement, increasing cooperative behavior and the likelihood of agreement.[4]

As the parties agree on each issue they "Tentatively Agree" or "TA" it, with representatives of each side initialing each change in the contract. This process continues until the parties have tentative agreement on all issues. When that happens, the parties formally announce they have reached tentative agreement on the contract. The union then conducts a ratification vote where the union members vote to accept or reject the proposed contract. If a majority of the voting members vote to accept the contract, it is ratified. In most organizations the tentative agreement must also be approved by a vote of the organization's board of directors. Once everything is finalized, the contract negotiation is officially complete.

BUT WHAT IF THERE IS NO AGREEMENT?

Although both labor and management have a legal obligation to negotiate in good faith over the mandatory subjects of bargaining, there are times when the parties come to impasse. When this happens, each side has "economic weapons" they may opt to use to try to force the issue. In the private sector, the most common is for the union to stage a **strike** against the employer.[†] The reasoning behind a strike is that it will impede, if not prevent, the employer from continuing its business operations causing economic harm, which theoretically will cause the employer's team to give more at the bargaining table. With one notable exception, strikes today typically don't have this result. A 1997 strike by the Teamsters against the United Parcel Service (UPS) proved successful for the union in converting 10,000 jobs from part time to full time and maintaining union control over the employees' pension fund.[5] The reality is if the employer is effective in planning for the negotiation, its team will have already considered the possibility of a strike and made contingency plans. From the employer's perspective, it becomes a matter of implementing the team's BATNA. The better the BATNA, the more likely the employer will be able to endure a strike.

[†]In the public sector it is generally illegal for employees to strike

While unions sometimes want everyone to believe that they will strike indefinitely, that seldom happens. When workers are on strike they lose their wages and benefits, and are not eligible for unemployment compensation. Even when the union has a "strike fund" to compensate striking workers, the payments are usually a small fraction of what the workers would have otherwise earned. In the UPS strike, the weekly strike benefits paid to striking union members was $55, and even that required financial support from the AFL-CIO.[6] Unfortunately for the workers, they still have bills to pay and most do not have large sums of money to tide them over. Some employers, seeking to break the union, take advantage of this by letting a strike continue. Over time the striking workers, needing an income, either find other employment or opt to cross the picket line and return to work. When the support for the union decreases to a minority level, the employer requests a decertification election under the NLRA. If a majority of the workers vote against the union, the employer becomes nonunion.

Another economic weapon sometimes used by unions is "**working-to-the-rules**." When this happens the workers continue to do their jobs, but they strictly follow all work rules and refuse to do anything that is not required. The net effect of this is slowing down operations so as to have a negative effect on the employer. This tactic has been used successfully in the airline industry, where slowing down operations can have a significant impact on air travel industry-wide. Unions may also encourage the members of other unions to honor their picket lines, again to put pressure on the employers by making it more difficult for them to continue operations. Finally, unions may try to involve the public by getting consumers to boycott the employer's products. This tactic can reduce the employer's sales, as well as bring negative publicity to bear on the employer.

While all of this makes successfully negotiating a labor contract sound like a dismal process that is doomed from the beginning, the reality is that neither side wants to get to the point of a strike or other industrial action. Strikes are bad for all involved and in the end no one wins. In most cases, before the parties get to the point of drawing their economic weapons, they will bring in a mediator, conciliator, or fact-finder to help them try to resolve the dispute. In the public sector, where most employees can't legally strike, an arbitrator may even be brought in to settle the contract. Fortunately, with or without the aid of a third-party intervention, most labor contract negotiations are successful. The focus then shifts to administering the contract and resolving disputes as they arise.

RESOLVING GRIEVANCES

A grievance is a formal written complaint alleging that the terms of the labor contract have been violated. Virtually all labor contracts contain a procedure for handling such complaints. While the parties are free to negotiate their own unique procedures, most specify how a grievance will be initiated, detail the requirements of each step in the process, and end with the arbitration of grievances that are not resolved at lower levels. Typically, each step involves progressively higher levels of management and union representatives, with time limits for completing each step. From a legal standpoint, grievance handling is considered an extension of the collective bargaining process. Thus, if management fails to abide by the grievance procedure, it is considered a ULP for failing to bargain in good faith.

Even though an individual employee files a grievance, once it is filed, the union "owns" the grievance. This means that it is up to the union to determine whether or not to pursue the grievance or take it to higher levels in the process. At the same time, unions have a "**duty of fair representation**" to their members. This means that the union has a legal obligation to represent all members and may not discriminate or show favoritism when it comes to pursuing employee grievances. If a union breaches this obligation, an employee can sue the union. Thus, unions sometimes pursue grievances in an effort to protect themselves from legal action. This is why if a grievance involves the termination of an employee, the union typically pursues it all the way through arbitration, even when it is fairly clear the employer was justified in terminating the employee.

Key Terms and Concepts

Duty of fair representation A union's legal obligation to represent all members and not discriminate or show favoritism when pursuing employee grievances.

National Labor Relations Act (NLRA) Federal law that regulates the labor/management relationship for private sector employers in the United States.

Strike The withholding of labor by a union.

Unfair Labor Practice (ULP) An illegal act under NLRA.

Working-to-the-rules An economic weapon used by unions where workers continue to do their jobs, but strictly follow all work rules and refuse to do anything that is not required in order to slow down operations and have a negative effect on their employer.

Endnotes

1. Benton, A. A., and D. Druckman. "Salient Solutions and the Bargaining Behavior of Representatives and Nonrepresentatives." *International Journal of Group Tensions* 3 (1973): 28–39.
2. Diekmann, K. A. "'Implicit Justifications' and Self-Serving Allocations." *Journal of Organizational Behavior* 18 (1997): 3–16.
3. Gruder, C. L. "Relationship with Opponent and Partner in Mixed-Motive Bargaining." *Journal of Conflict Resolution* 15 (1971): 403–416.
4. Stuhlmacher, A. F., T. L. Gillespie, and M. V. Champagne. "The Impact of Time Pressure in Negotiation: A Meta-Analysis." *The International Journal of Conflict Management* 9(2) (1998): 97–116.
5. CNN August 12, 1997. Teamsters: UPS strike will cost them $10 million a week. http://www.cnn.com/US/9708/12/ups.update/index.html retrieved 8/27/11.
6. *Ibid.*

Exercise A.1 Preparing for a Labor Negotiation

Instructions

Your instructor will provide a copy of a current collective bargaining agreement. Review the contract and gather additional information on the employer and the union. Prepare a report for the employer identifying at least five interests and issues and recommending opening demands and target and resistance points for each issue. Include the proposed contract language, the projected cost of each change, and the justification for your recommendations. Be prepared to share your results with the class.

Exercise A.2 Grievance Resolution

Instructions

In this exercise you will be assigned the role of the account manager, director of sales, HR manager, or observer. Your instructor will provide you with confidential role sheets based on your assigned role. Read all the information provided and complete the worksheet based on your knowledge of the situation.

Overview

Employment Resources Unlimited (ERU) is a placement agency that provides a wide variety of temporary and contract workers for medical, manufacturing, and general office positions in client companies, for both short- and long-term assignments. The business has grown steadily over its twenty-year history and currently employs eighteen account managers who have the responsibility of matching workers with employers and managing the ongoing client relationship. The account managers strive to develop good relationships with their clients, which encourages repeat business. The company policy is that client assignments will be allocated to employees who are qualified to service the client, but historically the new client assignments have gone to the account manager who has the most experience with that type of customer. All account managers report to Dixie, the director of sales. Dixie has held her position for several years, having come to ERU from a similar company in Texas.

Eric is a very successful account manager who has been with the company for seven years. He specializes in the medical field and prides himself in providing excellent service to his clients. Since coming to ERU, he has been the only account manager to work with ERU's nursing home clients. Recently, Eric found out that Dixie had given a new client, Meadowview Adult Care Facility, to Stephanie, an account manager who has been with ERU for less than a year. Eric told Dixie that he thought that Meadowview should be his client since he handles all nursing homes and has an outstanding performance record. Dixie replied that Stephanie is qualified to handle the Meadowview account and that she doesn't think one person should handle all clients in a particular industry. Eric was not satisfied with Dixie's response and filed a formal grievance.

Michael is the HR manager and is responsible for all internal human resource functions, including responsibility for resolving employee grievances. He has scheduled a meeting with Eric and Dixie to address the grievance.

Worksheet: Exercise A.2 Grievance Resolution

Account Manager, Eric

Interests: _____

_____

Issue	Opening Demand	Target	Resistance

Director of Sales, Dixie

Interests: _____

_____

Issue	Opening Demand	Target	Resistance

Manager, Michael

Interests: _____

_____

Issue	Opening Demand	Target	Resistance

APPENDIX B

Resumes and Cover Letters

RESUMES

A resume is a summary of your qualifications and experience. It functions as a personalized marketing tool for you, making a good impression and getting you an interview. A resume should demonstrate, through listing tangible results and accomplishments, that your knowledge, skills, and abilities are a good match for the position you seek, as defined in the job description.

There are two basic types of resumes: chronological and functional. Chronological is the traditional style of resume with sections for education, experience, honors/activities, and so on. Within each section, the material is organized in reverse chronological order so the most recent material is listed first. This type of resume works best for people with experience as it focuses on the person's career progression and growth. This resume type also highlights stability in employment, assuming of course there are no or minimal breaks in your employment history.

A functional or skills-oriented resume contains the same material, but instead of focusing on the chronological order that stresses how much experience the applicant has, it focuses on the skills the applicant possesses. The functional resume is often used when applicants are just beginning careers and don't have years of experience under their belt. It can also be a good choice when changing occupations or resuming a career after a break, such as after a period of staying home with small children.

Regardless of which type of resume you use, when creating your resume it is important to emphasize your skills using key words employers are looking for—especially since many employers today use software to screen resumes. Such software scans your resume looking for matches with employer-specified key words, usually taken from the job description. If your resume doesn't contain the specified key words, it is automatically rejected. Even employers who don't use resume-screening software generally spend only a few seconds initially reviewing resumes, so keep yours clear, concise, and error free.

Folklore in the office furniture industry holds that during an industry slump in the 1980s, the first screening criteria for applicants at Haworth Inc., one of the top three companies in the industry, was whether the applicant had spelled the company's name correctly. If the applicant spelled it *Hayworth* or *Heyworth*, or some other incorrect variation, the application was automatically rejected. On the surface this may seem like a poor criterion for hiring engineers or accountants, but given the high unemployment rate and small number of positions available at the time, managers needed a quick and objective way to determine who made the first cut. The logic behind it was that if an applicant didn't care enough about his application to correctly spell the company name, he probably wouldn't be particular about his job performance either.

After you draft your resume you should get input from knowledgeable others and revise it as needed. Understand that some of the advice you receive may be contradictory. This is to be expected since people have different opinions on how a resume should look. Ultimately it is your resume and you must be comfortable with it. You may even have different resumes for different purposes. Take the case of Kelly who was completing a degree in business. She really wanted to work in human resources and had a resume that focused on her skills in that area. She also had a more general resume that she used to apply for a variety of entry level jobs. As she neared graduation she was offered a job with a major resort hotel as an administrative assistant. While it wasn't really the kind of work she wanted to do, she was interested in the company and took the position to get her foot in the door. After six months as an administrative assistant she applied for an internal opening as housekeeping supervisor. She got the job and spent the next year learning as much as she could about that aspect of the business and demonstrating her management skills. With perseverance, she ultimately landed the job she really wanted in human resources.

While there is variation in resumes there are also some basics. The heading area of your resume needs to contain your name, permanent address, and, if applicable, your college address, along with your phone number(s), and email address. Think carefully about your voice mail greeting and email address, and the message they send to people trying to contact you. A student once left a message for a professor to call him. When the professor returned the call she was greeted with the following announcement: "This is Jeremy. There is one of three reasons I'm not answering the phone. Either one I'm out partying, or two the dog ate my phone, or three I just don't want to talk to you, and the answer is probably three. If you want to leave a message, go ahead and maybe I'll return your call." While this is certainly one of the more obnoxious voice mail greetings one could have, there are others that are milder but still don't convey an air of professionalism.

Think of the times you have called someone only to be greeted with music playing or where the greeting was recorded by the family's children. Even if the song happens to be your favorite or the children are really cute, most people don't care to be forced to listen to music or cute kids when they are trying to contact someone. Instead, they want a short message that lets them know they have reached the right person so they can leave their message.

Similar thought should be given to your email address. While you may like to let the world know that you are an "animallover" or think it's cute to be known as "beer-guzzler," many employers wouldn't have the same appreciation. You may even consider using a separate email account for your job search. Yahoo.com, hotmail.com and gmail.com offer email accounts that can be set up easily and at no cost.

In addition to the basic contact information, most people who provide advice on resumes recommend including an objective. An objective is a statement of the type of work you desire and what you have to offer and suggests you have purpose and direction in your job search. While an objective is usually only one sentence, it is something many people struggle with writing. Often this is because they are trying to select the perfect words to catch the attention of, and convey their potential contribution to, an employer for whom they would really like to work. However, there are also cases where the applicant simply needs a job, any job. Thus, your objective could be very specific if you are trying to land a particular job or it could be quite general if you are just trying to get your foot in the door. In either case you should be concise and to the point.

The next section on a resume is usually education. You should list your most recent, which is also usually your highest, degree first and work backwards from there. It is not necessary to include your high school education on your resume although some employers request it on their application form. You should also identify if you graduated "with honors," "high honors," cum laude or summa cum laude, and so on. Some even recommend including your actual GPA, if it is good. Of course people may define *good* differently, but most say anything over 3.5 is good.

After education, the next section is generally experience on a chronological resume and qualifications on a functional resume. In either format this is the area where you identify what you are able to do. This includes job-specific skills you have, such as the ability to write legal job descriptions or conduct performance appraisals, as well as transferable skills such as communication, writing, successfully working individually or in a team environment. Be sure to include all your experience. Even if your experience isn't in the area for which you are applying, it still shows that you are a reliable employee. Especially important is any supervisory or training experience, and any high-end technical or computer skills you have, as these may help distinguish you from other applicants. Employers are looking for evidence of your abilities, so focus on showing results and highlighting your accomplishments. It is more effective to use bullets, breaking the information into small bites, than to write lengthy paragraphs. Some suggest the PAR approach; using bullet statements, discuss a particular Problem you encountered, the Action you took to overcome the problem, and then the Results that were achieved. For example, "Customer complaints had been increasing, so I developed and conducted a customer survey, focused on improving the two most common complaints, and in three months, customer complaints decreased 65%."

It is also standard to include a section for honors/activities. This is where you list any professional certifications you may have or awards you have received. You would also list your professional affiliations and volunteer activities. Be sure to note any leadership responsibilities you have because leadership and high levels of involvement can set you apart from other applicants. In a tight job market employers can be much more selective and they are more likely to look for applicants who are highly involved.

The final section on a resume is usually references. Here there are two choices. If the job for which you are applying specifically asks for references, you should list the contact information for your references. If the employer doesn't request references it is acceptable to simply write "available upon request" in this section. Of course you should never list someone as a reference if you haven't asked her permission first. Even if it is someone who would say only wonderful things about you, you still don't want to have her caught off guard by someone phoning to check your references. It is also helpful if your reference has a current copy of your resume and some idea of where you are applying so she can give informed, specific responses.

Lastly, consider how your resume looks. It should be very clean and easy to read. In general you should use a 10- to 12-point standard typeface that is easy to read. Avoid decorative or overly artistic fonts. Remember the people who read your resume could very well be over forty and part of the "struggling with the fine print but not yet ready for bifocals" generation. If your resume is printed as opposed to electronic, it should be printed on a good quality, medium weight, neutral (e.g., white, off white, ivory) color paper. Always proofread, and have others proofread your resume.

COVER LETTERS

In addition to a resume you will also need a cover letter. The purpose of a cover letter is to get the employer to read your resume. If at all possible you should address the cover letter to an actual person instead of "HR Director." This shows that you are interested enough in the position to find the name of the person to send it to. It also improves the odds that the person receiving it will read it.

Your cover letter should show interest in the company and position, and show that you are a good fit by linking your qualifications to the job description. You should also ask for an opportunity to interview and state that you will be following up with the addressee by a certain date, usually within a week. Include your phone number and email address in the last paragraph.

In many cases you can accomplish all this in a standard three-paragraph format. The first paragraph identifies the job (using the title listed in the posting) and briefly clarifies your interest in and fit with the position. The second paragraph highlights two or three areas among your knowledge, skills, and abilities that you think would be attractive to the recruiter. Make it brief and make it interesting. Do not copy and paste parts of your resume. The final paragraph should reiterate your interest, clarify your contact information, and suggest (or ask about) next steps (e.g., interview, phone conversation).

As with your resume, it is critical that you proofread carefully so the letter is error free. A good cover letter will get the employer to read your resume and a good resume will take you to the next step in the process—an invitation to interview.

A Sample of Books on Resumes and the Job Search Available on www.amazon.com

Over-40 Job Search Guide: 10 Strategies For Making Your Age An Advantage In Your Career (Paperback) by Gail Geary (2004)

Job Search Handbook for People With Disabilities (Paperback) by Daniel J. Ryan (2004)

The Academic Job Search Handbook (4th Edition) (Paperback) by Mary Morris Heiberger and Julia Miller Vick (2008)

The Chicago Guide to Your Academic Career: A Portable Mentor for Scholars from Graduate School Through Tenure (Paperback) by John A. Goldsmith, John Komlos, Penny Schine Gold (2001)

The Elements of Résumé Style: Essential Rules and Eye-opening Advice for Writing Résumés and Cover Letters That Work (Paperback) by Scott Bennett (June 30, 2005)

Resume Magic: Trade Secrets of a Professional Résumé Writer (Paperback) by Susan Britton Whitcomb (September 2006)

101 Great Answers to the Toughest Interview Questions (Paperback) by Ronald W Fry (1991)

96 Great Interview Questions to Ask Before You Hire (Paperback) by Paul Falcone (September 1996)

301 Smart Answers to Tough Interview Questions (Paperback) by Vicky Oliver (March 30, 2005)

High-Impact Interview Questions: 701 Behavior-based Questions to Find the Right Person for Every Job (Paperback) by Victoria A. Hoevemeyer (October 2005)

The Vault Guide to Finance Interviews, 6th Edition (Vault Guide to Finance Interviews) (Paperback) by D. Bhatawedekhar (April 25, 2005)

Programming Interviews Exposed: Secrets to Landing Your Next Job (Paperback) by John Mongan, Noah Suojanen, and Eric Giguère (April 30, 2007)

What Color Is Your Parachute? 2007: A Practical Manual for Job-Hunters and Career-Changers (What Color Is Your Parachute) (Paperback) by Richard Nelson Bolles (August 5, 2006)

Career Anchors: Self Assessment (Paperback) by Edgar H. Schein (April 21, 2006)

Résumés for Dummies (Paperback) by Joyce Lain Kennedy (April 26, 1996)

Insider's Guide to the World of Pharmaceutical Sales, Eighth Edition (Paperback) by Jane Williams (July 31, 2005)

Job Interviews for Dummies (Paperback) by Joyce Lain Kennedy (April 25, 2000)

Guerrilla Marketing for Job Hunters: 400 Unconventional Tips, Tricks, and Tactics for Landing Your Dream Job (Paperback) by Jay Conrad Levinson and David Perry (September 29, 2005)

The Interview Rehearsal Book (Paperback) by Deb Gottesman and Buzz Mauro (March 1, 1999)

Cover Letters That Knock 'em Dead (Paperback) by Martin Yate (October 2006)

Working Identity: Unconventional Strategies for Reinventing Your Career (Paperback) by Herminia Ibarra (January 2004)

INDEX